The Newton Abbot to Kingswear Railway

by
C.R. Potts

THE OAKWOOD PRESS

First edition published 1989
Second revised edition published 2014

British Library Cataloguing in Publication Data
A Record for this book is available from the British Library
ISBN 978 0 85361 733 4

Typeset by Oakwood Graphics.
Repro by PKmediaworks, Cranborne, Dorset.
Printed by Gomer Press, Llandysul, Ceredigion.

Title page: Thought to be 1957 or 1958, as No. 1427 on the Brixham branch train was scrapped in September 1958, it is before then. Unfortunately details of the up express leaving Churston are not recorded but it is conveying 'foreign' coaching stock. In the summers of 1957 and 1958, train number 588 was the 10.20 am Kingswear to Crewe which, after Torquay, only called at Teignmouth and was then non-stop to Bristol (Temple Meads). *GW Trust (M. Hale)*

Front cover: On 19th June, 1961 'Castle ' class 4-6-0 No. 5059 *Earl St Aldwyn* hauls the combined load of four coaches from Paddington ('The Royal Duchy' '1.30 pm departure) and five coaches from Liverpool (9.05 am departure) up Goodrington bank en route to Kingswear. It is 6.40 pm and the sands are almost empty, but the carriage sidings (*left*) are full. These coaches should have formed separate trains from Newton Abbot 30 minutes apart, but the Liverpool train being late, they have been combined there. *Peter W. Gray*

Rear cover, top: '42XX' class 2-8-0T No. 5239 *Goliath* rests at Kingswear between evening duties during the Dartmouth Regatta period, 28th August, 2008. *Mark S. Wilkins*

Rear cover, bottom: On 10th September, 2013 the 11.05 Paignton to Paddington pulls out of Torquay up platform with power cars 43094 (front) and 43023 (rear) in charge. In the down platform the 08.00 Cardiff to Paignton is arriving formed of a 3-car class '150' unit and 153318 (rear). As can be seen, the former up sidings are now a housing development. *Mark S. Wilkins*

Published by The Oakwood Press (Usk), P.O. Box 13, Usk, Mon., NP15 1YS.
E-mail: sales@oakwoodpress.co.uk
Website: www.oakwoodpress.co.uk

Contents

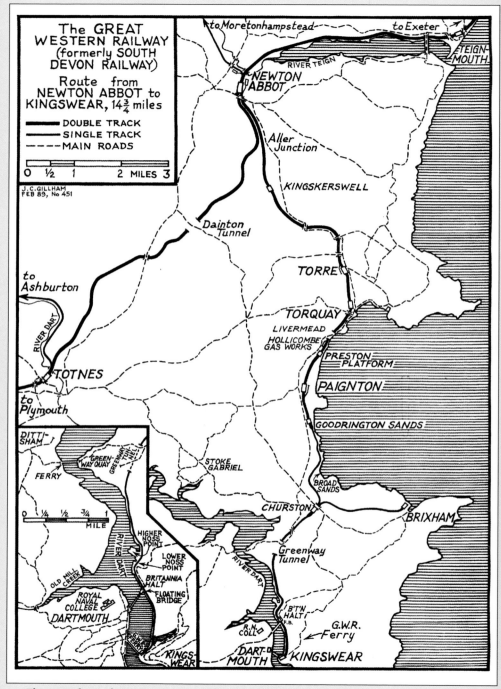

This map shows the Kingswear line at the period 1928-1947, although Preston Platform (closed 1914) is included for the sake of completeness.

The late John C. Gillham

Introduction and Acknowledgements

It is 25 years since the first edition of *The Newton Abbot to Kingswear Railway* was published and the book has been out of print for more than half of that time. I have been working towards a new edition for several years, off and on, with work slowly coming to a conclusion in 2013. On realizing that 2014 would be the 150th anniversary of rails reaching Kingswear, it seemed a good time for a new edition and fortunately my publisher agreed!

Much has happened in that time: rail privatization, a slow improvement in train services, a new steam railway station at Paignton and a halt at Greenway. The national railway service to Paignton could have been even better; First Great Western were proposing a half-hourly off-peak 'Metro' service to Torbay had not the franchising system gone into meltdown with the failure of the West Coast main line bid, so we may have to wait a few more years for our overcrowded local trains to be supplemented. However, unexpectedly in December 2013 the weekday service was increased by six trains each way, thanks to funding by the EU Interreg Citizens' Rail scheme. This gives a broadly half-hourly service between 9 am and 7.30 pm.

As well as much additional historical information uncovered since the first edition, the Great Western Railway (GWR) Locomotive Department water files for Torre and Kingswear have been unearthed. These reveal much fascinating information about severe problems at Kingswear ensuring that there was enough water for the engines working from there. At Torre, water was taken from a stream for several years until the millowner whose mill it supplied realized it and demanded the practice be stopped. Fortunately for the railway they were able to reach agreement with him. These files have since been scrapped and I think my photocopies are the only ones in existence. (Similar information for Brixham and Churston was incorporated in my *Brixham Branch* history in 2000.)

Another fascinating source of information was the letter book of a relief signalman based at Newton Abbot in the 1880s and 1890s. Although containing only (handwritten) copies of his replies to 'authority' demanding explanations for delays or incidents, they reveal much detail of how the railway worked in a period when little was available to the public. (I have published much fuller extracts in *At work on the GWR in the 1890s*, see the Bibliography.)

I have finally been able to put the question of whether Broadsands Halt was built to bed. Definite evidence has been found that it was NOT; in fact twice it was proposed but never built.

A file of train accidents in World War II was found which includes details of bombing and runaway barrage balloons as well as the customary derailments etc. Details of the less than transparent figures used to justify closure of the line between Paignton and Kingswear are taken from the closure files, also found since the first edition. The story is generally updated since 1989. Finally, there are additional memories from the staff, *see Chapter Twelve*. To make way for all the new material I have had to drop the chapter on Tramways.

Many new photographs are included and photographers are acknowledged as usual under each picture. Thanks go to Peter Gray for access to his excellent pictures and for the cover photograph, and to Derek Frost and Mark Wilkins for access to the collections of David Fish and John Attwood, as well as Derek's own photographs and Mark's pictures, including those on the back cover. Thanks also to Richard Woodley for access to Peter Bowles' photographs. Many thanks also to Brixham Museum and Totnes Image Bank for their help with or supply of photographs. Thanks go also to Jasmine Rodgers of the Science Museum for her help. The GWR and BR photographs, formerly marketed by OPC, are now in the care of the National Railway Museum

(NRM). These are credited NRM/SSPL (which is the Science & Society Picture Library). I have been unable to contact some photographers whose pictures were in the first edition and again used here; they have probably moved house (hardly surprising after 25 years) so I would ask that they contact me via the publisher.

The following have given new information or help with the new edition for which I am grateful: Alan Babbage, John Barcy, Bruce Bennett, Tony Cooke, Jack Eveleigh, Andrew Fiderkiewicz, Arthur French , Peter Kay, Martin Kelland, John Mann and Chris Turner. Finally, many thanks to my wife Sue who has had to retype much of the manuscript to incorporate new information. If I have missed anyone out, please accept my apologies.

Chris Potts
Torbay
2014

Bibliography

SDR and GWR, Board of Trade/MoT records at the National Archives, Kew
GWR and BR records at the BR Records Centre, Porchester Road, London W2
GWR, BR and Bradshaw's timetables
History of the Great Western Railway by E.T. MacDermot (revised Clinker) (Ian Allan)
The Locomotives of the GWR (RCTS)
A Regional History of the Railways of Great Britain Vol. 1 by D. St John Thomas (David & Charles)
Track Layout Diagrams of the GWR and WR Part 14 South Devon (R.A. Cooke)
Exeter-Newton Abbot: A Railway History by P. Kay (Platform 5)
The South Devon Railway by Roy Gregory (Oakwood Press)
The Brixham Branch by C.R. Potts (Oakwood Press)
At work on the GWR in the 1890s by C.R. Potts (editor) (Brixham Heritage Museum)
Passenger Steamers of the River Dart by Clammer & Kittridge (Twelveheads Press)
Estuary and River Ferries of South West England by Langley & Small (Waine Research Publications)
Torquay, a Bibliographical Guide; *Paignton, a Bibliographical Guide* (both) by John Pike (Borough of Torbay)
The Torquay and Paignton Gas Company 1834-1934 (J. Allan Hansom & Son, 1935)
The History of Torquay by J.T. White (Torquay Directory, 1878)
A Chronological Record of events relating to Torquay and Neighbourhood by Dymond & White (Torquay Directory, c.1880)
An Historical Survey of Torquay by A.C. Ellis (Torquay Directory, 1930)
Paignton in Six Reigns by F.R. Penwill (Paignton UDC, 1953)
Dartmouth by Ray Freeman (Harbour Books, Dartmouth)
The Chronicles of Dartmouth 1854-1954 by Don Collinson (Richard Webb)
Historic Dart by Eric Hemery (David & Charles)
On Guard [Devonshire Home Guard] by G.H. Lidstone (Battalion Publication Committee, 1945)
The Newton Abbot Blitz by A.R. Kingdom (Oxford Publishing Co.)
GWR Magazine
Dartmouth Chronicle and *Torquay Directory* files at Torquay Library and the British Library, Colindale
Herald Express newspaper, published in Torquay

Chapter One

The South Devon Railway
opens a Branch to Torquay

For Dartmouth the post-Napoleonic period was a period of stagnation that did not end until the coming of the railway in 1864 (and the arrival of the Royal Navy's training ship *Britannia* a year earlier). Whilst for most of Britain the depression period ended around 1830, Dartmouth was struck by commercial, financial and political disasters that prevented the town from advancing to prosperity along with the rest of the country at that time.

The first of these blows was the failure of the bank of Hine, Holdsworth in 1824, which affected both Dartmouth and Brixham, leaving a long term legacy of debt and aversion to investment. Then in 1840/44 came the chance of revival when Dartmouth was chosen by a Select Committee as the port for handling the West India Mails , despite the Committee's assumption that the mails would have to go to Bridgwater by road. As soon as the decision was announced, however, powerful interests in the competing ports of Falmouth, Plymouth, Southampton and Portsmouth set to work to alter it and succeeded in so doing. The status quo kept Falmouth as the Packet station for the West India Mails, although Southampton was allowed to continue as the arrival and departure point for the North America mails under the contract awarded to the Cunard line of steamships in 1837. The last calamity was a catastrophic strike of shipwrights in the port which lasted for some months and crippled the main industry of Dartmouth for a long while afterwards.

The topography of Dartmouth and its environs meant that natural communication was difficult, and cross-River Dart traffic was limited by the size of ferries available. To overcome this problem a Floating Bridge was constructed by Sir John Seale in 1832, the latter also building two miles of turnpike road on the eastern shore to the Brixham Road at Hillhead.

Earlier, in 1823, the last Governor of Dartmouth Castle, Arthur Howe Holdsworth, had supported a project to build a carriage road from the Quay at Dartmouth up the face of a 350 ft cliff along the crest of which ran a turnpike road. Prior to the completion of this road only pannier traffic could reach the town from the west whilst most goods of any size or volume had to come (or go) along the river to Totnes (10 miles) or be transported coastwise by small trading craft or collier brigs.

Despite these improvements, arrangements for transport of goods were still seriously restricted and the benefits that the building of a railway to Dartmouth would bring could readily be seen.

The first railway in the area was the South Devon Railway (SDR), authorized by Act of Parliament on 4th July, 1844. This allowed construction of a single track broad gauge line from Exeter St David's (the Bristol & Exeter Railway station) to Eldad, just outside Plymouth. After the passing of the Act the Directors decided to adopt the atmospheric system of propulsion, upon the recommendation of their Engineer, I.K. Brunel, and it was agreed at the first general meeting of the shareholders, in August 1844.

So much has been written elsewhere* on this choice of the atmospheric system that to repeat it here is unnecessary. But the fact that it was a failure is relevant to this book. The best part of £500,000 (something over £49 million at 2012 prices) was

* See for example *The South Devon Railway* by R.H. Gregory (Oakwood Press).

7

spent on atmospheric equipment, the scrap value of which raised only about £80,000. The company was left with a single line, no locomotives, steep gradients and very little money with which to improve or expand its network.

At about the same time as the South Devon Railway commenced its survey, a Prospectus was issued for a Torquay & Newton Abbot Railway, from Torquay Harbour to Aller Barn on the SDR. The Chairman was Thomas Kitson and the Engineer Robert Dymond an Exeter surveyor; the estimated cost of construction was £60,000. No more was heard of this scheme which was killed off by objectors, who thought a station at Aller to be close enough for Torquay.

There was no mention of a branch to Torquay or Dartmouth at the next (February 1845) meeting of the SDR, so a group of local gentlemen proposed a broad gauge line from Dartmouth to Aller (and a branch to Ashburton which was later deleted). It was proposed to work the line on the atmospheric method and the Engineer was to be W.R. Neale (an assistant to Joseph Locke, Engineer to the London & South Western Railway (LSWR)). In July 1845 this proposal, and a separate plan for a South & North Devon Junction Railway from Newton to Crediton, were swept into the narrow gauge camp by Joseph Locke with a promise of support from London. The Dartmouth Torbay & Exeter Railway began with separate branches from Dartmouth and Brixham which combined at Galmpton and continued via Torbay, Newton Abbot and 'the neighbourhood of' Moretonhampstead. At Exeter it would have joined up with intended 'narrow gauge' lines via Yeovil and Salisbury to London.

At last disturbed by these attempts at competition, the South Devon Railway presented a Bill to the 1846 Session of Parliament. This proposed a branch from the South Devon Railway at Aller to Kingswear routed through Torquay, Paignton, Churston and Brixham Quay. Some £45,750 was paid into the Court of Chancery in support of the Bill on 3rd February, 1846. The following day the competing 'narrow gauge' Dartmouth, Brixham, Torbay, Exeter and North Devon Junction Railway (to quote its full title) deposited £24,500 in the same Court on account of its Bill. However the 'narrow gauge interest' which included Richard Wolston who later built the Torbay & Brixham Railway, and Sir H.P. Seale and John Belfield, later to be Directors of the Dartmouth & Torbay Railway (D&TR), was defeated on technical objections; the Bill had been completed with too much haste. The South Devon Amendment and Branches Act received the Royal Assent on 28th August, 1846, but strong opposition from Paignton and Goodrington residents (who feared loss of access to the beach) had foreshortened the line and the Act showed it to terminate in field No. 23 in the parish of Tormoham (Torquay). The station was to be under Chapel Hill, at 'St Michaels' (Torre) but was named Torquay .

The failure of the 1845 Dartmouth proposed railway to produce any positive result, except for money lost in promotional and parliamentary expenses, soured the prospects for raising finance for new schemes until 1852/3 when a scheme for a line to Dartmouth from Torbay running close to Brixham was promoted. However, this too failed for lack of money pledged. The scheme failed to pass Standing Orders in Parliament and again considerable money was lost in survey and promotional expenses. The final scheme (1856/7) was more successful, as will be seen, particularly as Charles Seale Hayne* of Kingswear Castle was prepared to lead from the front using his not inconsiderable personal fortune.

The South Devon line southwards from Exeter was opened as far as Teignmouth on 30th May, 1846 and at first conventional locomotive power was used, hired from

---

* Charles Seale Hayne (1833-1903), grandson of Sir John Seale, Bt MP for Ashburton and Mid-Devon; Chairman Dartmouth Harbour Commissioners (1863-1885), Barrister, appointed High Court Judge 1886. Paymaster General 1892-1895 in Gladstone's last Cabinet. Founder of Seale Hayne Agricultural College, Newton Abbot.

the Great Western Railway. Newton (not called Newton Abbot until 1877) was reached on 31st December, 1846. Further extensions reached Totnes on 20th July, 1847 and a few weeks later, on 13th September, atmospheric power was introduced on the Exeter-Teignmouth section and extended to Newton on 10th January, 1848 (some trains in December).

Early in 1847, the SDR resolved to extend the Torquay branch as far as Morgan's nursery at Tor (on the site of the present day Town Hall at Castle Circus) and after negotiations the said Morgan agreed to part with his nursery for £2,300. This area would have been a mile nearer the town and powers were obtained by the South Devon Railway Act, 22nd July, 1847, for this short extension, which would have been on the lands of Sir Lawrence Palk who was in favour of it, and for a branch from the present terminus to Brixham. But the proposal brought strong opposition from the inhabitants of Dartmouth who feared that the new site favoured extension to Torquay Harbour rather than Dartmouth and the SDR agreed not to proceed with the Torquay extension at present.

The year 1846 had been memorable for a deficient harvest and the failure of the potato crop, causing a famine in Ireland and widespread distress elsewhere. Although the poor in Torquay were in great need, collections were taken for the Irish and over £600 was subscribed by private sources and chapels and churches. In May 1847, there were 'bread riots' about the quality of bread throughout Devonshire and on Monday 17th May disturbances broke out at Torquay. In his *History of Torquay*, published 1878, J.T. White says:

Rumours were current several days previously that a riot was meditated, ... but no preparation was made to guard against it. At half-past seven in the evening a mob collected in Lower Union Street, and at once made an attack on the bakers' shops, the contents of which were carried off by the women in their aprons. Owing to the economy of the Commissioners, no street lamps were permitted to be lit during the summer months, and to make matters worse not only the lanterns, but the burners had been removed. With a view to identifying the ringleaders, it was determined to turn on the gas at full; when the gas was lit each street lamp emitted a flame about a foot high, thoroughly illuminating the place. By this time several thousand persons were in the streets ...

Having attacked several bread shops, the rioters marched to Torre but here were met by a party of tradesmen and two magistrates; a scuffle followed. Following the reading of the Riot Act those who had been captured were locked up and a special sitting of the magistrates began at midnight. White continues,

Three men were committed for trial and despatched to Exeter, the others being remanded. At noon on Tuesday, while the magistrates were disposing of men in custody, a body of navvies, sixty in number, employed on the railway works above Torre, having been incited ... by persons belonging to the town, marched into Torquay equipped with pick-axes, crowbars and shovels.

At the Town Hall they were confronted by Mr H. March Phillips, one of the magistrates. A man named Hart, who appeared to be leading the navvies, demanded release of the prisoners and on being rebuffed it seemed that a rush on the Town Hall was imminent. Very bravely, Mr March Phillips seized Hart and held on to him, at which time a party of constables and coastguards arrived and several other rioters were secured, the remainder dispersing.

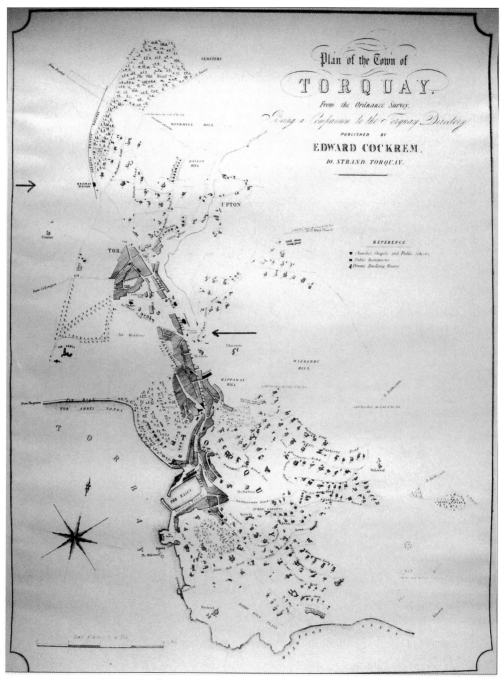

An early map of Torquay. The location of the railway station at Torre is top left (arrowed). The site of the proposed station in a more central position at Morgan's nursery is arrowed in the middle of the map. The harbour is towards the bottom, to the right of the compass marking.

Fearing further trouble, troopers were summoned from Exeter, more coastguards sent for and 300 special constables sworn in. The prisoners were sent to Exeter by steamer as a plan had been uncovered for rescuing the men if moved by coach. At the June Sessions Hart and another man got 14 days' imprisonment, considerably less than those who had incited them to riot who were awarded six weeks or a month's imprisonment. Towards the end of the month the SDR received a bill for £46 7s. 5d., in respect of 'the special constables expenses', which, after details had been supplied, they settled at £44 5s. The South Devon Railway papers indicate that the real ringleaders were Torquay men who enlisted the navvies because of the number readily available. The Court had recognized this and so dealt with the navvies leniently.

Despite this temporary interruption, building work continued on the Torquay branch. In February 1848 the Directors were pressing for completion of the work but had decided not to extend beyond the present terminus at St Michael's to Morgan's nursery, near New Church, Upton. Nor was the Brixham branch to be built (it was stated at the April Board) 'until the condition and prospects of the Company were in such a state as to warrant a further outlay'. The financial problems of the atmospheric operation were already being felt; the system was in fact abandoned from 9th September, 1848 and locomotives reintroduced on the following day.

The *Torquay Directory* 15th November, 1848 reported that:

The Torquay branch of the South Devon Railway is rapidly approaching completion, the permanent rails are laid as far as Kingskerswell and have been traversed by the engines conveying materials for the remainder of the line which is to be completed in a few weeks. The station at St Michael's is also in a forward state.

On 9th December the *Illustrated London News* noted that the railway from Torquay to Newton would be opened about '11th inst.' and could have been opened 'on the 30th ult. (but for) the incompleteness of the station'. The *ILN* may well have had a source 'inside' Whitehall, because the Board of Trade inspection was carried out on 9th December by Capt. Simmons and the important details from his report follow:

... I inspected the branch line of the SDR from the vicinity of Aller Farm near Newton to that of Torquay on the 9th instant, being a distance of 3 miles 75 chains. The works upon it are of a moderate nature, the only bridges ... carrying roads over the railway, seven in number. One of these called Law's Bridge carrying the Turnpike road from Newton to Torquay crosses the railway in a cutting about 25 ft in depth, the sides of which are supported by retaining walls, under 3 ft in thickness, built of rubble masonry of a curved section. The foundation behind seems to be a strong clay, but subject in places to the action of water, for which a system of drainage has been provided, but which appears in places not to be thoroughly efficient. The wall has therefore been forced very considerably from its original form, this was stated to have occurred some time ago, and the late rains have not affected it, but it appears to me that it will require to be watched very carefully so that should it give way, due notice may be given to trains before arriving at it[!] The masonry in the abutments of this bridge appear light considering the height of the bank to be supported ... Their sufficiency, as in the case of the retaining walls, depends on the nature of the material in the cutting ... the bridge however has been built nearly a year and the work appears sound.

There then followed a paragraph about two of the curves being altered slightly from the Parliamentary plans, to which no exception was taken, a note that the line was single, 'worked as a distinct branch from Newton Station' and that the electric telegraph had been erected alongside. Captain Simmons concluded (in a strangely complacent report) that subject to Law's Bridge being specially watched, the line might be opened.

Monday 18th December was decided upon as the opening day of the line and was observed as a local holiday. Poor people received 4,834 lb. of meat shared amongst them and the same amount of bread, the cost of which was raised by public subscription. A procession was formed up at Royal Hotel Square, at the bottom of Torwood Street, at about 11 am, and marched to Torquay (Torre) station to give a reception to the special train from Exeter (it left there at 12.05 pm). Chapel Hill above the station was not then tree-covered and was crowded with spectators who had a grandstand view of events.

Soon after midday the telegraph signalled the departure of the Directors' special from Newton and 'in about 10 minutes the train was seen approaching rapidly down the incline under Chapel Hill, decorated with flowers and evergreens'. Arriving at the station, 'a handsome and commodious building, principally of wood upon a limestone foundation' the party alighted. Led by the Chairman of the SDR, Thomas Woollcombe, the officials comprised the Directors, the Engineer I.K. Brunel and his assistants, and also numerous influential shareholders. A cheer went up , echoed by the multitudes clustered upon the surrounding hills. After a welcoming address given by Sir John Yarde Buller MP, 'in the absence of a gentleman of Torquay, who had undertaken to perform that duty [Sir Lawrence Palk?], Mr Woollcombe responded suitably. He referred to the current rather straitened circumstances of the company and hoped that, '... the completion of the branch in preference to other works which had long been in hand might be taken as a proof of the value which they attached to the Torquay line'.

Unfortunately, the Directors were unable to accept the hospitality offered to them but had to return to Plymouth for an engagement 'which it would be impossible for them to defer'. The newspaper report does not say so, but it is presumed they returned to Plymouth in the special in which they had arrived which was hauled by the locomotive *Taurus*.

An excursion to Newton had been arranged by the committee and, if the Directors used their train to return to Plymouth, this must have been another train, sent empty from Newton. Over 200 people had taken tickets for the trip and they filled the train which consisted of nine first and 15 second class 'carriages' according to the *Torquay Directory*, but this is generally assumed to mean 'compartments'. The five mile journey was completed in 13 minutes (there is a steep rising gradient immediately on departure from Torre). The Directory said of its destination , rather facetiously:

> . . . its occupants were duly landed at the station, but what they did during the awful hour and half which followed we are not at liberty to disclose. One thing is certain that no holiday had infected Newton - the roads were as dirty and the streets as dull as if no pleasure party had been expected and except by the power of contrast certainly added but little to their gala day.

The return excursion took 11 minutes to reach Torre, whence the more important participants proceeded to a dinner at Webb's Royal Hotel at 5 pm, at which it had been intended to entertain the Directors.

There is no doubt that this opening took place on 18th December for it is much reported in the local newspapers. But from the number of internal railway documents seen which quote 1st January, 1849, which was a Monday, as the opening date, it would seem that the timetabled train service started then. Unfortunately, this does not seem to have been recorded in the papers.

The first timetable published showed six arrivals and five departures on weekdays, and four trains each way on Sundays; a change of trains was necessary at Newton, although the branch enjoyed through carriages to and from London from the beginning [*Railway Times* 23.12.1848]. Writing in the *GWR Magazine* in February 1920, W.J. Scott said:

> On the Torquay branch (afterwards extended to Kingswear for Dartmouth) which from its opening always had through London coaches, which mostly were stabled at Newton; one or more branch trains either way were often made up of GW (or sometimes B&E) vehicles to be ultimately worked through to London, but meanwhile used for a local (branch) trip.

		am	*am*	*am*	*pm* NS	*pm*	*pm* NS
Newton	*dep.*	4.55	8.45	11.55	3.25	6.33	10.52
				pm			
Torquay	*arr.*	5.10	9.00	12.10	3.40	6.50	11.05

		am	*am* NS	*pm*		*pm*	*pm*
Torquay	*dep.*	8.30	11.13	2.05		6.18	7.40
Newton	*arr.*	8.42	11.25	2.17		6.30	7.52

NS - Not Sundays

Thomas Webb of the Royal Hotel was made agent for the collection and delivery of parcels. Stage coaches to Paignton, Brixham and Dartmouth, which met the Bristol Mail and London trains, were also started. Goods trains were not dealt with until 6th October, 1849, presumably the shortage of cash prevented provision of the necessary facilities at Torre.

The seal of the South Devon Railway.   *NRM/SSPL*

Chapter Two

The Years of Stagnation: 1849-1856

After the opening to 'St Michaels', which is well away from the business area of Torquay, although quite convenient for the residential areas of St Marychurch and Babbacombe, local pressure arose for the railway to be extended to the harbour. This would have meant tunnelling under Torre, emerging near Abbey Road and then following the line of George Street and Swan Street to the harbour. A Bill was placed before Parliament but was objected to by the inhabitants of Brixham who wanted the line extended to Livermead as a first step to reaching Brixham. Their objection was successful and the Bill was withdrawn. Unfortunately, this did not get the line to Livermead built - the SDR's financial difficulties prevented any such expansion.

In July 1849 a petition from the residents of Tormoham for a station at Kingskerswell arrived on the Boardroom table. The residents undertook to pay the costs of the platform but the Directors would only agree to stop one train in each direction each day 'for a short time as an experiment'. Not surprisingly the petitioners declined this offer which would have given them very poor value for their money. A further request for a station, in 1852, was also turned down.

As it had been intended to work the Torquay branch by atmospheric power an engine house had been erected not far short of the terminus. But atmospheric working was withdrawn before the Torquay line was ready so the engine house was never used. Now, in September 1849, a request was received from the Torquay Local Board of Health to use the building to house the families of cholera patients. The Directors agreed so long as they did not have to pay rates on the building while being used in this way.

In a year which had seen the value of the South Devon shares fall from £50 to £5 , further evidence of the enormous difficulties the SDR was facing in keeping afloat can be found in the December Minutes of the Board. There is a reference to approaching the Midland Railway to work the line , and also contact was made with the Bristol & Exeter Railway (B&E) in respect of 'a lease or otherwise'. However the Midland's terms, which are not detailed in the Minutes, appear to have been unacceptable, whilst the B&E Directors 'were not in a position to entertain such a proposal'. Full details of the SDR's financial problems at this time can be found in Roy Gregory's book *The South Devon Railway* (Oakwood Press).

Following the demise of the atmospheric railway, it had been necessary to hire locomotives from the GWR, because of course the SDR had not expected to need any. A workshop at Newton, designed for the atmospheric railway, was converted to service and repair the locomotives. Carriages and wagons were supplied by contractors and maintained and repaired by the GWR, probably at Bristol. This arrangement ceased from May 1849, when the Bristol & Exeter Railway took back the working of its own line from the GWR and raised high charges for the transit of SDR vehicles. From then on the SDR maintained its own vehicles at Newton.

The engines supplied by the GWR were not really suitable for the fierce Devon banks on the main line west of Newton, so the company was forced to consider alternatives . Contact was made with Charles Geach, a Birmingham contractor, who undertook to build twelve 4-4-0 saddle tanks for passenger trains and four 0-6-0 saddle tanks for goods trains. A minimum weekly payment of £298 was proposed and the contract would be for 10 years. These terms were better than the GWR offered and were accepted by the Board during 1850, and a contract signed in June 1851. Daniel Gooch's younger brother, W.F. Gooch, was installed as locomotive superintendent. The passenger engines (from four different builders) arrived between October 1851 and April 1853, whilst the goods engines, built by the Vulcan Foundry, were delivered in 1854 and 1855, after which it was no longer necessary to hire from the GWR. Notes of a meeting between the SDR and its locomotive contractors on 21st December, 1853 record: 'The maximum load for one engine with a passenger train is 9 coaches on the inclines or the Torquay branch and 18 coaches elsewhere'.

In September 1851, the SDR Traffic Minutes record a mishap to *Brigand*, one of the GWR engines, a 4-4-0 saddle tank of the 'Bogie' class, new in 1849:

Engine Driver Roland and Switchman Bidgood were reported by the Chief Superintendent for having got 'The Brigand' [*sic*] off the line at Newton station on the morning of the 22nd August, occasioning damage to the amount of £ … [blank in the minutes]. The switchman was ordered to contribute 20s. by installments of 2s. 6d. toward repairing the damage to the engine, but the accident appearing to have been caused by clumsiness and not by any inattention or neglect, the Directors ordered that the amount should not be recorded as a fine and should not affect his claim to premium.

On Boxing Day 1851 the 4.05 pm two-coach down train from Newton approached Torquay too fast, and overshot the terminus, the engine and the leading third class coach plunging down the embankment. As the *Torquay Directory* reported, somewhat melodramatically:

A passenger assures us that not long before reaching the station, he distinctly heard the signal for applying the 'breaks' [*sic*] twice, but that the motion seemed rather to increase than otherwise. To their dismay it swept by the station at a speed that rendered it all but certain that it would be carried over the slope in which the line terminates. Several attempts were made to leave the carriages, but without success, as the doors were locked, and the imprisoned passengers were hurried on in the dark to what seemed certain destruction.

The engine 'buried itself in a hedge', the third class coach was 'sadly broken', whilst the front of the rear carriage stopped on the crest of the slope, 'its front broken-in by blows received from the buffers of the third class carriage'. Fortunately the worst injury sustained was to a man and his daughter who received severe bruising. Driver Hutchins, his fireman and guard had to attend the next Board meeting in January. Following this enquiry it was resolved, 'that in future drivers were to shut-off steam at some considerable distance before reaching the summit of every incline which they have to run down'. At this time, of course, trains were controlled only by the application of hand brakes, or in emergency, the reversing of the engine's wheels and application of steam.

The SDR Board Minutes for March 1852 record that, on 15th March, an accident had disabled the engine of the 'up express'; the 'Torquay engine' had been sent to assist and Torquay passengers had been conveyed in omnibuses until it returned, at a cost to the SDR of £5 17s. 6d.

In the late summer of 1852 the SDR let it be known that they would be willing to consider any definite proposal made to extend the railway to Torquay harbour. This immediately caused great agitation in the town and a public meeting was held on 24th September to discuss the matter. Supporters of the idea referred to the 'great nuisance and delay occasioned by the change at Newton' and felt that Torquay, as the supplier of 'a great portion of the revenue of the Railway company ... received less consideration than any other town on the line'.

However, the majority of the meeting were fearful that great damage could be caused to the town, not just physical, but to its character. Furthermore, 'the hissing and snorting of the engine would ... in many instances hasten the death of the invalids who resided here'. A vote revealed a large majority against the extension into the town and a 'Protest' was sent to the SDR which pledged unqualified opposition to any such attempt.

The first shareholders meeting of 1853 learnt of the problems of running the (mostly) single track railway to Plymouth punctually:

> ... great difficulties ... keeping time and doing the work of the company satisfactorily ... owing to the station at Newton being constantly blocked. At that station there was no sufficient means of passing and as they now had a small amount of capital at their command, it was thought it would be best to construct a considerable portion of double line. (It was) determined to recommend the shareholders to authorise the Directors ... to double the line from the Torquay junction to Totnes.
>
> The Directors further contemplated the Newton station which they would recommend to be constructed after the plan of Didcot station, though of course on a smaller scale, so that the Torquay trains might come in abreast of the main trains and the inconvenience and trouble of travelling from one to the other of the two Newton stations might be avoided. (Could not estimate the cost of this yet.) With reference to the double line ... engineer's rough estimate was £30,000.

Although the doubling was started with Messrs Holmes as contractors the improvements of Newton station had to wait several more years.

Approached early in 1853 for a goods siding at Kingskerswell, the company at last decided to do better and install a station as well. £25 was spent buying land for the siding and Mr Peprall was appointed 'Booking constable' at a wage of 16s. a week. The station, 'a neat, though small structure', as the *Torquay Chronicle* described it, opened for business on Friday 1st July, 1853. The branch engine was bedecked with flags, flowers and evergreens that day, and great celebrations involving the firing of cannon and the enjoyment of sports, took place on a hill close to the new station. Within days, however, a petition to the SDR requested more trains calling on weekdays, but that 'a number might be reduced on Sunday evenings'. The Board agreed to stop two more up trains and a down train on weekdays, and that one up and one down Sunday evening trains should discontinue stopping there.

A few months later complaints of the inadequacies of Torquay station for goods traffic were finding their way into the local press. Delays of 24 hours in forwarding traffic tendered for dispatch were apparently common, 'because of the inability of the porters to find room for loading', and goods arriving at 7.30 am for delivery in the town, were not being unloaded until midday. Adverse comparison was made with the previous stage-wagons and the management of the station labelled 'disgraceful', for the want of a small expenditure to enlarge the station.

The passenger train service for the line shown on a timebill dated 3rd October, 1853 was as follows. Only the Torquay times are shown on the timebill and the Newton Abbot times are therefore estimated. As can be seen the line was worked as a shuttle to and from Newton Abbot, (the engine being shedded at Torquay) with the exception of those trains marked 'E' which were from or to Exeter.

		Weekdays							Sundays		
		am	am	pm	pm	pm	pm	am	pm		pm
Newton	dep.	8.40	11.50	3.55	5.00	7.55	10.50	8.40	4E10		7.55
Torquay	arr.	8.55	12.05	4.10	5.15	8.10	11.05	8.55	4.25		8.10

		am	am	am	pm	pm	pm	am	pm	pm	pm
Torquay	dep.	8.05	9.10	11.20	1.10	4.30	7.30	8.05	3.45	6E15	7.30
Newton	arr.	8.20	9.25	11.35	1.25	4.45	7.45	8.20	4.00	6.30	7.45

Timebills dated 1st February, 1854 and 1st December, 1854 show the same service still in operation.

Another attempt was made in the autumn of 1853 to extend the South Devon Railway to Torquay Harbour. The Board intimated that they would undertake the working of such a line if independently sponsored.

At about the same time another group, with John Belfield of Primley Hill, Paignton (now the site of Paignton Zoo), as its Chairman and the famous I.K. Brunel as its Engineer, was formulating a proposal for a Dartmouth, Torquay & South Devon Extension Railway with the principal intention of developing Dartmouth as a shipping port. Its Prospectus (much abbreviated) declared:

The objects of the Railway are to afford the important harbours of Dartmouth & Brixham the benefits of railway communication … and to make the harbours the ports of discharge for the increasing traffic with the Channel Islands, the south and west of France, Spain, Portugal and the Western Islands. It will also open to the tourist … the Dart and portions of the south coast of Devon hitherto all but inaccessible. Dartmouth … possessed the unrivalled advantage of being wholly free from Harbour dues and Dock charges and has great facilities for carrying on ship building … and is also admirably suited as a port of embarkation for passengers and emigrants.

Brixham which is the port and principal roadstead and post town of Torbay is also, as a harbour, extensive safe and commodious and the fortifications on Berry Head and the Admiralty establishment for watering the navy mark it as a place of importance.

The large and important district of the South Hams … will also add largely to the traffic.

Paignton has other but not less important attractions. In climate of equal salubriety with Torquay it possesses a large sandy beach nearly two miles in length admirably suited for bathing. Being in the centre of the bay it also embraces, within easy drives, all points of beauty and interest with which the neighbourhood so richly abounds …

The proposed line will be about 11 miles long [it looped towards Brixham] and the landowners for nearly the entire distance are unanimous in their desire for the Railway …

This railway would have run from a junction at the north end of Torquay (Torre) station to a point near Hoodown Ferry Passage House 'in the occupation of Mary Burgoine in the Parish of Brixham', with a branch to the Dartmouth Floating Bridge. There would also be a connecting railway at Torquay from the Western Quay of Torquay harbour with a westward-facing link with the proposed railway, the junction being near Livermead House, south of the present Torquay station; and a northward facing link which would have joined the proposed line south of the Torquay (Torre) station, about ¼ mile from the sea-shore.

The publication of this Notice of Application had two effects. First of all the SDR minuted their resolve not to allow running powers over their railway, nor subscribe to it.

There are no papers explaining the reason for this reaction which was entirely contrary to the view taken to earlier proposals to extend the line to Torquay Harbour. At the same time another public meeting was held in Torquay to support the part of the proposal to extend to Torquay harbour. The newspaper report of the meeting said, *inter alia*:

> The extension of the railway to Brixham and Dartmouth would confer privileges and facilities on these towns which hitherto had been alone enjoyed by Torquay; was it then a fitting position for this town to stand by inactive and see all those benefits filched and robbed from her?

Earlier plans had brought the railway through the town which had caused great objection because of the demolition of property involved. This latest plan had been completely altered by Brunel, and the Harbour branch would first head southward using the Dartmouth line and would then, according to the paper: '... be brought the greater part of the way through the sea , where no person could make a legal objection to it, except the Admiralty on behalf of the Crown'. But this line would have had to impinge upon the grounds of Torre Abbey, the home of the Cary family, and, presumably, be run to the Western Quay by means of a viaduct over the sea. It would have spoilt the attractiveness of Torquay's frontage for ever and fortunately was withdrawn before an Admiralty enquiry could be convened. Nor was the main scheme, the line to Dartmouth, successful in raising enough capital, or as the local paper rather descriptively put it: 'failed in turning that difficult corner for all railway undertakings, namely, the 31st of December when the capital had to be subscribed'. It also was abandoned. The failure of the 1846 scheme had cost local people dear and this time they kept their purses tightly shut.

Doubling of the main line between Newton and Totnes, 8¾ miles. meant that the two previously parallel single lines between Newton and Aller became down and up lines, necessitating provision of a junction at Aller, opened 29th January, 1855, and called Torquay Junction. The Board Minutes of 6th February, 1855 record that regulations for the switchmen at Torquay Junction and additional regulations to be observed by the Newton and Torquay switchmen were approved. On 3rd April, 1855, a double needle telegraph instrument, working to Torquay, was fixed at Torquay Junction by the Electric Telegraph Co.

Following another complaint of the 'general inconvenience of the arrangements at Torquay station' (particularly the shortness of the platform), the Board agreed in June 1855, 'an inexpensive extension of the platform at either end, and a shed over it, and that the end doors should be widened if necessary'. The 1855 train service was very similar to the timetable for 1853.

Christmas Day 1855 proved to be busy for the Superintendent of Police, Mr C. Kilby. On Christmas Eve Sir Culling Eardley and his family had left Paddington for Torquay, for the Christmas holiday, and his servants had placed four cases containing jewellery and other property under the seat of their reserved carriage. On arrival at destination the servants forgot these cases and the train had returned to Newton before the loss was discovered. Next day Superintendent Kilby went to Newton and Exeter in search of the carriage; at the latter place he learned that the vehicle was on its way to London. By using the telegraph the missing valuables were traced and returned to Torquay by the next train, being returned to their owner by Supt Kilby. In the present days of 'trainless' Christmas and Boxing Days this frenetic activity seems hard to believe.

Two of the switchmen were in trouble around this time. The Board Minutes of 11th March, 1856 record a fine of 2s. 6d. for switchman Sandford at Torquay Junction, for being asleep and delaying the 8.10 pm branch train: 'Sandford being a very old servant and very well reported of, his explanation that he was unwell was accepted ...' More seriously on the night of this hearing, 11th March, switchman Pound at Newton let the 8.43 pm down branch train out of Newton on the up line. He was reduced to a porter at 15s. per week and Mr Gooch was asked to fine the driver involved, for travelling to Torquay Junction on the wrong line. This illustrates the very rudimentary form of signalling in use at that time.

In April 1856 it was agreed to run an engine light to Torquay to form an additional weekday train, 3.45 pm Torquay-Newton to connect with the 2.30 pm express from Plymouth. The engine was presumably otherwise used for goods work because the Board Minutes record the superintendent's advice 'that during the summer when the Stoneycombe lime trains would be comparatively light there would be time to run such a train'.

To demonstrate that vandalism is not a recent phenomonem, on 14th May, 1856 'a large cable used for drawing carriages from the side rail at Kingskerswell was maliciously thrown across the main line. The up express passed over it at full speed and was much shaken'.

Another attempt was now made to get a Bill for a line from Torre to Dartmouth and a committee was formed with Charles Seale Hayne of Kingswear Castle as its head. He had not been connected with the 1853 scheme, as he was then under age, achieving his majority in 1854. Other members were Sir John Yarde Buller (later Lord Churston), William Froude,* John Belfield (Chairman of the abortive 1853 attempt), J.F. Luttrell and Henry Studdy. It is reported that the majority of shareholders invested their money without expectation of immediate profit, but expecting, rightly, that the railway would increase the value of land and house property. Impetus was given to the proposal with the granting of the Cape Mail contract to W. Shaw Lindsay† who decided to make Dartmouth his point of departure. Unfortunately his paddle steamers were underpowered and he lost the contract the following summer (1857).

At this time Dartmothians could only gain access to the railway after a tiring omnibus journey. After crossing the Dart in a rowing ferry they could catch an omnibus from the 'Plume of Feathers' Inn (later the site of the Royal Dart Hotel 1866/7) either the curiously named 'Why Not' leaving at 6.40 am or the afternoon 'Fairy Queen' at 12.45 pm. Both ran to Torquay (Torre) where trains awaited them. Alternatively would-be passengers could travel by boat to Totnes.

To ensure the prosperity of the line which would obviously depend greatly on long distance traffic from beyond Newton, the committee resolved to build a station for Torquay at Livermead. This would partially placate those who wanted a station at the harbour and also please the fish merchants of Brixham who had been clamouring for a quay at Livermead where the fish could be unloaded, thus avoiding the long road journey. But more than this it would also mean that passengers booking to Torquay would have to travel for a mile over the new line.

* William Froude (1810-1879) was a civil engineer, initially working with Brunel on the Bristol & Exeter Railway. He retired from professional life in 1846 and devoted himself to investigating the conditions of naval construction. In 1870 he built the first-ever tank for testing models of ships next to his house in Torquay. The results of his analysis on the rolling of ships ('Froude's Law') were used until the advent of computers in the 1970s. When he died in 1879 the Lord Commissioners of the Admiralty told his family they considered his death a national loss.

† W. Shaw Lindsay had obtained a contract for the Cape and India mails for five years in 1855 (prior to this all mails had been sent from Southampton). The service from Dartmouth started on 5th August, 1856 but was 'dissolved' before August 1857. On 12th October, 1857 the Union line of mail steamers took over the service from Plymouth.

The line was two miles shorter than the 1853 proposal, omitting the loop to Brixham. The Engineer was I.K. Brunel. The Prospectus was printed in the *Dartmouth Chronicle* for December 1856 (the paper was at that time printed monthly).

Remembering the money lost in the 1846 and 1853 proposals there was little local interest in the scheme until Seale Hayne and the Directors undertook to pay all expenses until 31st December, 1856 and anything over 10s. thereafter. After much canvassing it was just possible to raise the necessary 75 per cent of the capital by 29th December, 1856, two days before the deadline. £40,000 of this was contributed by 174 persons with a local interest (only £1,800 came from Brixham and nothing from Torquay which had more interest in a line to the harbour).

Late in November Brunel presented his estimate: the exact figure is not known but it was considerably in excess of the £80,000 capital the Directors had allowed for. Brunel was persuaded to revise his estimates to £90,000, which was all the Directors could afford, but it is unlikely that he had any faith in this figure.

After years of effort this time the Bill before Parliament was successful (despite opposition from Sir H.P. Seale and Mr Mallock of Cockington - the latter being placated by a promise of a coastal viaduct within Cockington parish), and the Dartmouth & Torbay Railway received the Royal Assent on 27th July, 1857. Just a few days before this the SDR decided to construct a lime siding at Torquay (Torre) at an estimated cost of £80, no doubt with a view to supplying ballast from its Stoneycombe Quarry. The year ended with a fire and Torquay goods shed was destroyed due to a faulty flue on a stove, even though this had previously been altered to meet insurance requirements.

South Devon Railway cash account for Torquay station – 1854.

Chapter Three

The Dartmouth & Torbay Railway: Torre to Kingswear 1857-1865

The Dartmouth & Torbay Railway Act provided for construction of a broad gauge railway,

> ... commencing by a junction with the Torquay branch of the South Devon Railway, at or near the north end of the Torquay station , at or near Torre ... and terminating at a point in a field or enclosure adjoining the River Dart belonging to John Fownes Luttrell,[*] and in the occupation of William Paige, in the parish of Brixham.

The line as then devised would have been 9 miles 2½ chains in length.

A large part of the Act allowed for the acquisition of the Dartmouth Floating Bridge company by the Dartmouth & Torbay Co. to enable the latter to control the ferry service to Dartmouth. The Floating Bridge Co. had for many years been managed by Sir Henry P. Seale, Bart as mortgagee. He was made a Director of the D&T Co. and received £2,000 in paid up shares as compensation for giving up powers bestowed by Act of Parliament by which he could prevent a competing ferry being established within three miles either side of the Floating Bridge. Other railway Directors were his nephew Charles Seale Hayne (Chairman), John Belfield, Henry Carew Hunt, Henry Studdy and Captain John Bulley. Working arrangements could be made with either the South Devon or Great Western companies, or both.

Capital was £90,000 in shares and £30,000 in loans. The *Dartmouth Chronicle* of July 1857 stated that £68,000 of shares had already been subscribed (but not paid for), of which 174 shareholders had a local interest. However, no less than £53,000 of this amount was by the Directors or the contractor (some in lieu of payment). No one would take the contract at first, but eventually Messrs Smith & Knight agreed to take it, but not at fixed prices, and indeed when offered part shares and part cash, Smith & Knight raised their schedule of prices still further!

The contract, dated 3rd April, 1858 was for £119,733 (i.e. almost exactly the total authorized capital of the company) and as this amount was exclusive of land and provision of rails, both of which were the company's responsibility, the latter was aware at an early date that its funding was inadequate. The contract required work to be completed, and the line ready for public opening by 1st January, 1860. Payment would be two-thirds cash, one-third shares; as originally envisaged there would be timber viaducts at Goodrington, Saltern, Broadsands and Hookhill. As will be seen, this desire for an early opening date greatly underestimated the amount of work involved in building the railway.

Although Sir Henry Seale and Charles Seale Hayne were related, they were on opposite sides politically. Sir Henry had been a Whig but became a Conservative and was Mayor of Dartmouth 16 times. Nephew Charles was an active Whig/Liberal and twice stood for Parliament as the candidate for Dartmouth. Sir Henry was accused of sharp practice when Mayor in 1852/3 by refusing the addition of opposing voters to the electors list. More seriously, in 1859, his nephew stood down as prospective MP in favour of an outsider who had promised to buy £3,000 worth of shares in the Dartmouth & Torbay Railway if elected. Furthermore, the

---

[*] A point between the Floating Bridge and Hoodown Ferry Passage House, 1,480 ft south of the Bridge and 1,320 ft (¼ mile) north of the Ferry Passage House.

latter had sent down a large sum of money in bribes. He won, but a fresh election was ordered which the Conservatives won unopposed.

The first evidence of negotiations with the South Devon Railway over working arrangements appears in the latter's Minutes for 10th November, 1857. The Dartmouth &Torbay wanted an allowance in respect of through bookings passing over the SDR but the minute records that the SDR 'was prepared to work the D&T for 7 years at 40 per cent of earnings, but not including terminal expenses [as wanted by the D&T] nor making any allowance to D&T for fares and charges earned over any portion of the SDR line'.

As soon as the Directors opened negotiations with the landowners they ran into trouble: 'friendly' landowners became antagonistic and placed extortionate demands. The Directors were forced to ask the Board of Trade to arbitrate and despite huge reductions in the claims made by the latter body (e.g. £5,000 reduced to £1,200), no less than £13,000 was eaten up by compensation claims before all the land to Paignton was secured.

The ceremony of the turning of the first sod took place on Thursday 21st January, 1858* at a field about 500 yards from Torquay (Torre) station, adjoining the turnpike road to Livermead. The day was enhanced by the most brilliant sunshine, more like May than mid-January and, bedecked by flags, Torquay was thronged by visitors and residents as the day was made a holiday. The MP for the 'Southern Division of the County', Lawrence Palk Esq (he and his father Sir Lawrence Palk owned much of Torquay) having agreed to turn the first sod, was met at the station at 12.30 pm and a procession formed up there, in the following order:

Constables
Navvies carrying the Barrow and Spade
Band
Engineer,
Supported by his Assistants and Staff
Contractors
The Directors and Officers
of
The Bristol & Exeter Railway Company,
and
The South Devon Railway Company
The Mayor and Corporation of Dartmouth
The Town Clerk
The Harbour Masters of Dartmouth, Brixham
Paignton, and Torquay
The Chairman of the Board of Health, Torquay
Lawrence Palk, Esq. M.P.
Supported by the Chairman and the Directors
of the
Dartmouth & Torbay Railway Company
The Shareholders of the Dartmouth & Torbay
Railway Company
Officers of the Company
Torquay Company of the Exeter and South Devon
Volunteer Rifle Battalion

---

* Not 31st January as usually recorded. The 31st was a Sunday and the event is described in a supplement to the *Torquay Directory* dated 27th January, 1858 ('last Thursday'). The *Dartmouth Chronicle* report gives the date, 'Thursday the 21st ult.'.

Charles Seale Hayne opened the proceedings by outlining the principal reasons for construction of the railway:

1. The provision of 'railway communication' to the magnficent harbour at Dartmouth which offered unrivalled accommodation to the large classes of steamer now in use.
2. The development of the traffic of the increasing port town of Brixham.
3. To place the beauties of the River Dart within reach of the numerous visitors to Torbay.
4. Erection of a station at Livermead would afford much better accommodation to the inhabitants of Torquay.

Mr Palk then turned the first sod which he wheeled away 'in a handsome mahogany wheelbarrow' and tipped. The Directors and others followed suit until the handle of the polished steel spade was broken by Thomas Woollcombe, Chairman of the SDR! In his speech Mr Palk forecast that just as Torquay had grown quickly, 'so would they see, on the banks of Dartmouth, vast stores, vast docks, vast commence , vast population'. They intended to open the line to Dartmouth by 1st September, 1860. Mr Woollcombe also made a speech and Sir Henry Seale, Mayor of Dartmouth, wound up this part of the proceedings by thanking Mr Palk 'most cordially for the part he had taken in the work'. A liberal supply of champagne, provided by the contractors was then used to toast 'success to the Dartmouth Railway'. A procession then reformed and 'proceeded through the principal streets of the town, headed by the Torquay Subscription Band. The rifle corps brought up the rear, followed by a long line of carriages whose fair occupants had been witnesses of the ceremony. The entire colonnade upwards of a mile in length halted at the Union Hotel where at three o'clock upwards of 250 gentlemen sat down to a dinner'. The *Dartmouth Chronicle*, from which this extract is taken, continued: 'Although [the dinner was] described by a contemporary as a "sumptuous repast" the less said the better. On the completion of the line to Dartmouth we hope to meet our Torquay friends at *this* end of the line and enable them to enjoy in reality what existed only in *imagination* on this occasion'[!]

The first half-yearly meeting of the company was held on 23rd February and was well attended. After detailing the receipts and costs incurred so far, Charles Seale Hayne advised the meeting that Brunel, the Engineer, wanted to alter the course of the line at Livermead (to save money). It was planned to cross the sands there on a viaduct but Brunel wanted to take the line inland. This later led to costly litigation with C.H. Mallock of Cockington Court, the Lord of the Manor, as his fields would be crossed by the resited line; which Mr Mallock lost. The deviation made necessary the construction of a short tunnel between Livermead and Preston. Land was being purchased sufficient for the line to be doubled throughout later, if necessary: about 10-12 acres of land per mile was necessary.

In April 1858 contractor's rails were heaped alongside roads and in a field at Livermead rows of stabling, forges, etc. were springing up. Two cargos of contractor's trucks and railway material had been landed at Torquay and a third cargo was expected at Paignton. The line was staked out west of Livermead House and the contractors only awaited possession of the land to start work.

During the first half of 1858 the SDR minutes have several entries concerning the rate to be charged the D&T for working the line. The SDR wanted more than 40 per cent of the gross earnings for working goods traffic and also suggested a temporarily higher percentage of the earnings for the 'partial openings' to the intermediate stations so as to make the D&T keep the pressure on the contractor for a speedy

The seal of the Dartmouth & Torbay Railway. *NRM/SSPL*

Cutting of first sod at Torquay, 21st January, 1858.

COMMENCEMENT OF THE DARTMOUTH AND TORBAY RAILWAY, AT TORQUAY.—

conclusion of the building of the line. In February they suggested a charge of 55 per cent of the gross earnings for working goods to Paignton only, reducing to 45 per cent when open to Galmpton (Brixham Road). But in March, having learned that it cost them 82 per cent of the receipts to work their own (i.e. SDR) goods traffic they went back with a new proposal to charge 70 per cent for working goods traffic.

This brought a furious protest from the D&T who complained of the conduct of the SDR Board throughout the negotiations. After due consideration the SDR agreed to reduce its charge for goods traffic to 65 per cent but would not 'reopen other matters already sealed' and gave the D&T the option of breaking off negotiations if it wished.

About a fortnight later, the Secretary of the D&T wrote accepting the SDR terms although the matter would have to be ratified at a 'special meeting' of 18th May. The 'intermediate opening terms' were later advised to the D&T as 87½ per cent whilst working goods to Paignton only and 82½ per cent to Churston Ferrers. On 15th June a meeting of the D&T proprietors accepted the SDR terms for working the D&T for seven years, and sealed agreements were exchanged in July 1858.

The working agreement, dated 15th June, 1858, described the line as terminating 'at the northern point of arrival and departure of the Floating Bridge over the river Dart [these days known as the Higher Ferry] in the parish of Brixham'. The railway was to be constructed by the D&T at its expense,

. . . with a single line of rails throughout , and with sufficient double lines of rails for insuring regularity and safety in working including the electric telegraph and all requisite sidings, passing places, stations and other accommodation …

A contract would be entered into whereby the SDR would work the line for seven years from the date of the line's completion. The D&T was to be responsible for maintenance of each section to be opened for the first 12 months, after which the SDR would assume this responsibility, and its costs. William Bell (1818-1892) was Resident Engineer of the D&T from 1857-1861; he had been engaged on the SDR widening works between 1853-1856 and was later Engineer for the construction of Hollacombe gas works and the Torbay & Brixham Railway.

An interesting part of the agreement relates to the provision of a station at Livermead to cater for Torquay traffic. The outlay for the D&T was stipulated not to exceed £1,500, but if, later, it was felt that a further outlay was required to improve 'communication with Torquay and bring more traffic to the line' the two companies would agree the improvements. The D&T would build the new accommodation (not to exceed £3,500 without its approval) but the SDR would pay £4 per cent per annum interest on the difference between £1,500 and the final cost, as long as the working agreement lasted. In the event the estimated cost of the station from the start was £4,000 because the SDR insisted on facilities worthy of this expanding 'watering place' and intended to make this the principal station. Eventually £5,000 was spent (see report of November 1865 meeting).

The South Devon Railway would provide the engines, rolling stock and all necessary staff, together with all stores and materials. For this, the SDR would retain a percentage of the gross earnings as follows:

	Passenger trains	Goods trains
Open to Paignton	55 per cent	87½ per cent
Open to Churston Ferrers	45 per cent	82½ per cent
Open throughout	40 per cent	65 per cent

The agreement said that gross earnings would include a proportion of all through traffic passing over any part of the South Devon line, the D&T proportion being based on the number of miles of D&T track traversed in relation to the number of SDR miles. The agreement was later described by Charles Seale Hayne as 'a most advantageous one, the percentage of receipts being slightly higher than paid by any Company in England'.

During the initial 12 months of opening of each section, when the D&T was responsible for its own maintenance, the SDR would allow an additional £2 per mile per week, in addition to the percentage of the gross earnings paid, to cover these costs.

The Board of Trade (BoT) received the sealed and signed agreement from the Dartmouth & Torbay Railway on 14th October, 1858, but that from the South Devon Railway was not received until 15th March, 1859. The delay is explained by the fact that the BoT were not satisfied that the SDR's shareholders had approved the agreement and they directed the SDR to call another meeting, which was not held until 24th February, 1859.

At the beginning of December 1858 the Board directed that policeman Rabbage at Torquay (of whom we shall hear more anon) be fined 5s. for leaving the points of the fish siding open on the night of 4th December, whereby a goods train was turned into the siding, damaging two trucks. In the early days railway signalmen were known as 'policemen', most of their duties being outside, their only shelter possibly a small hut. This led to signalmen being nicknamed 'bobbies' a term that is still in use today.

At the third half-yearly meeting held on 26th February, 1859, the Chairman said that it had been hoped to open the line to Paignton on 25th March. However, the continued rainy weather had delayed the works, although I.K. Brunel, the Engineer, in his report, said that this had helped to consolidate the embankments. The Chairman made extended reference to the various excessive claims for compensation made by landowners which had gone to arbitration; one for £18,000 settled at £1,200 and another for £1,500 settled at £515. Mr Mallock, a major landowner in Torquay, who 'from the first had shewn a disinclination to assist the undertaking in any way' had lost his attempt to stop the progress of the works but had added to the delay. Because of 'the peculiar circumstances of the case' the Directors were considering whether to apply for a supplemental Act to confirm the altered route at Cockington (*see plan*), but they had 'that day' received a fresh proposal from Mr Mallock which might avoid the need for this action. In fact this is what happened, agreement was reached with Mr Mallock, reported in the *Dartmouth Chronicle*, on 1st April, 1859.

In 1859, the telegraph wires which had been laid by the side of the turnpike roads between Torre station and Dartmouth as recently as 1857, were removed 'to their permanent place by the side of the railway'. The new station buildings at Livermead and Paignton were nearing completion at the beginning of June. The Traffic Superintendent at Plymouth wrote to the Torquay (SDR) station master (Mr Murch?):

Dear Sir

Changing Stations

On the opening of the line to Paignton you will have to take charge of the Livermead station and Mr Fowler will succeed you at the present Torquay station.

The opening of the line was delayed by a slight slip at the south end of Livermead tunnel. The local paper records that the first engine to run to Livermead station did so on 11th July, presumably on a ballast or materials train, or possibly a test train. For less than a fortnight later Col Yolland of the Board of Trade inspected the 3 miles 13 chains of new railway between Torre and Paignton:

> The line is laid single throughout on the broad gauge with sidings at Livermead and Paignton stations but the overbridge and two of the under bridges have been built for a double line … if required .
> The width of the line at formation level is 20 ft on the embankments and 17 ft in the cuttings and the permanent way consists of bridge rails weighing 62 lb. per linear yard laid on longitudinal sleepers 13 in. x 6½ in. with transoms 6½ in. x 4½ in. at intervals fastened with strap bolts. The rails are fastened to the sleepers by fang bolts with bed plates at the joints and four fang bolts to each joint. The ballast is of broken stone and is stated to be 18 inches deep.
> There are 20 bridges, one short stone viaduct 21 yds in length and a short tunnel 134 yds in length on the line - the latter is constructed for a single line with a brick arch throughout and the sides partly lined with stone set in blue Lias Mortar. Of the bridges 7 are over and 13 under - the whole of the overbridges with one exception are built of stone - the exception has stone abutments and a timber top. Four of the underbridges have stone abutments and timber tops - one with the largest span has wrought iron lattice girders (38 ft span) and the remainder are built of stone. The wrought iron lattice girder bridge is constructed for a double line and the centre girder is intended to support both lines of railway but as only one is at present laid in, it could not be tested with weights on both sides; it is sufficiently strong by calculation and exhibited no unusual deflections. All the other bridges and the viaduct are sufficiently strong.

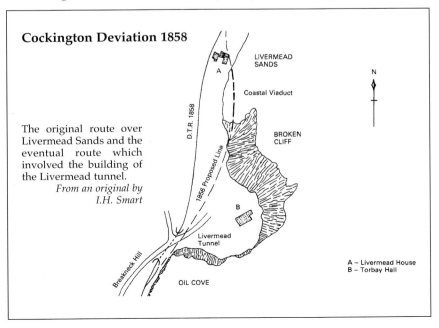

Cockington Deviation 1858

The original route over Livermead Sands and the eventual route which involved the building of the Livermead tunnel.
From an original by I.H. Smart

LIVERMEAD SANDS

A

Coastal Viaduct

N

D.T.R. 1858

1856 Proposed Line

BROKEN CLIFF

B

Livermead Tunnel

Breakneck Hill

OIL COVE

A – Livermead House
B – Torbay Hall

A leaflet produced and printed on 'Paignton Green' by John Robinson and sold for 1d. to celebrate the pudding and the opening of the railway to Paignton on 1st August, 1859. The quantities of ingredients differ from the report in the *Dartmouth Chronicle*.

CELEBRATION OF

THE OPENING

OF THE DARTMOUTH AND TORBAY RAILWAY, TO PAINGTON, AUG. 1st, 1859;

REVIVAL OF THE ANCIENT CHARTER OF

THE WONDERFUL PAINGTON PUDDING,

AND SOME PARTICULARS ABOUT IT.

THIS Pudding bore the form of a pyramid, and was gaily decorated. The ingredients were, 573 pounds of flour, 191 pounds of bread, 382 pounds of raisins, 191 pounds of currants, 382 pounds of suet, 95 pounds of sugar, 320 lemons, 144 nutmegs, and 360 quarts of milk, which made, in the aggregate, a total weight of two thousand one hundred pounds! The Pudding was made in sections, and was built up on a waggon. The procession was formed at Primley, the residence of John Belfield, esquire, at noon, from whence the cortege proceeded by way of Weston House, and through Winner-street, on by Matthews'-house, down by the Cross-road, and through Gerston-terrace to the Railway Station, and from thence to The Green, where about 3000 natives of the parish of Paignton, as well as the brave men who made THE LINE, all seated in a circle, partook of THE FEAST! The Pudding was a ton weight, and drawn by eight horses, there were, also, four waggon loads of beef, bread, and cider. Excursion trains ran from all parts of the county, several steamers made trips, and Mr. Anthony Nicks, the harbour-master, threw open the harbour, free. The bells sent forth merry peals. Hundreds of *pretty hats and bonnets* graced the fair forms of the daughters of Paignton, and the young gentlemen of Torquay took good care to *steal* their hearts before venturing on the green! Even the old men and women who partook of a like Pudding forty-two years ago were much exhilirated by the fun. A splendid band of music attended, and beaux and belles danced on the green, while the never-ceasing waves of the beautiful and glorious sea kept time.

ORDER
OF
THE PROCESSION.
—o—
Policemen.
Navies with picks & shovels.
Waiters.
Band.
Bread, in waggon with three horses.
Committee.
Beef, in waggon with three horses.
Committee.
Body of carvers.
Cider, in waggon with two horses.
Committee.

PUDDING
in waggon with eight horses.
General
Arrangement Committee.
Policemen.
Inhabitants.

Policemen.
Waiters with Flags.

Thousands of persons visited the scene of the festivities, and the whole must have formed a lasting feature in the memory of the youngest inhabitant! A great number of those who *walked* to the feast at *noon*, got an attack of *night-mare* in the *evening!* No accident of great moment occurred, save that which happened to a certain young lady, whose *crinoline was so large* that the carvers when getting near the bottom of the pudding actually took possession of it to keep the pudding from tumbling to pieces—a wise precaution on their part, considering the number of hungry boys from Torquay and Brixham who stood looking on with *open* mouths. So much for the utility of *Crinoline!*

But, as it is intended to say a word or two here about the beautiful sites for building, &c., at this delightful spot, I must now pass on. Paignton is about three miles from the pet-spot of Devon, Torquay, five from Brixham, five from Totnes, and eight from Dartmouth. It is situated in a remarkably rich and fertile district, and the scenery around it is very beautiful, consisting of wooded combes and gently rising hills, with the sea and the coast of Berry Head on one hand, and that approaching Portland on the other, to be seen from their summits. One of the great attractions of Paignton is its beautiful beach of smooth hard sand, which is nearly a mile in length. The ivy-covered ruins of a once magnificent palace are to be seen close to the church. Paignton is the second station of the Dartmouth and Torbay Railway. May PROSPERITY long attend it and THE PEOPLE OF PAINGTON!

PRINTED ON THE GREEN, AT PAINGTON, BY JOHN ROBINSON, OF TORQUAY.—PRICE ONE PENNY.

There are no unauthorized level crossings. There is an engine turntable at Torquay [Torre] belonging to the SDR but none has been created at Paignton and I am informed that the one at Torquay is never used to turn the tank engines with which the traffic is worked between Newton and Torquay. No tender engines are made use of by the contractors who supply locomotive power and as regards this short length of line I am of opinion that engine turntables may be dispensed with at Paignton. When the whole length to Dartmouth (9 miles) is open it will then probably be desirable to have engine turntables at Newton and Dartmouth as the same engine will probably run throughout the whole length of 14 miles.

In making my inspection I noticed that the timber trussed top and the approaches to an overbridge were incomplete.

An alteration was required in the mode of working the distant signals south of Livermead station and some bolts were required to be inserted at two places on the line - instructions were given for the alteration in the signal and I have since heard from the Resident Engineer that the bolts have all been inserted.

The line is to be worked by the SDR Co. and I understand it is to be worked by one engine in steam or two or more coupled together and forming one train.

As soon as their Lordships receive a satisfactory undertaking as to the mode of working I am of opinion that their sanction for the opening of the line for traffic may be given.

As is often the case, there is a little confusion about the actual date of opening of the extension. The *Torquay Directory* published Wednesday 3rd August, 1859 and written the previous day, Tuesday, says:

The first section of this truly beautiful line was opened for public traffic yesterday (Monday), and the inauguration was celebrated with the most marvellous festivities.

White's *History of Torquay* (pub. 1878) repeats 1st August as do P.R. Gale in an official GWR internal publication dated 1926, Penwill's *Paignton in Six Reigns* (1953) and the *Dartmouth Chronicle* of 2nd August, 1859. In favour of 2nd August are the half-yearly report of the D&T Railway (meeting held 31/8/1859), G.A. Sekon's *History of the GWR* (1895) and MacDermot's *History of the GWR* (1931). The 2nd August is the generally accepted date , but it is surely not possible that two local papers, writing the same week got it wrong, and the 1st August must have been a ceremonial opening (although the *Dartmouth Chronicle* does state 'public opening').

As usual the opening day was declared a local holiday, and in Paignton flags were hoisted, the houses bedecked with colours and 'trees planted in every principal street. From all directions thousands of persons poured into the streets'. The farmers interrupted their harvesting and neighbouring towns were deserted. Heavily laden excursions arrived from Exeter and Plymouth 'and numerous steamers plied from remote parts of the coast'.

The highlight of the day was to be the revival of 'the ancient charter of the Paignton Pudding' - an old custom that involved the distribution of a monster plum pudding to the poor and working classes. This custom took place every 50 years, the last such event being 1st June, 1819. Although 10 years short of the proper anniversary, it was decided the coming of the railway justified such a celebration.

So as to ensure the proper cooking of the pudding (the one in 1819 had been a failure) arrangements were made to bake the pudding in sections, being 'built together' afterwards. According to the *Dartmouth Chronicle*, the ingredients were 560 lb. flour, 180 lb. bread, 400 lb. raisins, 184 lb. currants, 400 lb. suet, 96 lb. sugar, 320 lemons, 150 nutmegs and one pint of milk to every pound of solid contents. It cost

£45, and weighed 21 cwt, measuring 13½ ft in circumference at its base and 5 ft at the top. As well as the pudding 1,900 lb. of meat and 1,900 lb. of bread, and an unlimited supply of cider, were provided. Twelve lines of tables were laid out on Paignton Green to feed the navvies and their families, and the poor of Paignton, Marldon and Stoke Gabriel. The whole event had been organized by John Belfield JP, one of the Directors and a Paignton resident, but unfortunately he had been forced to attend Exeter Assizes and so was not present.

At first all went well and the procession to the green moved off at noon, its most important features being a wagon of bread pulled by three horses, two wagons of meat, each drawn by four horses, two wagons of cider, each pulled by two horses, then the great pudding, drawn by eight horses. The people (some 700 men, women and children from Paignton, 150 from Stoke Gabriel and 300 navvies) took their seats and were served with bread, meat and cider by 'a number of gentlemen, farmers and tradesmen, who acted as carvers and waiters'. However, the pudding suffered a sorry fate, as recorded by J.T. White in his *History of Torquay*:

> The pudding was to have been cut up and served after the dinner; for that purpose the wagon containing it was brought within the rope fence which surrounded the tables, and placed in the centre. As the pudding was about to be distributed, the outside public clamoured for slices, and, breaking down the fence, attempted to help themselves. Five policemen mounted the wagon to protect the committee as well as the pudding. Seeing the turn affairs were taking, the navvies and others at the tables, imagining that they were likely to be deprived of the toothsome delicacy, left their seats and swelled the tumultuous throng by whom the unfortunate pudding, committee, and policemen were beleaguered. The mob literally swarmed round the wagon, and mounting the wheels, proceeded to demolish the pudding; alarmed at the menacing attitude of the crowd, the committee threw the pudding piecemeal amongst them. A disgraceful scene followed, in which men, women, and boys, struggled and fought for the possession of pieces thrown out from the wagon, and this continued until not a morsel was left. At three o'clock in the afternoon the first train came in with excursionists, but there were neither addresses presented nor speeches made, for the majority of the directors were in London. It was estimated that there were not less than eighteen thousand persons present at Paignton on that day. For weeks afterwards the Post Office was inundated with greasy packets, containing morsels of the pudding, sent off as so many souvenirs to distant friends.

After the First Edition of this book was published, Mr Arthur French of Ipplepen near Newton Abbot, kindly forwarded a copy of the leaflet printed by John Robinson to celebrate the opening of the line and particularly the 'Paington Pudding' (it was often spelled this way at the time). Accompanying this he sent a copy of a page from the diary of an 11-year-old girl, Jane Langler, who was visiting cousins who lived in Ipplepen, with her parents. Jane had left London on 22nd July: 'We started from Paddington half past nine and arrived by express at Torquay [i.e. Torre] about 4 pm'. Her diary entry for 1st August, 1859 reads:

> August 1st: I went with Mr Lamshead and Papa to Paignton to see the opening of the Dartmouth Railway 3 miles from Torquay. There was a procession in which figured a baked plum pudding 21 cwts drawn by eight horses; wagons laden with beef, bread and cider. Having passed through the town to the sea shore many hundreds of poor people had a dinner after which the great pudding was thrown in pieces among the people … As it was a fine day four or five thousand people were present.

The John Robinson report tends to bear out my conclusion that the 1st August was a ceremonial opening, although open to excursionists, with the timetabled service starting the next day.

The base for the navvies making the line to Paignton had been the five acres of land close to Torquay station which later became a recreation ground. Writing in 1923, William Winget in his article 'Reminiscences of an Octogenarian' had this to say:

> I can picture the scene when this ground was cleared for a move on to a spot beyond Paignton. Rats had found good quarters in this field, where there had been so much corn and fodder for scores of horses, so a kind of battue was arranged for a certain day, when all kinds of 'sportsmen' assembled - some with guns, many with dogs, but most with sticks - to give the rats 'what for'. Many of the vermin, of course, escaped, but over 200 were laid out upon the ground, some of them almost as large as cats. It was a field day and caused tremendous excitement … They must have cost the contractors something in food supply!

Now that there were two stations at Torquay, the original one was renamed Torre, and the new station, Torquay. There were two horse omnibuses a day from the Castle Hotel, Dartmouth to Paignton, and one per day from the Plume of Feathers Hotel, Kingswear to Paignton until the extension of the railway to Brixham Road in March 1861. The August 1859 timetable was as follows:

Down trains - weekdays
am

		previous calls
Torquay 8.47, Paignton 9.00		Kingskerswell, Torre
Torquay 10.50, Paignton 11.05		non-stop from Newton

pm

	previous calls
Torquay 12.17, Paignton 12.30	Kingskerswell, Torre
Torquay 2.40, Paignton 2.50	Kingskerswell, Torre
Torquay 4.20, Paignton 4.30	non-stop from Newton
Torquay 5.45 (terminated)	Kingskerswell, Torre
Torquay 8.02, Paignton 8.15	Kingskerswell, Torre

Up trains - weekdays
am

	also calls
Paignton 7.15, Torquay 7.25	Torre, Kingskerswell
Paignton 9.50, Torquay 10.00	Torre, Kingskerswell*
Paignton 11.15, Torquay 11.25	non-stop to Newton

pm

	also calls
Paignton 12.50, Torquay 1.00	Torre, Kingskerswell
Paignton 3.10, Torquay 3.20	Torre, Kingskerswell
(started) Torquay 6.10	Torre, Kingskerswell*
Paignton 7.00, Torquay 7.10	Torre, Kingskerswell

Down trains - Sundays
am

	previous calls
Torquay 8.47, Paignton 9.00	Kingskerswell, Torre

pm

	previous calls
Torquay 4.25, Paignton 4.35	Torre
Torquay 8.05, Paignton 8.15	Kingskerswell, Torre

Up trains - Sundays				*also calls*
am				
Paignton	7.15,	Torquay	7.25	Torre, Kingskerswell
pm				
Paignton	3.25,	Torquay	3.35	Torre
Paignton	7.00,	Torquay	7.10	Torre, Kingskerswell

* On 15th August the SDR Board directed that the Kingskerswell stop on these trains be withdrawn.

As soon as the new timetable came into force there was a great outcry at Torquay, firstly over the renaming of the stations and secondly because some trains did not even stop at the new 'Torre' any more, which affected the St Marychurch residents rather badly. The renaming meant that visitors to Torquay would naturally travel to the new station so the omnibuses to the town centre were diverted to and from that (Livermead) station, to the great detriment of the traders of Union Street. The latter formed an 'omnibus association' to run a bus between the Union Hotel and Torre station but this was dealt a death blow by the Turnpike Trustees who demanded £100 in lieu of tolls, in advance, and the association closed down after a month.

Public meetings were held at which many derogatory statements were made about the SDR. The local MP, Lawrence Palk, spoke of many wasted hours at Newton ('if put together would make many years!') waiting connections. He believed that if Newton 'were made a Borough town he should be entitled to a vote there on the score of residence', (*laughter*). The Commissioner for Bankruptcy said that on four occasions in the last four months to his knowledge, the London express had been so late that a special had been run from Bristol,

... but when the train had arrived at Newton, the officials well knowing by telegraph the London express to be fifty minutes behind, had refused to send on the Torquay passengers until its arrival , although there was ample time for the branch engine to proceed to Paignton and return to Newton in that time.

Other speakers failed to understand why the company should allow 'the principal appellation "Torquay"' to be applied to a station,

… not one third the size of Torre station, and so utterly inadequate to the wants of Torquay that even now in the summer season he had observed it crammed with persons waiting for the train.

Another speaker referred to an invalid lady who had to sit on a carpenter's box whilst awaiting the train, because of the entire absence of passenger accommodation. It can be inferred, therefore, that the line had opened before the buildings at the new station at Torquay, estimated to cost £4,000, had been built.

A petition signed by 1,000 people was forwarded to the SDR and a deputation met the Directors of that company, at Exeter, on 13th September, 1859. The Board Minutes record their understanding of the deputation's chief objectives:

1. The inconvenient situation of the new station.
2. The injury to Torre/St Marychurch from certain trains not stopping at Torre (most serious objection).
3. Want the names changed to Torquay Station North and Torquay Station South.

The Secretary of the SDR, W. Carr, replied to the Torquay deputation on 2nd November, 1859:

> That after a full consideration of all the circumstances laid before the directors by the different deputations in reference to the station at Livermead, the directors are of opinion that it would be inexpedient to discontinue the existing arrangements as to the stoppage there of the trains running in connection with the express trains, or to make any alteration in the existing names of the stations at Torre and Torquay.

Meanwhile the half-yearly meeting of the D&T Co., held on 30th August, had been given Brunel's report which said that some delay had been occasioned in completion to Paignton by 'a slip at Broken Cliff, near the south end of Livermead Tunnel'. This had been remedied and not recurred and all the works were in satisfactory condition. The contractors, Messrs Smith & Knight, were about to commence work at Goodrington and the company was anxious to reach Churston quickly, both to cater for Brixham's important fish trade and so as to obtain the additional 10 per cent of the earnings, under the Working Agreement. In the first three weeks since extension to Paignton, 4,728 passengers had booked at that place and a further 10,168 at Torquay and Torre, making a total of 14,896. (By the end of this year the combined total had reached only 21,104 , whereas 54,479 had booked tickets *to* Torquay and Paignton.)

At the South Devon's half-yearly meeting held a week later, Thomas Woollcombe acknowledged that the trains on the South Devon 'had been marked by great irregularity, occasioning great inconvenience'. Sometimes the causes of the delays originated on the GWR or Bristol & Exeter but,

> ... others arose from their's (the SDR's) being a single line, the sections being inadequate to the work, and to the engine plant not being sufficient. These matters ... would require a large outlay. They needed to enlarge the Plymouth terminus ... They also intended to remodel the Newton station which would prevent many of the irregularities at present complained of. It would be necessary to raise £300,000.

At this time Newton station consisted of three independent sheds, one for up trains, one for down trains (both of these on the same (north) side of the lines), and one for Torquay trains. The rebuilding changed it to a conventional double-sided junction station, and at the same time the locomotive sheds were much extended.

On 15th September, 1859 Isambard Kingdom Brunel, Chief Engineer to the South Devon and Dartmouth & Torbay railways, died at his residence 18 Duke Street, Westminster. His assistant R.P. Brereton succeeded him as Engineer to the Dartmouth & Torbay.

In November 1859 there was yet another proposal for extension to Torquay harbour, but this time starting from the new Livermead station, and building a railway or street tramway terminating at a station on Vaughan Parade. Nothing came of it.

At the end of January 1860, the SDR Board authorized the reconstruction of Newton station (in red Baltic pine) by Messrs Call & Pethick, at a cost of £9,222 10s. A fortnight later the contractor made a proposal to build the outer walls in brick for an additional £300 and this was accepted. The new station opened in 1861. The Board had also agreed to the expenditure of a further £1,000 on improvement at Torquay station by the Dartmouth & Torbay (including a refreshment room), for which the SDR was responsible for the interest payments.

On 1st February the *Dartmouth Chronicle*, reported that heavy rains were delaying work between Paignton and Brixham Road. The contractors were advertising for 150 men to make up lost time. On the last day of February the half-yearly Dartmouth & Torbay meeting heard that in the five months since the extension to Paignton opened, traffic revenue had amounted to £772 12s. 10½d. of which the D&T retained £344 10s. 8½d., after payment of SDR working expenses. December and January had been very wet, which, together with a shortage of manpower, had led to the opening to Brixham Road being delayed. Work so far had entailed the movement of about 280,000 cubic yards of earthwork to make embankments. In addition about 10,000 yards of masonry in bridgework or culverts had been formed, the stone being quarried locally, with 200 men working on this section of line. A tramroad from Lord Churston's quarry conveyed stone to Hookhills viaduct where the trucks ran down a steep incline. The weight of the loaded trucks descending raised the empties by a wire rope to the top of the incline. (The local paper observed a great and magnificent horse which worked the wagons exactly as needed on a single word of command: 'starting loaded wagons, and when they had sufficient impetus, jumping on one side and letting them pass him, and pushing empty ones forward with his broad chest, merely at the word of command'.) Sand had been obtained from nearby Broadsands beach.

An extra siding had been installed at Paignton, in anticipation of a considerable goods traffic, although this traffic did not commence until after the line through to Brixham Road opened for goods. Presumably it was not worth the Dartmouth company's while for the miserly 12½% per cent of goods receipts they could retain.

Possibly to help alleviate the effects of the 'irregular (train) working', £360 was authorized for a refreshment room at Newton and in June it was decided to adopt the room intended for a parcels office at Torquay as a first class refreshment room. This was additional to the general refreshment room for less important travellers - 'alternative arrangements' would be made for the parcels. In July the D&T Chairman attended the SDR Board with a request that the latter contribute to a bridge, proposed to replace a level crossing near Paignton. The SDR could afford only £100, which was declined, and the bridge was not constructed. On 1st August, 1860 the SDR assumed responsibility for maintenance between Torre and Paignton, in accordance with the Working Agreement. This also tends to confirm the actual opening date to Paignton as 1st, rather than 2nd August, 1859.

The August 1860 half-yearly meeting disclosed a profit of £372 18s. 6d. after SDR expenses. The Torquay refreshment rooms had been let to Mr Cash of the Queens Hotel at £50 pa for three years. A goods shed was being erected at Brixham Road and would be ready by the end of September.

More wet weather and a late decision to construct the viaducts in stone rather than wood (at the same price) - possibly Brereton's idea - had slowed down the building of the line to Brixham Road but it was hoped to be open by November. There had been considerable sinkage of the embankment at Goodrington bog; this was eventually overcome by buying up large quantities of the unwanted atmospheric pipes and laying them in wooden crutches as drainage ditches, as well as dumping spoil from the cuttings. (In 1993, workmen relaying a culvert beneath Goodrington beach dug up three 10 ft sections of atmospheric pipe. They were subsequently moved to Didcot Railway Centre for restoration and exhibition.) After a firm foundation was achieved it was found that the sinkage had been 40 ft against the calculated 12 ft! To date nearly 280,000 cubic yards of earthwork had been moved to form embankments and masonry construction totalled about 16,000 cubic yards. The arches of Broadsands viaduct were finished and those of Hookhills viaduct were well under way. The permanent way would soon be laid and Brixham Road station buildings were being built.

Expenditure so far totalled £93,000 for some two-thirds of the line, out of total capital of £120,000 (£90,000 shares and £30,000 loans). Concern was expressed by the Chairman that many shareholders had not responded to 'calls' (payment in instalments) and it had been necessary for the Directors to buy more shares, lend money and the company to take out temporary loans. For this reason and because of 'the very large sums exacted by the landowners as the price of their land' they must expect a delay before the line was completed to Dartmouth. When Brixham Road was open the company intended to concentrate on development of the line to that point. Extension to the envisaged terminus could only be contemplated if arrears of calls were paid (legal action would be taken if they were not) and more interest was taken by those who would benefit from the completion of the railway, in purchasing shares.

This news brought forth a petition from Dartmouth to alter the final section of the railway and divert it to Greenway Point, rather than the Floating Bridge near Kingswear. From here there were two possibilities - steamers into Dartmouth and eventually, perhaps, a high level bridge across the Dart to join a proposed South Hams Railway to Plymouth. The petitioners felt that such a proposal would save the D&T money, as costs had already reached £93,000 and the company estimated building costs to Kingswear at £80,000. The latter was persuaded by this argument and amended a Bill it had before Parliament seeking further capital, to include this deviation, but this was done without consulting the shareholders.

Not for the last time policeman Rabbage from Torquay had his name before the Directors, the following month. On 5th September an 'excursion' left Paignton at 9.20 am (its destination is not revealed) but on arriving at Torquay it was diverted into the fish siding instead of a platform. As the *Torquay Directory* has it:

(In the siding) were some trucks laden with bricks, flour etc. The momentum with which the train came on put the trucks in motion, the further one of which broke away the barriers, and a horse box was forced upon end, the buffers broke through the woodwork of the station and one or two of the trucks were damaged.

There was only one passenger on the train who was unhurt.

For causing this mayhem, Rabbage was fined 10s. The passenger was one of Lord Churston's servants, who was 'severely shaken'. The Board Minutes rather obsequiously record an offer 'to pay such small compensation as Lord Churston might consider proper'.

Some minor matters of business arising at this time were the acceptance of a tender of £60 for one year's rental of the refreshment room at Newton (rather more expensive than Torquay) from a Mr Bale of Bishopsgate. Also the SDR wrote to the D&T requesting provision of a turntable at Brixham Road, whilst that station was the temporary terminus. The D&T ordered the turntable on 4th October.

As late as September 1860 serious consideration was still being given to bringing another railway to Torquay and the ground below Upton Church was surveyed with a view to extension of the Yeovil and Exeter 'narrow' gauge line to that point. It will be recalled that this area was subject to consideration for a station (for the SDR) as early as 1847. There was still discontent with the facilities offered at Torquay as evidenced by this November 1860 letter to the *Directory* from 'A Traveller'.

Last night we had another specimen of the arrangements at this station, on the arrival of the down train due at 6, the train was late and had to draw up and discharge passengers on the further side of the line, the up train being on the station side (the side on which the rudimentary accommodation was built). No tickets were asked for and many carried away, and when the poor and rich (for all fared alike) were turned out in the dark, they had to get along the platform by the aid of a policeman's small lamp, and then had to cross the line just in front of the engine of the up train. Your readers may imagine the feelings of the invalids and nervous people among the passengers, and their ideas at this specimen of mismanagement on their first arrival at Torquay. It would have been reasonable to expect that it was the Company's interest to encourage passengers to move about by giving proper attention and accommodation, but at present that is far from being the case at Torquay Station.

One of the contractor's men was killed on Christmas Eve 1860 near Brixham Road when he fell in front of one of the tram wagons which were being hauled by a horse he was driving.

The half-yearly meeting of the D&T held in February 1861 informed shareholders that the opening to Brixham Road, which had been forecast for November (1860), but had been delayed because of the 'unprecedented character of the weather', was expected within a few days. Traffic had increased substantially over the Paignton section and the following figures were given:

	No. of passengers	Gross earnings	net earnings
Five months to 31.12.1859	75,583	£811 6s. 5d.	£383 3s. 3d.
Six months to 30.6.1860	77,582	£898 12s. 0d.	£422 18s. 6d.
Six months to 31.12.1860	104,577½*	£1,196 19s. 7d.	£579 16s. 10d.

* ½ = child.

The meeting was told of the plan to deviate the line to Greenway (or Dittisham) Ferry to reduce costs (£100,000 had now been spent on construction, land, etc.) and to enable the line to be extended across the Dart to Dartmouth at a later date. To build the line to the Floating Bridge involved tunnelling through Greenway and a viaduct and would cost a further £60,000 to £80,000; whereas the shorter line to Greenway was estimated to cost only £26,000. This, however, would be some two miles from Dartmouth and would require passage along the river for that distance.

The meeting was told that this proposal had aroused the strong opposition of the owner of Greenway, Mr Richard Harvey who had spent a large amount of money on improvements to his estate of 160 acres. Contemporary reports say that Harvey had an aversion to the railways but he was also a major shareholder in the Falmouth Dock Company, and therefore opposed to the development of Dartmouth. The meeting was not given the details of the works involved but when one reads the report of the Deviation Bill Hearing in the House of Lords it is hardly surprising that Mr Harvey opposed the scheme, even without his other objections already mentioned:

The estate is about three quarters of a mile from east to west, and the proposed railway is intended to be made through the extreme length of it, within about 22 yards from the mansion, destroying the woods and orchards. Moreover, having once intersected it through its entire length, the proposed railway is intended to be then carried back in a reverse direction, nearly parallel with the first mentioned intersection, and then again, by another nearby parallel line down to the river Dart. The effect would be to construct a railway of a mile and a half in length ... for the purpose of a communication between two points only three quarters of a mile apart ... Difficulties would arise in the working of the line from the necessity of adopting a system of shunting and turntables, all of which would take place on the estate itself; so that there would be the additional nuisance of every train ... being shunted twice within a short distance of the house.

The half-yearly meeting was adjourned until 5th April, by which time it was anticipated a decision would have been made on the Bill, which had passed Standing Orders.

Col Yolland the Board of Trade's inspector carried out an inspection of the line between Paignton and Brixham Road on 9th March, 1861. He was fairly complimentary, praising the substantial nature of the permanent way, the good quality and quantity of the ballast and the fact that the two viaducts 'of 72 and 148 yards ... with 40 ft semi-circular arches ... are very well constructed and sufficiently strong'. The section also contained four over- and five under-bridges, all except one being constructed in stone; the exception had a timber top. He noted an engine turntable was under construction at Brixham Road. He felt that the presence of 'several sharp curves render it desirable that it [the line] should be worked at moderate speed'. His only complaints were that some fencing needed repair and that in one place the line was too close to a bridge abutment, and, in another, too close to a level crossing gate post. Subject to these defects being remedied and the receipt of an undertaking as to the method of working, he recommended that opening be sanctioned. The company advised the BoT on 12th March that the line would be worked by One Engine in Steam.

The extension of the line was opened on Thursday 14th March, 1861, a special train leaving Paignton at 12.40 pm hauled by *Tiger*, a 4-4-0 saddle tank of the 'Hawk' class built by Slaughter, Gruning & Co. for the locomotive contractors who supplied

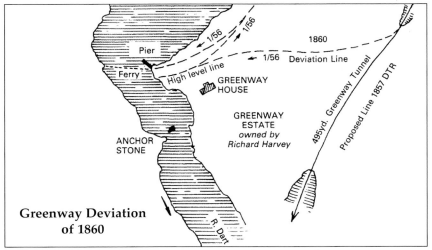

Greenway Deviation of 1860

The deviation to which Mr Harvey objected would have crossed his Greenway Estate in three places, descending at a constant gradient of 1 in 56 to the banks of the River Dart.

From an original by I.H. Smart

engines to the SDR in May 1860. Unfortunately, most of the Directors had been summoned to London to attend the House ot Lords Committee deliberating the D&T's Deviation Bill. In fact, John Belfield of Paignton, who had missing the opening to Paignton, was the only Director on the train, which also conveyed officials of the SDR, and D&T officials and representatives of the contractors.

The report in the following day's *Western Morning News* is included below. As well as being written in rather amusing style, it also gives a good description of the new line and some of the problems involved in its construction.

OPENING OF THE RAILWAY TO BRIXHAM ROAD

The railway was opened yesterday from Paignton to Brixham Road. This addition to the South Devon Railway is interesting, because it is another step towards Dartmouth, because it increases the railway accommodation of the sea port and extensive fishing station of Brixham, and because it places at the disposal of the traveller an additional three miles of a very pleasant and picturesque railway.

The Directors' train, which was to commence the regular running left the little town of Paignton at 12.40. At this place there was no public signs of rejoicing, which we presume the inhabitants thought could be very safely left in the hands of the Brixhamites themselves. Before hearing the screar of the whistle, we notice that our engine bears the rather queer name of 'Tiger' and that it intends taking five carriages - first, second, and third class, to the desired destination. Immediately after quitting the station the train proceeds along a made way - and indeed the whole two miles and 77 chains, which is the length of the line, consisting of either made ways or cuttings, consequently the engineering difficulties have been great, and the expense - that which has so sensibly touched the pockets of the directors - something which we should suppose would require a good passenger and goods traffic to make a remunerative interest - and over a level crossing which leads to the Paignton beach from the town itself. At this spot there is a house erected for the man in charge of the gate. It then goes on to the Goodrington-road, near which there is another level crossing. The rail here proceeds by the side of a high headland, which forms the Paignton Ridge, and is on the sea side the ground which looks on the waters of the bay. A little further on the rails are placed on a road which was found to be very difficult of formation. This place of which we speak is a peaty bog, and swallowed up an enormous quantity of 'filling'. From this spot is obtained the first of those magnificent views which so delight the travellers. It was near here that the old naval hospital formerly stood, and which was in use during the great Peninsular war, and at the conclusions of which, or rather after the final defeat of all at Waterloo, the modern Caesar himself might perhaps have seen in the distance as he stood on the deck of the Belerophon, while she lay in the bay prior to the conveyance of the mightiest spirit of these latter ages to the gloomy prison in which his proud, eagle-like soul, fretted itself away. Berry Head, beneath the shelter of which a number of merchant vessels are now lying, as did the Belerophon then, is very plainly seen standing out in bold relief against the clear sky. At this moment the sun shines out with a brilliancy to which we have been strangers for many a long day, and which our bons companions hope is an indication that better times are coming at last. But we are speeding onward, and have only time to express surprise and draw attention to the beauties of one scene, ere another breaks upon the view. A high embankment, something like eighty feet, says our traveller, now shuts out everything, but the oft-expressed remark that the engineers had rather hard work in the construction of the line. Over another level crossing and we are come to the Goodrington Marshes. This part was particularly troublesome in construction, and one portion sank twelve feet before the men got half-way through it. Those who may still prefer the 'old road', may feel grateful for our telling them that the raised way just here considerably shelters them from the unpleasantness of an east wind. We here catch an excellent view of the Ilsham Valley, the Orestone, and the Thatcher rocks, as well as the town of Torquay itself. Further on the whole of the town is seen, and the high hills stretching away to the left. An artist would say that this formed as exquisite a view as could possibly be desired. Passing by the side of the Sugar Loaf Hill, the line continues on to another deep cutting known as No. 28. At the bottom of this cutting is a place known as David's Grotto, and which was broken open some years since, in consequence of a ship being stranded on the spot. The line then passes at the foot of the old road at Rounding Hill, from which decidely the most varied and panoramic view of the entire neighbourhood can be obtained. It certainly surpasses anything that is to be seen out of Devon, although we fully admit the claims of our Cornish friends, The acqueducts [sic] then claim notice. The first we go over is that at Oakhill [Broadsands], and the second, which is just beyond, is styled the Great Acqueduct and is at Broadsand [Hookhills]. Both are built of solid masonry, though it was once stated that it was contemplated to construct them with wood. Between the two is a very short curve which discloses another 'scene', and as pretty a little bay at the Broadsands as the most timid swimmer could desire. Here stands the model farm of Mr Tully, tenant of Lord Churston. A little further on is his lordship's bathing cove, at a spot known to the inhabitants of the neighbouring places as Elbany. The remainder of the journey possesses no very special feature.

At the Brixham Road Station considerable preparations had been made for a reception. Having promised that the building itself is as unarchitectural as any Goth could wish, we must do the Brixhamites the justice of saying that though they did not expend much time or trouble in decorations beyond displaying a few flags, with such friendly mottos as 'Lord Churston' &c., they did that which was far more flattering to the Directors of the Dartmouth and Torbay Railway Company, they assembled *en masse*, and gave them a right English welcome, and expressions of hearty satisfaction at the successful conclusion of their labours up to this point.

The train entered the station at eleven minutes to one o'clock, the band playing the National Anthem, and the whole company breaking out into a prolonged cheer. The directors, J. Belfield Esq., and Dr Miller (of the Bristol and Exeter and South Devon Railway Company), and Mr Cockshott, the traffic superintendent, having alighted, Dr Brooking (who is commandant of the Brixham Artillery Corps [also present]) stepped forward, and in company with other gentlemen, read an address of congratulations, which was suitably acknowledged by J. Belfield, Esq., on the part of the Board of Directors. Mr Murch read a resolution agreed to by the Brixham Improvement Commissioners. After the speeches, three cheers were given for the directors. The directors and a number of gentlemen subsequently dined together.

The dinner for those participating in the opening was held in Wintle's London Inn, Brixham, and it has been related elsewhere* how it was that Brixham, the principal fishing port in the west, if not the country at that time, almost had no fish with which to serve its honoured guests! Brixham treated the day as a general holiday.

For the next three years that Brixham Road was terminus of the line, horse omnibuses linked the station with Kingswear and Greenway Quay, from which Dartmouth could be reached by river steamer (which called five times a day in 1861). A proper timetable was adhered to connecting with the trains. In 1862 Mr Harvey took legal action to stop the steamers calling at Greenway but lost the case. A railway-owned hotel was opened opposite Brixham Road station on 29th January, 1863. Its first tenant, Mr Carpenter, intended to carry on his business of Vetinerary Surgeon from there but cannot have been too successful as its lease was advertised for sale, with stables and outbuildings in July 1865.

On the very day that the line opened to Brixham Road the Hearing of Richard Harvey's petition against the Deviation Bill was heard in the House of Commons

---

* See *The Brixham Branch* (Oakwood Press, 2000) page 9.

and, without all the railway witnesses having been called, was upheld. Although the Engineer, Mr Brereton, said in evidence that the company considered the line far preferable in many respects to the authorized line of 1857, it is difficult to see that a line consisting of a zig-zag at its terminus would have been a practical proposition. Much was made in the local papers of the rejection of a scheme 'which might have led to the establishment of docks at Dartmouth', but in view of its financial position it is very doubtful the D&T would have bridged the Dart. Harvey probably did the company a favour by compelling them to return to the original, and workable, scheme of a terminus at Kingswear.

The adjourned half-yearly meeting was held on 5th April, 1861 where the Directors' reasons for wishing to deviate the line were explained as:

a) the impossibility of extending the line or crossing the Dart from Kingswear (the Admiralty would not allow a bridge below Greenway).
b) Greenway was the only place from which the South Hams extension could commence.
c) Greenway was more convenient for construction of wharves and quays than the Floating Bridge and also an attraction for tourists.
d) As a boat journey was involved to Dartmouth from either place the extra ten minutes travelling time was irrelevant.
e) 'as the greater part of the money subscribed had been intended for a line terminating at Maypool (the original plan) the Directors were not breaking faith ... in such a deviation'.

Nevertheless the Bill had been thrown out except for the section authorizing additional capital. The Chairman revealed that to date £145,000 had been spent on the line's construction (cash and loans received totalled £101,000) and also said, for the first time, that the estimates made were too low; he admitted that Brunel had told them this. Landowners had not been as liberal with their asking prices as expected and bridges had been constructed for a double line, although the estimates were for a single line. The cost of Torquay station was higher than expected, nor had they expected to pay £2,000 compensation to the owner of the Floating Bridge (Sir H.P. Seale). For the moment, work stopped until money could be found for the last section beyond Brixham Road, and the contractors were discharged. George Knight, being the largest shareholder, later became a Director in place of Sir H.P. Seale who had resigned.

It was agreed (by the SDR) that the D&T could construct a bank at Brixham Road for unloading timber 'as long as no more staff were required to deal with the shunting involved'. Paignton-Brixham Road was opened for goods traffic on 1st April, 1861 but no goods traffic was yet being worked to Paignton because of the absence of a goods shed at that point. Soon afterwards the D&T decided to provide a passing loop and second platform at Paignton.

Mr Bale of Bishopsgate, whom it will be remembered was renting Newton refreshment room at £60 pa, wrote to the SDR on 1st May complaining of poor business. The Board directed that the porters at Newton should notify passengers on up trains the length of time available for refreshments. At the same Board meeting it was decided to construct a crossing place and siding at Kingskerswell which the D&T company had requested.

The *Western Morning News* of 20th June, 1861 had a report that *Lion* the engine hauling the 2.30 pm train from Brixham Road, a sister engine to *Tiger* and built in June 1859, had run off the rails approaching Torre and hit the Torquay end of the platform. No injuries had occurred, but considerable delay was caused to the down express, due at Torquay at 3.55 pm.

A small waiting room was opened on Torquay up platform in August (the next shareholders' meeting was told 'the up platform has been covered in') and the D&T advised the SDR that expenditure there to date was £5,049 3s. 5d. Mr Chapman, Torquay's station master left the company's service in August and the *Torquay Directory* had this to say:

Under circumstances of no ordinary difficulty, with a third-rate station totally inadequate for the wants of the town, with an inefficient staff of porters and deficient accommodation - and we speak more especially of the period when he first entered upon his duties - Mr Chapman has conducted the traffic arrangements with satisfaction to the public. For his marked attention and solicitude for the comfort of passengers by the train, Mr Chapman has repeatedly received substantial tokens of acknowledgement. From the Grand Duke Michel of Russia he received a handsome diamond pin; and from his Royal Highness the Prince Frederick of the Netherlands a silver cup. In leaving Torquay, for, we hope, a larger sphere of usefulness, Mr Chapman takes with him the kind wishes and regards of a large number of friends .

The eighth half-yearly meeting of the company was held at the end of August and to the financial details previously reported was added:

	No. of passengers	Gross earnings	Net earnings
1st Jan.-13th March, 1861	26,472	£404 3s. 1½d.	£195 10s . 0½d.
14th March-30th June, 1861	75,444	£1,092 17s. 1d.	£521 9s. 10d.

Revenue at Brixham Road had increased in a few weeks from £400-£500 per week at the opening to £900 currently. Confirmation is given in the report that goods working to Paignton itself had still not commenced, but that the Engineer had been told to obtain tenders for the construction of a goods shed there.

The company, although gravely disappointed by the failure of its Deviation Bill, intended to proceed with the completion of the line to Dartmouth 'at the earliest possible moment' and would raise Preference Shares to pay for it.

The timetable for September 1861 is included below and is taken from the newspaper which only shows one time at each of the intermediate stations. The apparent head-on collision between Torquay and Paignton of the 3.33 pm ex-Newton and the 3.42 pm ex-Brixham Road is explained by the fact that the former arrived at Torquay at 3.50 pm and did not leave until after the arrival there of the up train, also explaining its apparent 15 minutes running time Torquay-Paignton. The underlined station times show where trains crossed. The passing loop at Paignton must have been ready by September - the timetable was recast and trains now passed there.

		Timetable – September 1861								
Weekdays		*am*	*am*	*am*	*am*	*pm*	*pm*	*pm*	*pm*	*pm*
Newton	*dep.*	8.10	8.30	10.45	11.55	2.20	3.33	5.10	7.00	7.40
					pm					
Kingskerswell		8.16	8.36	–	12.01	2.26	–	5.16	7.06	7.46
Torre		8.24	8.44	10.57	12.09	2.34	–	5.24	7.14	7.54
Torquay		8.30	8.49	11.02	12.14	2.39	3.50	5.29	7.19	7.59
Paignton		–	8.56	11.10	12.21	2.46	4.05	5.36	–	8.06
Brixham Road	*arr.*	–	9.05	–	12.30	2.55	4.15	5.45	–	8.15

Weekdays		am	am	am	am	pm	pm	pm	pm	pm
Brixham Road	dep.	7.22	–	10.00	–	1.30	2.35	3.42	6.10	6.55
Paignton		7.29	–	10.07	11.22	1.37	2.46	3.50	6.17	7.02
Torquay		7.36	9.35	10.14	11.29	1.44	2.53	3.58	6.24	7.09
Torre		7.41	–	10.19	–	1.49	2.58	4.03	6.29	7.14
Kingskerswell		7.48	–	10.26	–	1.56	3.05	4.10	6.36	7.21
Newton	arr.	7.57	9.50	10.35	11.44	2.05	3.14	4.19	6.45	7.30

Sundays

am	pm	pm	pm				am	pm	pm	pm	pm
8.20	3.05	4.13	7.40	dep.	Newton	arr.	7.57	4.05	7.30	8.25	9.00
8.26	3.11	–	7.46		Kingskerswell		7.48	3.56	7.21	–	8.51
8.34	3.19	4.27	7.54		Torre		7.41	3.49	7.14	8.10	8.44
8.39	3.24	4.32	7.59		Torquay		7.36	3.44	7.09	8.05	8.39
8.46	3.32	4.39	8.06		Paignton		7.29	3.37	7.02	–	8.32
8.55	3.46	4.48	8.15	arr.	Brixham Road	dep.	7.22	3.30	6.55	–	8.25

The 8.30 am arrival at Torquay would have been shunted to the middle siding to make way for the 8.49 arrival, and before forming the 9.35 up train.

In March 1862 the GWR introduced the 'Flying Dutchman' express to Torquay. This left Paddington at 11.45 am and reached Exeter in 4½ hours, a 45 minute improvement over the previous 9.20 departure. Torquay was reached at 5.44 pm, a minute under 6 hours: in the down direction the train continued to Brixham Road due 6 pm. In the reverse direction the train started from Torquay at 9.15 am and arrived in London at 3 pm.

The ninth shareholders' meeting of the company took place at the end of February 1862 and gross earnings for the 6 months to 31st December, 1861 were reported as £2,190 10s. 1d. (£1,218 19s. 5d. net). The goods shed at Paignton 'and other additional works' had been completed. Net receipts had quadrupled since 1859, despite their track mileage only doubling in the same period. The Chairman, Charles Seale Hayne, referred to a Bill before Parliament to enable the company to issue new shares and a loan, to pay for the extension to Dartmouth and said that unless more money was forthcoming the line could not be completed to Dartmouth and that Brixham might be chosen instead. Dartmothians were vociferous in their protests and Capt. John Bulley resigned, being replaced by William Froude of Torquay.

George Farrant was appointed porter at Brixham Road on 17th May, 1862. After a couple of minor misdemeanours (failing to trim carriage roof lamps in April 1863 and 'shunting carriages too quickly' the following month) he was appointed a switchman at Torre in July 1865. He could well appear in the 1866 picture with *Zebra* at that station.

The Dartmouth and Torbay Railway Act 1862 received the Royal Assent on 7th July, 1862. The Act authorized the creation of Preference Shares worth £52,500 and additional loans of £17,500 (authority received in 1861 to create £32,500 shares and £10,800 loans had not yet been exercised), together with power to lease the undertaking to the South Devon Railway. The railway had to be completed to Dartmouth within three years. An agreement was reached with Henry Fownes Luttrell, tenant-for-life of the upper part of Nethway estate, for the land required by the railway at a rent charge of £1 per acre.

In September 1862 a contract was let to Messrs Blinkhorn & Atkinson for extension of the railway to Hoodown, some little distance short of Kingswear and opposite Dartmouth, with work starting the following month.

By now it was fairly obvious that, with little money coming in for the new Preference Shares, the railway could not raise the finance to construct the jetties at Kingswear for the ferry authorized by its Act, and for shipping traffic. The Dartmouth & Torbay Directors hit on a novel idea* to raise the necessary cash - they would form themselves into Dartmouth Harbour Commissioners who would be able to obtain loans by alternative methods. Additionally they would obtain powers to raise tolls on goods shipped or landed at their jetties and charge for passengers similarly landing or leaving. As well as helping to finish the railway, the Commissioners would develop Dartmouth as a port which would bring prosperity to the town and, in turn, to the railway.

A Provisional Order (Dartmouth Harbour Order 1863) was obtained from the Board of Trade on 13th April, 1863 authorizing the appointment of Harbour Commissioners. Three special commissioners were appointed for life (C.S. Hayne, William Froude, George Knight - all railway Directors). Two were to be appointed by the Mayor of Dartmouth, one by Kingswear, three by the Board of Trade and two by the Dartmouth & Torbay Railway, a total of 11.

The Order authorized a road or tramway from the termination of the railway at Hoodown Ferry House across Waterhead Creek to the 'Plume of Feathers' Inn adjacent to Kingswear Ferry where a two-armed jetty would be constructed. A new road would be built from Kingswear Ferry into the existing Kingswear to Brixham road. Provision was made for all necessary sheds, warehouses, coal depots and other buildings.

Naturally provision was made to transfer or lease any or all of these works to the Dartmouth & Torbay Railway Co. Another part of the Order catered for the relevant harbour works including provision of beacons, buoys, mooring posts, and lighthouses, necessary dredging and so on. The Dartmouth Harbour Order allowed for costs of £14,000 to be obtained as a loan from the Public Works Loan Commissioners and was confirmed by the Pier & Harbour Orders Confirmation Act 1863. The actual costs of the works was £10,941 for the facilities at Kingswear and £2,997 for the demolition by blasting of Pin Rock in the Dart and for improving the harbour and placing buoys and lights, which work was carried out in 1864/5.

There were two serious accidents in February 1863. The first was to a porter named Manning at Paignton who died after falling between the platform and a carriage he was trying to board, whilst it was moving. A few days later several men were at work in a 12 ft deep ('West Hill') cutting, on the portion of line the Greenway side of the proposed tunnel, when the bank collapsed, burying William Blake and George Turner. Every effort was made to extricate them, but when they were uncovered Blake was dead and Turner seriously injured.

The eleventh meeting of the shareholders that month detailed another increase in revenue for the half-year to 31st December, 1862, although the summer traffic had been reduced by the attractions of the Great Exhibition in London and the poor weather. A decrease in the takings at Torquay and Paignton had been countered by an increase at Brixham Road. Mr Blinkhorn the contractor for the extension was pressing on with the work and there was every possibility of the line opening in the summer of 1864 - completion would be governed by the building of Greenway tunnel and viaducts alongside the River Dart. Mr Knight, one of the contractors for the line as far as Brixham Road, was elected a Director by the meeting. John Belfield acted as Chairman.

---

* It was more likely to be the idea of the East India Steamship Co. who were visiting Dartmouth at the time to assess its suitability for the departure and arrival of its steamers. No pier or other works existed at the time and they wanted to know what the D&T could do to help. Obtaining a Harbour Act was made easier after 1861 with the passing of amendments to the General Harbours and Piers Act of 1847.

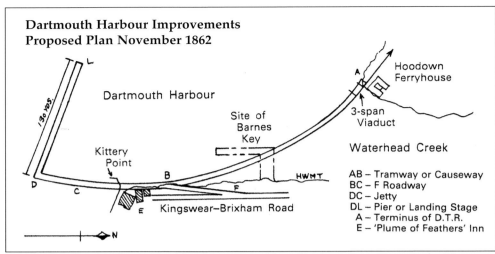

Dartmouth Harbour Improvements
Proposed Plan November 1862

Dartmouth Harbour

Site of
Barnes
Key

Kittery
Point

Hoodown
Ferryhouse

3-span
Viaduct

Waterhead Creek

Kingswear–Brixham Road

AB – Tramway or Causeway
BC – F Roadway
DC – Jetty
DL – Pier or Landing Stage
A – Terminus of D.T.R.
E – 'Plume of Feathers' Inn

The plan showing the proposed 'road or tramway' from Hoodown Ferry House to the 'Plume of Feathers' Inn. Doubtless it was always intended that a railway would be built.
From an original by I.H. Smart

The 'Plume of Feathers' Inn, mentioned in the Dartmouth Harbour Order 1863 and shown on the two plans of the Kingswear station site included in this chapter. Seen here *c.* mid-1864 to the end of 1865, in 1866 it was completely rebuilt as the Yacht Club Hotel, later the Royal Dart Hotel.
Courtesy Brixham Museum

The *Dartmouth Chronicle* gave a progress report on the works in its 2nd April, 1863 issue:

The cutting through Long Wood is about fifty feet above high water line. The coppice is all cut down and converted to charcoal on the spot, several kilns being at work. Substantial railings on both sides marks the space taken by the company. From the uneven character of the ground there are alternate cuttings and embankments, extending upwards towards Maypool, where the contractors - Messrs Blinkhorn and Atkinson - have constructed a roadway, lime kiln and apparatus for mixing the lime required at this point for the viaduct, which here crosses the valley. This will be a substantial erection of limestone, the centre arch upwards of ninety feet in height. The viaduct meets an embankment sixty feet high at the point of juncture, which forms the entrance to the tunnel, which is penetrated to the extent of sixty yards.

The stone for the viaduct is brought from the Greenway side of the hill, being carted up one side, and let down in trucks on a tram road, which has been laid down on a steep incline, worked by a wire rope, the weight of a full truck bringing up an empty one. The Greenway entry to the tunnel has just been commenced. The cutting here is very deep, and for some distance through solid rock. The line runs on an embankment, across a deep hollow which is being filled up from each end, the quantity of filling is so great that three months work is required before the two points will unite.

Passing under the turnpike road, which has temporarily been diverted, for the construction of a bridge, the line leaves the village of Galmpton on the left, and passing through three fields, effects a juncture with the portion left unfinished two years ago, after the opening of the Brixham Road station . The entire distance from the Floating Bridge will be on a stiff incline; from that point, however, it runs on a level by the margin of the river to Hoodown, which has been fixed on as the terminus. The point at which the station will be fixed in Dartmouth seems to be still undetermined.

An advertisement in the July 1863 edition of the *Dartmouth Chronicle* detailed the following connections at Brixham Road 'by the Royal Mail "Vivid" and other omnibuses', applicable as from 8th June. At Dartmouth the service (fare 1s. 6d.) ran from and to the Castle Hotel.

From Dartmouth	connects with	From Brixham Road	connects from
6.15 am	7.37 am to Exeter and Plymouth	9.00 am	First train from Exeter and Plymouth
8.45 am	(Carrying HM mails) 10 am to London and down mail to Plymouth	12.27 pm	(Carrying HM mails) North Mail, and 10.40 am from Plymouth
12.15 pm	1.30 up mail and down train to Plymouth	4.00 pm	(Carrying HM mails) London Day Mail, 2.35 pm express from Exeter and 1.45 pm from Plymouth
2.30 pm	(Fetching HM mails) 3.45 pm up express and down train to Plymouth	6.00 pm	3.55 and 4.25 trains from Exeter and 3.25 pm from Plymouth
5.45 pm	7.02 up train to Exeter and down train to Plymouth	8.20 pm	6.35 from Exeter and 4.45 from Plymouth

By August 1863 the earthworks had reached the Floating Bridge, 90,000 cubic yards of embankment having been formed. Greenway (Maypool) viaduct piers had been built and 3,500 cubic yards of masonry had been erected. Brereton reported that the best site for a station at Dartmouth would be the south of the New Ground, the area known as Spithead (*see Appendix One*).

Before the end of the year it had been decided to extend the railway beyond Hoodown, across Waterhead Creek to Kingswear Point under the auspices of the Dartmouth Harbour Commissioners. They concluded an agreement in October 1863 with the tenant-for-life of the lower part of Nethway estate, George Fownes Luttrell, conveying the land required at a rent charge of £1 per acre. The Hoodown Ferry House was to be purchased (for £300); the Lower Ferry together with foreshore properties at Kingswear (*see plan p.50*) was to be bought for £3,000.

These Heads of Agreement and those relating to the land belonging to H.F. Luttrell (now deceased) were not conveyed to the Dartmouth & Torbay Railway until 18th November, 1873, by when G.F. Luttrell had converted his tenure as a tenant-for-life into absolute ownership. In all the conveyances there was a clause that no one should challenge the absolute title to the property of G.F. Luttrell, but Seale Hayne, a barrister, insisted on inclusion of an indemnification clause as protection against possible claims from other parties.* The rent charge and an annuity from the Floating Bridge (to be paid by the railway if the bridge was abandoned) were offered for sale when Nethway and other Luttrell holdings in Kingswear were put on the market in July 1874, but failed to reach their reserve price.

The *Dartmouth Chronicle* of 1st December, 1863, said:

The Greenway Tunnel advances slowly, about one hundred yards being completed at each end, a solid mass of rock rendering the work necessarily tedious. The viaduct will be a noble structure when complete, which, should fine weather continue, be in about two months. At Noss the work seems to proceed more slowly, the pile driving machines having a tedious task in getting the huge piles driven to a foundation. The cutting in Lower Noss Field has made considerable advancement in the last few weeks, and the embankment now reaches the Floating Bridge. A gang of hands commenced at Hoodown last week and have already much altered the rural appearance of Mrs Burgoine's favourite cottage garden. It is intended to cross the Waterhead Creek on a solid embankment. A station is to be built about the site at present occupied by Mr Alford's building yard .

On 12th January, 1864 the 'early goods train' ran through the gates of Tanner's Crossing (Goodrington) - the cost of repairs was to be charged to the locomotive contractors.

In January also there was a little local difficulty with Sir Henry Seale (Bart) who was the mortgagee of the Dartmouth Floating Bridge Co. and also a shareholder (originally a Director) in the D&T, and it will be remembered, the Chairman's uncle. Despite having received compensation of £2,000 'for all injury sustained' in 1857, on hearing that the company had now decided to abandon the attempt to reach Dartmouth and proceed beyond Hoodown to Kingswear, Sir Henry Seale obtained an injunction to prevent the company from crossing the road leading to the Floating Bridge (which his father had built). The company was quite sure of its ability to win in court but could not afford the cost of litigation and so a compromise was reached: £150 compensation was paid to Sir Henry and the D&T dropped its right (under the 1857 Act) of acquisition of the Floating Bridge Co. For his part Sir Henry Seale waived his powers of preventing anyone from crossing the river within three miles of his Floating Bridge, thus opening the door to the D&T to provide a ferry service from Kingswear to Dartmouth (Spithead).

* In 1856 the life tenant of the Luttrell estates was John Fownes Luttrell (1787-1857), first son of John Francis Luttrell (1752-1816). In 1857 the life tenancy passed to his brother Henry Fownes Luttrell (1790-1867) and then to George Fownes Luttrell, first son of Francis Fownes Luttrell (third son of 'old John'). By some means George converted his life interest to an absolute holding, hence Seale Hayne's caution. I am grateful to Ivor Smart for information re the Luttrell family.

The next (thirteenth) meeting of the company took place on the last day of February 1864 and the shareholders were told of the intention to complete the line to Kingswear. Gross receipts for the last half-year were about the same as the corresponding period of 1862. The Directors bemoaned the fact that although passenger traffic on the line had increased, particularly to Torquay and Brixham, the traffic to Paignton had remained static. Despite the line to Paignton having been open for five years, little had been done to improve the town and it was hoped that 'local parties would take some steps to attract visitors'. The company were pleased to note a Bill in Parliament proposing the construction of an independent line from Brixham Road to Brixham and would give this every support.

Temporary loans had increased as the Directors had not yet issued the authorized Preference Shares (because no-one wanted to buy them!), but expenses had been kept down, in particular because the rails for the new section had been bought some time ago at advantageous terms. Expenditure to date was £192,337 of which construction costs accounted for £114,467. The Engineer, RP. Brereton, reported as follows:

> The works and permanent way between Torquay and Brixham Road Station continue in good condition. Upon the line between Brixham Road and Dartmouth the contractor has made great progress. The earthwork is nearly completed as far as the Floating Bridge, and from thence to Hoodown is in a forward state. The excavation upon the extension of the line to Kingswear Point has recently been commenced, possession of the necessary property having been obtained. The embankment across the Waterhead Creek, where there is a considerable depth of mud, is proceeding satisfactorily, being already upwards of halfway across. Altogether about 200,000 cubic yards of excavation have been taken to embankment. The masonry in bridges and viaducts is nearly completed, about 7,500 cubic yards having been executed. Two arches only of the Greenway Viaduct remain to be turned. At the Longwood Viaduct, in the river Dart, the heavy piling of the foundations has been completed, and the superstructure is in progress. At the Noss Creek the piling is proceeding satisfactorily, five sets only remaining to be driven. Bottom ballast has been laid for nearly a mile in length, and the permanent way has been commenced. At the Greenway tunnel the work is now proceeding rapidly, the entrances having heen built and 300 lineal yards out of 490 driven. The heavy ground at the south end, which has hitherto caused delay, is now passed through, and greater progress may be expected, about eight yards per week having hitherto been the average rate of driving. The station arrangements at Kingswear Point have been determined upon, and will shortly be proceeded with, as well as a landing place on the Dartmouth side.

Greenway (or Maypool) viaduct was built in stone whilst Longwood and Noss which were across creeks were built in timber on piles about 40 ft high, and 200 and 170 yards long respectively. In August the *Dartmouth Chronicle* reported that the mud at Waterhead Creek was so deep that 300 tons of hard material had to be tipped (over 30 days) before a foundation could be effected.

The embankment to the site of Kingswear station was completed by the beginning of May, obliterating the 'quaint' Alford's shipyard in the process. By the end of the month the contractors had started to build an 80 ft jetty at Spithead (Dartmouth).

On Saturday 28th May, William Carnell, a packer on the railway, while detaching a ballast truck between Torquay and Paignton, was knocked down and the train passed over him. He was taken to the Infirmary, but later died. The excavation of the opposite ends of Greenway tunnel met in mid-June and the viaducts were completed the same month. On 1st July the Secretary of the D&T wrote to the Board of Trade giving one month's notice of intent of opening between Brixham Road and

Noss viaduct, brand new in 1864; this was designed by Brereton. *Courtesy Brixham Museum*

The very basic facilities provided at Kingswear at first can be seen in this August 1864 photograph. It is unlikely it was taken on opening day because there is luggage on the platform, but was probably the scene at the Regatta, two weeks after opening, judging by the boats dressed with bunting. In any event the railway is new enough to attract the attention of onlookers leaning over the wall. The wharves for goods traffic are not yet built.

Totnes Image Bank

Kingswear (3½ miles). On 1st August the Engineer R.P. Brereton drove the first locomotive from the Floating Bridge to Kingswear (a number of people returned in the empty trucks to Brixham Road) and on the same day the pontoons for the ferry landing stages arrived from Plymouth. On 5th August the Secretary advised the BoT that the line was ready for inspection (it was actually completed on the 9th and had cost about £68,000) and that opening was planned for 15th August (a Monday); the line would be worked by One Engine in Steam.

To this sum must be added, however, the railway works at Kingswear which were paid for by the Dartmouth Harbour Commissioners who raised loans from the Public Works Loan Commissioners. At first the facilities were extremely primitive (*see 1864 photograph*) but after the provision of wharves (in 1865) and a steam crane (in 1866) the total cost of works at Kingswear had reached £10,941 (of which £830 was paid by the Dartmouth & Torbay Railway). The same contractor was employed for the Harbour Commissioners' embankment (Blinkhorn & Atkinson), but the station was built by Call & Pethick of Plymouth who had also built Newton station.

The formal opening of the last stretch of railway took place on Wednesday 10th August, 1864. A special train hauled by *Lion*, one of the 4-4-0 tanks, carrying the Directors and officials, left Brixham Road and arrived at Kingswear just after noon. Here, the station buildings were not completed, although the booking office was occupied. The party crossed to Dartmouth in the steamer *Newcomin* where they were received by the Mayor of Dartmouth, Sir Henry Seale, and the Corporation. After a welcoming address from the Town Clerk and reply by Mr Seale Hayne, the party adjourned to a luncheon provided by the townspeople of Dartmouth at the Subscription Rooms (now the Guildhall).

The Mayor in his speech praised the determination of the Directors ('he had been a Director himself for some time but had given it up as there was no standing the work' - (*laughter*)), and made public some interesting facts, not previously so clearly highlighted:

From the time that the first shovelful of earth was dug from the station at Torre an opposition (little thought of as the party was supposed to be friendly) arose, and the Directors were put to an enormous expense in consequence. The opposition continued for the whole distance to Paignton, and immense sums were expended in paying claims for compensation for imaginary damages, and in protecting themselves against exorbitant demands. [One can visualize the Directors exchanging knowing looks here!] This in a great measure accounted for the discrepancy between the calculated estimate and the real estimate.

Mr Seale Hayne in his speech referred to the additional passenger traffic which would be forthcoming thanks to the government having based the naval training ship *Britannia* at Dartmouth. Mr Woollcombe of the SDR reported that a new express train had been laid on by which a person could leave London at 4.50 pm and be in their home between 10 and 11 o'clock. He also said that the line between Newton and Teignmouth was being doubled which should reduce the delay in changing trains at Newton.

Col Yolland carried out his inspection on 11th August, 1864 and he noted that land had been purchased, and the overbridge constructed, for a double line if required later. The formation was 17 ft wide in cuttings and 21 ft wide on embankments and the 7ft 0¼ in. broad gauge track was, as usual, constructed in 62 lb. bridge rail on longitudinal timbers. There were two overbridges in stone and four viaducts (one stone, three timber), and a single line tunnel 492 yards long at Greenway (it is normally considered to be 495 yards long) with an engine turntable at Kingswear. Everything was in good order except for a portion of the double line at Kingswear station which needed attention

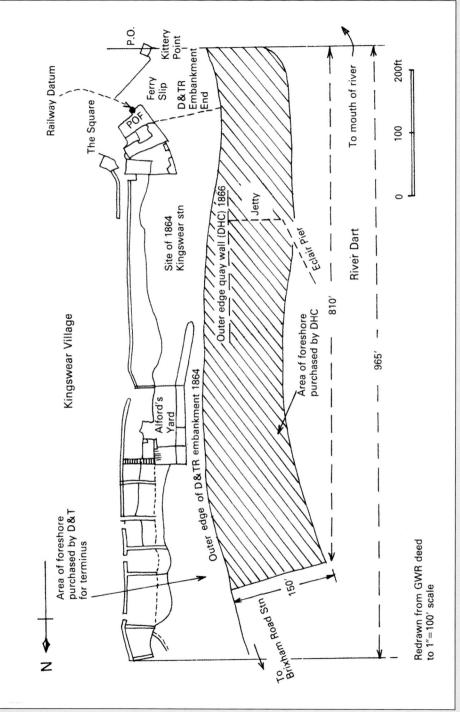

Kingswear station was built on the mud of the foreshore at Kingswear Point. Further foreshore was acquired by the Dartmouth Harbour Commissioners to enable the wharf and goods facilities to be added in 1865/1866.

From an original by I.H. Smart

(perhaps two or three days work). Once this was attended to the line could open to Kingswear and it did so on Tuesday 16th August. The new section of the line was 3 miles 36 chains in length, making the whole line from Torre 9 miles 46 chains.

So at long last the line was open throughout. At first there were six trains each way to Kingswear on weekdays and three on Sundays but by September 1864 a more complete service was in operation as follows:

Timetable – September 1864

		Weekdays										Sundays		
		am	am		pm	pm	pm	pm	pm	pm		am	pm	pm
Newton	dep.	8.25	10.50	...	2.20	3.31	5.08	5.50	7.35	10.50		8.25	4.05	8.10
Kingskerswell		8.31	10.56	...	2.26	–	–	5.56	7.41	–		8.31	–	8.16
Torre		8.39	11.03	...	2.34	–	–	6.04	7.49	–		8.39	4.17	8.24
Torquay		8.44	11.08	...	2.39	3.46	5.21	6.09	7.55	11.05		8.44	4.22	8.29
Paignton		8.51	11.15	...	2.46	3.53	5.28	_6.22_	8.02	11.12		8.51	4.29	8.36
Brixham Road		_9.06_	11.23	...	2.55	_4.01_	5.36	6.30	_8.11_	11.20		9.06	4.37	8.45
Kingswear	arr.	9.20	11.35	...	3.07	4.17	5.48	_6.42_	8.23	11.35		9.20	4.50	9.00
Dartmouth	arr.	9.30	11.45	...	3.20	4.27	6.00	6.50	...	–		9.30	5.05	...

		Weekdays										Sundays		
		am	am	am	am	pm	pm	pm	pm	pm		am	pm	pm
Dartmouth	dep.	7.15	8.40	9.40	–	1.05	3.40	5.45	6.30	7.40		7.15	2.50	6.55
Kingswear	dep.	7.28	8.54	9.53	–	1.18	3.53	6.00	_6.43_	7.55		7.28	3.03	7.10
Brixham Road		7.40	_9.06_	10.05	–	1.30	_4.05_	6.15	6.55	_8.11_		7.40	3.20	7.25
Paignton		7.47	9.15	10.12	11.30	1.37	4.12	_6.22_	7.02	8.21		7.47	3.27	7.33
Torquay		7.54	9.25	10.19	11.40	1.44	4.22	6.29	7.09	8.29		7.54	3.34	7.40
Torre		7.59	–	10.24	–	1.49	–	6.35	7.14	8.34		7.59	3.40	7.46
Kingskerswell		8.06	–	10.31	–	1.56	–	6.42	7.20	–		8.06	–	7.53
Newton	arr.	8.15	9.38	10.40	11.53	2.05	4.35	6.50	7.28	8.47		8.15	3.54	8.01

It is interesting to note the differences between 1861 and 1864 weekday services, starting with the down trains. In 1861 there had been two branch trains between 8 and 9 am, the first connecting out of an Exeter train, the second a Plymouth train. In 1864 the main line trains had been retimed and only one connection was needed. The 11.55 am ex-Newton in 1861 connected out of Exeter and Plymouth trains; in 1864 only the Plymouth train ran so presumably did not justify a Kingswear connection but leaving a 3½ hour gap in services to Kingswear. The 5.10 pm ex-Newton in 1861 connected out of the 6 am 'slow' from Paddington but its sister 5.08 pm in 1864 met the 11.45 express from Paddington, the 6 am ex-Paddington being even slower in 1864 and making a new connection at 5.50 pm from Newton. The main line trains from Paddington and Plymouth which connected into the 7 pm ex-Newton in 1861 did not run in 1864 and the new late train at 10.50 pm (1864) was the connection out of the 4.50 pm from Paddington, mentioned by Mr Woollcombe.

The up trains were not altered so much; the former 9.35 am ex-Torquay (1861) now started from Kingswear at 8.54. The 2.35 pm ex-Brixham Rd in 1861 connected to Bristol and Plymouth then; as these connections still ran in 1864 the branch train cannot have been worthwhile. The new (1864) 7.55 pm from Kingswear connected into an overnight service to Paddington which did not have its own branch connection in 1861. The crossing places are underlined in the timetable above, most use being made of Brixham Road.

The Sunday services were simplified and now could be worked with one set of coaches (and probably one set of enginemen, from Kingswear). The 3.05 pm ex-Newton (1861) was no longer needed because of main line adjustments; the 8.05 pm ex-Torquay

(1861) cannot have been justified, and in any case the 7.10 pm ex-Kingswear in 1864 was later than the 6.55 ex-Brixham Rd in 1861, so reducing the waiting time at Newton. Finally the 8.25 Brixham Road to Newton in 1861 did not connect with anything and was probably run for balancing purposes, not being required in 1864. Incidentally the Sunday steamer service between Kingswear and Dartmouth cannot have lasted long - there is no such service shown in the June 1865 timetable and Sunday passengers for Dartmouth would then have to use the private Kingswear Ferry.

An engine shed was provided at Kingswear, its dimensions being 70 ft 6 in. by 20 ft 3 in. and built in timber with a slated roof. Interestingly, engines entering had first to pass over a 23 ft 5 in. diameter turntable. An enginemen's cabin (also in timber) was attached to the end wall of the shed; this was fitted with a hot water boiler which supplied the foot warmers. The turntable was enlarged to a more substantial 55 ft 8 in. diameter in 1900.

Two large public meetings were held in Torquay and Newton in the middle of August where people expressed strong condemnation of the adequacies of the railway services between Exeter, Newton and Torquay. Mr Woollcombe attended both meetings and alluded to the improvements to be made in September (which we have just seen). He also said that it was intended to double the line between Newton Abbot and Teignmouth to reduce delays; this was done in 1865.

The half-yearly meeting was held at the end of August and gross receipts for the first half of the year were reported as £2,170 1s. 9d. (net £1,155 12s. 0d.), both figures being slightly up on 1863. Goods traffic could not run to Kingswear until the necessary landing places had been arranged by the Harbour Commissioners, and the passenger ferry service was being conducted by one of the river steamers, pending the arrival of their own boat which was imminent.

An encouraging note in the October *Dartmouth Chronicle* reported that receipts for the line exceeded £25 per mile instead of the £15 per mile estimate. In November the paper reported 'Kingswear passenger station may now be said to be complete'. Extension of the embankment across Waterhead Creek was now proceeding to provide space for construction of a goods station but this was unlikely to be ready until next Spring.

On Saturday 19th November, 1864 there was a collision at Kingskerswell. A special goods train consisting of only six or seven trucks left Newton for Torre at 8.30 pm. It failed to stop at Kingskerswell and ran on into the section to Torre and collided with the 7.55 pm from Kingswear. A second and a third class carriage on this train were derailed and several passengers in the second class coach were bruised and shaken, but nothing worse. The third class coach was being conveyed empty to Newton. After some delay a brakevan was removed from the goods train to convey the passengers to Newton, the engine subsequently returning with as many men as could be found to clear the line, which was done by Sunday morning. The other engine was severely damaged. The SDR Board Minutes only give details of the punishment meted out. Driver Hutchings was dismissed and Mr Dawe (station master at Kingskerswell?), 'to whom the accident is mainly attributable', was in future to be employed in the Stores Dept at a reduction of £5 per annum. The disparity in scale of the punishment seems unfair!

Early in 1865 the D&T asked to use the siding at Kingswear for mileage traffic, which the SDR agreed 'provided the percentage to be charged that company on goods traffic were not altered'. This means that because complete goods working to Kingswear could not be introduced the SDR continued to pay the D&T only 17½ per cent of the goods receipts (they would be entitled to 35 per cent when full goods working throughout was introduced). Mileage and mineral rates from this siding to SDR stations were approved in May.

Kingskerswell station 1865, looking towards Newton Abbot.
Courtesy Terry Lakeman

Kingskerswell church (1866) with broad gauge track in the foreground. The church is located between the two bridges shown in the 1865 picture. *Courtesy Terry Lakeman*

In March 1865 the new shipbuilding yard built at Hoodown was leased by Mr Alford whose previous establishment was now 'under the station'. (However, business declined as the yard was sold in 1867.) A gridiron was constructed on the river face of the station approach embankment which was used for overhaul of the ferry steamer and could be used by others on application to the station master (the first at Kingswear was James Paddon, appointed by the Harbour Commissioners in November 1865 - he was still there in 1886).

During the period June-December 1865 the Commissioners were in negotiation with HM Customs as to the use of the jetty and pier at Kingswear. A Customs House was erected at the junction of the pier and the wharf, partly overhanging the waters.

The March shareholders' meeting was full of optimism. Net receipts at £2,300 were almost double those for the same period in 1863. Application had been made to Parliament for a South Hams Railway Company which was intended to commence by a junction with the D&T below Greenway tunnel, bridge the Dart and run through 'the whole of the fertile and picturesque and now almost inaccessible county between Torquay and Plymouth' to reach Plympton on the SDR, 52 miles away. More benefit would come to the company with the introduction of a service (by the Dartmouth Steam Packet Co. owned by Charles Seale Hayne) between Dartmouth and Jersey and St Malo, for which a 400 ton steamer *Éclair* was being built in Glasgow; and promised to be in service by that summer. Finally the expected opening of the Moretonhampstead Railway would connect Dartmouth with the clay works and potteries.

The Chairman explained that the failure of the Harbour Commissioners (several of whom were D&TR Directors!) to provide the necessary landing stages, as yet, was preventing the carriage of goods to Kingswear. The Engineer advised the meeting that the following works were in hand, or completed:

– increased accommodation at Paignton (including platform covering)
– a second passenger platform at Brixham Rd and siding for iron ore traffic
– station buildings completed at Kingswear and approaches to floating piers, on both sides of the river, covered in

-    a coal siding and shipping place constructed near Hoodown
-    a reservoir and pipes for supplying water from Greenway tunnel to the engines [at Kingswear station, and also shipping at the harbour wharves]
-    the embankment for the wharves and deep water pier to be ready by early summer.

The following August (1865) the D&T suggested the erection of rooms over the exterior platform, at the southernmost end of Kingswear station, to which the SDR agreed. The latter also decided during this month to proceed with the erection of a larger goods shed at Torre, and in October a tender from J. Marshall of £2,075 for this was accepted. Work had been suspended following a proposal by Sir Lawrence Palk the previous November that the shed should be sited at Torquay.

There were insufficient shareholders present for the half-yearly meeting to be held on 28th September, but the Directors' Report was issued and confirmed that all the works mentioned in March had been completed, except the wharves 'nearly completed'. A goods shed and sidings were about to be constructed [at Kingswear]. The *Éclair* was running to St Malo.

The South Hams Bill fell by the wayside in April 1865 but the same Directors tried again in August 1865, this time with the support of the LSWR. This caused loud warning bells to ring in the SDR office at Plymouth, and Thomas Woollcombe, fearful of the 'narrow gauge' invading his territory offered the D&T the prospect of amalgamation. The eventual final cost of the line, including the debt on Debentures, was nearly three times more than the original estimate. The D&T needed the substance of the SDR behind them to arrest the growth of liabilities and to undertake the issue of Preference shares to pay off the loans involved in building the line.

The SDR was not in a position to take over the line immediately and offered a lease with eventual amalgamation. A key issue in the minds of the D&T Directors was that the amalgamation should have the effect of indemnifying them from the outstanding debts of the company, standing at about £200,000, and they refused to consider the SDR's proposal without such a guarantee. After a short withdrawal, Woollcombe agreed to this arrangement, although as will be seen, some years later he repudiated it , at great cost to the Dartmouth Directors. The South Devon, as the Torbay & Brixham later found out, was not to be trusted!

The lease would be in perpetuity but leading to eventual amalgamation. The agreement provided for annual payments to the D&T company, commencing with £6,150 in 1866 and increasing by annual increments of £1,000 for four years. From the fifth year onwards, the amount paid would be such as to cover the interest on the Debenture debt and the Preferential Capital of the company. The eventual agreement was summarized in a schedule to the South Devon Railway Act 1866 and this is included as an illustration in this chapter. The two companies agreed the terms, including the election of Charles Seale Hayne to the SDR Board. Accordingly, the D&T called an extraordinary general meeting for 23rd November, 1865, to enable the shareholders to approve the terms. This was fully reported in the *Torquay Directory* and is included in full below, as it gives much detail of the problems the company faced:

THE DARTMOUTH AND TORBAY RAILWAY COMPANY

An extraordinary general meeting of the shareholders of this company was held at Dartmouth, on Thursday afternoon, for the purpose of considering the report which recommended the adoption of an agreement, leasing the Dartmouth and Torbay Railway to the South Devon Railway Company, for ten years. Mr C. Seale Hayne occupied the chair.

The Chairman stated that the object of the agreement was to bring about a more intimate agreement with the South Devon Railway Company. The effect of the arrangement would be, that during next year the rent would be £6,100, and it would increase at the rate of £1,000 a year until it came to £10,000. The calculation was, that this £10,000 would enable them to pay the interest on the preference shares; and that at the end of ten years, whatever the surplus profits might be, the original shareholders should have the benefit of them. They would be enabled, with their South Devon guarantee, to pay off the debts of the company at a reasonable rate of interest, and the original shareholders would then have the advantage of seeing a dividend at an earlier date than if they raised the money on their own credit - (*hear, hear*). The first thing that might suggest itself might be how was it that there had been such a large expenditure in excess of the original estimate, and in order to explain this satisfactorily, he must call attention to the leading features in the history of the line. The Chairman then enumerated the difficulties which they had to encounter - first , in obtaining the necessary number of subscribers; then in obtaining contractors; and , above all, the high price exacted by the landowners for their land. The balance sheet, up to the last half-year, shewed that the total responsibilities of the company amounted to £200,000, including the debenture debt; and it was to pay interest on that sum that the arrangement he was about to submit had been under consideration - (*hear, hear*). On the balance sheet there was an item of £150,000 for the construction of works a sum which had been swelled in consequence of the contract with Messrs Smith and Knight, which was not so high when it was remembered that they agreed to take a large number of preference shares. Then nearly £40,000 was spent on compensation for land - an enormous sum, but the land could not be obtained for less. Parliamentary and law expenses were set down at £10,000, and this was chiefly occasioned by unavoidable litigation. Then there was £27,000 for interest and commission, arising from the capital not having been subscribed for, and because the public had no confidence in them. Then came an extra expenditure. They were to spend £1,500 on the Torquay station, but they spent, by desire of the South Devon Company, £5,000 on the station, the Dartmouth and Torbay Company receiving 4 per cent, on the outlay. Then came the deviation to Cockington, by which the advantage was gained of having the line carried further inland, but it involved a law suit which was expensive, although they gained it. In addition to these items there was the cost of the ferry steamer, and of the two landing stages. The extension from Hooe Down across the creek had increased the expenditure, but the Harbour Commissioners had enabled the company to effect a saving by having undertaken the expenditure at the wharf. The company had begun to cast about to make their financial position secure until the end of the arrangements with the South Devon Company, and two directors had made an offer of very large sums for that purpose, when the South Devon Company initiated the arrangement referred to in the report. The agreement so concluded was to take effect from the 1st of January, and provided for the following payments to their own company - in the year 1866 £6,150, an increase on this sum of £1,000 yearly for four years, and during subsequent years of such a sum as would pay the interest on the debenture debt and preferential capital of the company, not exceeding together £200,000 (*hear*). The agreement also provided that the South Devon Company should keep an account of the Dartmouth and Torbay Company's receipts for ten years, and deducting 50 per cent for working expenses, should pay in perpetuity such annual sum, in addition to that referred to, as the net earnings of the railway in the last three years of the ten should exceed the amount of the dividend and interest payable on the preference capital and debenture debt on the average of those years. The Chairman then spoke upon the advantages of Dartmouth harbour, and mentioned that every vessel had ridden out the gale there with a single anchor each; and referred to the favourable prospect of increased trade with the Channel Islands , as shown by the trade done during the past season by the steamer *Éclair*.*

---

*   Under pressure from the GWR and SDR, the steamer *Éclair* was withdrawn after two seasons and did not operate after 1867. The GWR was concerned about competition with its Weymouth route. The vessel ended up at Ilfracombe.

The South Devon Railway Act, 1866.

SCHEDULE referred to in the foregoing Act.

HEADS FOR AN AGREEMENT between the Dartmouth and Torbay Railway Company, herein-after called "the Dartmouth Company," and the South Devon Railway Company, herein-after called "the South Devon Company."

1. These Heads to be subject to the Sanction of Parliament.

2. The Undertaking, Railway, Property, and Powers of the Dartmouth Company to be leased to the South Devon Company from January 1, 1866.

3. The Lease to be under Section 18 of "The Dartmouth and Torbay Railway Act, 1862."

4. The present Working Agreement between the Two Companies of June 15, 1858, to be determined on January 1, 1866.

5. The Rent payable by the South Devon Company to be—

    (A.) For the First Year of the Term - - - £6,150
    For the Second Year - - - £7,150
    For the Third Year - - - £8,150
    For the Fourth Year - - - £9,150

    (B.) For each of the Fifth, Sixth, Seventh, Eighth, and Ninth Years, a Sum equal to the Amount of the Interest and Dividends payable by the Dartmouth Company for the respective Year on their present Debenture Debt and preferential Capital, and any further Debenture Debt and preferential Capital, if any, raised to pay off their present Liabilities, but not exceeding in the whole 200,000*l.*

    (C.) For the Tenth and every succeeding Year of the Term, a Sum equal to the Rent (B.), with the Addition thereto of a Sum equal to the Excess of the net Earnings of the Dartmouth Railway on the Average of the Eighth, Ninth, and Tenth Years over the Rent (B.)

6. If and whenever in any Year during the First Ten Years of the Term the net Earnings from the Dartmouth Railway exceed the Amount of the Rent payable for the respective Year, the Excess to be applied in or towards the Payment of the Arrears during the First Five Years of the Interest on Debenture Debt and Dividends on preferential Capital not met by the Rent (A.); and the Surplus, if any, to be applied in Payment of Dividend on the ordinary Capital of the Dartmouth Company.

7. In the event of that Excess being insufficient to meet those Arrears, the Deficit at the End of the Tenth Year to be converted into additional preferential Capital of the Dartmouth Company, and the Rent (C.) to be thenceforth increased by the Amount of the Dividend thereon.

8. The superfluous Land and Property of the Dartmouth Company to be sold under the Direction and with the Approval of the South Devon Company, and the net Proceeds to be applied in reduction of preferential Capital of the Dartmouth Company.

9. After the Date of these Heads no Debenture or preferential Share to be issued by the Dartmouth Company without the Approval of the South Devon Company.

10. For

Lease of the Dartmouth & Torbay Railway by the South Devon Railway, 1866.

10. For the Purposes of the Sixth Head the South Devon Company to keep and render to the Dartmouth Company, half-yearly, an Account of the Traffic Receipts of the Dartmouth Railway (under whatsoever Form or Name the same be collected), and Fifty per Cent. thereof, with the Addition thereto of the net Profits of the superfluous Land and Property of the Dartmouth Company, to be deemed the net Earnings of the Dartmouth Railway, the Balance of the Traffic Receipts being retained by the South Devon Company for Working Expenses.

11. The South Devon Company not to be liable to or responsible for any Expenditure incurred by the Dartmouth Company after the Date of these Heads, unless incurred with the Approval of the South Devon Company.

12. The Dartmouth Company to be, so soon as reasonably can be, amalgamated with the South Devon Company on Terms securing to the Debenture Holders and Shareholders of the Dartmouth Company Benefits equivalent to those which they would have under the Lease.

13. The Dartmouth Company not to promote directly or indirectly any new Line of Railway, nor enter into any Contract or Engagement in respect of any new Line, or on account of any new or additional Works, or other Source of Expenditure, without the Approval of the South Devon Company.

14. The Dartmouth Company, until amalgamated, to exist only for financial Purposes, and for facilitating the Exercise of any of their Powers to be leased to the South Devon Company.

15. Arbitration under the "Railway Companies Arbitration Act, 1859," on all Differences.

16. A formal Agreement, with all such Details and incidental Provisions as he thinks consistent with the Intent of these Heads, to be prepared by Mr. John Bullar, or, him failing, Mr. John Horatio Lloyd, whom failing, by some Counsel to be nominated in case of Difference by the Board of Trade, and to be executed under Seal by the Two Companies, and to bind both.

17. Parliamentary Sanction, so far as necessary, to be obtained by the South Devon Company, the Dartmouth Company giving requisite Assistance.

Dated the Tenth Day of October 1865.

C. SEALE HAYNE,
Chairman of the Dartmouth and Torbay
Railway Company.

THO. WOOLCOMBE,
Chairman of the South Devon Railway
Company.

LONDON:
Printed by GEORGE EDWARD EYRE and WILLIAM SPOTTISWOODE,
Printers to the Queen's most Excellent Majesty.   1866.

Lease of the Dartmouth & Torbay Railway by the South Devon Railway, 1866.

He expressed the opinion that had the directors at the outset had £150,000 in cash, that amount would have been sufficient to construct the works, and they should now be receiving a dividend of 4 per cent, increasing within a short time to 6½ per cent - (*hear*). The directors had done a difficult duty, and as the object of the shareholders was not to gain a dividend above all things, but mainly to benefit the district by giving to Dartmouth railway communication, they had not been disappointed - (*hear, hear*). He then moved that the heads of arrangement read by the secretary should be sanctioned, approved, and confirmed.

The motion was seconded by Mr Belfield and carried unanimously.

A vote of thanks to the Chairman concluded the proceedings.

The meeting approved the proposal and the lease of the Dartmouth & Torbay Railway took effect from 1st January, 1866. It was confirmed by the South Devon Railway Act 1866, which received Royal Assent on 28th June, 1866. Until this ratification, Preference Shares could not be placed* and Messrs Belfield and Froude made several personal loans to the company, with SDR agreement, which raised considerably the Dartmouth Co.'s liability.

Before the company lost its independence there were two accidents involving trains from Kingswear, although one was on SDR property. On 21st October, 1865, the 8.40 pm goods from Kingswear was diverted into the siding at Brixham Road, the points having been left in the wrong position by porter W. Lintern. SDR Break Van [*sic*] No. 24 and Bristol & Exeter truck 185 were 'much damaged'. Lintern was subsequently fined 5s. but as the driver overshot the platform, the SDR approached the locomotive contractor requesting they pay one half of the truck repair cost.

Then on 27th December after arrival at Newton at 7.28 pm with the 6.43 pm passenger ex-Kingswear, driver West detached the engine to take it to shed for turning before working the 7.35 pm thence to Kingswear (a tight 'turnround'). On return he unfortunately forgot the position of his coaches and collided heavily with them, severely injuring several passengers who claimed compensation. Driver West was severely reprimanded and fined £2.

The final meeting of the independent company took place in February 1866 to hear that for the six months to 31st December, 1865 gross receipts had been £4,553 5s. 8d. (an increase of £587 5s. 1d. over 1864), net receipts had been £2,682 19s. (some £380 more than 1864). The Harbour Commissioners had provided a steam crane (with a 6 ton lift costing £374) and would erect storehouses at Kingswear and it was expected to commence goods working there soon. Appended to the report was a balance sheet which detailed the outpayments since 1857 in constructing the line:

	£	s.	d.
Parliamentary and law expenses	10,981	17	10
Land and compensation	38,447	7	0
Construction of Works	158,671	13	7
Engineering account	5,859	3	11
Rails account	9,436	17	0
Interest and Commission	27,233	8	3
Salaries etc.	3,361	15	0
Printing, stationery etc.	932	17	1
Erection of telegraph	244	19	11
Purchase of ferry steamer	1,769	13	8
Auditors	141	13	6
	257,081	6	9

* The first £20,000 Preference Shares were eventually issued in February 1867.

Chapter Four

The SDR takes control: 1866-1876

At long last with the necessary goods shed, crane and fish quay provided, the line to Kingswear opened for goods traffic, on 2nd April, 1866, but too late for the Dartmouth & Torbay to receive 35 per cent of the goods receipts! The Dartmouth & Torbay Directors may have imagined they would continue to decide the future of their line, but after the lease to the SDR, their company's existence was a purely financial one. The Yacht Club Hotel at Kingswear (owned by the railway) opened in 1867 and was intended to accommodate passengers using the mail steamers leaving Dartmouth (these were switched to Southampton in 1891). The hotel's name later became the Royal Dart Hotel. The cost to the Harbour Commissioners of the works at at Kingswear had been just over £10,941, with £830 due from the D&TR.

Traffic developments during 1866 were an approach trom the Torquay Gas Co. for a siding at Hollacombe in June, for which a private siding agreement was drawn up on 26th July (*see Chapter Ten*). In August the Board approved construction of a siding at Aller for Mr J. Stooke, at his expense, and the private siding agreement was dated 16th October, 1866 and took effect from 1st January, 1867. The siding was used to convey sand excavated from a pit nearby.

On 1st July, 1866 the SDR's contract with the locomotive contractor expired and the SDR bought the engines and ran the fleet themselves. John Wright who had managed the locomotives for the contractor became locomotive superintendent for the SDR, still based at Newton. The SDR also supplied locomotives from its fleet to the Cornwall and West Cornwall Railways (Woollcombe was also Chairman of the latter).

A serious accident occurred at Hollacombe on 21st September, 1866 on the points leading to the new gasworks siding which was then being installed. The *Torquay Directory* gave a very full account:

ACCIDENT ON THE TORBAY AND DARTMOUTH RAILWAY
A very serious accident occurred to the 9.53 up train from Kingswear on Friday morning last, fortunately without injuring any of the passengers, but resulting in the destruction of about one hundred feet of the line. It happened close by the Torquay gas works at Hollacombe. The gas company are making a siding in connection with the railway, by which their coals will be brought up from Dartmouth by rail, and shunted direct into the manufactory. This siding was near completion, and on Friday morning Mr. Burrows, the contractor, with his foreman, Andrews, were engaged in laying down a 'switch'. It is said that only half an hour's work was required to make it complete when the train came up. The iron bar that connects the two points, and by which they are opened and closed had been fixed at one end, the other slipped between the rails and got jammed immoveably against the woodwork. The points are situated close by a bridge, from whence for a hundred yards in the direction of Paignton the curve is rather sharp. Whilst Andrews was getting the points in order, and which happened to be closed at that moment, the train came up at a quarter past ten o'clock at a full speed. The driver Charles Marsh and stoker William Kerswill seeing that there was something wrong immediately reversed the engine (the *Meteor*) and all the breaks were applied, but the space was too short within which to bring up the train. Andrews, aware of the imminent danger to the train. tried with all his might to open the points with a bar, but in consequence of the end of the connecting rod pressing against the inner side of the

When the *GWR Magazine* published this picture in 1911, it dated it as 1866 so it was probably taken at the same time as the one including *Zebra*. The gentleman in the top hat can just be made out standing in front of *Zebra* and behind the man sitting on a chair. It is thought the partly-obscured name board reads 'South Devon Railway'.   *GWR Magazine*

Torre station seen *c.*1866, looking towards Torquay, when the locomotive *Zebra* would have been brand new. The disc and crossbar signal (*left*) is the up starting signal.   *Torquay Museum*

rail, this was abortive. The engine, tender, four carriages and a parcel van came on, and knocked Andrews away, passed on to the siding, got off the rails, and ran into a bank of earth. The sleepers, the permanent way and the siding were broken to fragments and the rails bent in various shapes. It is believed that had not the engine been reversed as soon as it was, that the train would have passed over the embankment into the gas works, and the loss of life would have been terrible, for in addition to the ordinary passengers there was a considerable number who had been landed from the Channel Islands by the *Éclair*.

Another important and most providential circumstances was the fact that the siding had not been properly ballasted , and the rails sinking, threw the train off; otherwise, the impetus with which it came on must have carried the whole over the bank of earth. The concussion shook the passengers very much but they escaped without injury; one of them jumped out of the carriage and was cut in the face. Andrews, who was knocked down by the engine hurt his thumb. The carriages and van were uninjured and the damage to the engine was comparatively trifling. In the course of an hour a large staff of workmen and engineers arrived on the spot, and with powerful jack screws lifted the carriages off the siding to the rails. The traffic between Torquay and Dartmouth was suspended throughout the day, for this being the up train there was no engine between the scene of the accident and Dartmouth. A large party of excursionists were thus prevented from attending the Brixham Regatta. Traffic was resumed on Saturday.

A similar sort of accident involved the 11 am down goods train at Torquay on 10th January, 1867. Porter John Rodgers turned the down signal to 'all right' before he had correctly set a pair of points, derailing the engine. The porter was dismissed.

On 4th November the last down train, described as the 11.10 pm down branch train in the Board Minutes, ran through the gates at Paignton. Porter Bovey, in charge of the gates and station at the time was later dismissed 'for neglect of the signals and telegraph'.

Policeman Rabbage was again involved in an incident in December 1867:

Rabbage [by now not granted the courtesy of a rank] on duty at Paignton level crossing was reported for not having his signals at danger on 19th December whereby a collision between the 3.25 pm up goods train and the up 2.30 pm passenger train occurred. He appeared before the Committee and was dismissed from the service.

Mr Rabbage may have been reinstated, or in any case received his pension, because Pension Fund Minutes in November 1885 record R. Rabbage, living at 2 Church St, Torre, receiving 8s. per week pension, and record his death in March 1895.

A letter to the *Directory* in September 1867 makes it clear that the line was still worked as a branch from Newton, with passengers having to change there in each direction. After the 1861 reconstruction of Newton station, some of the Exeter-Plymouth (and vice versa) trains of the South Devon Railway may have conveyed through coaches to or from Paignton, later Kingswear. But, unfortunately, neither the public or working timetables make this clear. The September 1867 timetable was not much different from 1864, except that the best journey time to/from London was about ¾ hr slower, but there was a new early train at 6 am from Newton to Kingswear. This was 'mixed' and shunted at intermediate stations thus taking 2½ hours to reach Kingswear, arriving there only 50 minutes in front of the following 8.25 departure from Newton.

Between September 1867 and March 1868 the best journey times between London and Torquay were further worsened by the withdrawal of the 'Flying Dutchman' express so that throughout times were worse now than in 1861, as the following details show:

	Best time (down)	Best time (up)
September 1861	6 h. 30 m.	6 h. 31 m.
September 1864	5 h. 36 m.	5 h. 35 m.
September 1867	6 h. 24 m.	6 h. 25 m.
March 1868	7 h. 19 m.	6 h. 57 m.

The great deterioration in journey times over several years can be laid squarely at the door of G.N. Tyrrell, appointed GWR superintendent of the line in February 1864, who believed in economy not speed. With the monopoly of the Torquay traffic he could afford to do so.

After a test run on Christmas Eve 1867, the Torbay & Brixham Railway, two miles long from Brixham Road to Brixham, received its formal opening on New Year's Day, 1868. As described in my book *The Brixham Branch* (Oakwood Press) it unfortunately had failed its Board of Trade inspection (on 28th December) and had to close again after the New Year's Day excitement was over, pending BoT approval. It eventually opened on 28th February, 1868, and Brixham Road was renamed Churston. The opening of the branch involved the re-location of the goods shed at Churston.

Another accident occurred at Torquay on Wednesday 15th April, 1868 comparable to the one which had caused Porter Rodgers to be dismissed in January 1867, but with far more serious consequences. There were races at Torquay this day and an extra train was run from Exeter at 10.40 am with excursionists, arriving Torquay at 12.14 pm. After unloading the coaches were placed in the middle (through) siding and the engine, *Titan*, a 4-4-0ST of the 'Pluto' class ordered from the Avonside Engine Co. after the SDR bought out the locomotive contractors, and new in October 1866, ran to Torre to be turned. Returning, it continued on the up line over the single to double junction and was turned back into the middle siding by a second point south of the connection leading to the down platform. The policeman, John Chamberlain, had gone to lunch at 12.35, leaving porter Michelmore in charge. The latter was covering for a man named Coleridge, who, unknown to the station master, had gone to the races.

At about 12.45 pm Michelmore accepted the 11.20 am Newton to Kingswear goods from Torre, over the electric telegraph. This consisted of the locomotive *Lion* (involved in the minor accident described at Torre in 1861) hauling 10 trucks sandwiched between two brake vans. The driver was Charles Marsh and the fireman William Kerswell, both of whom had been involved in the 1866 derailment at Hollacombe. Charles Marsh was only 35 years old and had been stationed at Moretonhampstead since that branch opened in July 1866. The goods train left Torre at 12.46 pm and on reaching Torquay was diverted into the middle siding, for Michelmore had forgotten to re-set the points. Seeing that a collision was imminent the crew on *Lion* jumped off; sadly Marsh fell under the trucks and was killed, Kerswell escaped with only a fractured collar bone. *Lion* was severely damaged, *Titan* received a shattered buffer plank. Seeing driver Marsh cut to pieces, Michelmore ran off but eventually gave himself up on Friday and was charged with manslaughter. Charles Marsh left a widow and four children and was buried at Moretonhampstead on Sunday. The SDR Board ordered that the Torquay station master Robert Pearse be removed from Torquay to a position 'not in charge of a station'.

Colonel Yolland's report on the accident dated 6th May, 1868 is given below and makes very interesting reading:

The Torquay and Dartmouth branch, as well as the whole of the main line of the South Devon Railway, are worked with the assistance of the electric telegraph, and on the block system, and they have been so worked, I believe, since the first portion was opened for traffic. Two thirds of the main line between Exeter and Plymouth is now doubled, but the whole of the branches are still single lines, with passing places at certain of the stations.

In consequence of these arrangements, the signals on the South Devon Railway are generally limited to an up and a down station signal, either placed opposite to the facing points where the double lines commence, which are required for passing places, or some distance outwards from them.

At Torquay station, 3¾ miles from the junction with the main line of the South Devon Railway near Newton Station, there are three lines of way, two with platforms alongside of them, and a middle line of way in which empty trains and carriages are placed out of the way of up and down trains travelling on their respective lines. The total length of the passing place from the northern to the southern points is about 325 yards, the northern points , which are facing points to a down train, being somewhere about 170 yards north of the north end of the passenger shed on the eastern side of the line. The facing points for entering the middle line from the north are rather less than 80 yards south of the northern points, and they are situated on what is properly the up line of railway, so as not to present facing points to an up train travelling on that line. The down station signal, worked by a wire from the station, is placed on a bank on the western side of the line, nearly 125 yards north of the northern facing points. It is well seen for a considerable distance.

On the day in question some races came off at Torquay, and the South Devon Railway Company ran excursion trains to accommodate the public attending these races. One reached Torquay at 12 h 14 m pm from Exeter, and as soon as the passengers had got out of the carriages the empty train was placed in the middle line, and the engine was unhooked, and was sent to Torre station, ¾ mile north of Torquay station, to be turned on the engine turntable, with instructions to return to Torquay station in readiness to take the excursion train away. The engine left at 12 h 24 m pm and the regular station policeman quitted the station at 12 h 35 m having previously told porter Edward Michelmore, whom he left in charge while he went to get his dinner, that the engine would return from Torre before the down goods train, and that it was to run on the middle line, and that he would set the points right for it before he went to his dinner; he states that he also told him that after the engine had arrived he was to be careful to set the points right before he gave 'line clear' by telegraph to Torre station for the goods train, and that Michelmore answered 'all right'.

The driver of the engine of the excursion train found, on his return to Torquay from Torre, that the two pairs of facing points had been set right for him to run at once into the middle line, the station signal was at all right for him to enter the station, and the porter signalled him back, and coupled on his engine to the 10 carriages of the excursion train then standing south of his engine on the middle line.

He observed the porter next go towards the south end of the station, to see if the carriages stood in the middle line, quite clear of any train travelling on the down line, and after that he returned, and looked to see if the engine and carriages were also clear of the north end of the station; then he left, and the driver did not see him again until he heard him call out 'push back; the train is coming on your line'; or some such words, and on looking out he saw that the train had passed over both pairs of facing points, and was about half way between the middle points and his engine. He and his fireman had barely time to jump off the engine on the same side before the collision occurred.

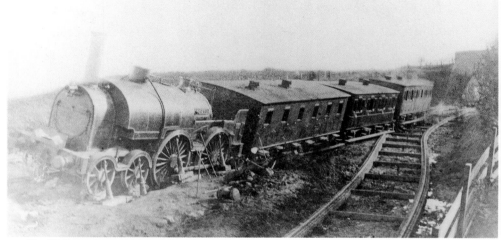

The Hollacombe accident of 21st September, 1866. 4-4-0ST *Meteor* and its three vehicles have
been derailed on the facing point leading to the Gas siding.   *Devon Library Services*

Opened in 1863, and originally railway owned, this building opposite Churston station has seen
several changes of name. Owned by Mr Harris, possibly from 1865, it was in the Harris family for
two generations until sold in 1921. Mr Harris's granddaughter said: 'Our house was used by the
gentry who played golf and by the side of the hotel was a tin hut where the golf caddies had their
food'. Her grandfather spent £800 fighting the railway for a right of way off the front doorstep;
'The railway used to close the hill from the bridge downwards once a year to claim ownership'.
The former hotel is now the 'Weary Ploughman' public house.   *Courtesy Brixham Museum*

The collision must have been a severe one, as the engine of the excursion train, which was at rest, was knocked back more than 100 yards, and the carriages behind it as much farther.

It appears from the evidence of the head guard of the goods train, which consisted of an engine, 10 trucks. and two vans, that it left Torre at 12 h 46 m pm. He rode in the van at the tail of the train and after they had come some way he heard the shrill whistle sounded, and on looking out he saw the down signal standing at 'danger', and then he put on his break, and the speed of the train was checked. He next saw the signal turned off, and put right for the driver to proceed 200 or 300 yards before they reached the signal, and he kept his break on until he saw a man under the over bridge, holding out his arm to the driver, signifying 'all right', and then he went to his van, and the break whistle was shortly afterwards sounded, and the collision took place before he could put his break on again.

There is a steep incline of 1 in 55 falling all the way from Torre to Torquay station, and although the speed of the train was checked in consequence of the down signal being on at 'danger' when it was first seen, still there would be sufficient space for the rate to be considerably accelerated in running down such an incline, when the signal was taken off, as the goods train, due at Torquay station at 5 h 5 m, was not appointed to stop there.

The evidence of the head guard and of other persons at the station is to the effect that the speed was about 10 miles an hour; but I think it more likely to have been at least double that rate. The driver, on observing that a collision could not be avoided, in consequence of the points being set open for the up and middle lines instead of for the down line or even the up line alone, jumped off on the left side of the engine, while the fireman jumped off on the other. The driver is believed to have fallen backwards and sideways under the wheels of the trucks, and was instantaneously killed. The fireman had his collar bone broken.

No blame attaches to either of these men; they were evidently doing their duty at the time, and there does not appear to be the shadow of a doubt that the collision was occasioned by the porter Michelmore having neglected to alter the two pairs of facing points after the engine from Torre had passed into the middle line. He seems to have observed the death of the driver, and immediately made off in a state of great excitement.

A verdict of 'manslaughter' has been returned against him at the coroner's inquest which was held on the body of the driver Charles Marsh.

He had been employed for about two years, and was in the habit of performing this duty occasionally when the policeman went to his dinner, and at other times to take charge of the station at night.

The man evidently forgot to turn the facing points before he took off the down station signals for the goods train to pass through Torquay station.

This is one of a class of accidents which may be entirely prevented by mechanical means.

At the time when this portion of the line was opened for traffic in 1859 the system of locking points and signals had only just been introduced, was by no means general, and had never been applied to the broad gauge lines of railway. Of late years they have been so applied; but a large portion of the stations on the South Devon and Cornwall railways are similar as regards their signal arrangements to the Torquay station. It appears to have been stated at the coroner's inquest that a similar accident occurred at the same station once before, when the signal was taken off before the points were set right, and the man who made the mistake was dismissed, and, in my opinion, the wonder is, that more accidents of this kind have not occurred. It shows that the company must have had very careful and good servants. But the best men are liable to make a mistake, and there cannot be any security from collisions of this kind unless the signalman, or whoever may be acting for him, is not prevented by mechanical means from turning off the station signal until the points are set right for the line on which the expected train is to travel. I think it is not only right as regards the public safety, but fair towards the men who are employed on this responsible duty. I am informed that there are difficulties in carrying out my suggestion as regards the Torquay and some other stations, inasmuch as the company mostly use the eastern or down line at Torquay for both up and down traffic, because there are many invalids arriving at

Dartmouth Branch.—Week Days.

DOWN TRAINS.

Distances	STATIONS.	1 §§ GOODS	2 Passenger.	3 Passenger.	4 GOODS	5 Passenger	6 Passenger.	7 Passenger.	8 Passenger.	9 Passenger.	10
		a.m.	a.m.	a.m.	a.m.	p.m.	p.m	p.m.	p m.	p.m.	
—	Newton Dep.	6 0	8 25	10 53	11 20	3 20	4 16	6 14	7 45	11 10	...
2	Kingskerswell	C. R.	8 31	10 59	11 30	3 27	4 22	*6 21	7 53	11 14	...
5	Torre	7 0	8 39	11* 6	12 0	3 35	4 29	6 28	8 1	11 20	...
5¾	Torquay... ...	7 5	8 44	11 11	12 5	*3 43	4 34	†6 33	*8 10	11 23	...
8	Paignton ...	†7 27	8 51	11 19	12 27	3 51	4 41	6 41	8 15	11 30	...
10¾	Churston ..	8 5	9 1	11 27	1 5	3 58	4 49	6 50	8 23	11 38	...
14½	Kingswear ..	8 25	9 15	11 40	1 25	4 10	5 0	7 1	8 35	11 48	...
—	Dartmouth Ar.	8 35	9 25	11 50	...	4 20	5 10	7 10	8 45	...	...

§§ This Train conveys Third Class Passengers.

UP TRAINS.

Distances.	STATIONS	1 Passenger.	2 Passenger.	3 Passenger.	4 Passenger.	5 Passenger.	6 GOODS	7 Passenger.	8 Passenger.	9 GOODS	10
		a m.	a.m.	a m.	p.m.	p.m.	p.m.	p.m.	p m.	p.m.	
—	Dart. Co's Pier	6 55	9 40	10 20	1 50	3 5	...	5 22	7 30	...	...
—	Kingswear Dp.	7 8	9 53	10 33	2 3	3 18	5 0	5 35	7 43	9 0	...
3¾	Churston ...	7 20	10 5	10 45	2 15	3 30	5 30	5 48	7 55	9 30	...
6½	Paignton ...	†7 27	10 12	10 53	2 22	3 37	‡6 9	‡5 57	8 3	9 45	...
8¾	Torquay... ...	7 39	10 19	11 3	2 32	*3 43	†6 33	6 9	*8 10	9 53	...
9½	Torre	7 44	10 24	*11. 6	2 37	3 46	7 5	6 15	8 19	10 25	...
12½	Kingskerswell	7 51	10 31	11.14	2 43	3 53	7 20	*6 21	8 26	10 35	...
14½	Newton ... Ar.	8 0	10 40	11 20	2 50	4 0	7 30	6 30	8 35	10 45	...

SUNDAY TRAINS.

Distances.	DOWN TRAINS.	1 Passenger.	2 Passenger.	3 Passenger.
		a.m.	a m.	p.m.
—	Newton Dep.	8 30	10 47	8 10
2	Kingskerswell	8 36	10 53	8 16
5	Torre	8 44	11 1	8 24
5¾	Torquay... ...	8 49	11 6	8 29
8	Paignton ..	8 56	11 13	8 36
10¾	Churston ...	9 6	11 22	8 45
14½	Kingswear ...	9 20	11 35	9 0
—	Dartmouth Ar.	...	...	..

Distances.	UP TRAINS.	1 Passenger.	2 Passenger.	3 Passenger.
		a.m.	p.m.	p.m.
—	Dart. Co's Pier	...	...	...
—	Kingswear Dp.	7 28	1 15	7 10
3¾	Churston ...	7 40	1 27	7 25
6½	Paignton ...	7 47	1 35	7 33
8¾	Torquay ...	7 54	1 42	7 40
9½	Torre	7 59	1 47	7 46
12½	Kingskerswell	8 6	1 54	7 53
14½	Newton ... Arr.	8 15	2 3	8 1

Passing and Crossing of the above-named Trains,

In Force on and after NOVEMBER 1st, 1868.

When the Trains named above are running in their proper course, they will **PASS** and **CROSS** each other as below :—

WEEK DAYS.

PASSING AND CROSSING.

The 5 35 p.m. Up Passenger Train will **PASS** the 5 0 p.m. Up Goods Train at Paignton.

The 7 8 a.m.	Up Passenger Train	and	6 0 a.m.	Down Goods Train		will **cross** at	Paignton.
,, 10 33 a.m.	,, ,,	,,	10 53 a.m.	,, Passenger		,,	Torre.
,, 3 18 p.m.	,, ,,	,,	3 20 p.m.	,, ,,	,,	,,	Torquay.
,, 5 0 p.m.	,, Goods	,,	6 14 p.m.	,, ,,	,,	,,	Torquay.
,, 5 35 p.m.	,, Passenger	,,	6 14 p.m.	,, ,,	,,	,,	Kingskerswell.
,, 7 43 p.m.	,, ,,	,,	7 45 p.m.	,, ,,	,,	,,	Torquay

The November 1868 Working Timetable. *Courtesy National Archives (RAIL 981/442)*

and leaving that place, who would complain at having to cross to the opposite platforms, and because there is frequently a very large amount of heavy luggage to be carried across. I do not dispute these facts; but if the Directors of the South Devon Railway company prefer to provide for the public safety, and wish to avoid collisions of this kind, which, if they do not even involve loss of life, are generally very costly, they will without delay instruct their engineer to connect the working of the points and signals at all their stations so that similar collisions may not again occur.

On 6th January, 1870, Richard Harvey, arch-opponent of the Dartmouth & Torbay Railway, died aged 62. Strong feelings remained in Dartmouth over this man's opposition to the railway and when his will was published in 1871, the *Dartmouth Chronicle* published a very strongly-worded editorial expressing pleasure at his passing, 'now no more in the land of the living to injure by his crochety obstinancy the development of the trade of a rich district'.* Whatever were Harvey's reasons for his total opposition to the railway, posterity lays the blame squarely on him for the failure of Dartmouth to develop. Writing in 1954 the historian famous for his history of Devon, W.G. Hoskins wrote 'the failure to bring the railway across the river at Greenway and down the west side of the Dart into Dartmouth itself, did untold damage to the town'.†

Another careless act caused an accident that could have been very serious but good fortune must have been smiling on 5th May, 1870 as no one was killed or injured. The 1.05 pm from Kingswear left the terminus and was accelerating for the climb to Churston when it was suddenly diverted into Hoodown Siding, about ½ mile from the station. The driver reacted very quickly, reversed the engine and sounded the brake whistle while the fireman applied the hand brake. The two guards applied brakes on the coaches but before the train could be stopped the engine ran on to a wagon turntable which was set away from the line on which the train was running. This derailed the engine, which was fortunate as the end of the siding overhung the harbour. Inquiries revealed that some permanent way men had placed their trollies in the siding and closed the gate but omitted to reset the points for the main line. The passengers, doubtless much shaken, were delayed until the arrival of the next down train at 1.47 pm, whose engine was used to take them to Newton. Mr Paddon, the station master at Kingswear, telegraphed for the engine of the down goods to be sent on from Paignton to take up the work of the engine which had substituted for the derailed engine.

Dartmouth and	Fares in July 1869									
	Single						*Return*			
	1st		*2nd*		*3rd*		*1st*		*2nd*	
	s.	*d.*	*s.*	*d.*	*s.*	*d.*	*s.*	*d.*	*s.*	*d.*
Churston	1	2	0	10	0	5½	2	0	1	5
Brixham	1	8	1	2	0	7½	2	10	2	0
Paignton	1	10	1	3	0	8½	3	3	2	1
Torquay	2	4	1	7	0	10½	4	0	2	8
Torre	2	6	1	8	0	11½	4	3	2	10
Kingskerswell	3	2	2	1	1	2½	5	6	3	6
Newton	3	8	2	5	1	4½	6	3	4	3

* An article in the *Dartmouth Chronicle* 1.4.1881 contained some notes about Harvey. He bought Greenway House from Col Carlyan about 1860. He previously lived in Torquay with an income of £7,000 pa. Was in partnership with the Williams family (copper and tin trade) when the partnership broke up. Harvey retired with capital of £¼ m. Left property on his death worth £½ m. Came from St Day in Cornwall where his father was a cooper.
† Dartmouth's population was 4,500 in the early part of the 19th century and remained static until the arrival of *Britannia* when it rose to approx, 5,500 (by 1871), rising to 6,500 in 1901 and only reaching 7,000 by 1914. By comparison Paignton's population was 1,796 in 1821, 3,590 in 1871 and 11,241 in 1911.

In July the Board decided to erect refreshment rooms at Torre at a cost of £200, to be rented by the Torquay Brewing and Trading Co. at £40 pa over seven years. The Torquay refreshment rooms were rented by Southern Cash, Hotel Manager, for three years at £50 per annum at the end of the following year. There were first and second class refreshment rooms and a kitchen.

The August 1870 meeting of the D&T was told that goods traffic from Kingswear showed steady increase, recently a collier had discharged 600 tons of coal within 48 hours. A quantity of Baltic timber had also been dispatched and there were now three cargos of grain waiting to discharge. A second steam crane had been ordered in 1867 (a third one was supplied in 1889). Further traffic was likely from Brogdens iron ore mine at Churston station which had recently resumed mining operations.

A matter of much concern to the D&T Directors arose from the SDR's decision back in December 1869 to repudiate their guarantee to the D&T in respect of those debts incurred after October 1865, bearing interest of over 5 per cent. On the strength of this 1865 guarantee loans had been raised (much of which was money provided by Messrs Belfield and Froude, D&T Directors, following the 'financial panic' of 1866), and large issues of Preference Shares made (£100,000 between 1867-1868). Further Preference Shares and debentures were issued, by agreement, in 1870 to cover £53,000 of outstanding loans. At the first half-yearly meeting of 1870 the D&T had decided that the amalgamation should proceed, the terms being an exchange at par of the D&T Preference Stock for South Devon 5 per cent rent charge stock.

Matters became acrimonious and arbitrators were called in and finally Sir Roundell Palmer was called in as umpire , under the terms of the arbitration, as the arbitrators had failed to agree. Realizing the weakness of its case the SDR took steps to limit his terms of reference to the amount of compensation the D&T should receive in lieu of rent.

Sir Roundell Palmer made his award in August 1871 and a summary is given in *Appendix Two*. Basically the award allocated South Devon 5 per cent Rent Charge stock to holders of D&T Preference Shares (including those issued in 1867-8) who would receive annual interest payments thereon, in lieu of rent. The Dartmouth Debenture debt would be added to that of the SDR. No provision was, however, made for £71,000 of ordinary stocks held by the shareholders, who were quietly forgotten, and a large part of the loans made by Directors Belfield and Froude was sacrificed. It was made a condition of the amalgamation that the SDR be indemnified against all the Dartmouth's liabilities.

In November 1871 Charles Seale Hayne resigned from the SDR Board in support of his Dartmouth & Torbay directorate having first ensured the SDR bought from the Dartmouth Harbour Commissioners the works they had undertaken. This cost the SDR only £697 14s. 6d. but they also took over the principal and interest on outstanding loans from the Public Works Loans Commissioners of £11,619 3s. 9d. Seale Hayne subsequently published the relevant correspondence with the SDR and although fairly lengthy this is presented at *Appendix Three*, as it does throw some light on a very complex matter. The Dartmouth & Torbay was amalgamated with the South Devon Railway on 1st January, 1872 .

The amalgamation was so little publicized that some ordinary shareholders did not find out until 1876, after the *intended* leasing period of 10 years had expired, that it had happened. Certain shareholders at that time served notice on the SDR to furnish an account of the D&TR earnings (in the absence of any annual statements) in accordance with the Heads of Agreement of Lease, and found out for the first time of the amalgamation! Sixty-eight shareholders petitioned Parliament to prevent the amalgamation of the SDR with the GWR in order that they might obtain some benefit from their D&TR shareholdings but the petition was declined.

In 1871, after a lapse of 13 years Dartmouth was selected as a channel port of call for 'an ocean line of steamers'. The ships of the Cape & Natal Steam Navigation Co. would leave London on the 1st of the month, and leave Dartmouth on the 4th day of the month. Calls would be made at Maderia and St Helena on the way to the Cape of Good Hope, Algon Bay and Natal, the throughout journey taking, it was anticipated, 35 days under steam. The local paper commented that 'the jetty erected at heavy cost in connection with the railway station at Kingswear will now be fully tested'. Several days' passage could be saved by taking the train from London to Kingswear and, doubtless, the SDR hoped this would lead to substantial increased traffic .

A customers' petition in April 1872 to the SDR, to prevent the removal of guards Smerdon and Mann, regular guards on the Kingswear line for many years, to other parts of their system was only partially successful. Guard Mann was retained but Smerdon moved to the new Totnes to Ashburton branch. In a commentary the *Dartmouth Chronicle* said the reason for removal was 'quite unaccountable - (it was) not promotion'.

It seems difficult to understand, but mails from Newton to Torquay and Brixham still went by 'mail cart' rather than train, as did those for Dartmouth (via Totnes and Halwell) even in 1882. Complaining about these Dartmouth mails in 1876, the *Dartmouth Chronicle* pointed out that passengers for Dartmouth arriving at Newton Abbot (off the overnight trains) at 4 am would not arrive at Dartmouth until 9.20 am. Passengers for Penzance would arrive there at 8.10 am. 'Passengers on this train for Dartmouth … have to wait until 8 am for a train … in a room containing a deal table, a hard couch, a Bible, a few tracts, a missionary book and no fire'. A similar complaint had been made in 1864, but Mr Woollcombe had said that when a train was run, on average it only contained a fraction of a passenger! In February 1873 the Torquay Magistrates gave notice of their intention of petitioning the Postmaster-General to send the mails by train. (That met with partial success for the up night mail went by train from June onwards.) Not long after this in March, a deputation from Torquay met the Directors to ask that the 11.45 am ex-Paddington be speeded up and that Torquay station be improved, which latter was agreed in the following month. During the summer, platform covering was authorized for Churston station.

Portrait of Charles Seale Hayne.

In November the Board decided there was a need for a third line between Newton and Torquay Junction on which the Torquay trains could be separated from those to Plymouth. They were certainly proved to be correct, for a month later on 11th December, 1873 the Board Minutes contain the following:

Reported on 4th instant the 4.30 am up goods train failed to stop at Torquay Junction although the signals were at danger and that the 7.08 am up branch train was at the same time approaching the junction, but that the driver reversed his engine and pulled up short of the main line. The committee ordered a telegraph wire (with gongs) to be fixed from Dainton to Torquay Junction, in order that the departure of up goods trains from Dainton may be announced to the man on duty at Torquay Junction, and that whilst up goods trains are running between Dainton and Torquay Junction, no up train be allowed to leave the branch line for Newton.

Following this decision, the telegraph was fixed by 12th February, 1874 and the survey for the new third line started on 31st December, 1873. Still dissatisfaction with the railway services rumbled on in Torquay. A November 1873 meeting sought to achieve the extension of the LSWR line to Torquay, and in December another meeting discussed, *inter alia*, the possibility of the line continuing beyond Paignton to Totnes, thus upgrading the line from branch line status. The Board's response to a deputation from the latter meeting was as follows:

11.45 am Paddington to be accelerated Exeter-Torquay	: *advised deputation of additional line Newton to Torquay Jn*
Improved station accommodation at Torquay	: *plans in course of preparation*
New railway line Paignton-Totnes	: *unlikely 'having regard to its inconvenience and great cost'*
Additional staff at Torquay	: *agreed if found to be required*
The limit of free delivery of goods to be extended	: *would have consideration*

Two more accidents were reported to the Directors in the first part of 1874. On 22nd January the '9.15 am up train' was derailed at Kingskerswell 'in consequence of Porter Moore being asleep - fined 2s. 6d.'. Another case of points being incorrectly set occurred on 24th April; the 9.48 am from Kingswear ran into the carriage siding at Paignton, the points 'having been left wrong by packers'. The porter in charge of the signal broke the wire in trying to turn the signal, not observing that the points were wrongly set. Station master Weeks was summoned before the Directors on 30th April, blamed for not properly training the porter and ordered to be removed from Paignton. Station masters on the SDR were not allowed to make a mistake!

On 14th September two coaches were derailed at Goodrington in an up train variously described as 2.28 pm ex-Dartmouth, 2.42 pm ex-Dartmouth and 3 pm ex-Kingswear. According to the local paper the vehicles ran for about ½ mile on the sleepers: no injuries resulted.

The *Torquay Directory* on 11th August, 1874 said that 'The SDR are making great progress with the additional line of rails from the station at Newton to the junction. This has been undertaken for the benefit of those who travel to and from Torquay …' Macdermot states that the third line of rails between Newton and Torquay Junction opened on 1st July, 1874 but it does not appear to have been ready by then. On 14th August, 1874, the Board authorized their Engineer, Mr Margary, to lay a fourth line between Newton and Torquay Junction, and a second line between there and Kingskerswell.

In October the Board authorized the widening of Ford Bridge at Newton and estimated to cost £2,500. This would enable the Torquay junction to be brought to the east side of the bridge (the physical junction at 'Aller' and the signal box there had been removed when the third line Newton-Torquay Junction was introduced).

In addition to this work at Newton the Board studied plans submitted by the Engineer for the improvement of Torquay, '… by carrying a carriage road over the railway and making the up station on the western side of the line'. The acquisition of two acres of additional land was required, and this was eventually bought for £1,087 10s. from Mr Mallock.

On 12th November, 1874 Mr Woollcombe, Chairman of the SDR for 26 years out of a total 30 years in their service, tendered his resignation. He was no longer able to give the close personal attention to the company's affairs the position demanded and needed to 'seek rest' but he asked to remain a Director. The Board reluctantly accepted his resignation and Alexander Hubbard was elected Chairman at the next meeting. His holding of the office of Chairman was to be of much shorter duration.

The year 1874 finished with a resolution by the Board that on and from 10th December no new works would be completed or undertaken on the broad gauge without the express sanction of the Board, the only exception being the doubling to Kingskerswell, which had been approved in August.

There was speculation in the local press in January 1875 that the long overdue improvements at Torquay station would be delayed because the SDR was under pressure to alter its gauge to 'narrow'. The paper felt that 'a change is nearer at hand than many people are inclined to think'. Obviously whatever pressure the SDR was able to bring, it was insufficient to influence the GWR, for another 17 years were to pass before the broad gauge was abandoned. The Board agreed on 28th January to enlarged booking and other offices on the downside, with 'a few waiting rooms and minor offices only on the upside'.

The train service for April 1875 is shown below (taken from the local paper):

Timetable – April 1875

Weekdays		am	am	am	am	pm	pm	pm	pm	pm	pm
Newton	dep.	8.20	8.40	9.43	11.36	3.18	4.16	4.55	6.00	8.05	11.10
Kingskerswell		8.26	8.46	9.49	11.42	3.24	4.22	–	6.06	8.11	–
Torre		8.34	8.55	9.57	11.50	3.32	4.31	–	6.14	8.20	11.23
Torquay		8.39	9.00	10.01	11.55	3.38	4.38	5.08	6.17	8.28	11.28
					pm						
Paignton		8.46	–	10.08	12.02	3.46	4.45	5.18	–	8.36	11.35
Churston		8.56	–	10.18	12.10	3.54	4.52	5.26	–	8.44	11.43
Kingswear		9.10	–	10.31	12.23	4.05	5.03	5.37	–	8.55	11.53
Dartmouth	arr.	9.20	–	10.41	12.33	4.15	5.13	5.46	–	9.05	–
Weekdays		am	am	am	am	pm	pm	pm	pm	pm	pm
Dartmouth	dep.	6.55	–	9.35	10.20	12.42	2.28	4.27	–	6.30	7.45
Kingswear		7.08	–	9.48	10.34	12.57	2.42	4.40	–	6.45	8.00
Churston		7.20	–	10.00	10.45	1.09	2.53	4.52	–	6.58	8.13
Paignton		7.27	–	10.08	10.53	1.17	3.00	5.00	–	7.06	8.20
Torquay		7.35	9.15	10.15	11.03	1.26	3.10	5.08	6.45	7.14	8.28
Torre		7.44	9.20	10.20	–	1.32	3.17	5.13	6.50	7.19	8.36
Kingskerswell		7.51	–	10.28	–	1.40	3.24	5.21	6.58	7.26	8.43
Newton	arr.	8.00	9.35	10.34	11.20	1.48	3.30	5.30	7.05	7.35	8.52

An early lithograph of Kingswear station with a couple of paddle steamers close to the 'Éclair' pier; one may be the *Dolphin* railway ferry to Dartmouth or could be a Dartmouth Steam Packet Co. boat.   *Devon Library Services*

South Devon Railway broad gauge 4-4-0T *Hawk* at Newton Abbot. The locomotive was built by Slaughter, Gruning of Bristol in 1859.   *J.B.N. Ashford courtesy A.R. Kingdom*

Sundays

am	am	pm	pm				am	pm	pm	pm
8.30	10.47	3.30	8.10	*dep.*	Newton	*arr.*	8.13	2.03	4.15	8.01
8.36	10.53	3.36	8.16		Kingskerswell		8.06	1.54	4.07	7.53
8.44	11.01	3.44	8.24		Torre		7.59	1.47	4.00	7.46
8.49	11.06	3.47	8.29		Torquay		7.54	1.42	3.55	7.40
8.56	11.13	–	8.36		Paignton		7.47	1.35	–	7.33
9.06	11.22	–	8.45		Churston		7.40	1.27	–	7.25
9.20	11.35	–	9.00		Kingswear		7.28	1.15	–	7.12
–	–	–	–	*arr.*	Dartmouth	*dep.*	–	–	–	–

The main service improvements (compared with 1867) were 10 weekday trains each way, rather than eight, and that Kingskerswell and Torre had a much improved service. In June the *Torquay Directory* reported that the GWR had started to run a newspaper train from London which reached Torquay at 1.32 pm.

Traffic continued to expand causing a constant expenditure on new works. In February 1875 the Board authorized construction of a 'shunt siding for down trains on the Exeter side of Newton station'; in April the enlargement of Torre parcels office was agreed. An additional crane was approved for Kingswear in May to deal with traffic for the Torbay & Dartmouth Paint Co. In the 1875 *Kelly's Directory* James Paddon, station master at Kingswear, was also noted as postmaster and piermaster!

In February 1875, the *Dartmouth Chronicle* reported that on Tuesday 23rd February, Sir Garnet Wolseley, who had been appointed interim Governor of Natal, accompanied by his staff, travelled down to Newton Abbot on the overnight mail train. Here they boarded a special train to Kingswear, arriving there at about 4.30 am. 'They were immediately conveyed to the *Walmer Castle* [Currie Line] by the ferry-steamboat'. This must have been the *Dolphin*, making a special and unusually early journey: it had been fitted with new engines earlier that month. The ship left at noon, after the arrival of the 'North Mail'.

1875 was a bad year for accidents and these started early on 7th January. The 11.36 am Newton to Kingswear hauled by *Orion*, a 4-4-0 saddle tank of the 'Comet' class built in February 1853, left Churston at 12.10 and after passing through Greenway tunnel had attained a speed of 30 mph. Running downhill, the front wheels of the locomotive ran into a large stone deliberately placed on the line and were derailed on to the longitudinal timbers supporting the rails. The driver reversed the engine and whistled for the guard's hand brake (the continuous brake was not yet standard), but because of the speed and the downwards gradient the train ran for a mile, passing over Maypool viaduct before coming to a stand at a point where the embankment is 70 to 100 ft above the River Dart. At this point the leading wheels had left the longitudinal timbers and were on the ballast and would surely have caused more wheels to follow (pulling the train down the embankment) had it not been stopped. The 30 passengers were detrained and guard Oliver walked to Kingswear where a spare engine and carriage were obtained which proceeded to the derailed train, and cleared its passengers to Kingswear. A gang of workmen was sent to the site and *Orion* was rerailed in about two hours but 214 timber transoms had been damaged by the derailed wheels. A shuttle service was run from Kingswear to the derailed train whilst *Weasel*, an 0-4-0 well tank built by Avonside Engine Co. in March 1873, ran a service from the Churston side of the derailment. Later that day the crank shaft of *Weasel* broke and passengers in the train it was hauling had to detrain and walk about ¾ mile to Churston station!

The next accident was much more serious and of the type normally only seen in feature films where a train is driverless, and runs at full speed for several miles, but it really happened in this case. Col Rich's report for the Board of Trade has been included in full because it has so much detail. The only information not included (which was reported in the newspaper) was that the passenger train was the 7.08 am from Kingswear, manned by driver Easterbrook and fireman Folland. The goods train was driven by Aaron Stillman with fireman J. Dennis; the accident happened on 16th August, 1875.

In compliance with the instructions contained in the order of the 19th ultimo, I have the honour to report, for the information of the Board of Trade, the result of my inquiry into the circumstances connected with the collision that occurred on the 16th ultimo, at Torquay station on the South Devon Railway.

A down goods train from Newton ran into an up passenger train from Kingswear.

Three passengers are reported to have been slightly hurt by jumping out of the train just before the collision occurred.

The railway is a single line, with sidings and loop lines for trains to pass each other. It is worked by telegraph, the fixed passing-places being changed by telegraphic messages when circumstances require it.

Torquay station is situated at the bottom of two inclines. The line from Torre to Torquay falls 1 in 54. There is a loop line for up and down trains to pass each other at Torquay station. This loop or double line is level at the station and is 325 yards long between the northern and southern points. There is only one down-signal, which is placed about 125 yards to the north of the northern points. This signal can be seen by a driver immediately after he leaves Torre station, but the signal is not very distinct, owing to a clump of trees in the background.

There is an up home-signal about 250 yards from the south points, which is provided with a repeater towards Paignton.

On the day in question. a goods train which consisted of two engines, 36 waggons, and two break vans, left Newton at 6.10 am. It stopped at Torre to leave and pick up waggons, and when it left that station about 7.33 it consisted of an engine, 18 loaded waggons, and two break vans with breaksmen. One of these breaks was about the centre, and the other at the tail of the train.

The engine-driver stated that he noticed the Torquay signal standing at danger against him immediately after he left Torre station; that he had only given his engine sufficient steam to start his train from the level at the station; and that he felt that he had lost control of it almost immediately after he got on the falling incline at the south end of Torre station . He then reversed his engine, put steam on, his fireman applied the break and he whistled for the guards breaks during the whole time that he was running from Torre to Torquay. These stations are about a mile apart. but he could not succeed in stopping the goods train before it ran into the up passenger train which had been standing at the down line platform at Torquay station.

It is customary for the up and down passenger trains to stop at the down platform at Torquay to prevent the inconvenience of carrying the luggage across the railway, and the danger of passengers walking across the rails.

When the occupants of the passenger train heard the whistling of the goods train and saw it running into the station, many of them jumped out on to the platform. The engine-driver of the passenger train was putting tallow into the cylinders of his engine at the time, and the fireman who was on the foot-plate pulled the engine into backward gear and opened the regulator. At this moment the engine-driver of the passenger train came on to the footplate. The fireman stated that the driver, when he got on the footplate, took the regulator from him; that he saw the passengers jumping out, looked again for his driver who had disappeared, and the fireman then jumped off the engine, leaving the regulator open and the passenger train running backwards.

The engine-driver appears only to have returned on to the foot-plate to jump onto the platform and run away through the station house door. This man has been discharged by the company, and I did not see him. The goods train struck the passenger train lightly as it was moving backwards.

The goods train came to a stand at the south side of the station, and the passenger train ran backwards towards Paignton, which it passed at great speed, and was brought to a stand on the rising gradient as it approached Churston station by two of the company's workmen, who were travelling in the train, and who, when they became aware that there was no one on the engine, resolved to make their way along the footboards, Edward Purcell to the engine, and Robert Harley to each of the coaches in rear of the one he was travelling in, so as to put down the breaks [sic]. These men appear to have shown great coolness and judgment in what they did.

The passenger train consisted of a tank engine and seven passenger carriages, each of which was provided with a break. The guard had been travelling in one of the coaches about the centre of the train. He was occupied on the platform at Torquay and left there, when the train ran away.

The engine-driver of the goods train got his engine uncoupled and followed the passenger train as soon as he could, but he did not overtake it till after it was stopped. It was then brought back to Torquay.

The accident was the result of working a goods train over a single line with very steep gradients, without sufficient power to command the train. I cannot altogether believe the engine-driver's statement, that he lost control of his train when starting with the greatest care from Torre station. I believe that he depended on the down-signal at Torquay being taken off, and his being allowed to run through the station, which would probably have been the case if the switchman at Torquay had been smart and had reached the point at the north end of the yard in time to turn them. This should have been done before the up home-signal was lowered for the passenger train to enter the station.

It appears that frequently when goods trains are stopped at Torquay, the engine drivers keep their trains on the falling gradient outside the station, so as to get a start for the bank at the opposite side. These methods of working are always attended with danger, and are resorted to by the servants and officers in charge, owing to the insufficient or defective means which are too frequently provided by the company for carrying on the traffic, the result being always more or less danger to the passengers who travel on the railway.

The engine-driver and fireman of the passenger train appear on this occasion to have behaved very badly. If those men had remained at their posts , a very slight collision would have occurred, and the very great danger which the passengers were subjected to, when the train ran back for several miles along a line of steep gradients with the engine in full steam, would not have happened.

The coolness, courage, and judgment of Purcell and Harley contrast strongly with the behaviour of the engine-driver and fireman of the passenger train.

I recommend that the South Devon Railway Company should not run goods trains which the engines attached to them cannot effectively control; that the line should be worked with the train staff as well as the block telegraph, which is now in use; and that the points and signals at Torquay and all other stations should be re-arranged and interlocked.

At the SDR Board meeting of 26th August four of the principal actors in the drama were summoned to attend. Torquay station master Masters and policeman John Metherell were blamed for having the points wrongly set at the Torre end of the station, but attribution of blameworthiness was to be deferred until after the BoT enquiry. (No subsequent record of punishment has been found.) Edward Purcell and

Dartmouth Branch.—Week Days.

DOWN TRAINS.

Distance	STATIONS	1 GOODS	2 Passenger.	3 Passenger.	4 Passenger.	5 Passenger.	6 GOODS	7 Passenger.	8 Passenger.	9 Passenger.	10 Passenger.	11 Passenger.	12 Passenger.	13
		a.m.	a.m.	a.m.	a.m.	a.m	noon	p.m.	p.m.	p.m.	p.m.	p.m	p.m.	
—	Newton dp	6 0	8 20	8 40	9 43	11 50	12 0	1 28	3 18	4 55	6 10	8 25	11 10	...
2¼	Kngskswll	C.R.	8 26	8 46	9 49	11 56	12 10	*1 34	*3 24	5 0	6 16	8 31	11 14	...
5	Torre ...	7 0	8 34	8 55	9 57	12 4	12 40	1 42	3 32	5 6	6 24	*8 40	11†23	...
5¾	Torquay	C.R.	8 39	9 0	10 1	12 9	12 45	1 47	3 38	5 8	6 27	8 48	11 28	...
7¾	Paignton	†7 27	8 46		10* 8	12 16	†1 10	1 54	3 46	5 18		8 56	11 35	...
10¾	Churston	8 5	8 56	...	10 18	12 28	1 25	2 4	3 54	5 26	...	9 4	11 43	...
14½	Kingswear	8 25	9 10	...	10 31	12 38	1 40	2 18	4 5	5 37	...	9 15	11 53	...
—	Dartmth a.	8 35	9 20	...	10 55	1 10	...	3 0	4 15	5 46	...	9 25	...	..

UP TRAINS.

Distances.	STATIONS	1 Passenger.	2 Passenger.	3 Passenger.	4 Passenger.	5 Passenger	6 Passenger.	7 Passenger.	8 GOODS	9 Passenger.	10 Passenger.	11 Passenger.	12 GOODS	13
		a.m		a.m.	a.m.	p.m.	p.m.	p.m.	p.m.		p.m.	p.m.	p.m.	
—	Dart. Pier	6 55	...	9 35	10 35	12 35	2 30	4 27	...		6 55	7 50	...	...
—	Ksgswr(dp)	7 8	...	9 48	10 40	12 50	2 43	4 40	5 45		7 10	8 5	9 30	...
3¾	Churston	7 20	...	10 0	10 52	1 2	2 54	4 52	6 0		7 23	8 18	9 55	...
6½	Paignton	†7 27	a.m.	10* 8	11 0	†1 10	3 1	5 0	6 15	p.m.	7 30	8 25	10 15	...
8¾	Torquay	7 35	9 15	10 15	11 10	1 20	3 11	*5 8	6 30	6 55	7 40	8 33	10 25	...
9½	Torre ...	7 44	9 20	10 20	11 16	1 26	3 17	5 13	‡7 8	‡7 0	7 45	*8 40	†11 25	...
12½	Kngskswll	7 51	9 26	10 28	11 24	*1 34	*3 24	5 21	7 18	7 8	7 52	8 47	11 35	...
14½	Newton ar	8 0	9 35	10 34	11 33	1 43	3 31	5 30	7 26	7 15	8 0	8 54	11 45	...

SUNDAY TRAINS.

Distances.	DOWN TRAINS.	1 Passenger.	2 Passenger.	3 Passenger.	4 Passenger.	Distances.	UP TRAINS.	1 Passenger.	2 Passenger	3 Passenger.	4 Passenger.
		a.m	a.m.	p.m.	p.m.			a.m	p.m.		p.m.
—	Newton Dep.	8 30	10 47	3 30	8 10	—	Dart. Co's Pier	...	...	...	...
2	Kingskerswell	8 36	10 53	3 36	8 16	—	Kingswear Dp.	7 28	1 15	...	7 12
5	Torre	8 44	11 1	3 44	8 24	3¾	Churston ...	7 40	1 27	...	7 25
5¾	Torquay... ...	8 49	11 6	3 47	8 29	6½	Paignton ...	7 47	1 35	p.m.	7 33
8	Paignton ...	8 56	11 13	...	8 36	8¾	Torquay ...	7 54	1 42	3 55	7 40
10¾	Churston ...	9 6	11 22	...	8 45	9½	Torre	7 59	1 47	4 0	7 46
14½	Kingswear ...	9 20	11 35	..	9 0	12½	Kingskerswell	8 6	1 54	4 7	7 53
—	Dartmouth Ar.	..	...	...	..	14½	Newton ... Arr.	8 13	2 3	4 15	8 1

Passing and Crossing of the above-named Trains,

IN FORCE ON AND AFTER JULY 1st, 1876.

When the Trains named above are running in their proper course, they will PASS and CROSS each other as below:—

WEEK DAYS.

PASSING.—The 6.55 p.m. Up Passenger Train will pass the 5.45 p.m. Up Goods Train at Torre.

CROSSING.

The 7 8 a.m. Up Passenger Train and 6 0 a.m. Down Goods Train will cross at Paignton.
,, 9 48 a.m. ,, ,, ,, 9 43 a.m. ,, Passenger ,, at Paignton.
,, 12 50 p.m. ,, ,, ,, 12 noon ,, Goods ,, at Paignton.
,, 12 50 p.m. ,, ,, ,, 1 28 p.m. ,, Passenger ,, ,, at Kingskerswell.
,, 2 43 p.m. ,, ,, ,, 3 18 p.m. ,, ,, ,, ,, at Kingskerswell.
,, 4 40 p.m. ,, ,, ,, 4 55 p.m. ,, ,, ,, ,, at Torquay.
,, 8 5 p.m. ,, ,, ,, 8 25 p.m. ,, ,, ,, ,, at Torre.
,, 9 30 p.m. Goods ,, 11 10 p.m. ,, ,, ,, ,, at Torre.

The July 1876 Working Timetable. *Courtesy National Archives (RAIL 981/453)*

Robert Harley, viaduct labourers, were informed that they would be presented with a silver watch and chain with an inscription and £25 each for their heroic action and also a public subscription was raised for these men. As the goods train was heavy, the minutes stated, 'the driver and stoker were not blamed for passing the signal as it appeared *they had done their best* to stop the train' [my italics] . The driver of the passenger train had absconded and was considered dismissed, the stoker was reduced to an ordinary labourer.

With the company reeling from the adverse publicity from this truly frightening accident, only a few days went by before a passenger train came into sidelong collision with a shunting movement at Newton. The Board of Trade investigation revealed a very haphazard working arrangement whereby a signal controlling the exit from the down siding to the down main line was not used or obeyed for shunting movements, although it was for engines coming off shed and the odd passenger train placed in the siding!

The 26th August Board meeting (already mentioned) also saw the attendance of station master Pratt and switchman William Caler of Newton. Mr Pratt was blamed for not having discovered that the signal referred to was not used during shunting and Mr Caler, the Centre switchman was given one month's notice of dismissal for not stopping the shunting before turning off the down line signals .

Immediately after receiving the BoT report on the Newton accident, the Board authorized expenditure of £3,375 for interlocking at Newton and £505 for Kingskerswell (the line was being doubled at the time) with Messrs Saxby & Farmer, signal engineers. Torquay had to wait until 1879 for its interlocking.

The company earned further adverse publicity at the end of August by the putting on trial before the magistrates at Churston Ferrers of the Paignton station master, William Henry Maunder (shown as 'booking constable' in the staff records) on a charge of embezzlement. Maunder, previously the issuer of tickets at Dartmouth, pleaded guilty to the charge, which involved the retention of 5s. 11½d., and received three months' imprisonment with hard labour.

In October 1875 the Bristol & Exeter Railway wrote to the GWR suggesting that either the latter purchased it or they would offer the company to the Midland. Having seen the Somerset & Dorset go that way, the GWR reluctantly undertook to take over the line (from 1st January, 1876); reluctantly, because the GWR knew they would be forced to pay more than its worth and they would have to cover its losses for some time. The SDR took this opportunity to approach the GWR with the result that an agreement was reached that the SDR was to be worked by the GWR for a period of 999 years as from 1st February, 1876. On that date, with control of the Cornwall and West Cornwall railways also passing to the GWR, the latter at last reigned supreme over the whole line from Paddington to Penzance and Kingswear.

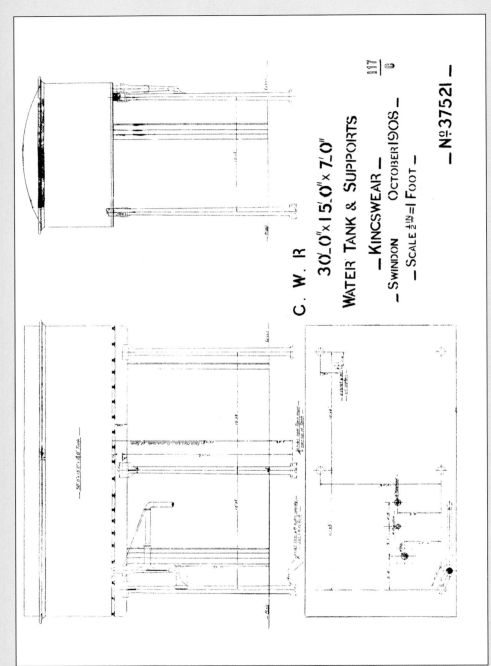

C. W. R

30_0" x 15_0" x 7_0"

WATER TANK & SUPPORTS

— KINGSWEAR —

— SWINDON   OCTOBER 1908 —

— SCALE $\frac{1}{2}$ IN = 1 FOOT —

$\frac{117}{C}$

— Nº 37521 —

Kingswear water tank.

Chapter Five

The end of the Broad Gauge: 1876-1892

Between 1870 and the end of 1875 the Great Western had reduced its broad gauge-only track from 563 miles in length to just 8 miles. At the same time its mixed gauge track had declined from 141 miles to 122 miles whilst 'narrow' gauge had jumped from 618 miles to 1,393 miles. Now with the coming in of the Bristol & Exeter Railway, the South Devon Railway and the Cornwall Railway, broad gauge mileage increased to 327 miles and mixed gauge track increased to 219 miles; this included the West Cornwall Railway which had no broad gauge-only track. Taunton to Exeter was quickly made 'mixed' and with some other such work elsewhere (in SDR territory), broad gauge mileage had dropped back to 268 miles by the end of 1876.

One other effect of the amalgamation, of no real significance then but destined to be a major influence on the GWR's locomotive policy, occurred at this time. George Jackson Churchward, born in Stoke Gabriel on the east bank of the River Dart near Dartmouth in 1857, had started work as a pupil of the SDR locomotive superintendent at Newton Abbot in 1873. Transferring to the GWR drawing office at Swindon, he later became assistant manager in the carriage works in 1881, subsequently assistant manager and later manager of the locomotive works. Finally, in 1902, he became locomotive, carriage and wagon superintendent (retitled chief mechanical engineer in 1916), a position he held until his retirement in 1921. Churchward never returned to his native Devon, living all his working life in Swindon and remaining there after retirement until his death in 1933 (aged 75), knocked down by a train whilst crossing the line to the works on a foggy day.

The SDR Minutes give the impression that negotiations with Mr Mallock over the purchase of land to extend Torquay station were concluded but an entry appears in the GWR Board Minutes for 1st March, 1876 which suggests otherwise. Doubtless the planned amalgamation with the GWR had aroused some uncertainty, however, by June Mr Mallock had agreed to sell for £1,087 10s. The August Board meeting accepted a tender from Henry Stevens of Ashburton to provide a new station (excluding the buildings, *see below*) and widen the bridge at the north end, remove an old stone bridge and replace it by a new bridge at the south end: cost £7,437 19s. 3d.

A new Floating Bridge was towed to Dartmouth arriving there on 24th February. This had been built in Plymouth and was, of course, no part of the railway; it provided competition with the railway-owned ferries running from Kingswear (*see Chapter Eleven*). In August the GWR received an application from traders for a siding at the Floating Bridge 'to avoid the necessity of going across the ferry and through the town'. This was declined as it would have led to loss of ferry tolls.

Since the First Edition of this book was published the Locomotive Department 'Water files' for the area have been found (sadly these have since been destroyed and I think my photocopies may be the only ones extant for this area) and there are now several references in this chapter to the parlous state of the water supply at Kingswear and Torre during some of this period.

A few months after it took over the SDR, the GWR learned of the precarious state of the locomotive water facilities at Kingswear. Divisional locomotive superintendent Luxmoore wrote to Swindon on 13th May, 1876, as follows:

Water tanks at Kingswear

There are two of these and both in a very bad state. They were received some years ago from Paignton and put up at Kingswear and were then very shaky.

The tanks were wooden and hold each about 6,250 gallons. My foreman tells me that the water company have been complaining of the leaky condition of these tanks and of the waste from them and they are both quite past repair.

It will be necessary to put up there an iron tank on pillars in our usual style and I shall be glad if you will arrange accordingly.

The water at Kingswear is self supplied but is not sufficient for our requirements and the deficiency is made up by water from the Water Company whose supply is also intermittent and consequently a large tank capacity is necessary.

Just two days later Joseph Armstrong, the locomotive and carriage superintendent at Swindon, responded agreeing to supply a 30 ft x 15 ft x 7 ft wrought iron tank, capacity 19,600 gallons, *see accompanying plan*. (The date of October 1908 on the drawing relates to the fact that, the following month, Barlow rails resting on wooden beams supporting the tank as originally built were replaced by steel joists at a cost of £63. 10s.)

Good progress was being made with the doubling of the line between the former Torquay Junction and Kingskerswell, and provision of the fourth line from Torquay Junction to Newton. The *Torquay Directory* stated that the double line from Newton to Kingskerswell was opened on 22nd May, 1876, which date is confirmed by papers in the Clinker collection at Brunel University.

Col Yolland made the inspection on behalf of the BoT on 18th July, 1876 and passed the new work satisfactory. Although there is no mention of a signal box at Kingskerswell in his report, there is one shown on the accompanying plan. The quadruple track between Newton and Aller (former Torquay Junction) was paired (from west to east): up and down Plymouth, up and down Torquay. At Kingskerswell the down distant signal was 280 yds in rear of the down home (gradient 1 in 125 rising) and the up distant 486 yds to the rear of its home signal (gradient 1 in 113 falling). The physical junction between the two pairs of lines was just south of the road overbridge at the Plymouth end of Newton station.

At the same time Col Yolland inspected the new signal boxes provided at Newton that had been authorized following the 1875 accident there. These had actually delayed the inspection of the Kingskerswell line because the interlocking was not ready until 14th July.

The portion of the BoT report dealing with Newton read as follows:

I have also inspected the alterations which have been made in the Newton station yard. Three new signal boxes have been erected from which the points and signals are worked. The whole of these are properly interlocked with each other. Two additional shunting signals, one of which is to be connected with a throw-off point, on the straight pair of shunting sidings at the eastern end of the passenger platforms [*sic*]. Orders have been given for these signals to be erected at once by Messrs Saxby & Farmer who have done the interlocking throughout the station yard.

An advanced starting signal has been put up at a distance of more than 600 yards from the cabin C in the fork between the main line and the Moretonhampstead branch. The signal is well seen from the cabin, but the distance is far too great and it is to be shifted to the bottom of the gradient of 1 in 132 falling from the station.

Exactly a year after taking over the SDR, the Great Western Board authorized the change to the present name of Newton, 'Newton Abbot', which was actually brought into effect in March 1877, according to C.R. Clinker. Meanwhile work at Torquay was proceeding apace as the *Torquay Directory* recorded on 21st February, 1877:

> The army of excavators and other workmen have effected a complete transformation in the neighbourhood of Torquay railway station. Scores of trees have been felled, hedges removed, bridges taken down, the railway cutting widened to about four times its original width, broad embankments have been thrown up and the line between Torre and Torquay is now being doubled. All this is preparatory to building the new station for the erection of which tenders have been invited. The directors of the Great Western are fulfilling the promise which they made to a very select deputation, which waited upon them one very cold night [in January 1876] in the little shanty which has done duty as a waiting room for so long a period on the up platform. While on this subject I may mention that I have heard that the directors propose building a goods station as well. I hope my information is wrong, because it would be very undesirable for many reasons for such a building to be erected there, especially as that which already exists so near at Torre is exceedingly suitable for the purpose and might be enlarged if necessary. If the Torbay road is to be preserved as a promenade for our visitors, the huge furniture and luggage vans must be kept away from it.

A week earlier the GW Board had accepted a tender for £17,430 from Messrs Vernon & Ewens of Cheltenham to construct the station buildings at Torquay but 'subject to alteration as the Company had decided to modify the design to save expense'. On 1st March the Board were presented with modified plans saving about £3,000 and also decided to exclude the cab shelter from the plans at a further reduction in cost of £500.* The *Dartmouth Chronicle* of 8th March, 1878 reported that a meeting of shareholders had agreed to a special expenditure of £15,000 on Torquay station. To assist in the doubling between Torre and Torquay which was already in mind, the Board arranged for Messrs Stevens to remove 3,250 cu. yds of spoil from the bank (upside) of Torquay station at a price of 1s. 4d. per cu. yd, to be spread between Torre and Torquay – new sidings were laid in the excavated area.

Among some improvements to the train service in July 1877 was a new 3.45 pm Newton Abbot to Torquay (connecting out of the North Mail), returning from Torquay at 4.30 pm and connecting into the down 'Flying Dutchman'. The 6.15 pm Newton Abbot to Paignton was extended to Kingswear, following pressure from the Torbay & Brixham Railway to prevent passengers having to wait at Newton Abbot until 8.25 pm. There was also a new 6.35 pm Kingswear to Newton Abbot, later retimed to 5.15 pm from October.

In September the GWR acquired premises at No. 2 Vaughan Parade, Torquay (on the west side of the harbour for use as a 'Receiving Office' as the company called it, for parcels and for booking passengers (the station being some way from the town centre and, in any case, being rebuilt).† Use of this block of buildings continued until 1948 when the office moved to nearby Palk Street, although at some later stage No. 7 Vaughan Parade became the British Railways (BR) town office until the 1960s.

Thursday 18th October, 1877 was a red letter day for Dartmouth (and the railway) for on that day the Prince of Wales, Prince Albert Edward, brought his two sons, Prince Albert Victor and Prince George Frederick, to enter HMS *Britannia* as naval cadets. The Royal party left Paddington in a special saloon attached to the 11.45 am from Paddington, the 'Flying Dutchman', but at Bristol a special train was waiting to which the saloon was attached. Arriving at Exeter at 3.50 pm the train was joined by the Chairman and other officials of the South Devon Railway and was then non-

---

* It was reinstated in March 1879 at an estimated cost of £685.
† The rent was £100 pa and the staff, a clerk and lad porter. Fittings cost £50.

HMS *Britannia* and *Hindustan*, moored in the River Dart, provided training facilities before the RN College at Dartmouth was built. This postcard, posted in Paignton at 8.30 am on 15th September, 1904 at a cost of a halfpenny, is addressed to a Mr Cole in Exeter and reads: 'Please Jack tell Perry to look out for me at Newton, am going to Plymouth for the day…Julie'. *Author's Collection*

Paignton station surrounded by fields, probably in the late 1870s (the three-storey white building by the level crossing is the Gerston Hotel, built in 1870). From left (Kingswear end) can be seen a coal merchant's office with roof sign, the goods shed, the small two-platform station and the Torbay Road level crossing and wooden footbridge. The photographer is standing on Roundham Hill (Keysfield Road). *Peter Tully Collection*

stop to Kingswear. However, the practicalities of the single line sections meant a 10 minute allowance at Dawlish awaiting the passage of an up train, Newton Abbot was reached at 4.27 pm and Kingswear at 4.55 pm. At Kingswear a platform had been specially erected at the level crossing leading to the Floating Bridge and here the Royal Train stopped to unload its Royal passengers. 'The platform, profusely dressed with flags, was covered with maroon carpet and backed with crimson baize' reported the *Dartmouth Chronicle*. An avenue of evergreens led from the platform to the boat which was to take the Royal party to *Britannia*. An estimated 5,000 to 6,000 persons looked on as the Prince of Wales and his sons alighted and some 300 boats filled the harbour.

The South Devon Railway had arranged an extra late return excursion from Kingswear so that residents of Torbay and Newton could enjoy the event and the bonfires, candle illuminations and torch light procession which followed in the evening. Over 350 return tickets were issued at Torquay alone which would have been far fewer without the late train, suggested by the Visit Reception Committee.

The following week's *Dartmouth Chronicle* was 'glad to hear that the Railway Company contemplate retaining the platform erected at the level crossing'. The 18th October, 1877, can therefore be regarded as the opening date of Kingswear Crossing Halt or Britannia Halt as it was known later; for many years it was only used by naval personnel and visitors to the *Britannia*.

After the misfortunes of 1875, 1876 had been an accident-free year (or at least none had reached either the Board of Trade or the local press). The company now experienced two accidents at Newton Abbot, on successive days. In the first accident, on 12th November, 1877 the head shunter was killed when he slipped as he stepped between the wagons and was squeezed between the buffers 'which were probably a little further apart than usual, owing to the side chains only being used for coupling the waggons together without the centre coupling'.

The next day the shunting engine was propelling a carriage and brake van (detached from the 9 am ex-Paddington), when the coaches broke away from the engine and collided with the local train to Torquay, to which they were to be attached. Six passengers were injured. The cause of this collision was the faulty method of coupling the engine to the carriages by a loose chain, which had become uncoupled during the reversing movement.

At the beginning of 1878 Sir Daniel Gooch and some of the Directors, accompanied by the General Manager J. Grierson, met the Chairman of the Local Board of Health, L.J. Bowring. The latter complained of the 'unreasonable delays' at Newton Abbot, that there was delay in dealing with passengers luggage at Torre and Torquay and, finally , that the express trains to and from Torquay were unpunctual and should be speeded up.

Obviously aware of the growing importance and great potential of this new resort of theirs, the GWR replied speedily by letter. They authorized additional trains at 2 pm from Newton to Torquay and 2.20 pm in the reverse direction to obviate the worst delay at Newton Abbot. Furthermore, the officers had been instructed to further improve connections whenever the main line trains were altered. They saw no need to increase staffing at Torre but admitted that delays in dealing with passengers luggage occurred at Torquay, particularly when the 11.45 am from Paddington and the 4.40 pm from Kingswear 'crossed'. Two additional porters would be employed (what a different outlook to that prevailing today!).

So far as punctuality was concerned the Directors admitted that during November and December the average late arrival at Torquay was seven minutes late. Following a special investigation appropriate instructions had been issued to prevent delay in future.

In the meantime the fine new station that had taken nearly 30 years to be built was nearing completion. In January 1878 the *Torquay Directory* reported:

> During the early part of January a portion of the new railway station on the up line was so far advanced as to be roofed in, and several villas between the railway station and Livermead were in course of erection. The up and down stations are of the same length, 224 ft, one storey high, with two waiting rooms and offices. The platforms extend 50 ft further, in the direction of Torre, and are covered so as to protect passengers from the weather.

The Board had approved construction of a house for the station master, at a cost of £700, the latter official paying £24 pa rent. A week later they approved a station footbridge (it was already partially constructed!). We must be grateful that provincial newspapers then took so much interest in developments on local railways, as witness this comprehensive report in the *Torquay Directory* of 27th February, 1878:

THE NEW TORQUAY RAILWAY STATION

The construction of the new Railway Station at Torquay is progressing satisfactorily, and now that the whole of the walls of the up-station are raised, some conception may be formed of the extent of the building. The station on the up-line will be 244 feet in length, and one storey in height; there will be two waiting rooms, a boiler house for supplying hot water tins for passengers , and apartments devoted to various uses.

The down station will be of the same length as the up, but the platform extends fifty feet further in the direction of Torre and is covered, so as to protect passengers from the weather. The refreshment room is on the down side, and its dimensions will be 25 ft 6 in. by 21 ft; the counter will be on two sides of the room, and have a marble top; the kitchen and other appliances are close to the refreshment room, and the stores are beneath. Here there are cloak rooms, lavatories, parcel office, telegraph office, also waiting rooms, and a variety of offices for the convenience of passengers and for those employed at the station - in fact the station will be more complete in its appliances than the generality of such buildings. Access is gained to and from the up and down platform either by the carriage road , or by the ornamental foot bridge which connects the two stations at the Livermead end.

The walls are of black marble, brought from Pomphlete, with Doulting stone dressings. The roofs of the platforms are supported by cast-iron columns; latticed girders rest on the columns, and to these girders ornamental cast-iron cantilevers are fixed, and these support the timbers of the roof. The roof projects so as to cover the entire platform; passengers will therefore be able to enter or leave the carriages under shelter.

On the approach side of both stations there will be a verandah, under which carriages will be able to drive up to the entrance. The work is being most substantially carried out by the contractors, Messrs Vernon and Ewings, of Cheltenham, and Mr James Jackson is the Clerk of the Works , on behalf of the Great Western Railway Company.

The approaches to the station are broad and substantial; but there is one defect about these which we must be permitted to point out. The approach to the down station, which is on the same side as the old station is very well arranged: but to get at the up station passengers have to go round and cross a bridge before they can reach it, and in the case of persons coming from Belgravia, Torre, and St Marychurch, they will be obliged to make almost a complete circuit before they can arrive at their destination. Unless there were engineering difficulties in the way, this might have been obviated by prolonging the approach road until it reached the first bridge, which leads direct into the Paignton Road.

(There are two variations in details between the January and February reports.)

After completion of the new platforms and buildings, the Board authorized a further £2,908 which would be needed for alterations to the permanent way, additional lines, locking and signals and the construction of a footpath alongside the downside approach road. The following month expenditure of £433 was approved for the construction of a siding and roadway at Torre, together with a weighbridge and office (the weighbridge and office was not actually proceeded with until 1882).

Thanks again to the good offices of the *Torquay Directory*, we know that the new station at Torquay opened on Sunday 1st September, 1878, but, even more precisely, the time:

> The railway station and booking office hitherto in use were closed on Sunday evening after the 7.32 train had passed up; and the first issue of tickets in the new station commenced with the 8.26 down train, the old structure is now in the hands of the contractors for demolition, and passengers for all trains must cross by the bridge to what will eventually be the up station, but which, while the station on the down line is being erected, will be used for traffic both ways.

The paper later reported that Saxby's patent signals were 'adopted' at the station on September 14th.

It is perhaps appropriate here to say a few words about the SDR signalling. Like the GWR the SDR employed disc and crossbar signals (see *MacDermot vol. 2 chapter XII for description and illustrations*) except that whilst the GWR apparatus was painted red, the SDR painted the front of the disc black with a broad white ring, and the backs of both disc and crossbar white (see *MacDermot vol. 2 p. 133*). The Great Western also employed 'Fantail' signals adjacent to the disc and crossbar signal which gave a third, 'Caution', indication to the 'Stop' or 'All Right' of the main signal. This caution aspect was displayed for a certain number of minutes (e.g. until 1852 after a train passed the 'Stop' indication was given for three minutes, then 'Caution' for another seven finally, 'All Right', trains being worked under the 'Time Interval' system). But MacDermot tells us that the SDR did not use Fantail signals (so called because of their arrow shape) except 'at a few special places like Newton or Plymouth'. The SDR did not employ the Time Interval system, using the telegraph to provide a space interval instead, from the outset. Because of the great height of the disc and crossbar signals, it was unusual to provide auxiliary, or distant, signals on the GWR but no comment is made in MacDermot's History as to whether the SDR did so. The SDR minutes for 1866 refer to the provision of an 'up check signal' at the west end of Newton station.

The broad gauge lines used the disc and crossbar system exclusively until 1865 when semaphore signals (which had been used on the 'narrow' gauge GWR lines) began to appear. The GWR 1876 Rule Book shows illustrations of both types of signal. It is the more modern semaphore that would have been installed by the signal contractor, Saxby, at Torquay in 1878.

The new signalling provided at Torquay included new signal boxes at the north and south ends of the layout (referred to as East Box and West Box on the Board of Trade plan), where previously only ground levers would have been available to move points and the one signal customary for each direction, and a hut for the policeman to shelter in. In December 1878 the Board agreed expenditure of £36 to provide bell communication between the two boxes and switching-out apparatus (for the telegraph equipment) at 'No. 1 cabin Torquay' (the north end box?). The layout, including 'new buildings on each platform, new down sidings at the south end and new up sidings at the north end, new platforms' and the two signal boxes, was inspected, and approved, by Col Rich of the BoT on 2nd September, 1879. From Plymouth Division staff records naming the signalmen at Torquay, it would appear the boxes opened on 9th April, 1879. Two of them, William Shiner and Samuel Holland, were still there in 1897. Signalman John Metherell was appointed booking porter (later inspector) at Torquay Receiving Office in August 1879; he stayed there until his retirement in 1913.

Guard Henry Mann, of Kingswear, whom it will be remembered had been saved from compulsory removal from the line by a passengers' petition in April 1872 was again in the news (literally) in June 1878. The *Dartmouth Chronicle* reported another petition against the GWR's decision to remove him to Gloucester for the heinous crime 'of allowing two gentlemen to travel with him in his box, into which they jumped. He will resign rather than submit to punishment'. He was a railwaymen of 31 years' standing, 20 years of which he had worked as a guard on the line. Another newspaper report mentioned his obliging disposition of making room for passengers and that 'he once saw Mann come into Newton station on the engine of the 9.15 am express from Torquay, as there were so many passengers that he was compelled to give up his own box in order to find room for them'.

Despite a 300 signature petition and intensive lobbying in the local press, alas, on this occasion, Henry Mann's backers were unsuccessful and he was moved to Moretonhampstead.

On 1st August, 1878 the SDR was officially amalgamated with the GWR, its working agreement concluded after only two of the 999 years allowed for. Alexander Hubbard, Chairman, and H. Brown, Director, were elected to the Board of the GWR.

In December 1879 the GWR Board received an approach from H. Cecil Newton of the 'Torquay and Plymouth Direct Railway' (and also Manager of the Torbay & Brixham Railway) asking for support for a Bill before Parliament. As the title of this railway suggests, the proposed company intended to build a line from Paignton to Totnes which would save a passenger from Paignton to Plymouth some 11 miles of travelling. The Torquay & Plymouth Co. (T&P) also wanted the GWR to work the line, and route all Plymouth trains by the new railway. This latter proviso, however, the GWR could not accept. Public meetings were held in Torquay in support of the 'Totnes, Paignton and Torquay Direct Railway' in February and September 1880.

The death knell of the Totnes & Paignton Railway came in the summer of 1883 because the GWR would not be committed to the company's proposal for routing of trains. Despite the GWR's offer to work the new line for 50 per cent of the gross receipts, the Totnes & Paignton Railway decided to obtain an Act for abandonment. Some indication of the GWR's close involvement in this scheme can be found in the latter's offer to pay £2,000 towards the T&P's costs. When the Act of abandonment was obtained in 1884 they also made an *ex-gratia* payment to the two Secretaries of the dissolved company 'for their labour and expense'.

The GWR had taken early steps to improve the precarious state of the water supplies at Kingswear. Now it was Torre's turn to have something done. Until September 1880 the station had been supplied by the Torquay Board of Health, 250,000 gallons per annum at 6*d*. per 1,000 gallons. It was then cut off, the papers available do not say why but state that the previous summer (1880) had been a dry one so possibly the local Board just could not spare the water. The dry summer had also caused the supply at Kingswear to fail. The divisional locomotive superintendent, Mr Luxmoore, then wrote to Mr Dean at Swindon in February 1881 asking for a railway supply at Torre.

Mr Luxmoore said that about 200 yds on the Torre side of the 218 mile post there was a good stream within the railway fence which he thought might be tapped. This was about 1,420 yards away and the water would drop about 50 ft in that distance. He requested permission to lay the pipes, sent a reminder on 22nd April and a final plea on 28th May, adding that owing to the scarcity of water he was having to use an engine to pump water at Paignton. This finally aroused Mr Dean who, on 16th June, told his works manager to put the work in hand 'quickly'.

The tank was brought into use on 2nd September, 1881, water running from a point 380 yds west of the 218¼ mile post through about 500 yds of 3 in. pipe to a 2,000 gallon mushroom tank at the station. In 1884 it was agreed to allow a hydrant to be fixed to the pipe to which a hose could be attached, in case of a fire in the yard shed. Now everything settled down for the next 10 years.

Under GWR management the November 1880 train service on weekdays provided 13 trains each way serving Torquay, as against the 10 each way of April 1875.

Timetable – November 1880

Weekdays		am	am	am	am	pm	pm	pm	pm	pm	pm	pm	pm	pm
Newton	dep.	8.20	8.40	9.45	11.59	1.02	1.40	3.15	4.00	4.57	6.22	7.58	8.27	11.10
					pm									
K'kerswell		8.26	8.46	9.51	12.05	1.08	1.46	–	4.06	–	6.28	–	8.33	–
Torre		8.36	8.56	10.01	12.15	1.18	1.56	3.27	4.16	–	6.38	8.13	8.44	11.23
Torquay		8.41	9.00	10.05	12.20	1.24	2.00	3.33	4.19	5.12	6.44	8.19	8.49	11.28
Paignton		8.48	–	10.11	12.28	1.31	–	3.41	–	5.19	6.51	8.29	8.57	11.35
Churston		8.58	–	10.21	12.38	1.41	–	3.51	–	5.29	7.01	8.39	9.05	11.43
Kingswear		9.08	–	10.31	12.50	1.51	–	4.01	–	5.39	7.11	8.49	9.15	11.53
Dartmouth	arr.	9.20	–	10.55	1.15	2.01	–	4.30	–	5.50	7.30	9.00	9.30	–

Weekdays		am	am	am	am	pm	pm	pm	pm	pm	pm	pm	pm	pm
Dartmouth	dep.	7.00	–	9.37	10.35	12.12	–	2.45	–	4.00	5.00	7.00	7.57	9.50
Kingswear		7.13	–	9.50	10.50	12.27	–	3.00	–	4.17	5.16	7.15	8.10	10.05
Churston		7.25	–	10.02	11.02	12.39	–	3.12	–	4.29	5.28	7.27	8.22	10.17
Paignton		7.33	–	10.10	11.10	12.47	–	3.20	–	4.38	5.36	7.35	8.30	10.25
Torquay		7.42	9.20	10.18	11.19	12.56	2.50	3.30	4.30	4.47	5.44	7.45	8.39	10.33
Torre		7.49	9.26	10.23	11.25	1.01	2.55	3.35	4.35	4.52	5.49	7.50	8.44	10.38
K'kerswell		7.57	–	10.31	11.33	1.09	–	–	4.42	5.00	5.57	7.58	8.52	10.44
Newton	arr.	8.04	9.37	10.37	11.40	1.18	3.08	3.48	4.48	5.06	6.03	8.05	8.57	10.50

Sundays

am	am	pm				am	pm	pm
8.30	10.47	8.05	dep.	Newton	arr.	8.16	2.06	7.51
8.36	10.53	8.11		Kingskerswell		8.10	2.00	7.45
8.46	11.03	8.21		Torre		8.02	1.52	7.37
8.51	11.08	8.26		Torquay		7.57	1.47	7.32
8.59	11.16	8.34		Paignton		7.50	1.40	7.25
9.09	11.26	8.44		Churston		7.42	1.32	7.17
9.19	11.36	8.54		Kingswear		7.30	1.20	7.05
–	–	–	arr.	Dartmouth	dep.	–	–	–

A c.1882 picture showing the embankment across Waterhead Creek and the twin embankment carrying the station and yard, the outermost portion of which was built by the Dartmouth Harbour Commissioners, together with the 'Éclair' pier jutting out into the Dart. The original pontoon for the GWR's steam ferry can be seen (bottom centre) with the covered-in passageway leading from it and passing behind the Royal Dart Hotel. The horse ferry slip is to the right of the hotel. Other features to be seen are the Customs House at the landward end of the pier (the horse ferry is moored beneath it). At right angles to the Customs House is the fish quay (roofed but otherwise open) and at its southern end the office later used by Renwick & Wilton (coal suppliers) and originally used by Mr Farley, Resident Engineer 1862–1866. Behind the water tank is the engine shed where the branch engine was stabled. The little building near the site of the later (1894) signal box is probably a weighbridge office.

Courtesy Brixham Museum

This extract is again taken from the newspaper; the service is still a 'shuttle' to and from Newton, apart from the following trains which appear to also convey through coaches, detached or attached at Newton:

Down (times from Newton)	Up (times from Torquay)
3.15 pm (9 am ex-Paddington	9.20 am
4.57 pm (11.45 am ex-Paddington)	11.19 am
7.58 pm (3 pm ex-Paddington)	2.50 pm
11.10 pm (5 pm ex-Paddington)	

The main event in 1880 was the GWR's decision to double the 3 miles 32 chains between Kingskerswell and Torquay at a cost of £14,300, including alterations at Torre. Later, in 1881, the authority was increased by £2,524 when the proposed Torre layout was improved by increased siding accommodation, provision of an up platform, footbridge and the lengthening of the existing (new down) platform.

The work to extend Torre station began in January 1882 and in March the GWR asked the BoT if the second line of rails could be used as this 'would greatly facilitate the works … at Torre'. This was agreed and the local paper reports that the double line between Kingskerswell and Torquay was used for the first time on Sunday 26th March. The new up platform at Torre was brought into use whilst work was continuing on extending the original (now down) platform and the original train shed was being removed, but necessary weather protection erected on each platform. Traffic to and from Torre was still very large and increasing.

Possibly envious of these improvements, the inhabitants of Paignton now raised complaints of the inadequacies of their station, or 'primitive little wooden house' as the *Torquay Directory* called it! Probably having been made aware of the local feelings, the GWR Board had just authorized a new waiting room and lavatory, alterations to the parcels office and erection of a verandah, all on the up platform at Paignton.* They were thus able to so inform their petitioners, adding 'this will form a portion of a larger scheme which will be carried out hereafter'.

Although Torquay had had the benefit of railway services for nearly 34 years, the need to change trains if travelling north of Bristol was obviously a major inconvenience and cause of delay. On 30th November, 1882 a deputation from the Local Board met the GWR Directors and made the following complaints:

1. Lack of through communication to the north
2. Delays at Newton Junction
3. Poor connections to/from Plymouth
4. Delay in transit of goods to/from Birmingham and elsewhere
5. Insufficient accommodation at Torre [still!]

All the GWR would concede at this stage was a promise to improve Torre, by covering the footbridge, making the upside waiting shed a waiting room and providing gentlemen's toilets on the up platform (as well as those on the downside).†

Col Yolland inspected the doubling track works on 9th March, 1883. He stated that new signal boxes had been provided at Kingskerswell (13 levers - 4 spare) and Torre (16 levers - 3 spare). (Not correct in the case of Kingskerswell as this had been built in 1876 for the doubling from Newton, see page 80). He required a catchpoint to be provided in the up line between Torre and Torquay, a train's length from Torre home signal. He also considered urinals were needed on the second platforms at

---

* At an estimated cost of £353 .

† At a price similar to the cost of the work at Paignton: £350 authority.

Up Trains.   TORQUAY BRANCH.   **Week Days.**

Distance from Kingswear	STATIONS.	1 — Empty Engine to run every alternate Friday.	2 Passenger.	3 Passenger	4 Passenger	5 Passenger	6 GOODS.	7 Passenger.	8 Passenger.	9 Passenger.	10 Passenger.	11 Passenger.
		arr / dep	pass	pass	pass	pass	pass	arr / dep	pass	pass	arr / dep	arr / dep
—	Dartmouth ...	a.m.	a.m.	a.m. 8 35	a.m.	a.m. 10 35	a.m.	p.m. 12 15	p.m.	p.m. 2 45	p.m.	p.m. 4 0
1	Kingswear ...	4 25	7 6	8 45	9 27	10 40		12 30		3 0		4 15
3¼	Churston ...	4 33	7 13 7 23	X8 57	9 40	11 2		12 45		3 12		4 29
6¾	Paignton ...	4 38	7 25 X7 33	9 0	9 52	11 10		12 51		3 20		4 38
8	Gas House Siding		7 31		10 1							
8¾	Torquay ...	4 43	7 38	9 20	10 6 X10 11	11 15 11 19	a.m.	12 56 1 0	p.m. 2 50	3 25 X3 30	p.m. 4 30	4 43 4 47
9¾	Torre ...	4 46	7 45	9 25	10 13 10 16	11 22 11 25	11 35	1 3 1 5	2 53	3 33 3 35	4 33 4 35	4 50 4 52
12½	Kingskerswell	4 52	7 56	9 30	10 23	11 32 11 33	11 47	1 12 1 13	3 2	3 43	4 41 4 42	4 59 5 0
13½	Aller Siding											
14½	Newton Abbot	4 56	8 4	9 36	10 31	11 40	11 55	1 29	3 8	3 48	4 47	5 6

Up Trains.   Week Days.—Continued.   SUNDAY TRAINS.

Distance from Kingswear	STATIONS.	12 GOODS.	13 Passenger.	14 Passenger.	15 Passenger.	16 Passenger.	17 GOODS.	18 Passenger.	1 Passenger.	2 Passenger.	3 Passenger.	4 Passenger.
		arr / dep	arr / dep	pass	arr / dep	arr / dep	arr / dep	pass	arr / dep	arr / dep	pass	arr / dep
—	Dartmouth ...	p.m.	p.m. 5 58	p.m.	p.m. 7 10	p.m. 8 27	p.m.	A 9 50	a.m.	p.m. 1 20	p.m.	p.m. 6 50
1	Kingswear ...	4 40	6 10		7 30	8 40	9 30	10 5	7 30	1 30 1 32		7 2
3¼	Churston ...	C. R. 6 20	6 22		7 40	8 50 8 57	9 55	10 15 10 17	7 40 7 42	1 38 1 40		7 9 7 11
6¾	Paignton ...	5 2 X5 20	6 29 6 31	7 20	7 48	X8 50	10 5	10 23 10 25	7 48 7 50		p.m. 4 5	
8	Gas House Siding	C. R.										
8¾	Torquay ...	5 34 6 15	6 37 6 40	7 25 7 27	7 55 7 57	9 4 9 6	10 23	10 31 10 33	7 55 7 57	1 45 1 47	4 10 4 12	7 16 7 19
9¾	Torre ...	6 26 6 36	6 43 6 45	7 30 7 32	8 2 8 4	9 10	10 30 11 25	10 36 10 38	8 2	1 50 1 52	4 15 4 17	7 22 7 25
12½	Kingskerswell		6 52 6 54	7 39	8 11 8 13	9 16	11 35	10 40 10 43	8 8 8 10	1 58 2 0	4 24 4 25	7 31 7 32
13½	Aller Siding											
14½	Newton Abbot	6 46	7 0	7 45	8 20	9 22	11 50	10 50	8 16	2 6	4 31	7 38

A   The Boat from Dartmouth to Kingswear in connection with this Train, will only be run for Passengers proceeding to Paignton and Station beyond.   For Passings and Crossings see page (18)

Working Timetable for July 1884 (up trains).

Down Trains.   TORQUAY BRANCH.   Week Days.

Distance from Newton Abbot	STATIONS	1 — To run every alternate Friday.		2 GOODS.		3 Passenger.		4 Passenger.		5 Passenger.		6 GOODS.		7 Passenger.		8 GOODS.		9 Passenger.		10 Passenger.		11 Passenger.	
		arr. pass	dep.	arr. pass	dep.	arr. pass	dep.	arr. pass	dep.	arr. pass	dep.	arr. pass	dep.	arr. pass	dep.	arr. pass	dep.	arr. pass	dep.	arr. pass	dep.	arr. pass	dep.
		a.m.	3 26	a.m.	6 0	a.m.	7 30	a.m.	8 20	a.m.	9 45	a.m.	9 55	noon	12 4	p.m.	12 10	p.m.	1 0	p.m.	1 40	p.m.	3 15
—	Newton Abbot		3 31		6 5	7 35	7 36	8 26	8 26	9 50	9 51			12 12	12 24	12 15	12 24		1 6	1 45	1 46		3 19
1	Aller Siding		3 37	c. R.		7 43	7 44	8 34	8 34	9 59	10	10 2		12 17	12 19	12 29	12 39	1 5	1 6	1 54	1 56	3 25	3 27
2¼	Kingskerswell		3 40	6 23	7	7 47	7 49	8 39	8 41	10 3	10 6	10 14		12 21	12 24	12 52	1 1	1 19	1 21	2 0		3 29 X3 33
5	Torre			7 10	7 12											1 30	1 32						
5½	Torquay		3 45	7 28	x8 5	7 54 X7 56		8 46	8 48	10 11	10 13			12 30	12 32	1 37	1 47	1 26	1 28			3 39	3 41
6¼	Gas House Siding		3 53	8 20 X9 12		8 3 8		8 56 X8 58	10 21	10 23			12 40	12 42	1 52	2 10	1 36	1 38			3 49	3 51
7½	Paignton		4 3	9 27		8 14		9 10	10 33				12 53		2 22	2 40	1 48					4 2	
10½	Churston		4 3			8 24		9 20	10 55				1 5		2 70		2 0					4 30	
14½	Kingswear																						
	Dartmouth																						

Down Trains.   Week Days.—Continued.

Distance from Newton Abbot	STATIONS	12 Passenger.		13 Passenger.		14 Passenger.		15 Passenger.		16 Passenger.		17 Passenger.		18 Passenger.	
		arr. pass	dep.	arr. pass	dep.	arr. pass	dep.	arr.	dep.	arr.	dep.	arr. pass	dep.	arr. pass	dep.
		p.m.	4 0	p.m.	4 55	p.m.	5 30	p.m.	6 23	p.m.	7 58	p.m.	8 30	p.m.	[1] 11
—	Newton Abbot			4 58		5 35	5 36	6 28	6 29		8 2	8 35	8 36		11 4
1	Aller Siding	5 4	4 10	5 4		5 43	5 45	6 36	6 38		8 8	8 43	8 47	11 21	11 23
2¼	Kingskerswell	4 14	4 16	6 5		5 47	5 49	6 41	6 44	8 10	8 12	8 49	8 52	11 25	11 28
5	Torre	4 19		5	5										
5½	Torquay			5 14 X5 16		5 55		6 49	6 51	8 17	8 18	8 58 x9	9 1	11 34	11 35
6¼	Gas House Siding			5 24 5 26				6 59	7 1	8 25	8 27	9 7	9 9	11 42	11 43
7½	Paignton			5 37				7 12		8 40		9 18		11 53	
10½	Churston			5 50				7 30		8 50		9 30			
14½	Kingswear														
	Dartmouth														

SUNDAY TRAINS.

Distance from Newton Abbot	STATIONS	1 Passenger.		2 Passenger.		3 Passenger.		4 Passenger.	
		arr. pass	dep.	arr. pass	dep.	arr. pass	dep.	arr. pass	dep.
		a.m.	8 25	a.m.	10 50	p.m.	2 30	p.m.	7 53
—	Newton Abbot	8 30	8 31	10 55	10 56	3 35	3 36	7 58	7 59
1	Aller Siding	8 39	8 41	11 5	11 7	3 45	3 46	8 7	8 10
2¼	Kingskerswell	8 44	8 46	11 7	11 11	3 48	3 50	8 12	8 14
5	Torre								
5½	Torquay	8 52	8 54	11 14	11 16	3 58		8 19	8 21
6¼	Gas House Siding	9	9	11 24	11 26			8 29	8 31
7½	Paignton	9 14		11 36				8 41	
10½	Churston								
14½	Kingswear								
	Dartmouth								

Working Timetable for July 1884 (down trains).

both stations, and, unusually, made this a condition of passing the work (which of course had already been in use for a year). However, due to a misunderstanding at the Board of Trade this stipulation was not passed on to the company; in any case the latter was already putting in an additional toilet at Torre. When, several months later, Yolland realised that no similar action was being taken at Kingskerswell pained letters passed to and fro until the matter was quietly dropped by the BoT. The second platform at Kingskerswell, as the GWR pointed out, was not even part of the doubling scheme, having been provided in 1876. The 'missing' toilet was actually installed in 1896!

In 1883 a young man of 19, born the year the railway reached Kingswear, and recently invalided out of the Royal Navy after suffering pneumonia, came to work at the railway's Yacht Club Hotel, Kingswear as 'Boots'. His name was John Lee and finding he did not like the work, he took a job as porter at Torre station. After only a few weeks there, however, he accepted an offer of a footman's job from a Col Brownlow of Torquay. Whilst the family was on holiday John Lee pawned some of the family's silver, was caught and sentenced to six months' hard labour in Exeter gaol. Released in January 1884 he was fortunate in being offered a job by an elderly lady, Miss Keyse of Babbacombe for whom he had worked as a pony boy five years earlier. On the night of 14th November, 1884 Miss Keyse was found murdered and John Lee was arrested and tried for the murder. He maintained his innocence and was completely calm throughout the trial which eventually found him guilty and sentenced him to death. On the day fixed for his execution three attempts were made to hang him but the apparatus would not work. The law did not allow any more attempts to take place and his sentence was commuted to penal servitude for life, which meant about 20 years. He was released in 1907. John Lee became known as 'The man they could not hang'.

(Interestingly in October 1930 the *Brixham Western Guardian* reported that a carpenter, who was in Exeter Prison at the time and was employed to help make the scaffold, had confessed to making the trap door with a slight slant. This caused the edges to fit together so that pressure from the top would wedge them. The greater the weight the more firmly the door would wedge.)

Twenty years after the opening to Kingswear, the residents of that village and their neighbours across the water at Dartmouth, also began to press for improvements. So began a long drawn-out struggle to modernize the facilities either side of the river, despite the views of the local authorities. For at this time Dartmouth Council and the Harbour Commissioners were locked in bitter combat over the construction of the south embankment. It is reported in the GWR Board Minutes that an invitation to both parties to attend a meeting was accepted by the Town Council but only if the Harbour Commissioners did not attend! Fortunately, perhaps, the latter did not feel the need to attend this particular meeting. In February 1885, following lengthy discussions, the GWR decided to order a new pontoon for Kingswear 80 ft long by about 27 ft wide, 10 ft further into the river than the present stage, linked by a connecting gangway 12 ft wide. The pontoon for Dartmouth was deferred 'until the views of the town authorities … were definitely ascertained'. The Kingswear pontoon was approved by the Board in February 1886 at an estimated cost of £3,000. (This opened for traffic on 5th January, 1888.) In March 1886 the two GWR representatives on the Harbour Commissioners resigned from that body and it took the involvement of the Board of Trade in the dispute in 1888 before all concerned could reach agreement regarding the Dartmouth pontoon (*see Appendix One*). Finally in October of that year following local agreement the GWR Board approved an estimate of £4,680 for new station accommodation on the embankment and a new pontoon. The two local authorities were by this time conducting their battle in the law courts, the Harbour Commissioners being the eventual losers.

The *Dartmouth Chronicle* for 4th April, 1884 reported that the chief clerk at Torquay, Henry Hill, had absconded two days earlier with the day's takings (about £80); but had been caught at Exeter!

The working timetable for 1884 still does not show through trains serving the Kingswear line, although some may have been portions off London trains. A very early arrival on Friday mornings was a connection for the fortnightly boat run by the Currie line to South Africa.

Other developments on the line at this time were mainly at Paignton where the promised improvements involving further extension of the platforms, widening of the (North?) level crossing and provision of an exit from the down platforms were approved in November 1884. The footbridge at Paignton North level crossing was reconstructed in iron in 1887 and in 1888 it was agreed to complete the up platform buildings, enclose the alcove on the down platform and (further) lengthen the down platform.*

There were two fairly minor incidents in 1886. On 7th January the 6.23 pm Newton Abbot-Kingswear approaching the terminus in charge of driver Daniel Durant failed to stop on an icy rail at the beginning of the platform (for ticket collection) and hit three coaches standing at the stop block. Major Marindin for the BoT suggested that driver Durant had been running too fast with a light 5-coach train, as the engine hand brake had been applied for 500 yds, and the two guards' hand brakes had been applied for 380 yds, yet the collision had occurred at about 7 mph. The driver was fined 20s. for not having his train under proper control. On 26th August the 11.25 am Torquay to Dartmouth (as identified by the local paper), 'was brought up near the tunnel at Livermead in consequence of the connecting rod of the engine having broken. Communication below Torquay was delayed about 3 hours'.

Also in 1886, on 31st March the Board declined Sir Bernhard Samuelson MP's request that the (foot) level crossing at Churston be replaced by an overbridge. However, on 15th July they did authorize the extension of the up platform there at a cost of £27. On 12th August, Messrs Browning & Wesley's tender for the tenancy of the refreshment rooms at Torquay and Torre for one year was accepted: £35 pa at Torquay and £25 pa at Torre. In September 1886, Kingswear's station master Mr James Paddon, who had been there since 1865, retired, following a heart attack.

Frank Hill, who was to be appointed station master at Churston on 7th November, 1898, was in 1886 a first class reliefman at Newton Abbot. In this post he relieved station masters, inspectors, clerks, signalmen (the bulk of his work) and guards so had to be very knowledgeable and flexible. In December 1886 he was relieving at Churston and was asked by the superintendent's office why the 7.07 pm ex-Churston was two minutes late in starting on 23rd December. His reply:

The above train was 2 mins late starting through a truck of fish coming in from Brixham not labelled, and by the time I had found the numbers (which was [sic] very dirty) and then found the Brixham guard to know where the truck was for, it was seven minutes after seven, 2 mins overtime.

At Churston again in October 1887 he had to report that on arrival of three bullocks from Exeter for Mr Pitts, Brixham on the 6 am goods from Newton Abbot,

---

* The November 1884 authority was £130; the footbridge in 1887 £230; the 1888 work was estimated to cost £755.

one of the three could not stand and was found to have a broken back: it was put down. The guard stated that the bullock had been 'down' when he took over the train and no shunting had taken place en route from Newton Abbot.

Mr Hill had to fend off a complaint from a senior naval officer when he replied to the station master at Newton Abbot on 1st February, 1888. On this occasion he was acting as guard on a train from Newton Abbot to Kingswear. The memo is as written by Mr Hill:

FH 150/1   *Best complaint*   *February 1st 1888*

Dear Sir

Referring to attached I deny being in any way rude to Captain Best. I may have spoken louder than would be required in ordinary conversation but the train was moving and a good breeze blowing which compelled me to do so, the facts were as follows at Paignton a gentleman asked me to stop the train at the Level [Britannia Crossing] on arriving at Churston I gave the driver the order and told him the carriages the passengers were in [,] some were in a third in front of the van and some in a first & second compo behind the van the train stopped with the third at the Level first and when the passengers were out and the doors closed I signalled the driver to pull ahead for the compo which was done and I passed out some luggage from the van for some cadets and when I came out of the van I looked up and down the train to see the doors right blew my whistle and started the train, then Captain Best jumped up and said we want to get out, I then said you should have got out Sir I cannot stop the train again, that was all that passed.

Mr Maggs

(From another letter copied into Frank Hill's correspondence book it seems that sometime in either February or March 1888 the GWR decided that trains would only stop at Britannia Crossing for first or second class passengers and not for third class passengers; they would, however, have the opportunity to pay excess to a higher class at Churston!)

Mr Hill seems a fairly fearless fellow because a month later he wrote to the divisional locomotive superintendent, no less, as follows:

FH 161/1   *March 4th 1888*

Dear Sir,

I beg to report to you that the Enginemen in this yard [NA] totally disregard the Rules as to carrying tail lights after dusk and in some cases they have neither head or tail lamps up your alteration to this will oblige.

J. Luxmoore Esq. [Locomotive Supt]

Commencing in 1889, the Post Office required a connection off the Night Mail train at Newton Abbot to Torquay; and on Sundays, Good Friday and Christmas Day a train to be run from Torquay to Newton to connect with the up Night Mail. The cost of these trains to the Post Office was £400 pa.

The Regulation of Railways Act 1889 required the railway companies to install block working and interlocking, where not already in use. In December 1889 the fairly large sum of £2,756 was agreed for this at Paignton which included a new signal box at each end of the station to work the level crossing gates (previously hand-worked); an additional siding, new goods office and further extension of the up platform and loop. An additional signalman was authorized.

In August 1890 the *Exeter Flying Post* recorded that Churston 'has recently had its platforms lengthened and a convenient waiting room for Brixham passengers erected'.

In November 1890 the Board of Trade issued an order requiring the GWR, *inter alia*, to install interlocking apparatus and new signalling west of Exeter and replace the telegraph and crossing order method of working single lines by the electric train staff, within three years. A signal box was ordered for Churston in September 1891. Although some GWR Maintenance records say that Kingswear box was 34 years old in 1924 (i.e. built 1890) it is more likely that the box opened in February 1894 as all other sources (including the Board of Trade inspector) state.* This is borne out by a report in the *Dartmouth Chronicle* of 10th February, 1893 which comments that 40 men were engaged in the station improvements including a new signal box.

Facilities at Torre were again expanded in 1890 by provision of an up siding and approach road, goods office and 10 ton crane and altered locking in the signal box (total £1,352). The work was passed on 18th November, Col Rich also inspecting the new works at Paignton the same day. The new North signal box there contained 9 working and four spare levers and the South box 14 working and three spare levers. (From a report in the *Exeter Flying Post*, it would appear that the signal boxes were in use from August 1890.) The lengthened loop now extended over the public roads at both ends of the station. However, Col Rich took exception to the new siding at the south end of the station as the junction points were only 50 yds from the stop signal protecting the gates there.

Frank Hill had been relieving the station master at Paignton, Mr Clampit, in July 1890. He had been lodging at Paignton and had to work from 7.15 am until departure of the 10.10 pm from Kingswear at 10.30 pm. A letter dated 17th July, 1890 in his correspondence book addressed to Mr Northcott, his inspector at Plymouth, asks to be allowed some overtime for these long days; his rate of pay was only 25 shillings per week. This was turned down and Mr Hill wrote again to Mr Northcott the following week:

FH 227/1   *July 22nd 1890*

Dear Sir

I am informed by Inspector Murrin that my overtime for week ending July 19th is struck out I think this is rather hard on me being that I worked 15½ hours per day and Paignton being an exceptional place for work also the Goods Booking Porter at Paignton is paid overtime every other week when he works this long turn. If I cannot be paid for working these long hours can I have next Saturday off duty in lieu of them I am not ordered away on that date and oblige.

Mr Northcott

Just before the new signal box was ordered for Churston (*see above*), Frank Hill wrote a letter to his inspector, Mr Northcott, complaining that the signalman's workload there made it impossible to carry out the company's rules and regulations. Apart from the fact that the signals and points were not yet controlled from a central signal box, entailing the signalman in doing a lot of walking, it seems he was expected to act as a shunter as well:

---

* A 'Nameplates Book', formerly kept at the BR Record Centre in Porchester Road, W2, recorded that nameplates were ordered for Churston and Kingswear signal boxes on 3rd March, 1891, which is the day after the GWR Board discussed work arising from the narrowing of the gauge (*see page 97*).

A Paignton-bound train leaves Hollacombe tunnel in 1889, the steep road, 'Breakneck Hill', crosses the railway here. The hills of Torquay are in the background.

'Torquay Directory', courtesy Brixham Museum

Dartmouth Regatta day, *c.*1889. Featured left is the store hulk of the *Windsor Castle* of the Castle Line which called at Dartmouth 1871-1891. The train in the foreground is made up of convertible clerestory stock hauled by a class 'B' 0-6-0ST converted to broad gauge. Moored just ahead of the locomotive is a spare horse ferry boat. Brereton's three-span wooden Waterhead viaduct can be seen at the right of the picture, while the building alongside is the ancient Hoodown Ferry House demolished during reconstruction of the viaduct in 1927. Just beyond the viaduct is the original Hoodown coal siding and shipping place (later called 'Forwoods'), together with the small shipbuilding yard built by the railway in 1865 to replace Alford's shipyard. Further up the river can be seen coaling hulks with vessels alongside and in the centre rear are HMS *Britannia* and *Hindustan* which preceded the RN college at Dartmouth. *The late I.H. Smart, courtesy Brixham Museum*

FH 254/1   *June 6th 1891*

Dear Sir
                    Duty at Churston 15th – 20th inst. Inclusive

I have been to Churston to relieve the signalman now for several years and I find that
the work is increasing each time I go, in addition to attending to the points and signals
the Signalman do [*sic*] the whole of the shunting, coupling and uncoupling in
connection with the Brixham train without any assistance whatever he also takes
number of trucks which arrive or leave Churston which on some days amounts to a
considerable number, the 6 am and 12.2 pm goods trains ex NA also put off their trucks
anyhow which on some days causes a considerable amount of shunting to pick out the
Brixham trucks. My object in writing … is to ask that the Brixham guard shall assist in
all the shunting in connection with his train as per Mr Compton's circular 575 of Oct.
28th 1890 or else one of the porters at Churston shall be appointed to assist the
signalman in this work, seeing the number of trains there is in and out of Churston and
the number of points to be looked after it is a matter of impossibility to carry out the
Company's rules and regulations and do the whole of the work. I have referred to you
trusting you will see into this matter and give me a favourable reply.
      Mr Northcott

     At this time there was an inspector at Churston, for Thomas Smith retired from
this post aged 69 on 31st December, 1893, so one wonders why the signalman was
expected to do so much on his own.
     The GWR had carried out a great deal of work on the Torquay line in the 12 years
of its ownership and obviously appreciated its revenue potential. So, following
representations from the Local Board, they agreed to run the Torquay portion of the
11.45 am ex-Paddington non-stop from Exeter to Torquay arriving there at 4.45 pm,
only five hours journey from London, via Bristol. This was declared to be an
experiment, commencing 1st January, 1891, for the rest of the winter service.
Correspondence in the paper spoke of the joy of travelling on a train which swept
through the intermediate stations 'at an excellent rate'. Dartmouth passengers were
saved further time by the collection of tickets between Churston and Kingswear,
rather than at Kingswear. Amongst other changes was a new train at 9.20 am from
Torquay to Moretonhampstead (during the summer) for the benefit of visitors to
Dartmoor. But the Board would not agree to the 3 pm ex-Paddington (7.58 ex-
Newton) stopping at Torre as there was little demand (although it had done in 1880,
see page 87) and 'it would interfere with the single line working between Paignton
and Kingswear, the margin at the present time being very narrow'.
     In 1892, Donald Currie & Co. (former Cape & Natal Steamship Co.) which had
been running a mail service from Dartmouth to Durban since 1871, moved its
Channel base to Southampton because of the more convenient rail facilities there.
This was chiefly at the insistence of the Post Office.
     A report by the General Manager on 'narrowing' the gauge was considered by the
Board on 2nd March, 1891. So far as the Kingswear line was concerned this also
involved the replacement of the single needle telegraph block working between
Torquay and Kingswear by electric train staff instruments. Additional staff (i.e.
manpower) costs of £342 pa would be involved for the Torquay and Brixham lines
and the following costs were identified for work at stations on the line (over and
above the trackwork costs):

An 1880s photograph of Torquay Gas Works at Hollacombe, showing the orginal horizontal retort houses and a line of trucks in the single siding. The broad gauge single track enters Livermead tunnel almost immediately under the photographer's feet; note the level crossing just this side of the first building. This may have given access to fields or possibly the beach. Paignton pier (built 1879) can just be made out in the bay.   *Peter Tully Collection*

Work at Torquay in connection with the narrowing of the gauge. Looking south at the station area; the track is still broad gauge.   *LGRP (NRM)*

Kingskerswell £686	Extension of siding and provision of toilets
Torre £1,760	New refuge sidings, alter sidings, extend goods shed
Churston £227	Extend platforms
Kingswear £3,732	Widen and extend platform, new sidings and cross-over road, new cattle pens and verandah [Kingswear's layout was virtually unaltered since 1866]

Newton Abbot received £5,000 for alterations and improvements in the station and Loco and Carriage works as well as another £15,000 needed to provide a larger locomotive shed. The 'narrowing' was found to be a convenient time for much of this overdue work, making it difficult to say how much the abolition of the broad gauge cost the Great Western Railway. Traders holding private siding agreements were advised of the change of gauge, as in many cases they would need new wagons. Sidings involved locally were Aller Siding, Kingskerswell and Gas House Siding, Torquay.

Monday 9th March, 1891 was the first day of a week of bad weather for the West Country which caused trains to be 'lost' in snow for days at a time, although not on the Kingswear line. The Great Storm, as it became known, began on Monday afternoon with sleeting snow and a keen easterly wind. During Monday night the snow fell heavily until six inches lay in the streets of Torquay and, whipped up by the winds, in many places it was much deeper. A tree was blown across the line at Lowes bridge near Torre station, with which an up train collided closing the line until the tree could be removed. Tremendous damage was done in the town, and to the pier and the sea wall, and the roadway to Torquay station looked 'as though a digging machine had gone over it'. Each train running was double-headed; the telephone and telegraph wires alongside the railway were brought down in many places. The 5 pm from Paddington which should have arrived at Torquay before midnight did not arrive until 9 am on Tuesday. Nothing passed through Newton Abbot after a train which had left Plymouth on Monday afternoon, which reached Newton Abbot on Tuesday morning. Two trains dispatched from Plymouth later on Monday got stuck between there and Totnes and three trains were held at Newton Abbot, unable to proceed. Snow fell during the whole of Tuesday and eventually blocked the Kingswear line stopping the traffic overnight. Snow stopped falling close to midnight and the weather became milder but on Wednesday morning the clearing skies revealed snow two feet deep. Early on Wednesday morning the GWR managed to clear a train stuck near Powderham Castle and ran a service from Exeter to Paignton, the first from Exeter since Monday night, and other local services were subsequently run. Later on Wednesday services resumed to and from Bristol and Paddington but the line was still blocked below Newton towards Plymouth (the LSWR line via Okehampton was also closed).

The snow thawed in the Torbay area on Wednesday so that a reasonable service could be run on the Kingswear line on the Thursday. The line between Newton and Plymouth was eventually cleared on Friday evening 13th March, having been blocked since the previous Monday; over 1,000 men had been involved in clearing the lines in Devon and Cornwall. The roads from Torquay to Paignton and Brixham were re-opened on Saturday, having been blocked since Tuesday. The telegraph communication between Dartmouth and Exeter was restored on Sunday. One presumes that the damage to the telegraph and telephone lines affected the signalling on the Kingswear line during this period, necessitating working by pilotman. Generally, Torbay had been far less affected than other parts of Devon,

The narrowing of the gauge at Noss viaduct, 21st May, 1892. The tents erected to house the navvies can be seen.   *Totnes Image Bank*

Some 40 of the navvies involved in the narrowing of the gauge pose with the station staff outside Kingswear goods shed, Tuesday 24th May, 1892. They have just had a 'substantial breakfast' paid for by the station master, Messrs Casey and some of the local residents and will leave in extra carriages attached to the 10.40 am train. The previous day (Monday) Messrs Casey had entertained them with a special river trip to Dittisham.   *Totnes Image Bank*

and the whole of Cornwall, the worst of the weather having passed by the Wednesday.

On 19th September, 1891 John Charles Neville was appointed station master at Kingswear. He did not stay long, moving to Devizes on 10th October, 1894. He seems to have done a swap, because the station master there, Thomas Abrahams, came to Kingswear on the same date.

On 19th January, 1892 goods guard John Thomas of Newton Abbot did not properly secure his train while it was shunting at Torre, causing it to run back to Torquay. He was subsequently fined 2s. 6d. for the mistake. Strangely, almost exactly two years later on 1st January, 1894 the same thing happened; this time brakesman Robert Henry Mitchelmore of Newton Abbot was fined 5s. for the same offence. These details are taken from staff records and there is no description of any damage caused, or whether the trains became derailed. Maybe there were other examples, for in November 1900 the sum of £131 was authorized to provide '[a] safety dead end and catch siding between Torre and Torquay'.

When the planning for the narrowing of the gauge took place it had been intended that the Torquay line would only be closed on the Sunday of the weekend involved. Early in 1892, however, it was decided 'that the line between Exeter and Torquay be entirely closed on Saturday and Sunday 21st and 22nd May'. The last down train on Friday 20th May was the 5 pm Paddington to Plymouth, hauled by *Iron Duke*, the famous 4-2-2, from Bristol to Newton Abbot. The portion off this train was the last down the Kingswear line and some 60 to 80 people waited at Torre to ride down to Torquay. The train approached, late, close to midnight and the 'last ride' was soon finished. Many of the passengers paid excess fares in order to retain their tickets as souvenirs but, to their chagrin, found they had been dated 21st May, 1892. The coaches returned as a special empty coaching stock at 12.45 am from Kingswear to Exeter hauled by locomotive 1566 with Inspector Hockaday in charge, forward thence to Swindon. All goods stock had been cleared by Thursday 19th and all passenger stock by 20th May.

The men were formed into gangs of just over 60 strong with three gangers and an inspector in charge. Inspector Venn of Bridgwater supervised to the 221½ mp (between Torquay and Paignton); from here to Churston inspector Cox of Weston-super-Mare was in charge, with sub inspector Luke of Newton assisting at Churston itself. The Brixham branch and from Churston to Greenway tunnel were dealt with by inspector Tazewell of Cheddar, whilst the remainder of the line and Kingswear itself were converted by inspector Sweetland of Taunton. Mr Hammett, divisional engineer Taunton, was in overall charge of the work between Exeter and Kingswear, including the Moretonhampstead branch.

Most of the men working at Torre and Torquay were housed in the goods shed at Torre. The GWR provided tentage (when required) and bedding and cooking utensils, together with oatmeal and sugar. Messrs W.D. & H.O. Wills of Bristol supplied each man with 2 oz. of tobacco and the *Torquay Directory* reported that the Torquay station master, Richard Masters, treated a gang of 70 men working locally to a cauldron of coffee. Twenty-eight men (from London and Didcot) were accommodated in Kingswear goods shed and a further 60 men in tents at Noss, between the two viaducts.

From dawn on Saturday the 'narrowing' commenced: so well had preparations been made that as early as 11 am work was completed as far as Teignmouth. The down line as far as Torquay was finished by 3 pm, Kingswear being reached a few hours later and completed by 8 pm. The up line was then started and by nightfall the

Right: Looking south from the incline to Torre, with Torquay North signal box (*left*). The track is still broad gauge.   *LGRP (NRM)*

Below: Looking in the opposite direction towards Torre with men laying the standard gauge rail in the up line track.

Courtesy Christopher Awdry

Bottom right: Another view looking from Torquay towards Torre. The up line (*left*) now has a third standard gauge rail throughout, while the down line has been narrowed but remains on its timber baulks with cross transoms. Note the up starting signal with lower 'shunt ahead' arm, both marked with an 'X', meaning not in use.

Courtesy Christopher Awdry

whole Torquay line was complete except for ballasting and packing which took place on Sunday.

Thanks to a most comprehensive report in the *Dartmouth Chronicle* of 27th May, 1892 we can follow the work of the Kingswear gangs in some detail:

COMMENCEMENT OF THE WORK

At 2 am on Saturday the men in the tents turned out and set to work with a will, commencing at the Churston side of the tunnel. They worked on until eleven o'clock by which time they had got down to Higher Noss viaduct, where they breakfasted. Starting again at 11.30 they laboured on without intermission until 6 pm by which time they had reached Kingswear station, having narrow-gauged the whole of their three miles in the short space of 15½ working hours, or an average of just over five hours per mile. In several places around curves and over the bridges both rails had to be shifted but in others it was only found necessary to move one rail. The work completed on Saturday included cutting the transoms, which had not previously been cut through, shifting the rails to the required gauge of 4 ft 8½ in. and re-bolting the whole together; and the only work left on the single line for Sunday was the necessary levelling and packing, or what is known as ballasting.

The men at Kingswear station started work on Saturday at 4 am and had a very different task to cope with than the alteration of a single straight line. All the points and switches had to be changed, and in many instances the rails cut on the inside of a curve in order to make them fit in their new places. The men worked on to 8 pm stopping only for breakfast and dinner, and by dusk had actually completed the work so far as shifting the lines, points and switches were concerned. The fastenings, of course, were not complete, but it is no exaggeration to say that by Saturday night an engine might have run over the whole of the points in the Kingswear Station, a truly remarkable piece of work, even in these days of engineering feats. During the day, Mr Neville (Station master at Kingswear) was in telegraphic communication with the Traffic Superintendent, Mr Burlinson, who was at Plymouth, concerning the progress which was being made.

On Sunday morning the men started again at 4 am and the tent gangs went over the whole of their previous day's work, for the purpose of packing the altered metals securely, while the station gang completed the fastenings of the points and switches, and then also commenced the final ballasting and packing work. The operations were watched on Sunday by a large number of people, many of whom came across from Dartmouth and strolled some distance up the line.

THE FIRST NARROW GAUGE TRAIN

At half-past eleven on Sunday morning, intelligence was received at Kingswear by wire that an engine and van would be able to run through in a very short time, and a few minutes before one o'clock a very heavy narrow gauge goods engine, pushing an engineer's van before it , made its appearance. The van was an open fronted one, and contained Mr Hammett (divisional engineer for Taunton division), his chief clerk, and an assistant engineer, besides Mr Maggs, station master at Newton Abbot, from which station the engine had started an hour or so previously, having run down at a very steady pace. The engine and van were met at the Hoodown siding by Mr Neville, who came in with it to the station, where a large number of spectators were drawn up to witness the arrival. The engine was tried on the straight line into the station running right back to the buffers, and afterwards it was shunted on to the right hand siding, and then on to the goods sidings. To general satisfaction the whole of the lines and points were found to be right, and Mr Maggs then issued a certificate to Mr Neville as follows:- 'This is to certify that the line between Kingswear and Newton Abbot is ready to be re-opened for traffic , and the ordinary working of the trains between these points can be resumed on Monday, the 23rd inst'. The engine and van shortly afterwards left again for Newton, and no further stock came down the line during Sunday. The men were at work packing, up to six o'clock on Sunday evening, when they knocked off. During the progress of the work, Mr Neville took journeys up the line to Longwood Viaduct in order to see what progress was being made. The whole of the men below the tunnel were in charge of Inspector Sweetland of Taunton, under whom Gangers Wilcox and Jones were in charge of the men at the station. Each man was furnished with a straw mattress, and a couple of blankets, and were more than satisfied with the accommodation which had been provided for them under the circumstances. The work was not without its humourous side, and on one occasion, while the men were asleep in the goods shed, one of them snored so loudly as to wake all his fellows up. One of the men thus rudely awakened from slumber said 'he thort that a narrer gage engine wor comin'.

RESUMPTION OF TRAFFIC

At 5.30 am on Monday morning, a train arrived at Kingswear from Exeter, composed of empty narrow-gauge coaches, and a nearly new engine. Several of the carriages were new, while others bore evidence of having been in use for many years, and had been shifted on to the narrow-gauge wheels. The new carriages were most elaborately fitted up, and decorated inside with photographs of local scenery, and of views around Plymouth, Exeter, and other towns on the Great Western route. The 7.13 am train from

A photograph taken at Kingswear a day or two before the narrowing of the gauge when the sidings were being dealt with. Alternate transoms have been cut and are lying discarded in the foreground. SDR locomotive No. 2123 *Pluto* has only a few more days of active life in front of her and her crew pose proudly for an historic photograph. Beyond the second building, which is reputed to have enclosed a simple ground frame, can be seen a grounded broad gauge coach body.   *The late I.H. Smart, courtesy Brixham Museum*

Torquay station probably photographed on 20th May, 1892, this view looks towards Torre. A gang of men is working on the track outside Torquay North signal box, which was reduced to a ground frame by 1903. Alternate transoms have been cut to standard gauge length, in preparation for 'narrowing'. *Torquay Museum*

Kingswear, was the first outward one to run, and afterwards traffic was continued in the ordinary manner. Both the 7.13 and 8.33 am were started punctually to the minute, but the 9.33 and 10.40 am were somewhat late, owing to a delay in getting the narrow-gauge coaches and engines down quickly enough. At noon on Monday, a special train of empty goods wagons was run down, in order that the goods traffic might be resumed on the following day, which was done. The Great Western Authorities are certainly to be congratulated upon having accomplished the undertaking so speedily and with so little inconvenience to the general public.

The goods traffic was resumed on Tuesday, when several goods trains came down to Kingswear, and on Wednesday everything was again in full working order.

I had hoped that Frank Hill might have recorded something about the abolition of the broad gauge but his correspondence only took the form of letters or replies to letters. However, he did act as guard in connection with returning the workmen from the Kingswear line and his letter is shown below. From this we know that the 6.30, and not the 7.13, as recorded in the newspaper, was actually the first narrow gauge train from Kingswear.

FH 263/2   *May 24th 1892*

Dear Sir
In accordance with your telegram I travelled to Kingswear with the 3.45 (?3.15) am empty coaches thence to Exeter with the 6.30 am workmen's train, we were obliged to stop at two places other than the booked ones first at the 227½ mp to pick up (?4) men and again at Paignton, the men that we should have picked up at the 223¼ mp had walked in to Paignton hence we were obliged to stop to pick them up, the empty coaches only left Newton at 5.3 am arrived at Kingswear at 5.40, attached please find the times from Kingswear to Exeter.
    Mr Northcott

On the last day of the broad gauge (20th May, 1892), an unidentified former SDR 4-4-0T leaves Torquay for Kingswear. Note the ornamental gas lamp with 'Torquay' engraved in the glass. The bookstall placards can be seen beyond the glazed partition on the up platform.

Torquay Museum

Seen through the entrance to the goods shed, an up local train leaves Torre hauled by an unidentified '3521' class 0-4-4T. It is thought that this photograph was taken just after the abolition of the broad gauge.   *Courtesy Torquay Museum (PR26227)*

		No. of men (?)	Time lost by engine	
Kingswear	6.30	12		
227½ mp	6.34-6.36			To pick up men
Churston	6.45-6.47	4		
223¼ mp	6.54-6.55	5		To pick up men
Paignton	6.57-6.59			To Paignton instead
Torre	7.7-7.10	9		
NA	7.22-7.34	21	2	Taking water
Exeter	8.31		20	

20 mins lost by engine Newton to Exeter

During the days of closure Torquay mails were conveyed from and to Exeter by coach. Passengers had a choice of road transport, or by sea to Exmouth. Connection with Paignton was either by horse omnibus or steam launch. Dartmouth mails went to Totnes by road and forward by road or river.

There were no accidents locally during the work but one local man responsible for a 2½ mile section became so worried about the responsibility resting upon him that he committed suicide. James Webber, a 34-year-old ganger, had complained to his wife over the pressure of the work which 'required a great deal of study', and was worried he would have insufficient tools for the men being sent down to do the job. On the Monday before the big weekend it appears that he walked off the cliffs at Hollacombe Gas Works. The coroner returned a verdict of 'suicide while suffering from temporary insanity'.

It is interesting to learn (*GWR Magazine*) that as late as 1910, there were still 63¼ miles of running line track laid on longitudinal sleepers on the GWR. Of this total, 1¼ miles was to be found on the Kingswear line.

This magnificent view of Torquay looking towards Torre was possibly taken in 1897 when the paving on the up platform was extended. Notice that the track through the platforms is still on wooden baulks with cross transoms. The station master, standing by the down home signal for the South box, keeps a watchful eye on the photographer.   *NRM/SSPL*

A view of the first engine turntable at Kingswear, which was of 23 ft 5 in. diameter and immediately in front of the engine shed. It was removed in 1896/97 and replaced by a 55 ft turntable in 1900. *Author's Collection*

Chapter Six

Water problems and doubling to Paignton: 1892-1918

On Friday 21st October, 1892 when the 7 am goods from Newton Abbot was shunting at Aller Siding the engine and four trucks were derailed, the engine falling on its side. Despite exhaustive enquiry no defect could be found in the permanent way and no definite cause of the derailment established. Single line working over the up line took place until the engine was rerailed on Sunday morning.

During 1892/3 the Paignton Local Board of Health attempted to persuade the GWR to substitute the level crossing at Sands Road (the south end) by a road bridge and footbridge (the GWR had donated two small pockets of land here in 1890 to enable the road to be widened). Unfortunately they expected the GWR to pay the cost of £4,300, although the Local Board would have provided the land (value £1,000). At the north end (Torbay Road) it would not be possible to close the level crossing but the Local Board suggested a bridge approach road to the station would divert a lot of traffic off the crossing, for which the local authority would pay half. These proposals, the first of many such, were, regrettably, not acceptable to the GWR (the crossings are still there today).

The years 1886, 1887 and 1892 had all been very dry leading to great problems with supply of water to Kingswear station. On 18th August, 1892 Mr Joseph Luxmoore the locomotive superintendent at Newton Abbot, made a personal site visit and found that water was running into the tank at Kingswear at the rate of eight gallons a minute, giving a total for the day of 11,520 gallons, whereas average daily consumption was 13,000 gallons but 15,000 in July, August and September. A check the following day revealed that the supply had reduced to five gallons a minute. He wrote to Mr Dean at Swindon asking that the parish be approached to lay down larger pipes to increase the supply. He had cause to send a reminder to Mr Dean the following January, and again in April (no action having been taken).

Finally the chief at Swindon awoke from his apparent slumber and dispatched one of his inspectors Mr J. Tonkin to Kingswear. The latter produced the following report, dated 27th April, 1893, extracts from which are of interest for their detail:

Report on Kingswear Water Supply
The supply at this station is from the Parish, who give us their surplus water from their village reservoir in winter and rainy seasons. The supply is brought from the village main into our tank through a ¾" pipe. This together with a pipe from a well was the original supply previous to one being laid from the Mill Leat. The pipe from the well was then taken off our tank.

The present supply pipe which was laid on to our tank 19th August 1887 is from the Mill Leat, the rights of which, together with the Mill premises, now pulled down, were purchased by the Parish some years ago.

A small weir is built in the course of the stream at Waterhead Brake Wood, up the valley, 1,298 yards from the tank, diverting a portion of the water into a catch-pit 6' 0" x 9" x 3' 0" from which it is fed in 2" galvanized iron pipes down the valley to near the site of the old Mill, or a distance of 462 yards , thence in 1½" pipes over the brow of the hill and then on an easy gradient down to our tank a distance of 886 yards. The fall from the catchpit to the tank is 27 feet.

The pipe after leaving the reservoir is laid at the side of a hedge, then through a small irregular culvert 35 yards in length, in an embankment carrying a road, not shown on the map.

The pipes when laid had to be drawn through this culvert with ropes as there was not sufficient room for a man to connect them. The pipes are then carried down to below the site of the old Mill sluice (now disused) and across into the road at the head of the creek, then following the road to within 119 yards of our tank where they pass on to G.W.R. property.

I estimate the consumption just 13,000 gallons per day at present as stated by Mr Owen and 15,000 gallons in the summer. The consumption however varies considerably according to the state of the water at Newton Abbot, which, when brackish, the engines take a full tank at Kingswear.

If it is decided to have an extra supply by means of new pipes the Parish authorities intend laying earthenware pipes from the catchpit some distance up the valley so as to collect free of mud or any sediment.

The G.W.R's own supply is a small spring at the Kingswear end of Churston Tunnel and the drainage from the tunnel itself.

The quantity now running into the tank [from the tunnel] is 4,000 gallons a day. This was formerly a good supply but first began to fail in June 1885 owing probably to a Mr Simpson having had a well sunk to supply his house close by.

I walked from Kingswear to Churston and I am of opinion that if a small heading was driven at the side of the tunnel we should get a better water supply from this source.

Noss Creek: A portion of this water is now used by the ship building firm of Simpson and Strickland but last summer they had to work their condensing engine at high pressure owing to the scarcity of their water supply.

As well as the locomotives and the station the water supplied the steam cranes and the SS *Dolphin*, the Dartmouth ferry.

Following negotiations with the Parish, it was agreed to increase the diameter of the supply pipe (to 3 inches), and the rate paid by the GWR to the Parish would go up from £25 to £35 pa (the latter had wanted £40) and a capital cost of £120 for the new mains on GWR property. The new pipe came into operation on 2nd October, 1893. (Also in 1893 it was agreed to tap into the locomotive water supply at Torre to give a supply to that station so as to wash out cattle wagons. Little did they know it, but the locomotive department was soon to receive a nasty surprise.)

Work carried out at Kingswear in 1893 included provision of a truck weighbridge and a timber ticket platform outside the station. This can be seen in the *c*.1905 photograph; arriving trains halted here while tickets were collected. Such ticket platforms were employed at a number of other terminal places including Plymouth Millbay. The one at Kingswear was out of use by November 1915. Additionally the station platform was widened and covering over the [main] platform was authorized at a cost of £416 9s. 4d.; this extended beyond the train shed.

Much of the alteration work carried out at stations after the narrowing of the gauge was inspected by the Board of Trade in the summer of 1893. In a report encompassing 19 stations, Major Marindin had this to say about Churston and Torquay;

Churston Station. The platforms have been extended and interlocking re-arranged. The new signal cabin contains 35 working and 4 spare levers and there is a subsidiary 2 lever ground frame. Approved.
Torquay Station: The loop has been lengthened, siding connections altered and interlocking re-arranged. The south cabin contains 13 working and 3 spare levers and the north cabin contains 10 working and 4 spare levers.
Requirement: at the north cabin safety points on the siding to be put in nearer to the main line than the present points and switch block. Approved subject to this being done within one month.

Work at two further locations was inspected in 1894 by the Major:

> *Kingswear:* this terminal station has been resignalled and the sidings have been added to and re-arranged. The new cabin contains 35 working levers, correctly interlocked and 10 spare levers and there is a subsidiary 2 lever ground frame bolted from the cabin.
> *Torre:* At this station the only new connection is that of a down siding. The signal cabin contains 16 levers correctly interlocked. Approved.

The siding at Torre had been installed by May 1893, for on 3rd May Frank Hill wrote to his inspector: 'The siding at Torre is working all right, after the siding was opened the PW people slewed the siding 18 inches towards the down line so I remained and put the 12.30 pm goods in the siding and see [*sic*] how it worked then'. (The *Exeter Flying Post* for February 1893 reported that this would be done by forming the siding out of the former down main line and then laying a new down line between the siding and the up main line: one of the benefits of a broad gauge formation.) The water tank, formerly opposite the goods shed, had already been moved to the station.

In November 1893 the large new engine shed was opened at Newton Abbot opposite the station. Built in stone the shed was 100 ft by 150 ft with offices adjacent and a 47,000 gallon water tank above the shed. The previous shed at the north end of the layout was so small that most of the locomotives must have been stabled outside.

The halt at Steam Ferry Crossing just outside Kingswear, which was at that time for the use of officers and men from, and visitors to, HMS *Britannia* the naval training ship moored in the estuary, was provided with a roof in 1894 (and new crossing gates in 1897).

In 1892 there had been correspondence with Messrs Hexter, Humpherson & Co. of Newton Abbot (a pottery and brick firm) for siding accommodation at Aller in which costs of £3,200 were mentioned. As this was a considerable sum for the time one envisages extensive works being involved, but this never happened. There was only a solitary siding at Aller which connected into the down Kingswear line, used by Mr Stooke under a private siding agreement dated 1866. Mr Harrison took over the tenancy in 1896 after Mr Stooke's death. Messrs Hexter, Humpherson also used the siding from 1899. Both Harrison and Hexter Humpherson agreements were terminated on 22nd June, 1917, when the GWR bought the siding for £75.

On 16th October, 1894, quite out of the blue, Mr Luxmoore received a letter from a Mr Floyde of Kingskerswell Mills to the effect that he had found that the GWR was taking water from his water course (the Torre station supply) and if it wasn't stopped at once he would take further proceedings. The GWR had been taking this water now for 13 years! (Perhaps not surprising, however, as the mill was over two miles away.)

Mr Luxmoore, writing to Swindon, said 'he [Floyde] complains of leakage of his mill stream and of our having put a pipe in to take water for our tank at Torre station. I will have the leakage stopped'. [There had been no mention of leakage in Floyde's letter.] Mr Luxmoore went on to explain that the 'leakage' had been caused by a heavy flood the previous Saturday morning, rain so heavy that a man working in the sewers at Torquay had drowned. Tellingly in the last sentence of his letter, Mr Luxmoore said, 'I am afraid however that the Miller means mischief'. On 23rd October, 1894 Luxmoore wrote to Floyde, 'the leakage shall be stopped as quickly as possible. It probably was caused by the flood of Saturday morning last'.

In early December a survey showed that locomotive use of water at Torre was only about 4,500 gallons a week. Now everything went quiet for nine months. To continue this story will take it out of the chapter's chronological sequence, but it is better to keep it together.

Mr Luxmoore received another nasty shock on 14th September, 1895 when another letter arrived from Mr Floyde: '... I find the pipe is still there therefore if it is not remove [sic] forthwith I shall then have to take more stringent measure to have it done as I want the water for the mill ...'

Mr Luxmoore in explaining the situation to Swindon said: 'I did not say [in October 1894] that the pipe should be taken out but that the damage to the bank of the leat, caused by the flood, should be made good, as the leat water was running to waste in considerable quantity ...' One gets the impression that Mr Luxmoore knew exactly what Mr Floyde wanted (to stop taking water) but chose to put his own interpretation on it! He said that average user was about 4,800 gallons for the locomotives and 600 gallons for the cattle wagons. On Mr Dean's instructions supply of water to locomotives was discontinued on 17th September, 1895.

Three years later, the water situation had deteriorated further. The divisional locomotive superintendent, now Mr B. Giles, wrote on 22nd September 1898, that 'the scarcity of water on this branch compels me to look about with a view of improving the supply'. He had, therefore, visited Mr Floyde to discuss the matter on 16th September. Mr Floyde had replied in writing, few days later, to the effect that would allow water to be extracted 'with care' for a payment of £5 pa payable half-yearly. Mr Giles was able to confirm that all water arrangements at Torre remained in place and were in working order.

Unsurprisingly, 'higher authority' quickly agreed to this, an official Agreement was drawn up and water was again taken at Torre, legally this time, from 21st October, 1898. The water charges, payable to Mr Floyde's successors at the Mill, were still being paid in 1962.

Returning to 1894, the Working Timetable shows a few through workings, although in most cases the trains are still to and from Newton Abbot only ('through coaches' are not, unfortunately, so described). The July edition shows an Exeter goods leaving Newton for Kingswear at 6.45 am. The 11.25 am Paddington express passed Newton without stopping at 4.20 pm and arrived at Torquay 4.30 pm. The only other through train shown was a North Express leaving Newton at 6.11 pm (only a few minutes behind a 6 pm to Churston). Both these through passenger trains ran to Kingswear. In the up direction the North Express left Kingswear at 9.10 am and a through goods to Exeter at 12.25 pm.

In 1894 for the weekday service Kingskerswell box was open between 7 am and 12.30 am daily; Torre box opened at 5.55 am Mondays and was open continuously until 9 am the next Sunday; Torquay boxes were open between 6.50 pm Sunday and 9.10 am the next Sunday; Paignton boxes and Churston were open for each day's train service shutting after the last train, and Kingswear opened at 6.30 am on Mondays until Saturday night. Kingskerswell did not open on Sundays; all the other boxes were open but closed between trains on Sundays, some of them doing so as many as four times.

Back in 1893 the GWR had received a 'memorial from colliery proprietors, ship owners and merchants' asking that the company's Kingswear wharf be extended; as examples the petitioners quoted 14 ships delayed 1,051 hours 'waiting a berth' between July and October 1892 at a cost of about £350. Doubtless the cramped Kingswear layout was being worked at full stretch. Now, in 1895, the GWR gained permission by the GWR Act 1895 to reclaim part of Waterhead Creek and make a new embankment to enable the layout to be extended. If was also necessary to construct the tall footbridge over the station (still there today), to enable local people to retain their rights of access to the foreshore.*

The GWR was obviously disturbed at the number of people using Kingswear station as a thoroughfare to the foreshore right up to the Floating Bridge, so in the 1895 Act they took powers to stop up all footways from Kingswear village to the foreshore and to substitute the footbridge from the Brixham Road to the bank of the Dart. The bridge was built in 1896/7 together with a footpath to the north side of Waterhead Creek; this was extended to the Floating Bridge in 1913, part of the cost being met by Totnes and Brixham councils. After 1889, on one day each year the GWR closed the gates of the Royal Dart Hotel archway so as to substantiate their rights to cut off public movements across the station site.

There was a macabre event at Kingswear on 10th December, 1894. The staff records note that porter Rundle was fined 5s. (out of a weekly wage of 16s.) 'for not discovering the body of a man named Glossop in the compartment of a return excursion from Weston-super-Mare'. This seems a savage penalty when compared to the damage caused by a blundering driver at Paignton, *see below*, who received only a 2s. 6d. fine. The *Dartmouth Chronicle* records that Mr Glossop was actually the station master at Newton Abbot; at the inquest a verdict of death by syncope (a fall in blood pressure) was recorded.

The coal traffic for bunkering and to Torquay gas works was obviously prospering for in 1895 the GWR spent £500 on an additional (fourth) travelling crane for Kingswear (one had also been bought in 1889 for £350).

To look after the passengers' comfort the Board agreed to provide £760 to 'fit appliances for heating the trains with steam' on the Torquay line and Moretonhampstead and Newquay branches. No details are given but I assume this means the fitting of the local sets of coaches with steam pipes and underseat radiators to replace the foot warmers then in use.

There was a minor accident at Paignton station on 10th June, 1895 and the Board of Trade report is interesting reading for the detail it gives of the men's duties and the hours they had to work. The train in question, the 12 noon Newton Abbot to Kingswear was staffed by a Kingswear-based crew. The driver George Hales, a 'third class engineman' of 25 years' service but with only four years as a driver, had booked on at 6.30 am to work until 5.55 pm. Fireman William Heath a fireman for 15 months only with 4½ years' service had started duty at 1 am and was due to finish at 1 pm. The guard, Henry Tribe, had eight years' service, four as a guard and had booked on at 6.40 am until 6 pm with an hour for lunch at Kingswear between 1 and 2 pm.

The 12 noon train on this day was hauled by No. 1564 an 0-6-0 saddle tank goods locomotive (of the '1076' class built in 1878 as 'broad gauge' and withdrawn in 1931) hauling six passenger coaches, a van and three fish trucks for Brixham. On arrival at Paignton the driver was asked to attach four empty coaches for Kingswear behind the engine. He did so but then complained to the inspector that the train was overloaded for the engine. In fact this class of engine was allowed to haul 84 wheels onwards to Kingswear and the train as it was now composed only totalled 56 wheels. However, it was decided to detach the fish trucks but instead of leaving them in the platform (there was another engine in the goods yard which could have cleared them later), the inspector told the driver to take the whole train over to the goods yard (behind the up platform) from which he had just brought the four coaches.

---

* The footbridge cost £888.

Kingswear about 1896 with the new carriage sidings beyond the engine shed in place, but the footbridge from Brixham Road to the foreshore not yet built. There is a line of coal trucks on the 'Éclair' pier, probably belonging to Renwick & Wilton Ltd, and an unknown vessel at the pier. *Dolphin* is waiting at Kingswear pontoon.   *Totnes Image Bank*

Another view, about 1896, looking in the opposite direction from the carriage sidings to the station.   *Courtesy Brixham Museum*

When moving back into the goods siding the driver travelled so fiercely that the guard had to apply the vacuum brake to prevent a collision with the trucks already standing there. The shunter then called the driver back whereupon he again made the shunt so fast that he collided with the leading wagon and jammed the six behind it against the stop blocks. Col Yorke of the Board of Trade found that:

> … the best excuse for the blundering manner in which he managed his train on this occasion appears to me to lie in the fact that his experience has mostly been gained with goods trains, which perhaps rendered his mode of shunting somewhat rougher than is permissible with trains conveying passengers.

For their misdemeanours the driver was fined 2s. 6d. and the fireman 1s. 0d.

The GWR was now thinking of doubling the section from Torquay to Paignton and in 1896 bought a small parcel of land from Mr Mallock (the Lord of the Manor) to enable the tunnel at Livermead to be opened out when this was done. A local petition asked that 'for St Marychurch and Babbacombe' be added to the name board at Torre station and this was agreed. Soon afterwards (1899) it was necessary to further extend the platforms here.*

Some staff changes at this time were the dismissal of the Torre station master, George Pullen, on 13th June, 1898 (no reason given in the records) and his replacement on 15th July, 1898 by William Smale, formerly at Bodmin Road. Then on 19th April, 1899 the Torquay station master, Richard Masters aged 64, resigned and was replaced on 1st June, 1899 by Alfred Peerman, formerly at Uxbridge.

Important work taking place at Kingswear was the installation of a 55 ft turntable in July 1900 followed by the building of an adjacent 40 ft engine pit and erection of a water column and its associated water mains. The 'water' element of this work was ready in August 1900 and cost £209.

There was a nasty accident on 3rd June, 1901. J.H. Harvey, an 18-year-old engine cleaner at Kingswear was helping to turn engine No. 1751 on the turntable there, when the turntable was turned slightly too far. In attempting to correct this, the handle bar fell on Harvey's right hand crushing three fingers which were afterwards amputated. He returned to (different?) work on 11th August.

On 16th July, 1901, Robert Clampit, station master at Paignton, retired aged 55 with 35 years membership of the Pension Fund, and a pension of 11s. a week. He may have seen the writing on the wall because earlier that year the GWR began consulting the men's representatives of the Pension Fund, which was in danger of going bust. It was too generous and, after many meetings, from March 1904 it was revised so that pensionable age became 65, although following strong representations from the men it was agreed that existing members might retire at 60.

Mr Clampit was succeeded as station master by Mr H. Morris who remained at Paignton for the next 11 years.

HMS *Britannia*, which had done duty in the Dart since 1863 as the training 'ground' for naval officers, was intended to be a temporary establishment until a permanent college could be built ashore. In 1877 the Prince of Wales had sent his two sons Prince Albert and Prince George to train there, thus starting a Royal tradition. In 1902, as King Edward VII, he executed the first ceremonial duty of his reign, except for the opening of Parliament, by travelling to Dartmouth to lay the foundation of a new Royal Naval College on the hill above Dartmouth. The building was to be 900 ft long and accommodate 300 cadets and was estimated to cost a quarter of a million pounds.

---

* The down platform from 300 ft to 365 ft and the up platform from 300 ft to 420 ft: cost £331.

'517' class 0-4-2T No. 1472 waits with the Brixham branch train at Churston in 1900. The 'tin hut' (*see page 64*) can be seen next to the Hotel.   *Brixham Museum (J. Holden)*

The south end (or west end as the GWR preferred to call it) of Newton Abbot prior to rebuilding, with a down train crossing to the down main (Plymouth) line; the pannier tank is shunting coaching stock. Newton Abbot West box can be seen extreme left, *c.*1900.

Lens of Sutton Collection

It had been ascertained that the King desired both outward and return journeys to be made non-stop. The GWR made sure that the new water troughs at Creech, near Taunton, were ready in time. As this was the longest run ever attempted on the GWR, a trial run was made from Swindon to Kingswear and Plymouth on 28th February and from Plymouth to Paddington on 1st March; both were satisfactory.

A special train conveying the King's horses and carriages left Paddington at 6.15 am on 5th March and arrived at Churston at 1 pm. This carried seven horses and one carriage and six servants. The entourage then travelled by road to the Floating Bridge, whence they crossed to Dartmouth and accommodation at Lady Freake's stables.

The Royal train, hauled by the specially re-named *Britannia* and formed engine, van, 1st class car, double saloon, Royal saloon and Directors' saloon, left Paddington at 10.30 am on Friday 7th March, 1902 and arrived at Kingswear two minutes early, at 2.53 pm. The journey of 229 miles (via Bristol) took 4 hours 23 mins, an average speed of 52½ miles per hour. At Kingswear the *Dolphin* was pressed into service as a pseudo – Royal yacht to convey the King and Queen to Dartmouth. Curtains had been hung at the windows of the saloon, the floor carpeted and the normal furniture replaced by four upholstered seats. Captain Beatty RN was on the bridge of *Dolphin* to give the signal to start. All this for a five minute crossing of the river! After the ceremony and the return crossing in *Dolphin* the Royal train left Kingswear at 4.03 pm for Plymouth, en route to another duty at Devonport to launch the battleship *Queen*. Several alterations had to be made to the timetable to accommodate these Royal trains on the Kingswear line. Thirteen special trains were run to Kingswear for the Royal visit, including two from Brixham, but no trains ran between Churston and Kingswear while the Royal Train was there. The College opened in 1905.

Other events locally were a new jetty and siding accommodation at Hoodown for Messsrs Forwood who were coal bunkering agents, trading as the Mersey Steamship Co. Ltd of Liverpool. They also ran a steamer service from London to Morocco via Madeira and the Canaries and called at Dartmouth for bunker coal. Several companies had hulks moored in the river to which coal was transferred and steamers moored thereat to recharge their bunkers (*see Appendix Four for fuller detail*). Forwood's agreed to pay £1,693 for the jetty and sidings which would be refunded to them by a 15 per cent rebate on their freight account (coal brought into Kingswear). When their outlay had been refunded Forwood's were to pay £50 pa rental and keep the works in good order. There had been one siding here since 1865, latterly double-ended, and a coal store, both removed to make way for the new works. The new jetty and two sidings were opened for traffic in October 1902. Some indications of the coal traffic brought in by rail can be gained from the fact that the firm had been refunded their £1,693 by January 1905. In 1903 Forwood's was bunkering 400 tons of coal per week, 20,000 tons a year, but it is not known if all of that came by rail. An electric capstan for positioning wagons was installed late 1903/early 1904. However, in August 1905 Forwood's gave notice that from January 1906 they would bring in coal by sea and not by rail.

In 1902 GWR Traffic Committee authorized expenditure of £1,305 on two new sidings and lengthening two others (to hold 48 more trucks) at Kingswear, this sum also covered the cost of extending the passenger platform by 66 ft. Despite the fairly constant expenditure on facilities at Kingswear, this cramped terminus was bursting at the seams and accommodation for goods wagons was quite inadequate. Often inwards traffic could not be brought in until outwards trains had left. A 70 ton weighbridge replaced an earlier 20 ton model in 1906; electric lighting was installed in 1912.

This picture can be dated post-1905 as it shows HMS *Britannia* (1863-1916) on its own, the *Hindustan* having left when the RN College opened. The iron battleship is possibly HMS *Espiegle* which replaced *Hindustan*.   *Totnes Image Bank*

An early view of Hoodown siding, sometime between 1892 and the rebuilding for Forwood's in 1902. Waterhead viaduct is in the centre with Hoodown Ferry House to its right. A third (former broad gauge) rail seems to have been left to the siding itself.   *Totnes Image Bank*

The *Dartmouth Chronicle* for 27th November, 1903 records the death of Charles Seale Hayne who had done so much to put Kingswear (and Dartmouth) on the railway map.

The lease of Forwood's Sidings (which was for seven years from 1st January, 1905) was re-assigned from the Mersey Steamship Co., now of 16 Helens Place, City of London, to Dartmouth Coaling Co. of the same address, from 24th June, 1908. The Dartmouth Coaling Co. only used Forwood's siding two or three times after June 1908, the last use being in November 1909. Sadly when the lease expired at the end of 1911, the Dartmouth Coaling Co. did not renew it 'as the railway rate on coal from South Wales does not compare favourably with the sea borne rates'. The associated coaling plant was not removed until 1921 and the capstan in 1924 at which time the owners, the Urban Electric Supply Co., endeavoured to persuade the GWR to replace its 'present horse labour' for shunting at Kingswear coal wharf by capstans (without success).

The *Brixham Western Guardian* for 1st May, 1902 reported that there was a new night train to London, leaving Kingswear at 12.15 am and Churston 12.27 am arriving at Paddington at 6.40. It is not known for how long this service continued to run.

Those present at a dinner held for the Paignton railway men in January 1903 heard some reminiscences of Paignton station 20 years earlier. The Churston station master, Mr Frank Hill, who had been there since November 1898, knew,

> There was room for improvement now, but it was a palace to what it was then. Only four trains left Paignton for London, and two were only first and second class. There were a lot of old open thirds, with scarce a foot warmer, and the wagon accommodation was 25, while there was no waiting room. His own little station [Churston] showed an increase for the past two years of nearly £2,000 in traffic receipts, 45,000 passengers being booked last year.

The *Paignton Observer* said sarcastically that 'to be told that the Paignton railway station is a palace compared with 20 years ago is not saying much for the accommodation then'. It continued: 'the [present] accommodation is very limited, and in wet or stormy weather the down platform is a sorry place on which to alight or embark'. A couple of months later the GWR Traffic Committee referred to representations 'as to the indifferent character of the accommodation at Paignton' and authorized expenditure of £6,757 to lengthen and widen the platforms at the south end by 100 ft, provide a down waiting room and toilets, verandah, erect a footbridge, provide additional sidings and extend the crossing loop. The new downside buildings and footbridge came into use on 6th February, 1905. Altogether a very comprehensive improvement scheme which involved a new locking frame for South box. The work was sanctioned by the Board of Trade in October 1905 (it was ready the previous March). No verandah, or very little, can have been provided in the event, to judge by subsequent comments in the local press.

As early as 1886 there had been requests for a footbridge at Churston to replace the foot crossing, but users had to wait until 1904 for its provision and probably got it then because of Lord Churston becoming involved in the matter and contacting the GWR Chairman, Lord Cawdor, in February 1902.

Meanwhile remedial work of a more urgent nature was occupying the attention of the local officials. On Tuesday night 3rd February, 1903 the cliff between Livermead tunnel and Torquay Gas Works subsided, having been undermined by the sea,

Two photographs taken following a major landslip near Torquay Gas Works in the late evening of 3rd February, 1903. The cliff was undermined by the sea, leaving the track hanging. Fortunately a watchman was employed there and stopped an approaching train in time. In the top view, looking towards Paignton, the damage is apparent, with the track having been slewed further inland. The additional tracks to the right are the gas works sidings. The lower view is looking towards Torquay. The section between Torquay and Paignton was doubled in 1910, at which time Livermead tunnel was opened out.   *(Both) Torquay Museum*

leaving the track hanging. A retired railwayman, Mr Bonning, had been stationed at the spot for the previous fortnight and thanks to him a disaster was averted. A correspondent to the *Western Daily Mercury* wrote in the following terms:

> It was entirely due to the attention and devotion of this watchman to his duty that the 10.30 pm passenger train from Newton to Kingswear is not at this moment lying at the bottom of the cliff. The last train to pass over the spot at 10.30 pm was the 10.05 pm passenger train ex- Kingswear. This train would cross the 10.30 pm ex-Newton near Torre. The man having examined the spot just before the 10.05 pm passed up and found it safe, many men I am thinking, would not have thought it necessary to again examine it during such a short period as would elapse after the passing of the up until the 10.30 pm passed down. But again examining it about three or four minutes after the 10.05 pm up, he arrived at the exact moment the ground was receding pretty nigh carrying him with it.
>
> Now a most serious state of affairs presented itself. To falter meant inviting disaster. That the down train from Newton was getting near he was well aware. That a train was following the last up he also knew to be possible. How many a man would lose his self-composure in such a crisis as his, and do just the thing that is wrong. But this watchman, although getting old and feeble, did the exact thing. The man first hurried towards Paignton for some distance, placing three detonators on the rails to stop any possible train, then, reversing his direction he hastened towards Torquay to intercept the train which he knew to be approaching.
>
> I saw the man this morning. In reciting is experience he told me that in hastening back to Torquay, stone dark was the night, he fell into the very chasm that was waiting to engulf the train, which at the moment was about to start from Torquay Station. That the man was frightened there is no doubt. He looked all that when I saw him this morning but with almost superhuman progress he continued his journey. On emerging from the tunnel the train is within sound. Detonators are placed on the rail, the ominous red light is held up; the frantic voice is resorted to. The three combined succeeded in stopping the train with its human freight.

The train was reversed to Torquay station whence the fortunate passengers completed their journey on foot or by charabanc.

Inspection the next morning revealed that the subsidence extended for nearly 100 ft; throughout the day vehicles from the stables of Mr Coombes and the Gerston Hotel, Paignton and Mr F.U. Webb of Torquay conveyed passengers between Torquay and Paignton, while 30 yards of line was relaid 'further inland making more of a curve'. Four great baulks of timber, each 70 feet long were inserted under the track bed so that in the event of future subsidence, the formation would be supported. Fortunately there was an engine and a set of coaches available at Kingswear so a shuttle service was maintained between there and Paignton. After several trains of ballast had emptied their loads at the spot, traffic was recommenced on Thursday 5th February, by the 11.25 am Newton Abbot to Paignton. A very expeditious repair job!

Divisional Engineer T.H. Gibbons later wrote:

> Before traffic was resumed the single line was slued inwards as far as possible, and underneath the permanent way were laid baulks of timber 70 ft long by 16 to 18 inches square. These supported the line safely under the weak place had been made good by forming a natural slope of rubble stone down to the beach 60 ft below. The sea shakes this slope into a permanent angle of repose, and rubble is added from the top as required. This method of withstanding the action of the sea has proved effective hitherto, and would be applied should another similar case of coast erosion have to be made good.

Kingswear

A view of Kingswear station sometime between 1897 and 1916 (when the card was posted). Compare it with the 1882 view in Chapter Five. *Author's Collection*

No. 3408 *Ophir* seen here at Kingswear *c*.1903/05, was built in October 1901 as a member of the 'Atbara' class but was rebuilt with a larger boiler in 1907 and became a 'City' class. She was renamed Killarney for the first Paddington-Killarney day excursion in 1907 and that name remained with her. There are three fine paddle steamers from the River Dart Steamboat Company's fleet in the background. *Devon Library Services*

At a meeting of Paignton District Council in March 1903, the Chairman considered the landslip had occurred because of the wholesale cartage of sand from the beach.

On 13th May, 1904 porter W.J. Symons (age 19) lost control of timber trucks being shunted into a siding at Churston causing them to strike the stop blocks and one wagon becoming derailed, two wheels. Symons, who was on a wage of 16s. a week and had moved to Churston from Coryton in December 1902, was cautioned.

On 1st October, 1904, Newton Abbot, the line to Kingswear and the Brixham branch, all of which had been in the Plymouth division, became part of the Exeter division. John Campfield, who had been Exeter superintendent since 1879, retired and was replaced by S. Morris from Penzance, which division was then abolished.

To shorten the long block section between Newton Abbot and Kingskerswell a new 19-lever signal box at Aller Siding was ordered in April 1905. The July 1905 timetable shows the new box open continuously except between 6 am Sunday and 6 am Monday, so the two signalmen would have worked 12 hour shifts (quite normal in those days). The weekday openings for the other boxes were: Kingskerswell 6.50 am-midnight; Torre and Torquay (now only one box, the former North box having been downgraded to a ground frame by 1903) open continuously; Paignton North and South 6.45 am-2 am; Churston 6.35 am-1.35 am; Kingswear 6.30 am-2.30 am. As in 1894 all the boxes shut between trains on Sundays (Kingskerswell shut all day) but Torre and Torquay remained open after 7 pm Sunday night whereas the other boxes closed from about 9.30 pm until Monday morning. Only Aller Siding, Kingskerswell and Torre were fitted with block switches.

The July 1905 Working Timetable was comprehensive and by now occupied several pages which there is not room to reproduce, so it is included in condensed form:

Down trains	Weekdays	Sundays
To Torquay/Paignton	4	4
To Churston/Kingswear	17	5
Goods (including 'RR')	6	2
Seasonal excursions (mostly Sat. only)	5	–

The first down train was the customary 3.50 am Newton Abbot to Torquay Mail which returned as empty coaches. The last train arrived at Kingswear at midnight on weekdays. On Sundays there were two 'RR' paths for coal trains (to Kingswear).

Up trains	Weekdays	Sundays
From Kingswear/Churston	16	5
From Paignton/Torquay	5	4
Goods (including 'RR')	6	–
Seasonal excursions (days varied)	4	–

The first up weekday train from Kingswear was at 6.45 am and the last the 12.05 night goods. The box stayed open until 2.30 am for shunting purposes. In 1894 it had stayed open all night although nothing ran after midnight so presumably the 2.30 am closure was an economy.

RR = Run as required.

Kingskerswell station from the roadway above, the station building is to the right. The tall down home signal can be seen among the trees, left, *c.*1905.   *Totnes Image Bank*

A pre-1906 view of Kingskerswell, looking towards Newton Abbot, the two-storey main station building is to the left.   *Totnes Image Bank*

A snowy scene *c*.1905/06. Kingswear ticket platform located between the single arm signal and the signal box can be made out with difficulty under its covering of snow. The turntable is the 55 ft model installed in 1900.   *Courtesy A. Fiderkiewicz*

An up local service, hauled by '1076' class 0-6-0ST No. 1617, pulls into Torre in 1907. This locomotive had a long life, being built in 1880 and withdrawn in 1934. *The Ken Nunn Collection*

Another early photograph at Torre. This down local service is hauled by 2-6-2T No. 2169, which was built in 1907 and renumbered to 4508 in December 1912. *The Ken Nunn Collection*

It is worth pausing for a moment to describe the motive power that was working these trains. After the abandonment of the broad gauge, double-framed 0-6-0 saddle tanks had worked the bulk of the Kingswear line passenger services. No. 1562 of the '1076' or 'Buffalo' class (originally broad gauge) was stationed at Kingswear for some years whilst inside-framed 0-6-0 goods tank engines of the 1701, 1801 and 2701 series ('1854', '1501' and '655' classes respectively) worked the freight trains, as did '2301' Dean goods tender engines. Brixham saw the little 0-4-2 tanks of the '517' class, including Nos. 204 and 205. In the first decade of the 20th century the biggest class of engines allowed on the Kingswear line was the 'Duke' class, and these normally only worked on the few through stopping trains from Exeter to Kingswear.

From 1906 onwards the '2161' class of 2-6-2 tanks, later re-classified '45XX', displaced these old engines from Newton Abbot and No. 4514 became the Kingswear engine. Other engines remembered at Newton Abbot about 1913 were Nos. 4535, 4540, 4542, 4548 and 4549. These engines, being new, were in first rate condition (although there were to be some problems with metal failures a few years later, *see below*). They worked the passenger service almost exclusively and were kept spotlessly clean. Heavy trains were the order of the day in the summer and the '45XX' engines were worked very hard on the banks to keep time. After 1914 No. 2050, a domeless 0-6-0 saddle tank of the '2021' class usually worked the Brixham goods, occasionally No. 2074 the Ashburton engine took its place or a '1901' series of the '850' class 0-6-0T was substituted.

Later on, when the route was upgraded by the GWR from 'yellow' to 'blue' (a colour coding denoting engine route availability, ranging from 'uncoloured' (greatest availability) to 'red' (the most restricted)), '3100' (2-6-2T), '4300' (2-6-0) and 'Bulldog' classes could be seen on the passenger services and '2600' 'Aberdares' on the goods trains.

There was a fire on Longwood viaduct in 1905 which was put out by a chain of men from Simpson, Strickland's Noss works with buckets of water from the river and from the tender of a train which had stopped when the driver saw the flames. The GWR later sent a sum of money to the shipbuilding works to be shared among the men who had saved the viaduct.

Line capacity was still a problem and in March 1906 Paignton Council protested at the inconvenience of the single line between Torquay and Paignton, and quoted instances in the summer when return excursionists had lengthy delays at Torquay as several trains terminated there. The GWR appeared to be sensitive to complaints from authorities in Torbay, for not long afterwards, in January 1908, Traffic Committee agreed to spend £19,810 on doubling the line between Torquay and Paignton and in April 1908 to extend Paignton's platforms to 600 ft and to extend the down platform cover (£1,546). On 10th November, 1908 authority was given to take out the wooden beams of the water tank at Kingswear and insert steel joists at a cost of £63 10s. Also in 1908, the sum of £800 was authorized to renew telegraph poles over 30 years old throughout the length of the line. The cost was exceeded by £150 'owing to bad weather prevailing at the time the work was carried out'.

The company was also aware that Newton Abbot station was too small to deal with the growing traffic to and from Torbay. The first thing to be done was to move the goods shed and sidings to a new site on the Moretonhampstead branch involving the purchase of 15 acres of land from Lord Devon. No less than £27,665 was to be spent on the new goods station and this was authorized on 30th October, 1907. The works included a second line on the Moretonhampstead branch for about ⅜ mile and this required an additional signal box on the branch, opened in 1911. The

A down stopping service pulls away from Torquay prior to 1910, when the section to Paignton was doubled. At the extreme left-hand edge of the picture the staff setting-down post for up trains can just be seen.   *Lens of Sutton Collection*

Built in March 1909, No. 2182 (*seen here*) was renumbered 4521 in December 1912 so this firmly dates the picture in this period. A fine portrait of Kingswear shed, which closed in 1924, and its environs.   *J.W. Chillman, courtesy Brixham Museum*

next stage was provision of additional marshalling sidings at Hackney; the new goods station opened on 12th June, 1911, and Hackney on 17th December, 1911.

Sadly, there were two fatalities at Torre within a matter of months. On 27th July, 1909 porter Arthur Hoare, who had only been employed for only a few weeks, was crossing the barrow crossing with a hand truck when he was hit by the 7.20 am train from Newton Abbot. In February 1910 guard Frank Hole left his goods train which had been shunted into a siding and, when crossing the rails, was hit by the 7.50 pm from Newton Abbot. The *GWR Magazine* reported that about 17 years earlier his father had been knocked down at Dunball (Somerset) while attempting to save his daughter, both being killed; an unlucky family indeed.

In May 1910 the local paper reported the presentation to the late guard of the 'Torbay Express', Mr Sam Taylor, at Churston station. Some £88 had been raised by public subscription for Mr Taylor who had retired the previous Christmas. Among those at the presentation were the station masters of Exeter, Newton Abbot, Torquay and Kingswear. Just over a year later, in July 1911, it was the turn of the Kingswear station master, Mr Thomas Abrahams, to retire; he had been there since 1894.

The next few years saw much work on the Kingswear line. Doubling was proceeding between Torquay and Paignton, followed by extensions of the platforms at Paignton, Torquay and Kingskerswell. The doubling work involved widening of six steel underbridges, a new underbridge of 30 ft span and the opening out of Livermead tunnel (133 yards), entailing the diversion of the public road carried over the top of it for a length of 270 yards. The opening out of the tunnel produced 70,000 cubic yards of spoil which was sent to Newton Abbot in trucks and used for the new goods yard alongside the Moretonhampstead branch. (Messrs R.T. Relf and Son were doing the doubling and also constructing the goods yard at Newton Abbot.) There were no problems at the site of the 1903 slip at the Gas Works, although they had been anticipated. The second line was installed and ready for use by December 1909 when the GWR asked that it might be brought into use (as a single line) to enable the bridges under the old (up) line to be dealt with. A new signal box at Torquay Gas Works Siding, intermediate between Torquay and Paignton, enabled a new down line (and double line working) to be introduced between the Gas Works and Paignton (1 mile 4 chains) on Sunday 24th July, 1910, the first train over the new up line leaving Paignton at 12.50 pm. The public road at the site had been doubled in width during these works. The complete section from Torquay was first used as a double line on Sunday 30th October, 1910 and in November the GWR requested the BoT to inspect the new works (the BoT had approved the introduction of double line working prior to inspection).

Before the BoT could carry out the necessary inspection, however, there was a landslide at Livermead Hill by the side of the old tunnel which had been opened out. Over a lengthy period there had been a tremendous amount of rain, and in the weeks before Christmas the landslide occurred, forcing the closure of the new down line. This was used to remove the fallen earth and rocks, single line running over the up line being resumed. However, as a new signal box had been provided at Torquay Gas Works as part of the new works, it is possible that down trains crossed to their proper line here. The ever resourceful GWR sent 3,700 cubic yards of the material from the slip to form an embankment at the new Newton Abbot goods yard.

It is not clear when the double line reopened but several months certainly passed before the line was ready and on 27th July, 1911 Colonel Yorke at last inspected the new works:

NEWTON ABBOT, TORQUAY AND DARTMOUTH.

Week Days.

(Down services)

		a.m.	a.m.	a.m.	a.m.	a.m.	a.m.	a.m.	a.m.	p.m.	p.m.	p.m.	p.m.	p.m.	p.m.	p.m.	p.m.	p.m.	p.m.
Newton Abbot	dep	3 50	7 5	8 18	9 15	9 53	10 45	11 30	12 7	12 45	1 40	2 22	2 40	3 26	3 53	4 55	5 40		6 10	6 48
Kingskerswell	,,	...	7 11	8 27	9 24	10 0	...	11 36	12 14	12 52	1 48	2 48	2 57	3 40	4 10	5 2	5 55		6 18	6 56
Torre	,,	4 6	7 22	8 37	9 32	10 8	10 57	11 46	12 24	1 0	1 58	2 34	3 1	3 43	4 13	5 12	5 58		6 27	7 6
Torquay	arr	...	7 25	8 39	9 36	10 13	11 6	11 49	12 27	1 4	...	2 38	3 7	3 46	4 16	5 16	6 1		6 32	7 8
,,	dep	...	7 27	8 40	9 38	10 16	11 0	11 51	12 29	1 2	2 3	2 40	3 10	...	...	5 18	...		6 35	7 10
Paignton	,,	...	7 35	8 50	9 46	10 22	11 16	12 8	12 40	1 10	2 9	2 46	3 13	3 56	4 22	5 26	6 8		6 44	7 50
Churston	,,	...	7 45	9 2	...	10 34	...	12 20	12 48	...	2 18	3 2	3 25	4 6	...	5 36	6 18		6 51	7 31
Kingswear	,,	...	7 55	9 15	...	10 45	...	12 32	1 0	...	...	3 12	3 36	4 18	...	5 48	6 30			7 40
Dartmouth	arr	...	8 7	9 25	...	11 0	...	12 45	1 15	...	...	3 25	3 50	4 35	...	6 5	6 45			7 55

Sundays.

		a.m.	a.m.	a.m.	a.m.	p.m.	p.m.	p.m.	p.m.	p.m.	p.m.	p.m.	p.m.	p.m.	p.m.
Newton Abbot	dep	3 50	8 45	9 30	10 48	1 30	3 40	...	5 45	7 53	8 50
Kingskerswell	,,	...	8 52	9 35	10 55	...	3 46	...	5 52	8 5	8 57
Torre	,,	...	9 0	9 44	11 6	...	3 56	...	6 0	8 14	9 5
Torquay	arr	4 5	9 3	9 46	11 8	1 44	3 58	...	6 4	8 18	9 8
,,	dep	...	9 14	9 48	11 16	1 46	4 0	...	6 11	9 18	...
Paignton	,,	...	9 24	9 53	...	1 52	4 6	...	6 20	9 25	...
Churston	,,	...	0 36	...	11 26	2 0	4 15	...	6 32	9 35	...
Kingswear	,,	...	9 45	...	11 36	2 11	4 25	...	8 47	...
Dartmouth	arr	...	...	...	11 50	2 25	4 40	...	6 45	9 0	...

Week Days.

(Up services)

		a.m.	a.m.	a.m.	a.m.	a.m.	p.m.	p.m.	p.m.	p.m.	p.m.	a.m.	a.m.	p.m.	p.m.	p.m.	p.m.	p.m.	p.m.	p.m.	p.m.
Newton Abbot	dep	7 18	7 52	8 58	9 30	10 Y 5	10 35	11 F	11 55	12 10	12 37	1 35	2 5	3 35	...	4 20	...	5 M	5 50
Kingskerswell	,,	7 20	8 0	9 42	9 45	10 Y 20	10 42	...	12 10	12 16	12 43	1 50	2 20	3 50	...	4 40	...	5 20	6 6
Torre	,,	7 23	8 8	9 50	9 57	10 Y 35	10 50	...	12 17	12 20	12 46	2 2	2 35	4 2	...	4 50	...	5 35	6 20
Torquay	arr	7 33	8 12	9 54	10 5	10 Z 40	10 54	11 31	12 10	12 22	12 43	2 10	2 45	4 2	4 35	5 0	...	5 46	6 30
,,	dep	7 36	8 14	9 18	10 11	10 Z 54	10 56	11 32	12 19	12 20	12 46	2 15	2 52	4 13	4 41	5 8	...	5 50	6 45
Paignton	,,	7 46	8 20	9 26	10 2	11 Z 7	11 1	11 40	12 25	12 30	12 52	2 17	2 54	4 20	4 23	5 15	...	5 52	6 38
Churston	,,	7 56	...	9 35	10 16	11 Z 15	11 11	11 49	...	12 35	1 0	2 24	3 0	4 23	4 47	5 30	...	6 0	6 43
Kingswear	,,	8 6	...	9 46	10 26	...	11 25	12 0	...	...	...	2 33	3 27	...	4 54	5 23	...	6 9	...
Dartmouth	arr	8 25	...	10 0	10 40	...	11 35	12 10	...	...	1 6	2 40	3 10	4 40	5 3	5 30	...	6 15	6 55

Sundays.

		a.m.	a.m.	a.m.	a.m.	a.m.	p.m.	p.m.	p.m.	p.m.	p.m.	p.m.	p.m.	p.m.	p.m.	p.m.	p.m.	p.m.
Dartmouth	dep	...	7 6	8 10	9 46	...	12 20	2 10	4 25	...	6 20	8 15	...
Kingswear	,,	7 10	7 20	8 25	10 5	...	12 30	2 25	4 40	...	6 35	8 25	...
Churston	,,	7 22	7 35	8 36	10 17	...	12 42	2 36	4 50	...	6 47	8 35	...
Paignton	,,	7 27	7 46	8 45	10 25	5 10 50	12 50	2 43	5 0	...	6 55	8 45	9 30
Torquay	arr	7 27	7 53	8 50	10 30	5 10 56	12 56	2 50	5 6	...	7 0	8 50	9 35
,,	dep	7 30	7 59	8 55	10 31	9 2 10 57	12 57	2 51	5 8	...	7 1	8 56	...
Torre	,,	7 34	8 5	9 0	10 37	9 6 10 17	1 4	2 56	5 15	...	7 5	9 0	9 35
Kingskerswell	,,	7 43	8 13	9 6	10 45	8 14 10 23 11 6	1 10	...	5 22	...	7 14	9 6	...
Newton Abbot	arr	7 48	8 18	9 13	10 50	8 20 10 30 11 17	1 17	...	5 30	...	7 20	9 12	9 45

X—Calls at Kingskerswell to pick up passengers for Bristol and beyond on notice being given by the passenger to the Station Master at Kingskerswell not later than 10.30 a.m. Y—Conveys passengers for Exeter and beyond only and not local passengers except from Dartmouth and Kingswear for Brixham. Z—Conveys passengers for London only. †—Paignton arrive 12.0 noon.

The summer 1910 timetable.

… Torquay Station Box where the former loop points from single to double line have been abolished and a new crossover road between the up and down lines substituted, now contains 19 levers, all in use. Owing to the gradient runaway catch points have been provided outside the down home signal.*

At Paignton Station North Box similar alterations have been made and the Box now contains 10 levers in use, 2 spare levers and 1 gate wheel.

A new intermediate signal box which takes the place of two ground frames has been built at Torquay Gas Works, containing 20 levers in use and 6 spare levers.

Owing to the gradient runaway catchpoints have been provided on both … lines … The arrangements being satisfactory … I can recommend the BoT to sanction use of the widening.

The work eventually cost £23,742, the additional cost arising after the GWR agreed with Paignton Council to widen three bridges, and it had been found necessary to divert two gas mains in Livermead Road, plus the additional work caused by the slip.

On the same day as he inspected Torquay-Paignton, Col Yorke also examined the extended platforms at Kingskerswell. These had been doubled in length at the Kingswear end to 600 ft,† involving the removal southwards of the existing crossover and the repositioning of the connection to the up siding, also provision of a new (second) crossover at the Newton Abbot end of the layout:

The signal box is old but a new locking frame has been placed in it which contains 17 levers, all in use. Owing to the gradient runaway catch points have been provided outside the home signal on the down line. Recommended for sanction.

A few days earlier, on 24th July, the GWR had opened a new halt at Preston Platform at 221 m. 13 ch., close to Seaway Road. Traffic Committee had voted £965 to construct this halt to compete with the new tram service between Torquay and Paignton which had started on 17th July. The halt which consisted of two 300 ft platforms, 8 ft wide, was not connected by a footbridge, the road under the line being used as necessary. The halt was served by a railmotor service, introduced the previous November (1910) and involved an extra 108¼ train miles per day, superimposed on the existing timetable.

A two-day national strike at the end of August 1911 did not seem to attract much support locally, apart from the Newton Abbot drivers and firemen of whom 47 out of 95 struck, according to the local newspaper. 'The loyal engine drivers, firemen and signalmen who finished their day's duty [at Newton Abbot] during Saturday were provided with meals on station premises, arrangements also being made for the men to sleep there.' No one struck at Torre or Torquay and the Brixham branch continued to run although some trains were cancelled on both lines. However, the last day (Saturday) of the Dartmouth Regatta was severely damaged by the lack of excursionists.

The following month the local paper recorded the departure of Paignton station master Mr W.H. Morris to Penzance, on promotion, to be replaced by Mr H.F. Mogford who was SM at Hengoed in South Wales.

The October 1911 public timetable showed an almost identical service of railmotors to that illustrated for 1910 (except the 10.13 pm Torre to Kingswear did not run). With the addition of 'ordinary' trains Preston Platform enjoyed a weekday service of 17 down trains and 14 up trains; there was no Sunday service.

* This was incorrect, the gradient was falling towards Torquay, as the GWR pointed out to the BoT.
† At a cost of £1,719.

Two poor quality views of the opening out of Livermead tunnel in 1910.

GWR *Magazine courtesy John Maule*

Torquay station at an unknown date, looking from the upside towards the Grand Hotel in the background. There is a line of empty coal trucks in the middle siding. The upside siding platform was used to load Theatrical traffic (scenery) amongst other things. *Lens of Sutton Collection*

The railmotor service introduced on 7th November, 1910. *Courtesy National Archives (RAIL 937/104)*

Kingswear and Brixham Branches.—New Rail Motor and Train Service (week-days).

STATIONS.	B Motor a.m.	B Motor a.m.	B Train a.m.	B Motor a.m.	B Motor noon	B Motor p.m.	B Motor p.m.	B Motor p.m.	B Motor p.m.	B Motor p.m.
Newton Abbot ......dep.	7 50	9 17	10 17	...	...	...	4 20	...	...	...
Kingskerswell ...... „	7 56	9 23	10 24	......	....	...	4 26	....	....	....
Torre .... { arr.	8 3	9 30	10 31	...	...	...	4 33	...	...	...
{ dep.	8 4	9 32	10 33	....	12 0	3 20	4 35	6 45	8 30	10 13
Torquay.......... { arr.	8 7	9 35	10 36	...	12 3	3 23	4 38	6 48	8 33	10 16
{ dep.	8 8	9 37	10 39	....	12 5	3 25	4 40	6 50	8 35	10 17
Paignton .... { arr.	8 14	9 43	10 44	...	12 11	3 31	4 46	6 56	8X41	10 23
{ dep.				10 55	12 13					X 10 25
Paignton S'th Crossing	....	....	...	CS	CS					CS
Churston............arr.	...	...	...	X11 4	12X22	...	...	...	...	10 34
Churston ....dep.				11 12						
Brixham............arr.	...	...	...	11 18	...	...	...	...	...	....
Churston ....dep.					12 25					10 35
Kingswear............arr.	...	...	...	...	12 35	...	...	...	...	10 45

STATIONS.	B Motor a.m.	B Motor a.m.	B Motor p.m.	B Motor p.m.	B Motor p.m.	B Motor p.m.	B Motor p.m.	B Motor p.m.
Kingswear............dep.		...	1 35	...	...	...	...	11 0
Churston ....arr.	....		—					11 10
Brixham............dep.	...	11 25	...	...	...	...	...	...
Churston ....arr.	....	11 31						
Churston ....dep.	...	11 36	1 46	...	...	...	...	X11 12
Paignton S'th Crossing	....	CS	CS	....		....		CS
Paignton .... { arr.	...	11 42	1 52	...	...	...		11 18
{ dep.	8 18	11 43	1 54	3 45	5 25	7 5	9 35	11 20
Torquay.......... { arr.	8 25	11 50	2 1	3 52	5 32	7 12	9 42	11 27
{ dep.	8 26	11 52	2 2	3 54	5 34	7 14	9 44	11 29
Torre .... { arr.	8 29	11 55	2 5	3 57	5 37	7 17	9 47	11 32
{ dep.	8 30			3 59				11 34
Kingkerswell ...... „	8 37	...	...	—	...	/ ...	...	11 41
Newton Abbot....arr.	8 42	...	...	4 10	...	...	...	11 46

8.50 p.m. Newton Abbot to Torquay (Sundays).—To be extended to Paignton.
9.30 p.m. Torquay to Newton Abbot (Sundays).—To start from Paignton.

	arr. p.m.	dep. p.m.			arr. p.m.	dep. p.m.
Torquay	9 8	9 10	Paignton		—	9 23
Paignton	9 15	—	Torquay		9 28	9 30

Kingswear and Dartmouth Steamers—Additional Trips.

	p.m.	p.m.			p.m.	p.m.
Dartmouth ....dep.	1 25	10 45	Kingswear ......dep.		12 40	10 55
Kingswear .... arr.	1 30	10 50	Dartmouth ......arr.		12 45	11 0

Work being carried out at Churston in 1912 to extend the platforms to 700 ft, looking towards Paignton. The loop points at this (Kingswear) end of the layout were worked from Churston ground frame adjacent to the footbridge on the down platform.   *NRM/SSPL*

Another view of Churston in 1912, with the ground frame visible. The point rodding in the foreground led from the signal box and bolted the levers in the ground frame so that they could only be worked with the signalman's co-operation.   *NRM/SSPL*

Torquay's platforms later were extended from 500 ft to 600 ft (at the northern end) at a cost of £796. On the upside three short sidings fanning out from a wagon turntable were replaced by two conventional sidings. The former North box, which had been downgraded to a ground frame by 1903, still had 12 working levers for points and shunting signals, released from the Station (former South) box. The work was inspected in June 1912.

In January 1912, a dispute having arisen between the GWR and Messrs R.T. Relf & Son over the cost of the Torquay-Paignton doubling and the construction of the new goods yard at Newton Abbot, Mr Walter Armstrong, new works engineer at Paddington, was appointed to act as arbiter. He awarded the payment of £28,768 7s. 10d. in full settlement.

Included in a GWR Bill in the 1912 Parliamentary Session was a proposal to double the line between Paignton and Kingswear but it was not proceeded with.

A miners' strike in March and April 1912 resulted in no less than 28 of the 62 daily trains on the Kingswear line being withdrawn, according to the local paper. On the Brixham branch there were no trains before 8.25 am from Brixham or after 6.50 pm from Brixham and 8.05 pm from Churston. There was no service to Preston Platform and a May timetable supplement stated 'Preston Platform will remain closed for the present'. The October 1912 public timetable showed no times against Preston Platform, nor does the May 1913 Working Timetable. Did it actually reopen?

On 20th February, 1913, '45XX' class 2-6-2T No. 4510, hauling the 2.24 pm Newton Abbot-Kingswear, failed at Paignton South with a broken left-hand driving axle pin (due to a flaw in the material); the train was delayed for 30 minutes.

Expansion at Churston, including a new signal box on the down platform resited from a position beyond the road overbridge, was ready in early 1913.* The new signal box opened on 9th February and inspection was carried out on 28th April:

> ... extension of the loop in the direction of Kingswear, slight† lengthening of up platform, widening of down platform, sluing of down loop, provision of a down refuge and general re-arrangement of connections. The new signal box has 45 levers in use and 5 spaces (it was actually a 48 lever frame). Owing to the gradient on the north side of this place no goods train should be allowed to stop at the down home signal. In other words no down goods to approach Churston from the Newton Abbot direction unless it can run unchecked into the down loop. Subject to this condition ... recommended for approval.

For Whitsun 1913, the *GWR Magazine* reports 'a new venture' in that a non-stop excursion train was provided for Torquay passengers only on Saturday 10th May, leaving Paddington at 1.25 pm 'and was the first train to run on the Torquay branch without stopping at Newton Abbot'. In 1913, Mr Peerman was still station master at Torquay.

In 1914 and 1916 there were several more engine failures caused, two out of three, by defective material in the connecting rods; all concerned the relatively new '45XX' class. On 31st January, 1914 No. 4502 working the 3.35 pm Torquay-Kingswear (probably the continuation of a through London service after an engine change at Torquay) lost its right-hand trailing coupled wheel spring due to a broken spring buckle when near Kingswear. On 17th April, 1914, No. 4527 working the 2.25 pm Newton Abbot-Kingswear suffered a broken left-hand connecting rod near the entrance to Greenway tunnel; this caused subsequent breakage of the cylinder cover

---

* This work cost £4,386 and included track circuiting on the Brixham branch and main lines.
† The accompanying plan indicates a 400 ft extension of each platform. They were now 700 ft long.

The newly resignalled Churston station in 1913, with central signal box opened in February of that year. The Brixham train in the bay platform will have to run-round before returning to the port.   *Courtesy Brixham Museum*

Another early, but post-1913 view of Churston, included because it shows the stone-built upside shelter.   *Lens of Sutton Collection*

and piston and 65 mins delay. On 18th January, 1916, the same engine was working the 8.40 pm goods from Kingswear to Newton Abbot when, on Longwood viaduct, the left-hand connecting rod again broke, also damaging the piston and cylinder cover; several trains were delayed. Strange that all three failures occurred between Churston and Kingswear. (There was a similar failure involving No. 4500 at Torre in October 1919.)

The GWR's thoughts were still firmly fixed on a new station for Newton Abbot. In 1913 a modest enlargement of the up main and middle platforms took place, together with a sizeable expansion of Hackney Yard caused by the provision of a new down through line at the passenger station which displaced several goods sidings. Parliamentary powers were sought and received for a flying junction at Aller and the cost of this work, including land, was estimated at £14,562. Here is how the *GWR Magazine* described this scheme after the relevant Bill received the Royal Assent on 31st July, 1914:

Newton Abbot (Aller Loops). These loops authorized as Railways Nos. 3 and 4 and having a length in all of 1¼ miles from flying junctions between the South Devon main line and the Kingswear Branch, and are devised with the object of minimising the occupation of the former . The section of the up branch line between Aller Junction and Newton Abbot station will be utilised for down main line trains, which will rejoin the existing main line by Railway No. 3, while up branch trains will be taken over the new down main on the high level by means of Railway No. 4 to the present down main line at Aller Junction, running thereon to the station.

On 30th July, 1914 Traffic Committee authorized a new station for Newton Abbot, at a cost, including the flyover at Aller of £125,200. Unfortunately both schemes were stopped, the Aller proposal for ever, by the onset of World War I on 4th August, 1914. Also postponed was a major expansion of Torre consisting of extending platforms, improved waiting room and office accommodation, extension of refuge facilities, new shunt spurs and an additional goods shed and siding accommodation estimated to cost £10,079. This scheme proposed a new signal box on the down platform (the existing box was on the north end platform ramp on the upside), whereas when Torre was eventually extended, after the war, the new box was built on the up platform. A further postponement was a plan to deviate the line between Churston and Kingswear to enable reconstruction of Longwood and Noss viaducts west (river side) of their present positions, which had been authorized in July 1914 at £71,370.

Another example of the excursions the GWR was running pre-war took place on 27th June, 1914. An excursion left Paddington at 8 am, running via the Berks & Hants line, non-stop to Newton Abbot arriving there at 11.25 am. Here passengers for a tour of Dartmoor detrained and after lunch at the Globe Hotel boarded seven 'cars' to accommodate 196 passengers. Meanwhile the train left for Torquay where passengers for a River Dart trip left for lunch at the Queen's Hotel, before rejoining the train at 2.15 pm. Reaching Dartmouth at 2.50 pm, there was time for a look round before the boat for Totnes left at 4.30 pm. Here they were given tea at the Seymour Hotel and then joined a special train for Newton Abbot at 7 pm.

The Dartmoor tour finished up at the Queen's Hotel, Torquay for tea and rejoined the excursion train there at 7.05 pm while the River Dart passengers boarded at Newton Abbot at 7.25 pm and everyone reached Paddington at 11 pm. What a splendid day out. The train comprised 11 coaches including a dining car reserved for a particular group.

Broadsands viaduct with the beach beyond and Elbury cove the second bay. Berry Head (Brixham) is on the horizon. Had the halt been built, it would have been to the right of the viaduct.   *Totnes Image Bank*

An unusual pre-1914 view of Kingswear looking towards Dartmouth. The 1900 turntable can be seen, extreme right. There is a 3-masted sailing vessel at the Éclair pier and *Dolphin* is at the Dartmouth pontoon.   *Totnes Image Bank*

Compare this view of Noss viaduct with the 1864 picture. Messrs Simpson & Strickland completed their move to Noss shipyard in 1893 so this photograph was taken sometime between then and 1923. The signal is the down distant for Britannia Crossing.   *Totnes Image Bank*

A horse-drawn cab stands in front of a GWR motor bus operating between here and Torquay (Vaughan Parade), outside the Gerston Hotel. The north level crossing at Paignton is just out of shot to the right.   *Author's Collection*

G. W. Railway Station, Paignton.

Paignton down platform at an early date; luggage from a previous train awaits clearance to the parcels office.   *Lens of Sutton Collection*

A poignant scene from 1914, possibly the first troop train to leave Paignton after war was declared in August 1914.   *Totnes Image Bank*

Just before the demands of war production and government control curtailed expenditure on all except absolutely essential projects, Paignton at last got approval for an approach road to the down platform, and authority was given for Kingskerswell to be re-equipped with gas lighting instead of oil, but this may have been postponed as electric lighting was installed in 1922.

A very early casualty of the war was the halt at Preston Platform which closed on 21st September, 1914, and never re-opened (but as I have suggested, may have actually closed much earlier than this). The railway's infrequent service of trains between Torquay and Paignton cannot possibly have been as convenient as the regular 25 minute service of trams. So the war probably saved the GWR the embarrassment of shutting it for lack of traffic.

At the beginning of the war (the details are actually for October 1914) the Kingswear line enjoyed a weekday service of 27 down trains (17 ran to Kingswear) and 25 up trains (17 from Kingswear) . In addition five down and six up goods trains ran.

A landslide at Kingswear in January 1915 resulted in the demolition of a considerable portion of stone wall and a section of the main road. The debris fell upon the GWR engine shed below, completely wrecking it. There were no engines inside as there had been signs of the landslide for days before.

In 1907 the GWR had obtained Parliamentary powers to double the line between Torquay and Churston although only the two miles to Paignton had been dealt with. Early in the war, Traffic Committee debated the doubling below Paignton: on 8th July, 1915 that body discussed the acquisition of land for doubling but doubling beyond Paignton (and then only to Goodrington) did not occur for another 13 years.

A minor accident occurred at Churston on 12th August, 1915 when the Brixham branch engine collided with the rear of the first up train from Kingswear (the 6.35 am) with considerable force. A few passengers were badly shaken up but no injuries occurred. There was a 15 minute delay because the engine and rear coach became buffer-locked.

A report in the local paper mentioned that attempts were being made to arrange for china clay to be loaded at Kingswear as the bunkering trade had practically ceased causing the coal lumpers to be unemployed. The coal lumpers were paid only 2*d*. a ton and had struck in 1914, without success, to obtain 3*d*. a ton. No further mention is made of this proposal. The great reduction in steam ships during the war meant that coal lumping never resumed its former importance in Dartmouth.

The local newspaper, in January 1916, reported that Brixham had had its heaviest fishing catch for the last 15 years, with 400-500 tons dispatched in one week. The GWR had run special trains through to London. Obviously this was a great help feeding the nation in wartime.

Over the winter of 1915 the old *Britannia* training hulk was prepared to be towed from Dartmouth for breaking up - it finally left on 7th July, 1916 to a 'standing ovation' from the College and town and school children were given a holiday.

There was a fatal accident at Kingswear on 19th August, 1916. William Boobyer, a 53-year-old carriage and wagon examiner was nearing the end of his 6 am to 6 pm shift. He examined the coaches of the 5.23 pm departure from Kingswear, and as it pulled out, a little late, walked off the platform ramp to cross the line to his cabin. He was slightly deaf in one ear and could not have been concentrating for he walked into the path of an engine hauling two coaches making a shunt from the carriage sidings to the bay platform. Although the engine driver was a first-aider and helped staunch the flow of blood, and even though the victim was immediately transferred to Dartmouth Hospital, the poor man died 1½ hours later. His son was a porter at Kingswear station and was on duty on time.

On 1st December, 1916 the Government warned 'Don't travel unless it's really necessary' and also exhorted traders to avoid delaying wagons. Despite this the Dartmouth local paper reported that the Christmas passenger traffic was considerably up on 1915, 'owing principally to the shipping in the harbour'. Many of the passengers were for London, and a fair number for Scotland and the North. Although no pheasants or other game were forwarded by rail, turkeys and other poultry were much in evidence. Train services ran as normal but delays were common. For example the last train due at Kingswear at 12.55 am on Sunday morning 24th December did not land its passengers at Dartmouth until 3 am.

The same issue of the paper reported big reductions in services from 1st January, 1917. The 'Cornish Riviera Express' would disappear and be replaced by a 10.15 am departure which would convey a portion for Kingswear, this portion replacing the 12 noon from Paddington to Kingswear. The 1.30 pm from Paddington to Penzance would run via Bristol leaving at 1 pm and the 3.30 pm Paddington to Penzance would be withdrawn. Certain branches would close on Sundays, including, locally, the Ashburton, Brixham and Moretonhampstead lines.

The fairly generous level of weekday services for October 1914, described above, was reduced from January 1917 to 15 down and 14 up trains (13 of each ran to/from Kingswear) and five down and six up goods trains. The service was still fairly comprehensive in that the first up train left Kingswear at 6.35 am and the last down train arrived as late as 1.07 am (for which a ferry connection was provided).

Because of this a comparison of the signal box opening hours in October 1914 and January 1917 indicates a practically identical situation, despite the fact that the workload was obviously much reduced in 1917:

January 1917		*Block Switch*
Newton Abbot East	Continuously	No
Newton Abbot Centre	Continuously	No
Newton Abbot West	Continuously	No
Aller Siding	4 am (6 am Mondays)-Midnight weekdays. Closed Sundays	Yes
Kingskerswell	9 am-7.30 pm weekdays* Closed Sundays	Yes
Torre	6 am Mondays-6 am following Sunday	Yes
Torquay	3.30 am Mondays-6 am following Sunday. Then 9.15 am-10 pm Sunday	No
Gas House Siding	7 am-5 pm weekdays† Closed Sundays	Yes
Paignton North ⎱ Paignton South ⎰	5.30 am-1.30 am weekdays. Open for train service Sundays 9.45 am-1 pm, 1.45-4.30 pm, 5.30-9.45 pm	No
Churston	6.15 am-1.30 am weekdays; closed 12.50 am Sundays then open 11.10 am-1.30 pm and 1.50-9 pm Sundays	No
Kingswear	6.15 am-2.15 am weekdays; 11.15 am-2.45 pm and 4.10-9.15 pm Sundays	No

* 7 am-9 pm in 1914
† 9 am-7 pm in 1914

The 12.20 am from Newton Abbot to Kingswear (2.10 pm from Liverpool) arriving at Kingswear at 1.07 am was terminated at Paignton in March 1917, however. Over a year later Dartmouth and Brixham Councils were trying to get it reinstated to avoid servicemen returning home on leave having to stay overnight at Newton Abbot or Paignton, but the GWR maintained the train had carried little traffic, and would not oblige.

In November 1917 signalman W. Horsham of Churston retired after 42 years' service. He received a purse of money, pipe, tobacco pouch and a walking stick from station master Mr Reed. A letter was read from Lord Churston which said that he was sad to see Mr Horsham retire, 'from my earliest youth I have been accustomed to look out for him as the train was coming into the station. He was my harbinger of home …'

In March, 1918, a melodrama was enacted on the line between Paignton and Churston worthy of a silent film plot. On Saturday, 6th March, Corporal Frederick Thornton aged 32 of the Canadian Mounted Rifles was visiting his father-in-law's home at Kingswear in an attempt to persuade his estranged wife to come back to Canada with him (he was due to receive his discharge after being wounded on active service in France) but she would not do so, as he had no home there for them. He left the house that morning, saying he was going to London but after joining a train at Kingswear, he got off at Paignton and deposited his kit bag in the luggage office.

Several hours later the crossing keeper at Tanner's Crossing saw a soldier walking towards him down the line from Paignton. This was not an unusual sight as many hundreds of soldiers had been allowed to walk along the line to the coast during the war 'and he had received no instructions to stop them'. So when Corporal Thornton asked to be let through the gates, the crossing keeper did so with a warning to look out for trains. A previous up train had just cleared the section from Churston; it was now about 5 pm.

At 5.48 pm the down Liverpool express left Paignton on the last leg of its journey to Kingswear – it was running about half an hour late. After passing Tanner's Crossing it climbed the steep gradient towards Churston but was still managing about 35 mph as it entered a deep cutting about half a mile beyond Goodrington. The line here is constantly curving and as the driver looked ahead he saw a soldier running away in front of him towards Churston. Almost immediately the engine struck two sleepers placed across the line, but the driver made an emergency brake application and the train stopped just before reaching two more sleepers placed across the line some 30 yards or so further on. The driver got down and asked the soldier how the sleepers got there but the latter said he didn't know.

When the guard appeared he had a shock – the soldier, Corporal Thornton, was his son-in-law! And this was the key to the whole incident. The soldier had married his daughter the previous December but she had returned home to her parents in January. Corporal Thornton followed her but not long afterwards had to be banned from the house. Father-in-law Henry Tribe* was a guard who always worked one day outward from Kingswear to Liverpool, returning the next day. Determined to have his wife back and feeling that his father-in-law was trying to prevent it, Corporal Thornton decided to try and derail the train so as to incapacitate his father-in-law.

The corporal was conveyed to Churston where he was handed over to the station master and then to Brixham Police Station. After a hearing before the magistrates he was committed in custody for the Assizes. At the Devon Assizes in June 1918 Corporal Thornton was sentenced to three years' penal servitude. One wonders if he was ever re-united with his wife after such an action!

* The same Henry Tribe who was involved in the 1895 accident at Paignton?

Kingskerswell looking south (towards Torquay).   *Lens of Sutton Collection*

Kingskerswell *c.*1920; an up stopping service has just left for Newton Abbot. The appearance of this station hardly altered over the years, apart from the lengthening of the platforms in 1911.
Peter E. Baughan Collection

Chapter Seven

Expansion and Improvement: 1919-1939

After World War I things slowly returned to normal although from now on the railway was to face ever-increasing road competition from army surplus vehicles driven by demobilized soldiers. There was a national railway strike from 26th September to 5th October, 1919, during which entire period the Brixham branch was closed. A modification of the 1914 scheme for Torre was approved in July/December 1919 and work was completed in 1921.* A new signal box on the up platform was also provided in 1921.

The company was still faced with replacing Brereton's timber viaducts between Churston and Kingswear, Longwood of 15 spans and Noss of 13 spans. These were expensive to maintain and similar viaducts elsewhere in the West Country were being replaced by masonry structures. At this location, however, a cheaper alternative was available, the deviation inland of the railway on a new section 60 chains long mostly on embankment.

In a letter dated 13th August, 1918, the Plymouth divisional engineer Mr H.D. Smith wrote to Mr Grierson, the Chief Engineer, at Paddington: 'Longwood viaduct was repaired between October 1915 and September 1916 and I fully expect more timber will have to be built into this viaduct if it is not reconstructed by 1920. The repairs to Noss viaduct were completed at the end of last year, and this would probably require further repairs towards the end of 1920'.

The Chief Engineer responded on 12th September: 'Referring to your letter of 13th ultimo, you will be aware that in connection with possible ship building developments, the War Office suggests that the Railway should be deviated at the point in question, and consequently the centre line was pegged out as shown …' (Although it appears from this isolated scrap of correspondence for the deviation to be a War Office idea, the author has been informed by a railway bridges and structures professional that he thought the railway intended to get rid of the viaducts anyway.)

Excavation of some 100,000 cubic yards of cutting was involved and this could be used for the embankment. The new works were being constructed with room for subsequent doubling should it become necessary and, in fact, the authority (April 1919 £58,871) did include £12,000 for doubling between Britannia Crossing and Greenway viaduct but this was never carried out. A policy document issued by the GWR in 1920 showed 'Paignton to Kingswear, doubling' as deferred; this refers to the doubling proposed in the Bill submitted in the 1912 Parliamentary Session.† The contract was let to Messrs Relf & Son in November 1919, at £34,281 and work started the following month with an average of 40 men employed. In November 1922 a progress report showed that £33,000 of the contract amount had been spent, with an average of 55 men employed. In 1924 the GWR made an ex-gratia payment of £2,000

* Lengthen and widen the goods platform, erect a redundant awning from Newton Abbot old goods station and construct 2 new up sidings , shunt spur and weighbridge road. The work was estimated to cost £13 ,089 in 1919. There was some 12 months' delay in building the sidings owing to difficulty in obtaining the land.

† This was a time of extremely high inflation.The value of the pound was higher in 1914 than in 1661 but then dropped rapidly; 1661 price levels = 100, 1914 = 91, 1915 = 116, 1916 = 146, 1917 = 193, 1918 = 207, 1919 = 222, 1920 = 270, 1921 = 167. Not until the 1970s did inflation again accelerate at such a rapid rate (Source: *The Economist* 13/7/1974).

Kingswear Deviation

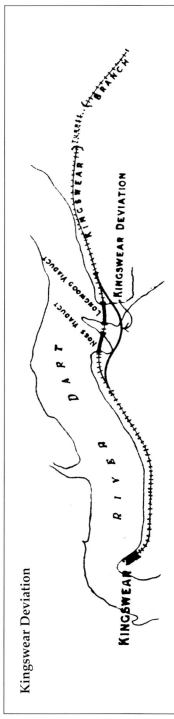

A sketch map showing the 'Kingswear Deviation', avoiding the replacement of Longwood and Noss viaducts.

Panorama of the Noss works in 1921. In the background the ex-German cruiser *Stuttgart* is being broken up for scrap. The post-war decline in shipping demand led to many vessels being laid up in the River Dart.

Courtesy Brixham Museum

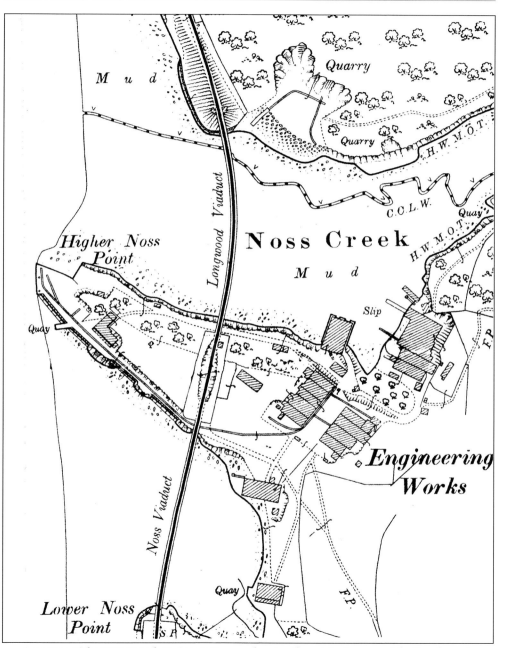

A portion of the 1904 25 inch Ordnance Survey showing the original course of the line through Noss shipyard.

Crown Copyright

The disused Longwood viaduct is in the background as a train traverses the deviation, *c.*1923, hauled by one of the 2-6-2 tanks that were the mainstay of the passenger service until Waterhead viaduct was strengthened.   *Totnes Image Bank*

Noss (*left*) and Longwood viaducts *c.*1921; the scar on the hill at the right edge of the picture is the beginning of the deviation excavation. Messrs Philip & Sons shipyard is in the centre of the picture, bisected by the railway.   *Dartmouth Museum*

to Relf who had made a loss on the contract. The eventual total cost of the works without the doubling was £43,264.

The *GWR Magazine* for July 1919 records the retirement of Mr W. Smale, station master at Torre for the last 21 years and his replacement by Mr H.F. Mogford from Paignton. The latter was replaced by Mr A.C. Foster, SM at Liskeard. In December, Mr H.L. Chaddock was promoted from Panteg in S. Wales to be station master at Kingswear. In April 1920 Mr H.J. Haly became station master at Newton Abbot (from Westbury) and in June Mr F. Vowles took over at Kingskerswell (from Bishops Nympton).

In April 1920 the GWR turned down a request for a halt at Greenway as the location was on a steep gradient on a single line and the extra time involved in stopping would mean connections at Newton Abbot would be missed. Nearly 100 years later the Dartmouth Steam Railway has built the halt, but some of the up trains will not call there because of the gradient.

In its edition for 3rd March, 1921, the *Brixham Western Guardian* reported that Dittisham boy William John Charles White, aged 14, working for Messrs Relf on the deviation works at Noss had been killed by a fall of earth. He was point turning and greasing wagons. Deceased was bringing a loaded wagon out of the tunnel when the stump of an old tree root caught the last supporting timber at the tunnel mouth, dislodged it, and a fall of earth occurred. Mr Owner, inspector of factories, suggested a loading gauge. He said the loaders were working in a dark tunnel and if they had a gauge showing the exact height to which a wagon could be safely loaded, such accidents would be avoided. The Coroner said there was no evidence of culpable negligence on the loaders' part but there was an error of judgement. The mouth of the tunnel was lower than the loading spot and he agreed a loading gauge was necessary. The jury found 'accidental death' with no blame attached to anyone but recommended introduction of a loading gauge.

In May 1921, station master Foster at Paignton took the now familiar route with promotion to Penzance, being replaced by Mr A.J. Bannister, formerly station master at Ross.

The *Brixham Western Guardian* reported in its 12th April, 1923 edition that the railway deviation near Kingswear was,

> … nearing completion. Work commenced in January 1920 and was expected to take 12 months but difficulties were encountered in building the embankment across the creek. Large quantities of stone, earth and rubble were tipped and it was necessary to go down 40 or 50 feet to get a foundation below the mud. There are two cuttings and the one nearest Kingswear is through solid rock necessitating months of blasting. The deviation should have opened at Easter but a landside at Teignmouth diverted workmen away. The work would enable larger, heavier trains and bigger engines to reach Kingswear.

The Noss Deviation opened for traffic on 20th May, 1923. This was 61.23 chains long and, as already mentioned, mainly embankment but with some cuttings. The alignment was curved throughout on a minimum radius of 14 chains and the formation was of sufficient width to allow for doubling. (Interestingly, at this stage the GWR was considering a crossing loop between Churston and Kingswear on the deviated section. The divisional traffic manager at Exeter asked the station masters at Churston and Kingswear to keep a record of delays that would be saved if a crossing place 'existed on the deviated line approximately six minutes from Churston and four minutes from Kingswear'.) In October 1923 a ground frame was put in at the Kingswear end of the new line to permit the removal of the old line and viaducts. Major Hall of the Ministry of Transport inspected and passed the line on 22nd February, 1924.

Torquay station, looking towards Paignton in 1921.   *Lens of Sutton Collection*

Torquay station, looking towards Torre, also in 1921, before the platforms were lengthened at the
signal box end which meant the removal of the down siding, seen here.   *Lens of Sutton Collection*

In March 1922 the Engineering Committee authorized £5,300 for sea protection works between Torquay and Paignton: 'Due to encroachments of the sea … defence works are requisite for protection of the line at several points'.

In August 1922 the local newspaper reported that 'a Brixham lad' had joined a train at Churston en route to Torquay to meet some friends. Thinking that Torre station would suit him better he remained on the train but found it was non-stop to London. On arrival there the officials accepted his story and sent him back by the next train! One wonders whether their charity extended to the provision of any food.

Paignton's goods facilities were authorized for improvement in 1922 at a cost of £1,507, including a new goods office. The ferry pontoon at Kingswear was replaced the same year at a cost of £7,020 and both pontoons were strengthened in 1924/5 so as to carry GWR parcels lorries on *The Mew*. When the work was completed and *The Mew* adapted, the horse ferry agreement was terminated *(see Chapter Eleven)*.

In the first half of 1923 the Board approved the plans for a new station for Newton Abbot, to replace an inadequate station ('practically in the same form as that in which it was built in 1846') with only three through platforms. A 1922 census revealed 147 passenger and 60 goods trains stopped or passed daily. The submission to the Board (from which the above quote is taken), in drawing attention to its importance as a junction, said that in 1922 the Kingswear line had booked approximately 750,000 passengers, a revenue of of about £500,000. The latest plans included more sidings at Hackney and at the goods station, genuine four-track working between Newton Abbot and Aller (rather than two pairs of double lines, not connected) and a new signal box at the latter place. The flyover of the earlier scheme had been dropped, but costs had almost doubled, the estimate being £247,100, later reduced to £233,783. Work started in November 1924. Not part of this scheme (and authorized in advance of it) was the reconstruction of the River Teign bridge at Newton Abbot.

Also not part of the Newton Abbot authority, plans were issued in 1923 for an east to west loop from the Torquay line to the Plymouth line just south of Aller Junction which would have formed a triangle there; nothing came of this.

A major expansion of Paignton was agreed at the start of 1924. The booking office was to be enlarged, a new parcels office, waiting shed for 'road motor' passengers erected, toilets, additional platform verandahs, a mileage siding provided and a new loop built at Paignton South box. The double line at that time finished at 222 m. 28 ch. and it was extended to 222 m. 36 ch., a new two-way loop being formed on the downside, and brought into use in June 1924. Included in the authority was a new 41-lever frame at South box, the box being extended, and three new track circuits installed. This work was estimated to cost £9,500, but actually cost £1,000 less than this. Later that year authority was given to adapt the up platform to deal with down trains, as the single down platform was unable to cope with the number of additional trains run for holidaymakers (known then as 'excursions') during the summer. Similar delays were occurring at Torquay and here also the up platform was to be signalled for two-way working, both platforms lengthened and the loading bank on the upside adapted to deal with fish traffic. And because at busy times trains were being delayed at Kingskerswell waiting acceptance from Torre, it was agreed to provide an additional home signal and track circuit at the latter place. All this work was intended to be completed in time for the 1925 holiday season.*

Some 60 years after the opening of the line, Kingswear engine shed closed on 14th July, 1924. In future total responsibility for provision of locomotives and traincrew for the service over the line lay with Newton Abbot. The shed was demolished *c.*1930/1.

---

* Authorities were: Paignton £2,122, Torquay £3,222, Torre £330.

We must be grateful to the unknown photographer who captured the working scene at various points along the line in 1921. The absence of activity on Kingswear wharf may mean that this view was taken on a Sunday. Note the three steam cranes and the coal screening apparatus behind the line of trucks (*centre*).   *Lens of Sutton Collection*

Maypool viaduct, looking towards Kingswear, seen in 1921.   *LGRP (NRM)*

A down local service leaves Torquay, passing the up home signal, hauled by '31XX' class 2-6-2T No. 3131, *c.*1922. This locomotive was renumbered in the '51XX' series in 1929.

The Ken Nunn Collection

Before the line between Paignton and Goodrington was doubled or Goodrington Halt built, '45XX' 2-6-2T No. 4540 has just passed Paignton South's starting signal (with Tanner's Lane lower arm distant) with a down local service *c.*1922.

The Ken Nunn Collection

A fine shot of Torre in the early 1920s, before the closure of the 1921 signal box and installation of reversible signalling over the up line. The goods shed can be seen beyond the down platform (*right*).   *GW Trust (P.J. Reed)*

The first signal box at Torre, which closed in 1921, is seen here in use as a bungalow at Kingskerswell in 1994. It, and the land on which it was located, was bought by a railway clerk in 1922.   *Peter Kay*

The passenger station at Paignton, pictured on 28th September, 1922, looking towards Kingswear. Despite its importance to the GWR, the station remained with only two platforms during the company's life and is still the case today.   *NRM/SSPL*

The opposite view looking towards Torquay on 28th September, 1922, before the reversible signalling over the up line was installed. This caused the crossover to be relocated further along the platform towards Torquay.   *NRM/SSPL*

An interesting early photograph (28th September, 1922) of the cramped goods handling facilities at Paignton before the new goods shed was opened. Coal for Paignton Gas Works in Mill Lane was dealt with here until the gas works was closed down in the mid-1920s, gas thereafter being supplied from Hollacombe (Torquay Gas Works). *NRM/SSPL*

There were also limited goods handling facilities on the down side of Paignton station, behind the down platform, seen here on 28th September, 1922. *NRM/SSPL*

Work on the Paignton and Torquay reversible signalling and the Newton Abbot rebuilding and associated resignalling was progressing well. A new facing crossover was introduced at the north end of the Torquay station layout on 15th March, 1925. This and the associated signals were worked from a substantial ground frame with 14 working levers (the former North signal box) released from Torquay (station) box. At the same time an additional up (outer) home signal 614 yds from the signal box was installed, to enable an up train to be accepted from Paignton with the up platform occupied. At Paignton North a similar facing crossover was brought into use on 29th March, 1925. When Col Pringle made his inspection for the Ministry of Transport (MoT) on 22nd April, 1925, he was not happy with the arrangements at Paignton and reported as follows:

At Paignton the works also include those reported in the company's letter of the 22nd March 1924. At the south end of the station there is a new end-on facing point connection with the down loop which leads into an extension of the loop for goods purposes, the goods loop extension being provided with trap points at the north end. There are two facing connections with the single line, one for passenger working situated about 100 yards south of the signal box, and the other for goods working, the facing points in the single line in this case being about 340 yards distant. The old up main home signal is now used as an inner home and at the far end facing points new outer up home signals have been provided, also a new down main advance starting signal. There is track circuiting on the single line between the down main advance starting signal and the up inner home signal. At the south end of this station there are two starting signals applicable to the down direction on the up loop line together with a calling-on signal. These new connections and signals are worked from Paignton South signal box, which has been extended and contains a new frame with 39 working levers and two spaces, also a gate wheel for operating the gates over the public road level crossing (Sands Road) and two small wicket levers.

I drew the attention of the Company to the fact that the new calling-on signal under the starting signal in the down direction at the south end of the up platform is not apparently intended for use in the manner described in the Requirements para. 3, nor in accordance with General Rule 43a. Since it is necessary that the use of calling-on arms should be strictly reserved for the purposes enumerated, unless the Company are prepared to restrict the use of this calling-on signal, as well as that under the down main starting signal, to occasions when there is an obstruction in the road between the starting signal and the signal next in advance (immediately north of the level crossing gates), the calling-on arm should be removed. The interlocking between the starting signals in the down direction from the up and down platforms and the level crossing gates should also be removed, in order to give greater freedom to the gates of the level crossing for public purposes, as I understand no trains are intended to pass through the station either on the up or down platform which will not be required to stop at the platforms.

At the north end of the station there is a new facing crossover which with the old trailing crossover forms a scissors crossing. The necessary additional signalling has been provided for working down trains through the new facing crossover on to the up platform. This new connection and signal are worked from Paignton North signal box which contains an old frame with 13 levers all in use, and a gate wheel for opening and closing the gates over the Tor Bay Road adjoining level crossing. Additional track circuits have been provided on the up loop line which cover the distance between the up main home signal and the Sands Road level crossing.

The offending 'calling-on' arms were removed in August.

A view from the south end of Newton Abbot on 31st October, 1923 showing three platforms sharing two running lines.   *NRM/SSPL*

Another view on 31st October, 1923, this time from the north end and showing the soon to be displaced Middle signal box.   *NRM/SSPL*

The street frontage of Newton Abbot station on 31st October, 1923. The posters (*left*) are interesting: the top one is for a rugby match between Exeter Argyle and Newton Town at Exeter; the middle one advertises an entertainment in the Alexander Hall featuring Jan Stewer; and the bottom one exhorts 'Vote for Vicary' in the County Council elections.   *NRM/SSPL*

Newton Abbot in October 1924 bore a strong resemblance to several other West Country stations which had an overall roof. The need to enlarge this station is quite obvious. Looking north, up main line to left, middle line in foreground, the down main line is out of sight behind the roof supports, right.   *NRM/SSPL*

The rebuilding work progresses at the south end of Newton Abbot station, looking towards Aller Junction, photographed in March 1925. *NRM/SSPL*

Hoodown or Waterhead viaduct, looking towards Kingswear station, seen in 1926 with work progressing on enlarging it to carry two lines. *NRM/SSPL*

At Torquay, as well as the signalling work already outlined the platforms had been extended southwards by 170 ft. Col Pringle made his approval subject to the resolution of the points he had made about the calling-on arm and the interlocking at Paignton.

In connection with the work proceeding at Newton Abbot Middle signal box closed on 1st March, 1925, its work taken over by additional signals and locking alterations at East box. West box locking etc. was altered so that the up main line could be slued to make way for a new West box, which opened on 3rd April, 1925.

While this work was continuing, on Monday 9th March a collision occurred at 7.30 am at Newton Abbot station between the 6.20 am stopping train from Kingswear to Exeter and an empty train that was leaving a siding, prior to working to the Torquay line. Luckily both trains were travelling very slowly. The engine of the empty train caught the middle coach of the Kingswear train 'which had not completely crossed over to the middle points on which it was due to enter the station'. In this carriage there were between 30 and 40 passengers. The middle coach was damaged and derailed. Some passengers received a nasty shock but were able to continue their journeys. Owing to the rebuilding of the station the West signal box was temporarily out of commission 'and the lines were being worked by flags from the points outside the station' (as the local paper described it). Shortly after midday the services were almost back to normal.

On 24th May Aller Siding signal box closed and a new Aller Junction signal box opened. The lines between Aller and Newton Abbot West were altered as follows, reading from north to south:

Previous	*New - Normal routing of junction*
Up Plymouth	Up Main - From Plymouth
Down Plymouth	Up Relief - From Kingswear
Up Kingswear	Down Main - To Plymouth
Down Kingswear	Down Relief - To Kingswear

New connections were laid in at Aller Junction enabling the signalman there to signal an up train to either up line, immaterial of its starting point; similarly a train received from Newton Abbot on the 'wrong' down line could be crossed to its proper route (e.g. a down train for Kingswear signalled on the down main could be crossed to the down relief thence to the Kingswear line). The signal notice detailing the opening of the new box stated that it would be switched out between 4 am and 6.30 am on weekdays, 4 am to 7.30 am on Sundays and 11.15 pm Sundays to 6.30 am Mondays. During these hours trains to and from Plymouth could run normally, but although a down train could run to Kingswear from the down relief, it was not possible for an up Kingswear line train to run to the up relief.

For the period 12th July-20th September, 1925 the signal boxes were open as follows:

		Block switch
Newton Abbot East	Continuously	Yes
Newton Abbot West	Continuously	No
Aller Junction	Continuously	Yes
Kingskerswell	10 am-6 pm weekdays only	Yes
Torre	3.30 am Monday-3.15 am Sunday and	
	6.15 pm-10.15 pm Sundays	Yes

Britannia Crossing *c*.1925, photographed from the Floating Bridge. The rear vehicle of an up train has just passed (*left*). *GWR (BR Records Centre)*

The approach to Kingswear gangway and pontoon, *c*.1925. The following dimensions are given on the back of the picture: width of archway 17 ft; width of gangway (at entrance) 10 ft; width of roadway (from collector to stone) 21 ft. The roadway to the right leads to the goods yard.
GWR (BR Records Centre)

		Block switch
Torquay	7.25 am-11.25 pm weekdays and	
	9.50 am-11.50 am Sundays	Yes
Gas House Siding	1 pm-4 pm weekdays only	Yes
Paignton North	5.50 am-2 am weekdays; open for	
	train service Sundays	No
Paignton South	5.50 am-2 am weekdays; open for	
	train service Sundays	No
Churston	6 am-1.30 am weekdays; open for	
	train service Sundays	No
Kingswear	6 am-2 am weekdays; open for	
	train service Sundays	No

From 12th August Kingskerswell's hours were altered to 8.30 am-4.30 pm weekdays. Torquay was opened earlier at 6 am on Saturdays and Gas House Siding became 7.30 am to 11.05 am (or after departure of 9.25 am goods ex-Newton Abbot) on weekdays only.

Since its goods facilities were last upgraded in 1921, traffic at Torre had increased from 74,721 tons annually to 93,350 tons (compared with 63,800 tons in 1913). Traffic Committee were told on 25th March, 1926:

A comprehensive reorganization is necessary, involving an additional goods platform and covered berthing space, a new goods office, 20 ton cart weighbridge and permanent way alterations to allow down trains to run to the up platform to avoid interference with goods yard shunting (there being no shunting spur) and enable other trains to pass while large quantities of parcels and PLA is being performed at the down platform.

The sum of £6,340 was duly authorized to be spent on this work, but in the end only £4,340 was spent, with a £1,700 underspend on 'engineering', so the work was somewhat curtailed (possibly in the goods shed). The new reversible signalling over the up line (as at Torquay and Paignton) was inspected and sanctioned in 1927 (*see below*).

Other happenings in 1925 were the takeover of goods and parcels delivery work in Torquay by the GWR from their appointed agents Messrs Gilley Ltd at a cost of £1,200. Following an appeal from the local Chamber of Trade, the GWR agreed to extend the limits of free delivery to all except the most remote and least populated areas of the town. At the end of the year £244 was authorized to renew the electric staff instruments between Paignton-Churston-Kingswear, then 33 years old.

The new 206-lever East box was installed at Newton Abbot on 25th April, 1926, superseding the 73-lever box opened in 1893 and at the same time displacing the Goods Yard box of 12 levers, opened only in 1911. This was the second biggest box on the GWR, only beaten for first place by Reading Main Line West which received a 222 lever frame in 1912. Newton Abbot West box, which opened on 3rd April, 1927, had 153 levers.

During May 1926, of course, the General Strike affected Great Western affairs very badly. There are few references to Torbay in the superintendent of the line's log for the complete strike period but it does feature briefly on 7th and 8th May. On the former date Mr Padmore, the district traffic manager at Exeter, reported there was only one signalman working on the Torquay line so he couldn't run a service, but that on the following Monday (10th May) if more men returned to work he intended

Paignton post-1925 ; there is a mountain of luggage on the up platform.
Great Western Trust (P.J. Reed)

An unidentified 'Castle' class 4-6-0 enters Paignton with an up express train. The date is unknown, but certainly post-1925 as the resited crossover indicates that the reversible signalling has been installed. *The late R.H. Clark*

to run an autocar service from Newton Abbot to Paignton and back, five trips each way. As soon as possible thereafter he would replace the autocar service by an ordinary train service through to Kingswear, subject to men returning to work and being persuaded to work at stations other than their normal one.

R.H. Nicholls, superintendent of the line, was not impressed by this report and, next day, asked why the station masters had not been sent to work the signal boxes as had happened elsewhere (at Weston-super-Mare, for example the station master was working both boxes as well as attending the station duties!). Mr Padmore replied that the level crossings were causing difficulty but stated that as two men had resumed work he would be running a service of three trains to Kingswear and back from Sunday 9th May onwards.

In its 20th May edition the *Brixham Western Guardian* reported:

> At Churston railway station the porter duties were carried out by Capt W.L. Ferrier, of Torquay, Mr Hugh Goodson, son of Sir Alfred L. Goodson, Bart, of Waddeton Court and Messrs H. Clayton and Evans. In the signal box was a student from London University. On Thursday one of the fish trains got derailed, but the volunteer staff remained on duty until late in the evening. Asked how he got on for tips, Capt Ferrier smilingly replied, 'Today (Saturday) we got 10*d.*, yesterday a lady tipped us with 2*s.* and earlier in the week we had sixpence. We are thinking about sending in an application to be placed on a station where tips are more plentiful'.

Amid their duties, the amateur staff gave the porters' room, the parcel office and the railway bridge a good 'spring cleaning'.

In August the paper reported that the ticket collector at Dartmouth station had been presented with a purse of money in appreciation of his remaining on duty during the strike.

During the summer of 1926 it was decided to reconstruct Hoodown viaduct, a timber structure just outside Kingswear, in concrete and steel, to carry double track instead of its present single line, and to take the heaviest locomotives of the GWR. Previously such trains as the 'Torbay Express' had to change locomotives at Torquay or Paignton as they were barred from passing over this viaduct at Kingswear. Whilst the work was underway (it was completed in 1928 at a cost of £5,809) it was also agreed to replace the 55 ft turntable at Kingswear by one of 65 ft diameter. This was authorized at £3,300, but was executed for £2,189.

In May 1927 the local newspaper reported a presentation to Mr W.J. Reed, Churston station master who had retired last February. He was presented with a gold watch suitably inscribed in recognition of 48 years' service, for 10 of which he was station master at Churston. Mr Reed made reference to his earlier service at Churston from 1881 to 1885 when he often acted as guard on the fish trucks attached to the night mail train, travelling from Churston to Paignton especially to put on the handbrakes. Mr Reed entered GWR in 1879 as a lad porter at Lydford, Churston 1881-85, Horrabridge 1885-1889, parcels office Tavistock 1889-1893. After a short period with the chief inspector at Plymouth, he was appointed SM at Gara Bridge in December 1893 and transferred to Heathfield in 1897 and then to Churston in 1917 on retirement of Frank Hill.

Without doubt the biggest event of 1927 for South Devon railways was the opening of Newton Abbot's new station on 11th April. This replaced the second station of 1861 which itself had ousted the original three-shed station of 1846/48. This second station consisted of three narrow platforms 400 ft long and just three lines, two for through trains and one for trains on the Torquay line and the

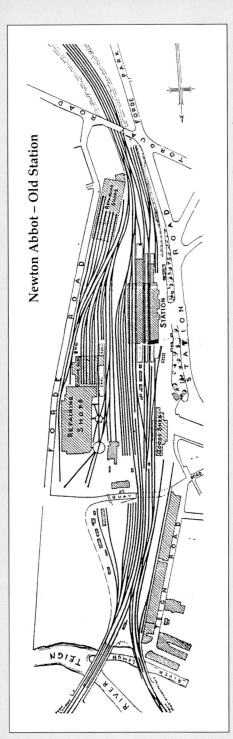

Newton Abbot – Old Station

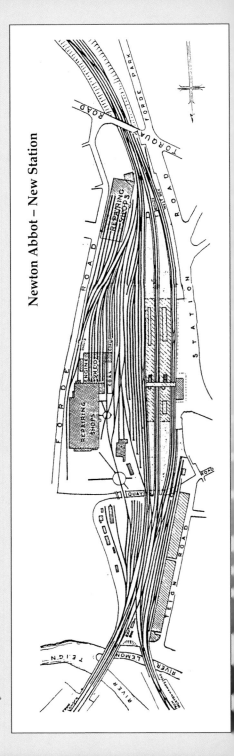

Newton Abbot – New Station

Between the repairing shops and the 'old station' at Newton Abbot were goods sidings: these were moved on to the Moretonhampstead branch (*bottom left*). The goods shed was moved to Hackney. The new passenger station is still on a rather cramped site but is a huge compared with its 1861 predecessor.
Courtesy National Archives (RAIL 268/49)

Moretonhampstead/Teign Valley branches. The station roof was of the overall type, 300 ft long and with a short verandah extension which had been the only alteration since the station was built. For many years inadequate for the traffic on offer, a decision was made to rebuild the station in 1908 and the first stage was the removal of the good depot at the north end (*see plan opposite*) to a new position on the Moretonhampstead branch. As already mentioned this opened in May 1911. Next came the laying down of marshalling sidings at Hackney to replace sidings between the passenger station and the locomotive depot. Work had just started on the passenger station in 1914 when the outbreak of war caused the work to he suspended.

After the war fresh plans were prepared and the principal features of the new station were:

- two island platforms 1,375 ft long and very wide (42 ft down platform, 56 ft up platform) covered by verandahs for 570 ft of their length
- a separate 320 ft long Bay platform for Moretonhampstead/Teign Valley trains
- six running lines, three in each direction (down and up through lines bypassed the platforms)
- scissors crossovers midway along the outside platform faces on each side, permitting these platforms to be divided into two
- spacious platform buildings linked by a wide footbridge and electric lifts for luggage
- revised signalling arrangements

The Council had given up some gardens in the approach to the station to enable a large circulating area to be constructed.

At the entrance to the station an imposing three-storey building had been erected; this had been built in red Somerset bricks with Portland stone dressings. The ground floor was a spacious booking hall and booking office together with parcels office and cloakroom. The first floor consisted of a dining/tea room 66 ft by 19 ft with separate access to the street, and the second floor was the headquarters offices of the South Devon divisional locomotive superintendent. The station was electrically lighted and centrally heated.

At the suggestion originally of the *Mid Devon Advertiser*, the townspeople had presented a large electric clock to the company, and this had been installed in the centre pediment surmounting the building.

The station was formally opened by Lord Mildmay of Flete, a Director of the GWR, accompanied by Viscount Churchill, Chairman of the GWR, the Deputy Chairman, Felix Pole, the General Manager and most of the chief officers of the company. In drawing attention to the importance of Newton Abbot as a trading centre and 'gateway to Dartmoor', Lord Mildmay remarked that the town housed no less than 900 railway employees, entailing a yearly wage bill of £200,000. As well as being the largest business, the GWR was also the biggest ratepayer and Lord Mildmay remarked, rather ruefully, that unfortunately much of the rates contributed by the company had been spent on improving the Newton Abbot to Torquay road! But Newton Abbot was not alone 'in this peculiar form of sin'. Some three-quarters of a million passengers used the station annually and it would be the company's job to improve upon that figure with the wonderful new facilities on offer.

The final cost had been £184,216, considerably less than the estimate. The signal department work was underspent by some £20,000 so there had been a major change of mind in this part of the scheme (*see below*). Incidentally, during the rebuilding it was found that Newton Abbot station sat upon a bed of pure china clay.

Work almost complete at Newton Abbot, 1927; the magnificent station building which formed part of the 1927 rebuilding can be seen, *right*. On the ground floor were the booking office, parcels office and left luggage office, whilst the first floor was a splendid dining room. The divisional locomotive superintendent had his headquarters on the top floor.   *NRM/SSPL*

A close-up of the Éclair pier which was demolished in 1930; Kingswear signal box is in the background.   *Totnes Image Bank*

As part of the rebuilding the broad gauge engine *Tiny*, an 0-4-0 well tank built in 1868 and which since 1883 had been used as a stationary engine at the locomotive shops, was placed on exhibition on a pedestal on the down island platform, a truly unrepresentative example of the broad gauge era!

Col Mount did not get around to inspecting the new facilities for the Ministry of Transport until 1930 and an abbreviated version of his report is given below:

> The station is operated from two new boxes, the East and the West , built respectively in the fork of the Moretonhampstead junction, and at the west end of the up platforms, the distance apart being about 31 chains. Both boxes command an excellent view of the approaches, and they are well sited to control operations generally at each end, movement being considerable and of special character, having regard to the amount of tail working involved here in the making and breaking up of trains.
>
> The signalling, by running, shunt and calling-on indications, has correspondingly been fully provided for. It was, I understand, at first proposed to install power working; but it was subsequently found that mechanical frames were more economical and they have therefore been adopted, the signalling layout and the works in connection therewith being an interesting example of an up to date and well designed plant of this nature, operating I understand with entire satisfaction.
>
> Track circuiting has been installed on the six platforms and running lines through the station, as also in rear of the advanced starters in each direction, the latter circuits extending back as far as the connections.
>
> Both boxes exercise control over the trailing crossover between the down main and up relief lines in the centre of the two platforms, the points themselves and shunt signals concerned being worked mechanically from the West box.
>
> The central up and down scissors crossings and the relevant starting, shunt and calling-on signals are worked respectively from the West and East boxes, the points of the latter crossings being operated by motor. Altogether respectively these boxes also work electrically 15 and 19 running and shunt signals. Track circuit indicator, and running and shunt signal repeater equipment, in each box, appears to be adequate.
>
> The East box contains 174 working levers (including 2 detonator placers) 5 spare levers and 21 spare spaces, with 6 permanent spaces, a total of 206. The West box frame comprises 145 working levers (including 3 detonator placers) with 5 temporary and 3 permanent spaces, a total of 153.
>
> In connection with the West box. I particularly noted the siting of the up inner homes, 3 signals applying to each main and relief line, on bracketed posts, the former located outside the up siding and the latter on the right-hand side of the lines, a considerable distance away outside the down siding. To provide for these signals on an overhead gantry would have considerably added to expense, and though the near-up view, particularly in respect of the relief line, might thereby have been improved, the view of approach would not have been materially affected. As therefore their present location has not been the subject of any criticism by drivers and having regard to the time which has now elapsed since installation, these signals may in the circumstances be considered as satisfactory.
>
> There are a number of calling-on signals throughout the yard, particularly in connection with the working of the West box. These signals are used strictly in accordance with Rule, and only in respect of movement into an occupied section ahead. I noted however, that they do not conform in colour to the latest standard, and the normal light is red instead of white. The latter I understand will be changed forthwith.
>
> I have no other remarks to make in regard to these large and interesting works, which are throughout of first class construction and in good order.

Great Western Railway

PAIGNTON
SOUTH DEVON
FOR ILLUSTRATED GUIDE APPLY:-
DEPT P., ENTERTAINMENTS MANAGER, PAIGNTON.
PADDINGTON STATION, LONDON W2   FELIX J C POLE GENERAL MANAGER

Railway publicity posters.   (All) NRM/SSPL

Great Western Railway

TORQUAY

THE
ENGLISH RIVIERA
Official Guide Free
J. M. Scott, Spa Director,
TORQUAY

PADDINGTON STATION LONDON, W2

Great Western Railway

SUN
AIR
SEA
HEALTH-GIVERS THREE
AT
TORQUAY

New two-way working facilities at Torre, similar to those already provided at Torquay and Paignton, were inspected on 24th June, 1927. A new facing crossover at the north end of the station, and a new trailing crossover at the south end, together with associated signalling enabled the up platform also to be used by down trains. The box now contained 40 working levers and 2 spaces, plus a small detonator placer lever. The work was approved subject to a 15 mph restriction over the new crossover. Yet more siding accommodation for 43 trucks (and a 12 ton fixed hand crane) was authorized at Torre in 1929; the cost £2,205.

Traffic for Torbay was very heavy at Easter 1928. On Maundy Thursday 5th April the 12.00 noon Paddington to Kingswear was run in three parts. The first part ran non-stop to Paignton and also conveyed passengers for Churston, Brixham, Kingswear and Dartmouth. The second part ran to Torquay only, whilst the last train called at Exeter, Newton Abbot, Plymouth (North Road) and stations to Penzance. Between them the three trains conveyed 170 first class and 1,211 third class passengers.

Hookhills and Broadsands viaducts were strengthened with concrete to take heavier loads in 1928. The larger (Hookhills) viaduct had been completed after several weeks of strenuous work, carried on both by day and night, and on Sundays the service between Churston and Paignton had been superseded by though bus connections, the Brixham branch train carrying out the connections between Kingswear, Churston and Brixham. The local paper reported a first sighting of a 'King' class locomotive at Kingswear in June 1928 following the strengthening.

The Board also decided to double the line between Paignton and Tanner's Lane crossing at an estimated cost of £7,017. This involved over ¼ mile of double line, plus a new up goods loop between the two places, a new engine spur at Paignton South and a footbridge at Young's Park crossing. A new signal box at Goodrington would replace the ground frame and crossing keeper at Tanner's Lane. In his application to Traffic Committee on 22nd March, 1928, the General Manager detailed delays to summer traffic at Paignton, including one day in July 1927 when 12 trains were delayed a total of 134 minutes 'outside the station', and another day in August when 12 trains were delayed a total of 111 minutes. This was having a very prejudicial effect on the working of the heavy and developing Torbay traffic. Despite marshy ground, this work was carried out rapidly, being authorized in March and some of the work was ready by 5th July, 1928, including the new signal box at Goodrington. (The final cost, in 1930, was less than estimate at £6,676, despite extra expenditure because of the marshy ground and the need to widen the road at Tanner's crossing.) The existing electric train staff working between Paignton South and Churston was replaced by electric token working between Goodrington and Churston.

On 9th July, 1928, a new halt with a single 600 ft platform and staffed booking office was opened at Goodrington costing £640. This was on the single line beyond the crossing and signal box. An Engineering Dept notice gave details of this halt and another at Broadsands (1 m. 28 ch. from Goodrington).

Readers of the First Edition may recall that I expressed doubt that Broadsands Halt was ever built. In this new Edition I can confirm that Broadsands Halt was *NOT* built, contrary to statements in many other books. John Mann, latterly regional structures engineer with Network Rail at Swindon and formerly a long serving railwayman with BR, has fortunately preserved many engineering documents in his private archive and produced for me copies of a letter dated 15th February, 1939 from the GWR Chief Engineer's file. This gave the history of decisions on (not) building Broadsands Halt from 1924 to 1939. The principal reason that the halt was

The view towards Torquay (*left*) and Plymouth (*right*) photographed from Aller box on 15th October, 1930. At the extreme left is former Aller Siding and its loading bank.   *NRM/SSPL*

The opposite view, looking towards Newton Abbot on 15th October, 1930. Aller Siding (*right*) is still laid on timber baulks with cross transoms as it would have been in broad gauge days.   *NRM/SSPL*

The interior of Aller Junction signal box, photographed on 15th October, 1930.   *NRM/SSPL*

not built was because landowner Lord Churston did not want the area developed and would not agree to public use of the land which ran under the viaduct and gave access to the beach. As the matter was protracted over 15 years, stopped by the war and never again resuscitated, I give more detail in *Appendix Seven*. If this evidence were not enough, the new works put forward in March 1934 (*see below*), also contained in papers preserved by John Mann, include a proposal to build a halt at Broadsands (also turned down), providing further definite evidence it was not built in the 1920s. Goodrington, renamed Goodrington Sands in 1929, is still open in the summer months, under the private ownership of the Dartmouth Steam Railway.

From 12th December, 1928 the GWR began a motor lorry service to collect and deliver parcels between Kingswear and Dartmouth, also farms and premises in the surrounding districts'.

The following year, 1929, there was a serious train accident at Aller Junction which resulted in the death of a railway employee. At 3 am on the morning of 23rd April, 1929, Edgar Yabsley (who was employed as a craneman, and lived at Newton Abbot) made his way by train to Plymouth, to travel with a 12 ton hand crane which was to be conveyed on the 5.50 am Tavistock Jn to Bristol goods train from Cornwood. Delayed by the need to attach the crane, the goods was running about ½ hr late. As the train was completely 'unfitted' (not fitted with the automatic vacuum brake) it was necessary to stop at the top of inclines to pin down sufficient wagon brakes to hold the train on the gradient, and stop again at the bottom to release the brakes. The train consisted of 47 vehicles mostly empty coal trucks, the rear three being the 12 ton hand crane, a match wagon and a 20 ton brake van in which Yabsley rode with the guard. The weight of the train was about 450 tons and it was hauled by 2-8-0 locomotive No. 2865.

At Aller Junction that day relief signalman Saffin was on duty and had worked the early turn there for the previous six days and was a very experienced man with 21 years signalling experience, the last five years of which had been as a first class relief signalman at Newton Abbot. He had worked Aller Junction when required since it opened in 1925. After receiving 'Train Entering Section' for the freight from Dainton signal box the relief signalman asked 'Line Clear' to Newton Abbot West on the up main line. He pulled off all his up main signals, although the train would have to halt at the stop board adjoining the up starting signal to pick up the wagon brakes pinned down at Dainton, 2½ miles away at the summit of a steep 1 in 50 (average) incline. At 8.27 am, before the goods train arrived, he accepted 'Is Line Clear' from Kingskerswell for the 8.10 am ex-Paignton which would be signalled to Newton Abbot on the up relief line.

The goods train arrived at the stop board at 8.32 am and when the brake van passed the up main inner home signal (the clearing point), the relief signalman gave 'Train Out of Section' to Dainton and was immediately offered the 7.10 am Plymouth to Newton Abbot, which had been delayed a few minutes by the late running goods. This he intended to hold at the up main home signal 578 yds in rear of the inner home until the Paignton passenger passed, and cleared Newton Abbot, when he would divert the Plymouth train on to the up relief line, thus passing the freight between Aller and Newton Abbot.

'Train entering Section' was received from Kingskerswell for the Paignton passenger at 8.34 am and after receiving 'Line Clear' for it from Newton Abbot West along the up relief line, the experienced relief signalman made a fatal mistake. He pulled off the up relief starting signal No. 12, and by a fatal mischance pulled off the up main inner home (No. 3), home (No. 2) and distant (No. 1) instead of the appropriate relief line signals, (Nos. 11, 7 and 6). Normally the interlocking would have prevented the up main distant coming 'off', but the up main starting signal was still 'off' for the freight train so 'off' came the distant.

One can imagine the scene. The relief signalman was probably writing in the train register when his concentration was interrupted by a long whistle from the Kingskerswell direction as the Paignton passenger approached the up Torquay line home at danger - this signal was almost ½ mile from the box and only about ¾ mile from Kingskerswell so it would only take two or three minutes for the train to reach it. For a split second the relief signalman would have been puzzled, then a quick glance at the lever frame would have revealed his terrible mistake!

The 7.10 am from Plymouth thus approached Aller under clear signals and at a speed of between 45 and 50 mph; approaching Aller on the up main line, vision was limited by an overbridge adjoining the up home signal, some 700 yards from the box. The line here forms a left-handed curve of some 28 chains radius, and between the home and inner home signals it was possible to look along a chord of the curve and see vehicles standing for some distance in rear of the up starting signal. But it was quite impossible to tell which line - main or relief - the vehicles were standing on: and remember, both starting signals were off.

Just after the train passed the inner home signal, 126 yds from the box, the driver saw the signalman waving his arms as a sign of danger, and at the same time his fireman, who was first to see the obstruction from the left-hand side of the engine, shouted 'Whoa'. Despite an immediate full brake application the passenger train consisting of five coaches hauled by 4-6-0 No. 4909 *Blakesley Hall* smashed into the goods (which had just started to move) at between 40 and 45 mph.

No. 4909 struck the brake van of the goods and 'entered it as if it were a shed', the engine chimney cutting through and standing above the roof. The wheels of the crane wagon were torn off and the crane thrown into a field. The leading vehicle of the passenger train fortunately was a brake van, and although the first two vehicles were telescoped to a limited extent, none of the 18 passengers was injured. Edgar Yabsley, travelling in the brake van, was killed; the goods guard had a lucky escape – he was walking back from the front of the train to rejoin his van. The driver and fireman of the passenger train were injured, the latter suffering a broken left leg.

Help was close at hand for only 100 yards or so away was a row of cottages occupied by railway workers who were soon on the scene, as were the emergency services from Newton Abbot. Trains kept running on the remaining two down lines whilst the wreckage was removed, which only took a few hours. The local paper reported that a member of the Torre station staff, Mr Morgan, was travelling on one of the passenger trains and assisted other passengers.

Signalman Saffin had to bear full responsibility for the accident, but in his report Col Trench of the MoT said that the accident would have been avoided had there been a track circuit to the rear of the up main starting signal. When occupied, this would have locked the signals in rear at danger, and in view of the distance of the signal from the box and the existence of the overbridge which was 'distinctly prejudicial to vision', Col Trench recommended such a track circuit be provided. Col Trench's report is dated June 1929 and in the Traffic Committee minutes for 10th October, 1929 is an entry 'Aller, Track circuiting £250' so it would appear the GWR carried out this request. A further £130 was authorized on 27th March, 1930: 'Aller Junction, track circuiting and signal alterations'. (Incidentally, Mr Saffin was appointed assistant district inspector at Exeter in 1941.)

Just three months later, on 22nd July, 1929, the engine and two coaches of an empty excursion train returning from Torquay to Newton Abbot early in the morning were derailed at Aller causing considerable disruption. The line to Plymouth was also obstructed and it was several hours before the vehicles were rerailed and normal working resumed.

Single needle telegraph instruments were still in use on the Torquay line as late as 1929 but only for communication purposes, not for train signalling. That year £405 was authorized to be spent on replacing them by telephones. Also, the distant signals on the line were converted from red arms and lights to yellow arms and lights, during March 1929.

Following on from the doubling of the approaches to Kingswear over Hoodown viaduct, which allowed shunting to be carried out without fouling the single line, it was decided in 1929 to extend the island platform to 850 ft in length. This involved extensive layout/signalling alterations, and additional carriage sidings requiring filling in part of Waterhead Creek. The former engine shed was demolished at this time. In May 1929, Hoodown siding was extended by 130 yards to enable the 'Torbay Express' coaches to be stabled there. Two 3-ton electric grab cranes were authorized to replace the existing steam cranes and expedite the unloading of coal from boats berthed at the wharf.* The timber wharf was reconstructed in concrete in 1930/1, at which time the Éclair pier was demolished (it had gone by August 1930). The *GWR Magazine* for August 1929 reported the retirement of foreman John Harvey after 53 years' service, all at Kingswear.

In connection with the major layout alterations at Kingswear, and the demolition of the engine shed, the water tank was moved to a new position east of the public footpath across the line. The works manager at Swindon carried out the work and in August 1929 asked the chief mechanical engineeer, Collett, whether the town supply which had not yet been connected to the tank's new position could be discontinued: 'Due to the fact that there has been no shortage of water during the very dry season at Kingswear, there is every evidence we shall not be troubled in future'. [A surprising conclusion, bearing in mind past history!]

Collett referred this to Christison, the divisional superintendent at Newton Abbot, who quickly responded:

> … there has been no shortage of water. This was no doubt the result of the Kingswear Parish Council employee looking after our interest. In addition, a field not previously drained, has been drained this year and is running into our supply [presumably at the tunnel], this might be stopped at any time when we might be short.

Mr Christison recommended that the tank be connected to the Totnes Urban District Council supply and that a meter be fixed so that the payment could be per thousand gallons used, rather than a fixed payment of £35 pa. This was never done, however, and the £35 annual payment continued to be paid until the arrangement was discontinued in June 1968.

Forced to do the job, the works manager reported in January 1930 that the inlet main had been found to be badly corroded and that it had been necessary to lay 670 yards of new main. Additionally when resiting the tank the ground was found to be very unsatisfactory for foundations and these had to be put in deeper than expected and required six concrete columns rather than four. Finally the top of the tank, which was 7 ft deep, was so badly corroded it had to be cut off and the tank made 8 ft deep 'in accordance with our standard practice' All this led to the original £950 authority being exceeded by £418, requiring fresh approval from the Locomotive Committee.

* The station work cost £8,006, the two new cranes £3,877.

Thought to be early 1930s, this photograph has many items of interest in it. Immediately in front of the signal box is the gridiron on which the ferry boat was berthed for repairs (presently occupied by the bottom half of a pontoon, the top half lying on the foreshore). The gridiron could also be used by others, the station master raising the appropriate charges. Just in front of the three-arm signal is Hoodown viaduct, now carrying two lines, and beyond that (*left*) Forwood's sidings, now used for stabling passenger vehicles. Hoodown siding, used by the Torbay Express vehicles, is to the right of the single line and in the distance (*top centre*) the slip to the Floating Bridge at Britannia Crossing may just be discerned. Beyond that the river is heavily occupied by laid-up shipping.   *Devon Library Services*

This 'official' was taken in June 1932 to record the opening of the new ferro-concrete wharf and two electric cranes installed at Kingswear. The 'Éclair' pier has been demolished and one of the steam cranes can be seen extreme right. Two Bibby Line troopships are moored nearby.

NRM/SSPL

A new siding and ground frame-worked connection at Noss (227 m. 51 ch.) was provided for Messrs Philip & Son, giving rail access to their ship yard for the first time. Opened on 2nd May, 1929 the main line connection was on a rising gradient of 1 in 87 (towards Churston) and so when traffic worked there, the engine was always kept on the Kingswear end of the train. The connection had cost the firm £409, to be repaid to them by a 5 per cent rebate on their transport charges, but by 1937 they had only received £288 back.

The Noss shipyard began life as the works of Simpson, Strickland who moved here in 1893 from Sandquay, Dartmouth. The firm made steam launches and pleasure craft; the Ordnance Survey map (*see page 147*) shows the layout of the yard in 1904, the bare nature of Noss at this time can be seen in the plan and in the photograph showing operations at the change of gauge. Simpson's works were situated on the eastern edge of the water north and south of the Noss peninsular. The boats were launched parallel to the viaducts and then towed through their piers in consequence, until the 1923 Deviation removed these obstructions to the yard's great benefit.

In 1917 the firm went bankrupt and the works became the property of Philip & Son who expanded it greatly by filling as can be seen from the 1950s plan (*overleaf*). This clearly shows that the Deviation curve embankment was built over the now demolished buildings of the former Simpson, Strickland yard. Only two parts of this remained; the house on Noss Point (probably used by F.C. Simpson himself as a residence) and part of the old boat yard in North Noss creek.

After the 1929 connection was installed, an extensive network of rail tracks was built up serving various parts of the Philip & Son works. Traffic brought in by rail included steel (both plates and sections), timber, castings, pipes and machinery. Material required at the Sandquay works (Dartmouth) would be loaded onto a barge and towed across, later being loaded to a lorry and using the Floating Bridge. The GWR loco limit is shown on the 1960 diagram on page 312, which shows the final state of the private sidings (which closed in 1965). Wagons within the yard were shunted by one or other of two mobile cranes.

An analysis of the summer 1929 timetable indicates the importance placed by the GWR on the Torbay holiday towns, judging by the number of through trains from different parts of the country, surely the best served GWR resorts. There were 21 trains from Newton Abbot to Kingswear (Saturdays excepted), all with Dartmouth connections, in itself quite a demanding workload with a single line beyond Goodrington box and severe gradients on both sides of the intermediate crossing place at Churston. Another 16 trains terminated at Paignton. On Saturdays a further four trains ran to Paignton, one to Churston and two to Kingswear.

The London route was the most important and best served with seven down trains through to Torquay, the best of which were the 11 am 'Torquay Pullman', on Mondays & Fridays only, non-stop to Newton Abbot and arriving Torquay at 2.40 pm and the non-stop 12 noon 'Torbay Express' (arriving 3.30 pm). The 'Torquay Pullman' had a very short life being introduced on 8th July, 1929, and withdrawn in September 1930. The Agreement with the Pullman Car Co. was that they should supply 'not less than 12 First Class and not less than seven Third Class Pullman cars' to form Boat Trains as required and the Torquay Pullman. The Pullman Supplement was not popular with patrons who could enjoy a fast service using the 'Torbay Express' without additional charge. There were six up through trains to London with two extra Saturday-only trains, the latter including the long running 9.45 am

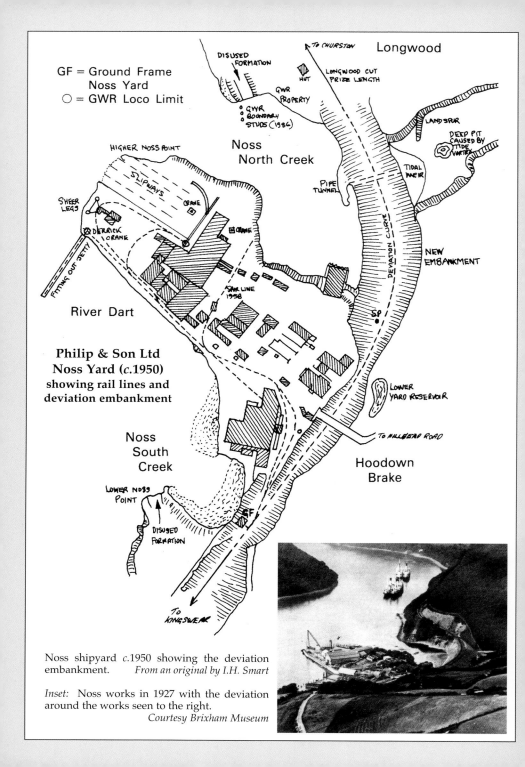

Noss shipyard *c.*1950 showing the deviation embankment. *From an original by I.H. Smart*

Inset: Noss works in 1927 with the deviation around the works seen to the right.
Courtesy Brixham Museum

Churston-Paddington which left Torquay at 10.15 and ran non-stop to Paddington (due 1.55 pm). (On Saturdays the up 'Torbay' ran in two parts; a 12 noon Torquay-Paddington and an 11.20 am Kingswear-Paddington which left Torquay at 12.10 pm.) In the evening on Mondays and Fridays there was the 'Torquay Pullman' at 4.38 pm, followed only 5 minutes later at 4.43 by another express for those who did not want to pay the Pullman supplement. The Pullman arrived in London at 8.30 pm and the 4.43 at 9 pm. (From September 1929 the Pullman also ran on Saturdays; in summer 1930 it ran daily.)

There were through cross-country services between the following starting points and Torquay and corresponding return services: Wolverhampton, Liverpool, Manchester, Bradford, Carmarthen. The first three places had more than one daily train in each direction.

On Sundays in the summer there were 25 trains each way on the line (seven to Kingswear, one to Churston, four to Brixham and 13 to Paignton, the latter including two through trains from Ilfracombe.

An interesting example of how the railway could provide special services in emergency was printed in the 9th January, 1930 edition of the *Brixham Western Guardian*. On Monday 6th January the Plymouth agents of an oil company wired their London office that the SS *Wasaborg* at Dartmouth was unable to proceed for want of oil: 2½ tons was required. A telephone call to the GWR resulted in a special van being attached to the 'Torbay Express' to convey the oil and the ship was able to sail the same night!

In 1929 unemployment was high and the Government passed the Development (Loan Guarantee and Grants) Act, which granted power to the Treasury to guarantee loans, or make grants towards the interest on loans, raised by public utility bodies on schemes of development or reconstruction. The aim was to alleviate unemployment and, in those days, Government had a high regard for the railways and gave many grants of financial assistance under the scheme. The GWR alone prepared schemes involving expenditure of £5 million, of which £4 million came from Government in the form of grants towards the interest on capital, necessary before the scheme became fully productive. Included in the list was a new goods depot and reconstruction of the passenger station at Paignton.

This major scheme involved lengthening the platforms at Paignton, new carriage sidings behind the down platform, a brand new goods station between Paignton and Goodrington and extensive carriage sidings for which five acres of ground had been bought from the council in 1927. The double line was extended beyond Goodrington signal box (222 m. 60 ch.) to 222 m. 76 ch., thus allowing trains to run to Goodrington Sands Halt (where a second platform would be provided), without waiting for the single line section to be clear. Paignton South box needed a new locking frame.

As usual work proceeded quickly and it was possible to open the new passenger facilities for summer 1930, the additional sidings at Paignton on 6th May, and the second platform and double line at Goodrington on 4th July. Automatic train control was introduced between Aller Junction and Goodrington in April 1931.

Meanwhile work was proceeding on the new goods station between Paignton and Goodrington. This large site was chiefly marshland and no less than 50,000 cubic yards of filling was necessary to bring the ground up to the required level. The building was erected on 152 concrete piles driven through the marsh to the shale base, at depths of between 20 and 30 feet. After this a concrete framework was constructed across the tops of the piles.

The new goods station at Paignton is being built on the left, 12th December, 1930.

NRM/SSPL

The lorry loading bank at Paignton goods station, a few weeks after opening on 15th July, 1931.

NRM/SSPL

An interior photograph of Paignton goods station on 15th July, 1931. Note the overhead crane.
NRM/SSPL

The arrival of 'King' No. 6023 *King Edward II* and the 'Torbay Express' is impressive enough to attract the attention of the little girl on the up platform at Churston, sometime in August 1931.
The late R.H. Clark

A spacious building was erected, in its own way as splendid an asset to the conduct of the goods business as the new station at Newton Abbot was for passenger traffic. The architect designed it 'with due regard to the desirability of preserving the amenities of the surrounding property'. Excluding the line through the shed there were five other sidings with room for 150 trucks, all with road access. The shed was nearly 300 ft long, with an upper floor warehouse for half its length, connected by an electric lift. The shed platforms were 25 ft wide with a verandah covering projecting 20 ft over the vehicle loading roadway. Overhead runways were provided to give electrically-powered lifting facilities with a capacity of 1 ton, and there was a 12 ton hand crane in the yard. Roomy accommodation was provided for the staff who would work there, including an office capable of housing 20 clerks.

The site had been selected as suitable not only for Paignton and district, but also for its convenience for serving Brixham, Churston, Kingswear and Dartmouth by railhead distribution schemes or country lorry services. The new depot opened for business on 1st June, 1931. The old goods shed at Paignton station was converted into a concentration point for all passengers' luggage in advance (PLA) for Torbay, whilst much of the ground area was taken up by the extension of the up passenger platform. The total scheme cost £73,127. Although all the work was completed by August 1931 the MoT did not get around to inspecting it for almost a year and Col Mount's report follows:

I have the honour to report for the information of the Minister of Transport that, in accordance with the Minutes of the 31st July, 1928, 22nd August 1928, and 8th August 1931, I made an inspection on 14th June, 1932 of the new works at and between Paignton and Goodrington Sands on the Great Western Railway.

Those works completed in 1928 comprise the doubling of the line on the down side between the South box, Paignton, and Tanners Crossing, Goodrington, the provision of a 2-way loop on the up side between these crossings, and the provision of a halt platform on the single line at the latter place.

The works completed in 1931 were those included in the Company's scheme No. 12, carried out under the Development (Loan Guarantees and Grants) Act 1929. As shown on the plan submitted, they comprise the reconstruction of the south end of the station, the provision of a new goods yard, shed, and rail head depot, and the extension of the doubling southwards beyond Tanners Crossing, to serve new up and down platforms at Goodrington Sands Halt, in place of the platform which had been built in 1928.

These platforms are formed of built up concrete walling, and are surfaced with slag and limestone screenings. They have been constructed mainly in red shale cutting. They are 600 ft long and 8 to 9 ft wide. The southern end is in bank, constructed of old sleepers and suitably fenced. The platforms are lighted by oil lamps, but the halt is only open in summer. Shelters 20 ft x 8 ft have been provided in the centre of each, and they are approached by wickets and short paths from Tanners Crossing, where a booking office has been provided in the cottage.*

At Tanners Crossing new double gates worked by wheel have been provided (in 1928) giving a clear roadway width of 30 ft. There are also controlled clap-Wicket gates, with fencing long enough to admit of the passage of bicycles.

The adjacent box (Goodrington) has a new frame of 29 working levers, one gate wheel, one space, and two small wicket levers. Owing to the steep rising gradient in the down direction, the instructions are such that after a train has left (movements are signalled from the up as well as from the down platform) the single line facing points must remain set for the down line until the out-of-section signal has been received , there being spring catch points in the lead.

Rail movements amount here to 35 to 40 each way during the 16 hours while the box is open, and road movements in summer are heavy. An auxiliary electric token instrument

* A report in the *Railway Gazette* in 1933 says that there was now a timber booking office at the entrance of the down platform. A new footbridge had been built to replace the former foot crossing at the site of the new goods yard and a new pathway constructed alongside the line from this bridge.

is provided at the south end of the down platform. The locking permits of as much latitude as is possible. There is permissive working on the single line up and down goods loop, operation being controlled by the usual release levers in Goodrington and Paignton South boxes. Track circuits have been installed in rear of the up home for Paignton South, the occupation of which locks No. 27 the up inner home line [sic], and in rear of the down home here, controlling the advanced starter for the South box and the block.

Paignton South box contains an old frame of 53 working levers, 7 spaces, a gate wheel, and two wicket levers. 8 track circuits have been added as shown on the plans. Here also the locking between points and the gate control is such as to give the maximum possible latitude to road movement.

The signalling has been considerably modified in accordance with the new layout and 2-way working is provided on the up platform line by means of interlocked release levers. The calling-on signal No. 53 should be painted in standard colours and have a white light in the normal position.

The down platform has been lengthened at this end by 240 ft. It is fenced with iron fencing and lighted electrically. The up platform has also been lengthened at the south end by 140 ft. Additional sidings for holding carriage stock have been provided on the east (down side) and a down (stabling) siding has been added between the South box and Tanners Crossing [this was actually a loop, into use 3rd February, 1931].

At the North box, little has been done. It contains an old frame of 13 working levers with a gate wheel. The level crossing here is still more heavily used than the others. A down outer home signal has been added for acceptance purposes while an up train is being despatched from the down platform, for which a new starter has also been added. The interlocking lever for 2-way operation on the up platform is also new.

The works are of heavy construction throughout and are in good order, and the arrangements generally appear to be satisfactory. Subject, therefore, to the minor requirements with regard to the calling-on signal and to the addition of any further facilities in connection with the new halt, depending upon the development of traffic, I recommend that these new facilities be finally approved.

In May 1931, with the retirement of the Brixham station master, the Churston station master took control of both stations. Two-way working over the down loop at Churston was introduced in February 1934. From the winter timetable of 1932, Goodrington Sands Halt remained open during the winter months. This arrangement continued until the war years but winter 1940 was the last time this happened and thereafter Goodrington became a summer-only halt.

In 1932 some much updated freight facilities were unveiled at Kingswear. The *Éclair* pier had been demolished in 1930. The timber wharf was demolished and a new wharf, constructed in reinforced concrete and some 360 ft long, was built 10 ft further out into the river, making deeper berths available for the vessels. Three steam cranes and one hand crane were superseded by two new electric cranes which worked on a 7 ft gauge track straddling the nearest siding to the wharf edge; one steam crane was retained. Many thousands of tons of coal were imported through this wharf each year. The ferry pontoon at Kingswear was renewed in 1934.

An internal GWR document dated 17th April, 1935 gives the following shipping charges for coal and coke traffic unloaded at Kingswear:

Cranage by GWR electric cranes	7½d. per ton
Wharfage	3¼d. per ton
Weighing	6d. per ton
Pier dues on registered tonnage	1½d. per ton
Harbour dues on registered tonnage	3d. per ton
(All except harbour dues accrue to the GWR)	

An unidentified 'Prairie' tank passes Torquay Gas Works with a down train, probably in the 1930s. Note that the first vehicle has a clerestory roof. In the gas works the wagon tippler is emptying a wagon.   *The late R.H. Clark*

Torquay Gas Works looking towards Paignton in 1934. Despite the atrocious smell, staff are cultivating allotments just below the railway line, middle left.   *British Gas*

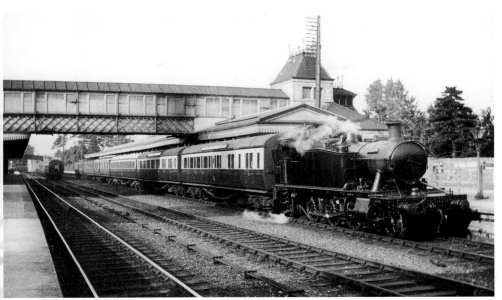

A down local service conveying a portion from an express about to leave Torquay hauled by a very clean '45XX' 2-6-2T, probably in the 1930s. The middle siding contains some coaches which will probably be used to strengthen an up train.   *The late R.H. Clark*

The down 'Torbay Express', hauled by 'Star' class locomotive No. 4054 *Princess Charlotte*, prepares to leave Torquay after the down platform was extended, probably 1930s.
     Author's Collection

An up train, hauled by '45XX' 2-6-2T No. 4530, prepares to leave Torquay and climb the 1 in 55
to Torre, *c.*1930s.   *GW Trust (P.J. Reed)*

A down local service, containing a motley collection of vehicles including two with roof
headboards, leaves Torquay in the 1930s, hauled by an unidentified 'Bulldog' class 4-4-0. This
was the location of the collision between two passenger trains in August 1962.
                                                                            The late R.H. Clark

Left: The station bookstall on Torquay's up platform, *c.*1930s. The placard for the *Spectator* advertises 'The Means Test for the Unemployed'. *Author's Collection*

Below: The down 'Torbay Express' hauled by a 'King' class 4-6-0, climbs the bank out of Goodrington Sands in August 1935. *GWR (BR Records Centre)*

This picture of Churston crossroads in 1936 is included because it shows the station master's house (*right*), some three-quarters of a mile from the station which is located on the road going away from the camera. The road width is just the same today and double-deck buses pass perilously close to the house.   *Courtesy Brixham Museum*

The Brixham branch train in August 1935 is headed by 'Metro' 2-4-0T No. 1415, which was built in 1878 and scrapped a few years after this photograph in April 1938.   *Peter Clare*

On 23rd May, 1934 representatives of all the major departments toured the Kingswear line and at a divisional meeting on 7th June, 1934 the following important new works were proposed:

Torre, extend platforms as far as possible up to 1,000 ft (£16,194)
Torquay, extend platforms to 1,000 ft at Newton Abbot end and provide accommodation footbridge (£3,600).
Preston, full station facilities to be provided and 1,000 ft platforms (£5,600)
Paignton, a new station (*see below*).
Goodrington, carriage sidings in goods yard (£6,810); extend halt and provide carriage sidings (£22,157). Tanner's Road crossing would be replaced by an overbridge.
Doubling between Goodrington and Churston was turned down as too costly, but a crossing place at a new Broadsands Halt would be considered (£5,170).
A crossing loop Churston side of Britannia Crossing, which would be switched out in winter (later costed at £1,700).

Most of these proposals were approved by the superintendent of the line, H.L. Wilkinson, although Goodrington's carriage sidings in the goods yard, Broadsands Halt and the Britannia loop were all deleted and the Torre scheme had to be made cheaper. However, in January 1935, the divisional superintendent, Exeter suggested that the line between Britannia Halt and Kingswear should be doubled for which the divisional engineer estimated £7,500 would be required. This resulted in the Britannia loop again being put forward by the Chief Engineer instead; this would be 900 ft long and cost £1,470.

In the event, none of these ambitious schemes ever saw the light of day, except Goodrington carriage sidings and Tanner's Road bridge were built after the war. The new station at Paignton is dealt with below.

Paignton's cramped two-platform station would be replaced by a five-platform station extending beyond Sands Road, capable of accommodating the longest trains on the line. New station buildings on the upside would be provided and the footbridge at Torbay Road replaced by a pedestrian subway. Sands Road level crossing would be closed and traffic diverted by Whitstone Road and a widened Roundham Road bridge. There would be a pedestrian subway at Sands Road, however.

Following negotiations between the council and the GWR it was agreed to construct a dual carriageway at Sands Road on a reinforced concrete bridge 60 ft wide carried over the extended station platforms. This entailed demolition of some houses at the bottom of Whitstone Road, which was done.

On 5th June, 1935, an excursion train ran from Kingswear to Paddington for Derby Day. It left Kingswear at 12.35 am (there was a special connection from Brixham at the same time) and arrived at Paddington at 6 am. The homeward train left Paddington at 12.30 am early on 6th June – all this for a fare of 16s. 6d. (the same excursion ran in 1936, leaving Kingswear and Brixham at 12.45 am).

On Sunday 29th September, 1935 at about 10.30 pm shunting operations were in progress to prepare for the departure of the last train from Kingswear. The train was being reversed from the platform when the three rear coaches became derailed; the engine was blocked in. Just before midnight the breakdown party arrived from Newton Abbot and speedily got to work. All three coaches had been rerailed by 3 am. The work was made all the more arduous because of the very high wind and heavy squalls of rain. The portion of line involved was considerably damaged and during Monday morning the trains were controlled by flagmen and not until 4 pm was normal working reintroduced. On Sunday evening the stranded passengers left by a requisitioned bus.

-G.W.R. PAIGNTON STATION-

— PROPOSED ALTERATIONS, —

The plan for the proposed five-platform station at Paignton (1937), but never built.

The strengthening steel ribs, supported by concrete, that were added to Greenway tunnel, photographed on 26th August, 1936. *NRM/SSPL*

Greenway tunnel inspection vehicle, photographed on 26th August, 1936. *NRM/SSPL*

It was reported to Engineering Committee in December 1935 that there was serious distortion of a portion of the masonry lining in Greenway tunnel and £2,500 was authorized to rectify this. During the work some additional strengthening was found to be necessary and an extra £415 was authorized in January 1937, after the work was satisfactorily completed. These are the steel ribs, supported by concrete, seen in the photograph.

In July 1937 Torquay Council complained to the GWR about the forthcoming winter timetable; '(there was) only one train a day from London which could be called a train'. Mr C. Hove of the Imperial Hotel said that he had to send his hotel bus to Newton Abbot as guests arriving there (and presumably changing trains) would not come on to Torquay. The Town Clerk said that it took an hour to cover 26 miles from Torquay to Exeter and 'that, in these days, was out of date'. In response the GWR superintendent of the line said that the timetable was at the printers but he would bear these points in mind for the future.

Traffic Committee approved the cost of the the Paignton and Goodrington scheme (£138,550) in February 1937. The works order stated that the work would be done in-house using the divisional engineer's staff, except for buildings which would be contracted out. Before the station could be rebuilt the track had to be widened between Sands Road and Roundham Road bridge, and the old stone bridge at the latter place was demolished on 21st July, 1938. Track widening, including the necessary abutments, was then carried out (also a recess for a new, repositioned, South box, never built, which recess can still be seen today) and the new steel Roundham Road bridge was erected in March 1939. This entailed the closing of the line between Paignton and Churston, while the work was done, passengers being conveyed by bus.

'Castle' class 4-6-0 No. 5040 *Stokesay Castle* leaves Kingswear with a 7.00 pm departure in July 1937.   *The late I.H. Smart*

'Hall' class 4-6-0 No. 4901 *Adderley Hall* pauses at Goodrington Sands Halt on a down stopping service in April 1939.   *R.G. Nelson*

That there was a need for such a large station in the 1930s is borne out by the fact that on August Bank Holiday Monday 1938, 20,000 people arrived at Torquay by train, as had occurred on the same day the previous year. Eleven thousand arrived on the Saturday and no less than 50 excursion trains on the Sunday from London, South Wales, Bristol and the Midlands. The congestion at Paignton, hemmed in between two level crossings, where most of these trains would have reversed and returned empty to Newton Abbot for servicing, just cannot be imagined these days when only 71 trains a day serve Paignton (and just a few more on Summer Saturdays).* But the problems would have been well known to the GWR management, and no doubt the five platforms were fully justified.

At Goodrington the abutments and embankments for the new overbridge at Tanner's Road and some levelling and drainage work at Clennon Valley had been finished when World War II broke out and all work stopped.† Many years later, as will be described, the new works at Goodrington were finally completed, but Paignton never got its grand five- platform station. Perhaps it was just as well, as all the houses on the left-hand side of the Dartmouth Road from below the Congregational Church to Sands Road would have been demolished, and a slice taken off Queens Park. The station would have been further south than the one it replaced with its entrance between the bus station and Curledge Street. But by the 1970s most of the enlargement would have been redundant, just as proved to be the case with the Goodrington scheme.

For the summer seasons of 1938 and 1939 (at least), the 11.0 pm train from Kingswear on Sunday nights conveyed sleeping cars for London. There was no apparent inwards, balancing service; presumably the empty vehicles would have been detached at Newton Abbot off a down service or worked up empty from Plymouth.

---

* It was only 45 trains a day when the First Edition was published in 1989, so things have improved!
† The new station at Paignton etc. authority was £88,100 of which only some £1,150 was spent. The Goodrington portion authority was £50,450 of which some £39,000 had been spent when the books were closed in December 1953 (£34,000 had been spent when the war started). The 'new' Goodrington scheme (*see next Chapter*) was authorized on 26th August, 1954.

The wartime emergency timetable which commenced on 25th September, 1939.

NEWTON ABBOT, TORQUAY, PAIGNTON AND DARTMOUTH.

Week Days.

	a.m.	a.m.	a.m.
Newton Abbot .... dep.	4 15	6 6	6 40
Kingskerswell "		6 26	
Torre arr.	4 25	6 27	7 0
Torquay { dep.		6 29	7 4
Paignton		6 42	7 18
Goodrington Sands Halt "			
Churston (for Brixham, see p. 30) "		6 52	7 26
Kingswear "		7 0	7 38
Dartmouth arr.		7 11	7 50

Week Days—contd.

	a.m.		11 night
Newton Abbot .... dep.	8 40	10 5	11 8
Kingskerswell "	8 46	10 11	11 14
Torre arr.	8 54	10 20	11 22
Torquay { dep.	8 56	10 22	11 24
Paignton	8 58	10 24	11 31
Goodrington Sands Halt "	9 7	10 30	
Churston (for Brixham, see p. 30) "	9 18		
Kingswear "	9 29		
Dartmouth arr.	9 40		

F—For Brean Sands and Lympsham.

M—One Class only.

DARTMOUTH, PAIGNTON, TORQUAY AND NEWTON ABBOT.

Week Days.

	a.m.	a.m.	a.m.
Dartmouth .... dep.	6 50	7 55	9 50
Kingswear "	7 2	8 10	10 5
Churston (for Brixham, see page 30) "	7 12	8 21	10 15
Goodrington Sands Halt "			10 21
Paignton "	7 21	8 30	10 25
Torquay { arr.	7 30	8 35	10 30
	7 33	8 37	10 32
Torre { dep.	7 33	8 43	10 37
Kingskerswell "	7 40	8 50	10 44
Newton Abbot arr.	7 44	8 57	10 48

Sundays.

	p.m.	p.m.	p.m.
Dartmouth .... dep.	4 55		
Kingswear "	5 10		
Churston "	5 22		
Goodrington Sands Halt "			
Paignton "	5 33	6 50	7 40
Torre "	5 38	6 55	7 45
Kingskerswell "	5 40	6 57	7 47
Newton Abbot arr.	5 52	7 3	7 52

M—One class only.
F—For Brean Sands and Lympsham.

W—Calls at Ivybridge at 8.35 p.m. to pick up passengers for Bristol and beyond on notice being given to the Station Master at Ivybridge not later than 7.15 p.m.

Chapter Eight

The Blitz and BR: The War Years and Nationalization 1939-1959

The coming of another war at the beginning of September 1939 meant the curtailment of holidays and the removal of all non-essential trains from the timetable to save fuel. The 'Evacuation from London' timetable (over four days) did not have a huge effect on the Kingswear line. The 'Torbay Express' was cancelled and instead ran to and from Penzance, the other main changes being to the local trains connecting out of massive 15-coach trains from London via Bristol to Penzance (six coaches being detached at Newton Abbot). There was, however, a special evacuation train from Acton to Torquay and Paignton on day three. There were many adjustments to the timetable in 1940 until the service was the best that could be provided in the circumstances.

The importance of Newton Abbot as a railway centre was forcefully brought home to its inhabitants on Tuesday 20th August, 1940. It had been a nice summer's day when three enemy aircraft (Heinkel IIIs) approached the station at 6.45 pm, just three minutes after the 10.32 am Crewe to Penzance had left. Only a 'yellow' warning had been issued so that people were moving about normally, not sheltering as would have been the case had a 'red' warning been sounded.

Six bombs were dropped on the station, five of which exploded. Two bombs dropped in the down relief and down through lines in the centre of the station, causing severe damage to the downside building and partial demolition of the platform. The estimated cost of restoration of the station buildings was £6,200. There were a number of casualties in the 7 pm Newton Abbot to Plymouth stopping train which was standing in the down main platform. Much damage was done to coaching stock stabled in the carriage sidings between the platform and the locomotive depot, and three members of staff working in the sidings were killed.

The other three bombs which exploded all fell south of the coaling stage which was located west of the engine shed. Extensive damage was caused to the locomotive stock including Nos. 6010 (from machine gun fire, the bomb which landed near it failing to explode), 2785, 5915, 6801 and 9311. A row of railway cottages between the carriage works and the road bridge was also destroyed. Fortunately, the last broad gauge engine in existence, *Tiny* an 0-4-0 well tank exhibited on Newton Abbot down platform, had been removed to Swindon for storage the previous June.

All in all 14 person were killed (including four GWR employees) and 15 people received serious injuries (five of whom were railway employees). Another 46 people were subject to minor injuries. Five engines were severely damaged, another 10 received lighter damage. Figures for coaching stock were 26 (severe) and 25 (light) whilst 10 wagons received heavy damage and another 12 light damage. The railway shut for 10 hours whilst the unexploded bomb was made safe and removed, to be blown up elsewhere.

Since the First Edition was published, a file of wartime accidents has been found and details of these now follow. Although some are obviously the result of wartime conditions, it should not be thought that accidents were significantly higher in number in this period. These accident reports have been fortuitously preserved while those for other decades have not.

On 18th September, 1940 after the 6.30 pm passenger train from Kingswear to Taunton consisting of four coaches and an empty dining car came to a stand at Churston up platform, the porter-signalman admitted the engine of the 6.15 pm Brixham to Newton Abbot goods onto the single line towards Kingswear, for the purpose of running round its train after departure of the passenger train. After this movement the porter-signalman pulled off the up home signal, at which the light engine No. 5798, was standing, in mistake for the up starter. He immediately realised his mistake and before the lever was fully pulled over threw it back, but the driver, seeing the signal arm lower, moved ahead and collided with the rear of the Kingswear train, causing some damage to the dining car No. 9555, which was, however, allowed to proceed to Newton Abbot. The porter-signalman was blamed for the collision but a joint inquiry ruled that the driver was not blameless and should have been keeping a better look out.

Wartime bombing also affected the Kingswear end of the line but, thankfully, in a less major way than the raid on Newton Abbot. On 12th April, 1941, at 12.20 am, six high explosive and one incendiary bombs were dropped at Kingswear, five falling in the village and one onto the retaining wall of the jetty undermining No. 1 siding alongside the wharf and closing access to No. 2 siding. A crater approximately 20 ft diameter and 10 ft deep was formed affecting the sidings to an extent of 50 ft at the north end. There was no boat in or due; repairs were carried out immediately and the sidings were back in use by noon on 14th April.

At 5 am on 24th May, 1941, a bomb was dropped at 227m. 3 ch.,between Churston and Kingswear, about 3 ft from the line on the river side. No air raid warning was in operation but sirens sounded at Kingswear at 5.5 am. An engine with porter left Churston at 6.5 am to examine the line and discovered a crater 30 ft wide by 15 ft deep, but the line itself was undamaged. At 7.37 am the ganger walked the line and on arrival at Kingswear gave a certificate that trains could pass, subject to being cautioned at Churston and Kingswear. The 4.15 am Newton Abbot to Kingswear terminated at Churston and formed the 6.58 am Kingswear from there; the 5.55 am Newton Abbot to Kingswear was held at Churston until 7.48 am, returning as the 8.10 am Kingswear 15 minutes late. After repairs, normal working resumed at 12.15 pm.

It was necessary to reverse the positions of the two facing crossovers between up main and up relief lines at Aller Jn, in connection with work arising from the provision of a new down goods loop, on the Plymouth line, just beyond the divergence of the two routes. This work took place in early 1941, with the loop opening that June.

Obviously with holiday traffic set aside for the 'duration', Traffic Committee meetings, once so full of items of expenditure on the Kingswear line related to the prosperous passenger traffic, now tended to deal with facilities for increasing goods traffic. Entries in the minutes for the Kingswear line are few and far between during the war years but, conversely, Newton Abbot as a major junction and traffic centre, features often.

During 1941 a jetty was built on the station side of Forwood's siding at Kingswear to refuel motor torpedo boats. Whilst this was under construction in the summer, a lorry crossing the line on its way to the construction site got stuck and was run into by a train due at 11.11 am killing the lorry driver.

Before 1941 and all through the 1930s Goodrington Sands Halt had remained open throughout the winter, although unstaffed, but from 6th October, 1941, it was closed for the winter and this practice was repeated in subsequent years.

Les Folkard of Torquay was an interested observed of the wartime local railway scene and recorded the following notes on traffic and locomotive workings:

SR 'Remembrances' Nos. 2329 and 2331, both in clean green SR livery, were active on local freights from late 1941. LNER (ex-GER) 'F4' 2-4-2T Nos. 7174 or 7177 hauling an armoured train made occasional appearances during 1941.

The wartime equivalent of the 'Torbay Express' left Torquay for London at 12 o'clock each weekday – one of Newton Abbot's 'Castles', or 'Kings' on five brown bow-ended corridor coaches was the usual formation, the same two rakes of coaches being kept for this working.

A daily working to and from Shrewsbury ('the Salop') regularly brought in a SALOP-based 'Castle', often No. 5050 which was kept in clean condition.

Another noteworthy train of the period was the morning Kingswear-Bristol (8.38 am off Torre) which was often worked by an interesting engine, with no particular pattern to the workings. The locomotive could be anything from a 'Bulldog' to a 'King', and among those recalled on it are No. 6014, still with bull-nose smokebox door, No. 2989 *Talisman* (a loco rarely seen in the area), while Newton Abbot's No. 4012 *Knight of the Thistle* was often used. In the absence of anything else, one of Newton Abbot's 'Granges' Nos. 6801/8/13/14/22 would be used. The rear two coaches on this train (and a corresponding afternoon working) were reserved for Torquay Grammar School pupils (one for boys and one for girls). These two, numbered 1388 and 4397, were the only non-corridor coaches seen on the line at the time. This was their only duty, and they otherwise stabled at Newton Abbot. All other coaching stock in use at the time on the line were the varying types of standard GWR corridor vehicles, though clerestory coaches were extremely rare.

Freight traffic was busy on the line, several daily trains being run, with pannier tanks often to be seen shunting at Torre and Goodrington, one proceeding light to Goodrington at high speed each afternoon. The afternoon Torre shunt was the preserve of Newton Abbot's oldest pannier, No. 1736 with open cab, being superseded after its withdrawal by No. 1751, 1761 or 1795. Nos. 3603, 3606, 3794 and 5798 were all commonly seen.

A variety of 2-6-2Ts, together with larger engines (even an occasional '47') appeared on local passenger trains, and during 1940-3 NA's stud of 2-6-2Ts included No. 3151, 3183, 5113, 5119, 5150, 4109, 8108, 6100, 6107 and small-wheeled 4526, 4545, 4547, 4582, 4587, 5551, 5552, 5557 all of which were very familiar on branch trains. One of the '45s' usually worked a freight down in the morning which stopped to shunt at Torre on the down side. The '31s', '61s' and '81' left the area early in the war and were replaced by more '51s' (the principal duty of the large-wheeled tanks was banking on Dainton).

Standard types rarely or never seen were Collett and Dean 0-6-0, Aberdare 2-6-0, ROD 2-8-0, 2-8-0T, 2-8-2T, 'Duke' and 'Earl' 4-4-0, 0-6-2T, auto-fitted 0-6-0PT and non-auto 0-4-2T. A coal train from South Wales to Hollacombe gas works which arrived on Sunday mornings sometimes worked a rare South Wales engine right through - 'Aberdare' No. 2669, 2-8-0T No. 5225 and 0-6-2T No. 6602 are all remembered on this turn.

After the 8.35 pm passenger train from Kingswear had passed Britannia Crossing on 18th October, 1941, the gates were opened for ferry traffic. Shortly afterwards Mrs Ashton the keeper heard 'Train out of Section' for the up train almost immediately followed by 'Is Line Clear?' for a down train, which was the 6.45 pm Exeter to Paignton specially extended to Kingswear on this date. She did not, however, hear the 'Train Entering Section' signal although both signalmen involved stated that it was sent.

It was a dark and stormy night and the driver on the down train missed Britannia's distant signal and claimed he slackened speed to 20 mph but still missed

Damage to the upside buildings at Newton Abbot, following the air raid on 20th August, 1940.
NRM/SSPL

Work on the receiving hopper for the wagon tippler at Hollacombe Gas Works, August 1941.
British Gas

the lamp on the crossing gates which he ran through (although he felt no impact and continued to Kingswear). On arrival at Kingswear he discovered the lamp and parts of the gate on the front of engine No. 6146. The driver was blamed for the accident and criticized for failing to stop; there was no criticism of Mrs Ashton as she was entitled to have the gates across the railway with a train in section if circumstances demanded it, this being a busy crossing.

Three days later, 'King' class No. 6021 working the 4.45 pm passenger Kingswear-Newton Abbot was detached at Torquay at 5.20 pm to pick up a truck of mails in the up siding, and became derailed four bogie wheels over the handpoint in the siding. A fresh engine was obtained from Torre, the train suffering 19 minutes delay. After the breakdown vans attended No. 6021 was rerailed at 7.55 pm.

An interesting example of work made necessary by the war was the authorizing in March 1942 of £110 to be spent at Torre on 'provision of a hut complete with four 2-tier bunks, coal stove, drop table, gas lighting and blackout for firewatchers and trailer pump crew'. Completed in August, it came in just under budget at £107.

Because of its shipbuilding yards (Philip & Son spent the war building naval vessels) and the Royal Naval College in its prominent position on the hill above Dartmouth, the town suffered quite badly from bombing in World War II. In September 1942 two bombs were dropped on the College (fortunately, the cadets were on leave) and there was a direct hit on Philip's Shipyard killing 20 workmen. Following this the naval cadets were moved to Cheshire, although the College continued to house WRNS. In February 1943, enemy aircraft dropped four bombs demolishing several historic buildings and killing 14 civilians. During the war the Royal Dart Hotel became a shore naval establishment, HMS *Cicala*, apart from the ground floor bar which remained in public use.

Also in September 1942, on the 4th, several enemy aircraft flew in from the sea over Torquay and Paignton at approximately 6.55 pm dropping one bomb near Paignton South box, also one on either side of the line between Torquay and Torre station. In addition machine gunning and cannon fire was used. Paignton South suffered superficial blast damage and telegraph wires were affected between Torquay and Torre causing block failure. The 6.15 pm ex-Kingswear suffered damage by blast while travelling between these stations and one girl passenger suffered a cut knee. A gas holder at Torquay gas works was set on fire but it was well away from the line. A number of bombs were dropped in Torquay and Paignton causing considerable damage and some fatalities, one plane a Focke Wulf was brought down by a searchlight battery at Torquay crashing into the beach at Torre Abbey Sands. Torquay signal box was kept open all night and block working was restored at 9 am on 5th September.

Commencing 5th February,1943, an additional connection, on Friday and Saturday nights only, was given off the 6.30 pm ex-Paddington (via Bristol). This left Newton Abbot at 12.35 am calling at Torre (12.47), Torquay (12.50) and terminating at Paignton at 12.58 am. This was experimental and would be reviewed in May.

During shunting operations with the 9.35 am Hackney to Kingswear goods at Torquay at 10.5 am on 23rd April, 1943, engine No. 5552 was derailed on the south end crossover. It had left its train on the up main line and was crossing back to the down line to proceed into the middle siding but moved back along the down line before the reversing of the crossover was completed. An engine obtained from Torre cleared the up line at 10.22 am when single line working (SLW) between Torquay and Gas House Siding was put into operation. Breakdown vans attended from Newton Abbot, and No. 5552 was rerailed at 11.20. There were minor delays to two up trains.

On Kingswear box being opened at 9 am on Sunday 25th April, 1943 it was found that the block instruments and telephone had failed and it was subsequently discovered that a runaway barrage balloon's cable had become entangled in the wires near Britannia Crossing. S&T and service personnel cleared the cable and restored communication at 11.15 am. The 8.30 am Newton Abbot-Kingswear terminated at Churston, restarting from there in the time of the 10 am ex-Kingswear and a special was obtained from Newton Abbot to work between Churston and Kingswear under pilot working conditions.

At about 2.55 am on 23rd May, 1943, the Torquay police informed the Newton Abbot platform inspector that a military lorry had fallen down the embankment at Lawes Bridge (218 m. 36 ch.). The Kingswear line was closed at this time, but the station pilot No. 4526 was sent out from Newton Abbot at 3.10 am to investigate and found the Army Austin lorry across the up line. It was cleared by rolling it over and subsequently moved to Torre by permanent way trolley. The driver was uninjured. The line was cleared and the engine returned to Newton Abbot at 4 am.

During shunting operations with the 3 pm freight ex-Kingswear in the downside lower yard at Torre on 17th September, 1943, LMS open No. 287267 became derailed fouling the down main line. SLW was opened between Torquay and Torre at 5.53 pm, breakdown vans sent for at 5.10, arrived 5.50, rerailed 6.35 and normal working was resumed. The cause was found to be a defective check rail at the points. There were minor delays to three down trains.

When Churston and Kingswear boxes were opening at 5.20 am on 28th September 1943, it was found that the token instruments had failed but the telephones were working. Pilot working was arranged with the pilotman walking through the section and arriving at Churston at 7.05 am. The lineman was called at 5.33 and arrived at 7.09. The instruments were restored at 8.05 and pilot working cancelled at 8.35 am. The failure was caused by a cable from the barrage balloon fouling the wires. Four trains were delayed, up to 64 minutes.

At 10.16 am on 22nd May, 1944 the engine of the 9.35 am Hackney to Goodrington goods failed about 1¼ miles from Kingskerswell. As no assistance was available, single line working was set up on the up line at 11.08 am commencing with the 10.30 am ex-Paignton. Later two assistant engines were sent from Newton Abbot and the disabled train was taken on to Torre at 1.10 pm and the other engine took the failure, No. 7222, back to Newton Abbot. Single line working was cancelled at 1.20 pm. Subsequently it was found that 7222's safety plug had fused, owing to mismanagement by the footplate crew. The only substantial delay was of 34 minutes to the 9.38 am Exeter-Kingswear.

Trains ceased to call at Goodrington Sands Halt from 22nd May, the start of the summer timetable, and from which date a supplement suspended a large number of trains throughout the GWR, including eight on the Kingswear line - presumably because of the critical state of the war.

At the request of the Military authorities, the railway ferry to and from Dartmouth was suspended between 31st May and 6th June, 1944 (preparation for D-day). One presumes that foot passengers used the lower vehicle ferry during this period.

On 22nd September, 1944, the 7.20 pm Newton Abbot-Kingswear consisting of eight coaches and an Asmo (motor car van) hauled by No. 5150 arrived at Paignton at 7.56 pm. After station work was completed the train (still containing passengers) was shunted to the upside to detach the Asmo in the middle siding. Owing to the driver coming back too fast the movement collided heavily with the stop blocks, causing three coaches to become buffer-locked. Only the three coaches nearest the engine were undamaged and passengers were transferred to these and the train left for Kingswear at 8.27, 28 minutes late. The 7.32 pm ex-Kingswear to Newton Abbot was also delayed 11 minutes. The breakdown vans arrived at 11.48 pm, the coaches were released and the vans returned to Newton Abbot at 1.20 am. The damaged coaches were van third 3422, composite 7317, van third 4682, third 5003 and van third 4628.

During shunting operations at Kingswear on 23rd February, 1945 at about 9.10 am, 'Hall' class 4-6-0 No. 4983 was pulling corridor third No. 3614 and four vans from No. 3 Forwood's siding towards No. 1 Loop for the engine to run round. When approaching disc 30, the driver sounded the whistle for it to be lowered but unfortunately the signalman reversed points 29 (sidings to up/down main) between the bogies of the coach causing the rear bogie to be derailed all wheels, together with two wheels of the following vehicle, NE Mink No. 182078, fouling the running line. Breakdown vans were ordered at 9.20 am and arrived at 10.32. The main line was reopened at 12.30 and rerailing completed at 1.30 pm. During the obstruction, 9.30-12.30, Devon General operated a special bus service from Churston to Kingswear. The following trains terminated at/restarted from Churston: 8 am Exeter, 9.38 am Exeter, 10.45 am Kingswear, 11.25 Kingswear, 12.30 pm Kingswear.

At noon on 27th July, 1945 the empty stock of the 9.38 am Exeter-Kingswear was shunted from Kingswear station to No. 1 Forwood's sidings for the purpose of detaching two vehicles. While passing over the handpoints leading to the siding, the third vehicle (van third No. 1597) became derailed four wheels and lock-buffered with the fourth vehicle (composite No. 7742). Breakdown vans were ordered at 12.20 pm and arrived 1.37 pm, the vehicles were rerailed at 3.0 pm and normal working resumed. Upon investigation it was found that the point lever had been moved by a naval rating attached to the Reserve Coastal Forces, Dartmouth. The divisional superintendent wrote to the man's commanding officer asking him to accept liability for the costs incurred. The latter, Thomas T. Carnie, replied on 10th August:

I visited the scene of this incident accompanied by Mr Bovey, station master at Kingswear, and we both formed the opinion that to move the points lever would require considerable physical effort. In view of this rating's statement and my remarks I shall be glad if you will give this case your sympathetic consideration as [G] is young and supporting a widowed mother ...

The rating's statement read:

At about noon on 27th July I was coming off the Torpedo Jetty but was prevented by a train of coaches being shunted. I stepped back to lean on the Shunting box and in doing so I touched the points lever with my back. I am under the impression that it was then in a vertical position. On my touching it the lever fell over, moved the points and resulted in the train being derailed. I realise the difficulty of moving a points lever in the ordinary way as I have in the past worked for the LMS at Belfast.

Somewhat contradictory statements? The papers do not show how the matter was concluded.

Once the war was over passenger traffic levels began to return to normal. In October 1945 the timetable showed a fairly generous service of 23 down and 24 up trains (14 ran to/from Kingswear) on weekdays. Bearing in mind this is the winter service, trains ran at remarkably close intervals, for example leaving Paignton (up) at 8.00, 8.26, 8.50, 9.05, 9.35, 10.05 am. On Sundays there were 13 down and 12 up trains of which six and five respectively served Kingswear. The first up service, 5.55 am ex-Paignton, only ran to get the stock to Newton to form the return 6.30 am to

A series of photographs all taken on 17th July, 1946 (*continuing on page 204*): Paignton North level crossing and signal box; pedestrians use the footbridge on a rather wet day as the crossing is closed for an incoming train.   *NRM/SSPL*

Paignton North level crossing looking from the down platform towards the north.   *NRM/SSPL*

Paignton and called intermediately at Torre only. On both weekdays and Sundays the last up train was the 11.55 pm Paignton to Newton Abbot and connected into the overnight sleeper to Paddington.

Upon completion of shunting operations at Gas House Siding on 14th November, 1945, at about 4.25 pm the engine of the 2.45 pm Kingswear to Newton Abbot freight 'Castle' class 4-6-0 No. 4077 *Chepstow Castle*, came out onto the up main line and points 14 were reversed for the engine to set back onto its train. Seeing the points reversed the shunter called the engine back whereupon the tender (leading) became derailed. Breakdown vans were ordered and arrived at Torquay station at 5.10 and on site at 5.45. Single line working over the down main, Torquay-Paignton North, was put in operation at 5.00 pm. The tender was rerailed at 7.20 pm and single line working cancelled at 8.15 pm. Delays were minimal except for the 5.30 Paignton-Newton Abbot, 37 minutes. The shunter was blamed for not checking the points were correctly set before calling the driver back.

The February 1946 *GWR Magazine* reported that Mr F. Barton, lengthman Churston, had retired after 36 years' service, all of which had been spent at Churston. He was presented with a pipe rack, pipes, and tobacco by Mr C.V. Williams, station master, from the staff at Churston and Brixham.

By the summer of 1946 holidaymakers were flocking back to Torbay in large numbers. On Monday 17th June, 1946 the 8.25 am Paddington to Paignton express, comprising 'Hall' class 4-6-0 No. 4984 *Albrighton Hall* hauling six coaches containing 74 passengers, was nearing the end of its journey but it never reached its destination that day. As it approached Lawes Bridge, not far from Torre station, driver Pope of Newton Abbot saw to his horror a freight train (engine No. 9633, 14 wagons and brake van) in advance on the same line; the latter was stationary at the stop board just over ¾ mile from Torre. A collision could not be avoided and the express smashed into the van of the 12.25 pm Hackney to Brixham local freight toppling it from the line. As had happened at Aller in 1929, the guard, Cecil Sussex, was fortunately outside, pinning down brakes before the freight commenced the steep descent to Torquay. A number of passengers, and driver Pope, were treated for shock.

Both lines were blocked and the GWR summoned a fleet of buses from both Devon General and Western National to run a shuttle service between Newton Abbot and Torre, where passengers resumed their rail journey to Kingswear or intermediately. On this Monday afternoon in June, starting at 2.10 pm, between 3,000 and 4,000 people were ferried by bus to or from Torre. The up line was clear at 6.50 pm when an up local train was passed, and at 8.17 pm the down line was also cleared, the first train being a Bradford-Torquay express.

What had happened was that in advance of the freight train was the 12.45 pm Newton Abbot passenger train which called at Torre station. To enable the signalman (a relief signalman in this case) to give the train-out-of-section signal (TOS) for a long down train calling at Torre, or should an up train be passing his box and blocking his view of the tail lamp, a large mirror was erected on a post to the rear of the box. When the signalman saw the tail lamp of the train he gave TOS to Kingskerswell and accepted the goods. But after the train had finished its station work and moved off, the signalman forgot he had already 'cleared it' and gave TOS again. As the section to Kingskerswell was fairly short this cannot have aroused any doubt in the mind of the signalman there, and he offered forward the 8.25 am Paddington express, which Torre accepted. The stage was now set for calamity as the first rule of absolute block signalling had been broken: 'only one train in a block section on the same line, at the same time'. Fortunately there were no serious injuries and the line was reopened the

Paignton South level crossing (Sands Road) and signal box.   *NRM/SSPL*

Looking through the level crossing gates at Paignton South (*left*) towards the station. From the
debris on the ground it appears that the gates have been renewed.   *NRM/SSPL*

same evening, as already mentioned. The divisional superintendent investigating the accident deplored the relief signalman's attempts to blame the Kingskerswell signalman who had a trainee with him. (The 'trainee' was actually a 64- year- old man who had been a special class signalman at Newton Abbot West for 20 years, resuming work after a month's illness, presumably on light duties.) He recommended that the track circuit to the rear of the down home signal should be extended by 574 yards to a point 200 yards in the rear of the stop board.

A more minor mishap occurred at Goodrington on Sunday 4th August, 1945. The 7.30 pm Goodrington to Taunton, formed engine No. 7316 and 10 coaches, was standing at the up platform at Goodrington with the rear van slightly fouling the Churston end of the crossing loop having been shunted there after arriving at the down platform with a terminating service. The 9 am Bradford to Kingswear was passing at slow speed when the 'King' class engine No. 6004 *King George III* came in contact with van third No. 5365, with very slight damage. The 7.30 pm Goodrington left at 7.52 pm (detaching the damaged vehicle at Newton Abbot) and the 9.00 am Bradford was delayed from 7.29 to 7.54 pm. The man who carried out the shunting of the Goodrington service was a temporary porter (acting shunter), an employee of only six months' service, and it was the first time he had carried out this operation. The Paignton foreman was criticized for employing such an inexperienced man on such duties. There was no track circuit or fouling bar at the Churston end of the layout to enable the signalman to see that a train was not fouling the down line.

The winter of 1946/7 was exceptionally severe and the GWR was very badly affected, particularly in South Wales, the source of its coal supply, and of course the supplier of much of industry. The worst weather came from January onwards and lasted until March. A blizzard, the worst in living memory on Tuesday 4th March, 1947, severed communication with 200 collieries in South Wales producing half a million tons of coal week. On the Wednesday only 192 coal wagons left South Wales compared with a normal movement of 2,000 wagons. The blizzard continued until Thursday and on the Friday some 3,000 wagons were cleared from the collieries. But coal shortage now reached crisis proportions and the GWR was forced to make drastic cuts in express services to save fuel - even the 'Cornish Riviera' was withdrawn from 17th March having until then run continuously since 1906, except for part of World War I. In Parliament the Minister of Transport told the Member for St Ives that the withdrawal of this train would save 110 tons of coal a week. The 'Torbay Express' was also withdrawn, as were 31 other main line and 156 local services. As late as May 1947 the GWR only held five or six days stocks of coal, and it was necessary to reduce the summer 1947 timetable by 10 per cent compared with 1946, or a 25 per cent reduction on the pre-war level of service. So concerned was Sir James Milne, General Manager of the GWR, that the system would be dangerously overcrowded that summer that he wrote an article for the *News of the World*, outlining the railways' problems.

In 1947, introduction of Zonal Collection and Delivery arrangements meant that 'smalls' goods traffic was in future sent to Paignton (Newton Abbot in the case of Kingskerswell) and delivered from there by road. However, full truck loads continued to be sent to the nearest station for that traffic.

Following the election of a Labour Government at the end of World War II, nationalization of the railways became inevitable and despite the strong opposition of the 'Big Four' the Transport Bill became law, receiving the Royal Assent on 6th August, 1947. Many of the GWR officers retired, including the General Manager, Sir James Milne, rather than face the prospect of nationalization, and the new,

A '4575' class 2-6-2T starts away from Paignton with an up local train in June 1951. The British Transport Advertising billposter is at work nearby. *Revd P.L. Baycock*

An excellent official photograph of Aller Junction signal box interior taken on 26th October, 1952. At the left-hand end of the block shelf are various signal repeaters and beneath them numbered plungers to release electric locks on the relevant signals. Attached to hooks above the repeaters are the metal lever collars which reminded a signalman not to pull a lever (these also doubled as egg cups at breakfast time!). In the centre of the shelf are block bells and block instruments, *left to right*, Kingskerswell, Newton Abbot West (Relief line), Stoneycombe and Newton Abbot West (Main line). The box contained 46 levers. *NRM/SSPL*

somewhat demeaning, title of chief regional officer. At midnight on 31st December, 1947, the GWR became the Western Region of British Railways.

On 10th September, 1949, a heavy sea mist prevailed between Goodrington and Churston when the signalman at Churston accepted a light engine from the former just before 6 am. The 4.15 am Newton Abbot to Kingswear mail train was standing at his down platform, but he was permitted to accept a following train (not a freight) under Regulation 5 (the 'Warning arrangement') in clear weather. As it was still possible to see his fog marker point he did not need to introduce the more restrictive 'fog and falling snow' conditions and accepted the engine. Unfortunately the driver missed the down home signal and ran into the back of the mail train, which was standing with brakes off preparatory to leaving for Kingswear. There were no injuries; the driver of the light engine was blamed for proceeding without sufficient caution in the prevailing conditions. Guard H. Beer had a narrow escape as he was about to board his brake vehicle when the accident occurred. A parcels van in the middle of the train was 'lifted from the rails' and single line working over the up platform line then took place until repairs were effected.

The following month Cecil Williams, station master of Churston and Brixham for the last 14 years, retired and was succeeded by Mr L.F. Nickels, formerly of Watchet.

There was a presentation at Churston in November 1950 to George Snell (signalman) retiring after 49 years' service, 33 years of which had been in Churston box. He was presented with a pipe and an automatic lighter and a handbag for Mrs Snell. Mr Penwarden, former station master, caused roars of laughter with his reminiscences of work on the fish platform at Brixham - engines arriving without their trains, and the primitive signalling arrangements of the early days [he was first there about 1892]. Many of the men who had worked with him had gone far in the railway service.

Another coal crisis early in 1951 reduced a very comprehensive winter service of 31 trains in each direction on weekdays (18 down and 18 up ran to and from Kingswear) and 16 down and 17 up on Sundays (seven each way served Kingswear). From 12th February, 1951 the following weekday trains were suspended (some of the trains had been withdrawn in an earlier supplement):

11.10 am	Newton Abbot-Paignton	7.45 am	Paignton-Newton Abbot
2.30 pm	Newton Abbot-Paignton	1.20 pm	Paignton-Newton Abbot
3.00 pm	Newton Abbot-Kingswear	3.55 pm	Kingswear-Newton Abbot
		-	to start from Paignton at 4.30 pm
4.55 pm	Newton Abbot-Paignton	6.55 pm	Paignton-Newton Abbot
		7.20 pm	Paignton-Newton Abbot
7.30 pm	Newton Abbot-Paignton	8.15 pm	Paignton-Newton Abbot
9.55 pm	Newton Abbot-Paignton	10.20 pm	Paignton-Newton Abbot

Even with these trains withdrawn, in most cases the gaps in the service were not too large and one wonders why some of the trains were run at all in a winter period.

The Brixham branch passenger service was withdrawn between 12th February and mid-April. In February a BR spokesman at Exeter told the *Brixham Western Guardian* that '(they) had been making representation to keep this line open for passenger traffic, but we have been overruled at a very high level.' The Brixham-based driver, Reg Westaway, was temporarily transferred to Newton Abbot.

There was a protracted correspondence from February 1952 and lasting for over a year, between the various departments regarding the carriage cleaning staff

An unidentified 'Castle' class 4-6-0 arrives at Churston with the down 'Torbay Express' in June 1951. The fireman has the token ready for the signalman.   *Revd P.L. Baycock*

'Star' class 4-6-0 No. 4060 *Princess Eugenie* rests between duties in Hoodown siding, Kingswear, June 1951. The locomotive was scrapped the following year.   *Revd P.L. Baycock*

'Star' class locomotive No. 4007 *Swallowfield Park* stands at Kingswear with the up 'Torbay Express' on 1st June, 1951. The toilet roof tanks on the second coach are being refilled. A down train is arriving at the bay platform.   *R.G. Nelson*

A light engine runs through Britannia Halt en route to Kingswear, June 1951. *Revd P.L. Baycock*

'Castle' class 4-6-0 No. 5011 *Tintagel Castle* has just left Hookhills viaduct with an Exeter-Kingswear local service and despite the stiff gradient is blowing off as it approaches Churston, July 1954. *The late J.W.T. House*

'14XX' class 04-2T No. 1402 was a Cheltenham-based engine but came to Newton Abbot works for a 'light casual' repair in August 1952, hence its possibly unique appearance on the Brixham goods, here at Churston, on 23rd September, 1952. The engine spent almost its entire life at Cheltenham or Gloucester, being scrapped in 1956. *Derek J. Frost*

messroom at Kingswear. Apparently this was in a dilapidated condition and needed replacement. As letters passed to and fro, the operating superintendent at Paddington (Gilbert Matthews) asked whether a condemned passenger brake van might be found for temporary use, but no such vehicle being available, the carriage and wagon engineer at Swindon proposed stores van No. 1070, in use by the Hotels Executive, as a suitable replacement. This had been built in 1897 as a brake van in the new Royal train! However, in July 1953 the new mess room with boiling ring, drying room and lavatory was authorized at a cost of £820, without making use of No. 1070. The work was completed in December 1954.

It will be remembered that the 1935 scheme for a new station at Paignton envisaged new carriage sidings at Goodrington. Now, in June 1952, a submission was put to the British Transport Commission (BTC) for approval in principle (pending full costing) that these be provided and the unfinished road bridge at Tanner's Road be completed. The submission stated that the present carriage sidings could hold 103 coaches but the maximum demand required 150, necessitating some trains being worked to other places for stabling. The BTC very quickly approved the scheme on 1st July, 1952.

The variation between an already generous Monday to Friday service and the Saturday service in the summer can be gauged by considering the 1953 service, for example. Summer 'Saturdays' often actually started late on Friday nights during late July and August with trains of returning holiday passengers who had to make their way home earlier than the Saturday, for one reason or another, Torquay box which normally closed at 9 pm stayed open until 11.30 pm to deal with these extra trains (although they did not run in 1953).

Summer Saturday trains started early, but certain trains only ran for a few weeks. For example, the very early first down arrival at Torquay (at 4 .15 am) only ran on three Saturdays in September. The next train, 4.15 am Newton Abbot-Kingswear, ran all the year round but was principally for parcels and newspapers and never did call at Torquay, this traffic being dealt with at Torre, for which 25 minutes was allowed. The next down service 4.25 am Newton Abbot-Paignton (10.10 pm ex-Leicester) availed itself of the reversible signalling at Torre and passed the 4.15 using the up platform. Kingskerswell and Torquay boxes which normally opened between 6 and 6.30 am, switched in at 4 am on Summer Saturdays to cope with this early morning stream of traffic. Gas House Siding box between Torquay and Paignton, and normally open only for freight trains shunting at the sidings, was opened between 6 am and 6 pm on Saturdays only. This helped with any late running on the down road and enabled up trains to leave Paignton at close intervals (and remember there were empty coach trains and light engines to fit in between the advertised service).

There were some unusual Saturday-only trains, particularly in the up direction. Many trains did not call at Newton Abbot (which entitled them to a special signalling bell code 3-3-1 rather than the usual 2-2-4 (up express calling at Newton Abbot). Examples were the 10 am Torquay to Wolverhampton (which was first advertised stop Banbury) and the 10.30 am Torquay to Paddington (non stop to Paddington). The coaches for the former came empty from Paignton, but for the latter from Torre (the coaches were stabled there each Friday) using the ground frame-worked facing connection to the up platform at the north end of the station. In between these two was the 9.45 am Churston to Paddington (non stop Paignton to Paddington). The coaches for this service normally spent the week stabled in Churston down refuge, being worked down from Newton Abbot on a Monday.

On 25th April, 1952, 'Grange' class 4-6-0 No. 6822 *Manton Grange* on the 11.40 am Newton Abbot to Kingswear has been using the up platform at Paignton and is crossing to the down line at Paignton South box. The carriage sidings on the right are now the site of Queen's Park steam railway station.   *Derek J. Frost*

A fine view of Kingskerswell signal box, of Saxby & Farmer design, on the up platform.
                                                                      Great Western Trust (M. Hale)

'14XX' class 0-4-2T No. 1466 takes the daily Paignton-Moretonhampstead through working past Torre up advanced starting signal, *c.*1953.   *L.F. Folkard*

A very clean Newton Abbot '28XX' class 2-8-0 enters Goodrington Sands Halt with the 9.05 am Kingswear to Swansea in either 1956 or 1957. One hopes this engine was in fine fettle because after leaving Torquay it did not make a station call again until reaching South Wales, even Bristol being passed non-stop.   *Great Western Trust (M. Hale)*

'Britannia' class 4-6-2 No. 70022 *Tornado* is turned at Kingswear on 10th September, 1953.
T.G. Wassell (Hugh Davies)

Although the glass plate is damaged, I could not resist including this photo of 'Britannia' class 4-6-2 No. 70022 *Tornado* leaving the Brixham branch at Churston. The locomotive was not permitted on the branch, so I assume the train (possibly the 'Torbay') had been recessed on the branch line for some reason (it is not the one described by Jack Eveleigh in Chapter Twelve as that was an up train). Mark Wilkins, who now holds the David Fish collection, thinks the date can be narrowed down to 1955/56 (*Tornado* left Newton Abbot in 1956). Does anyone know the date and circumstances of this event? *David Fish courtesy Mark S. Wilkins*

Most Brixham passengers for this service came from the holiday camps and were brought to Churston by special coaches, rather than the branch train, Brixham station being rather remote from these camps. Other unusual workings were 11.30 am Torquay-Paddington and 1.30 pm Paignton-Paddington (both non-stop) and 1.55 pm Torquay-Paddington (called only at Newbury). The 2.40 pm Paignton-Paddington called only at Torquay, whilst the 4 .15 pm Paignton-Paddington called at Torquay and Slough.

Travel on most of these Summer Saturday up trains required compulsory, free, seat reservations, later referred to as Block Regulation Tickets. Their purpose was to guarantee the holder a seat, but not a specific seat thus spreading the return load over the train service available; they had been introduced in 1952. A new seat reservation office to issue these tickets was authorized for Torquay in 1953 at a cost of £1,138. At Paignton £344 was spent on adapting the existing luggage and enquiry office as an enquiry and seat reservation office and provision of a new timber building for passengers' luggage. At both Paignton and Torquay large queues were formed up outside the station for the respective trains, and passengers were not allowed on the platform until the previous train had loaded. At Torquay where there was an up inner home signal, at which the next following train could be held only just to the rear of the platform, it was quite possible to admit the next train to the platform before all the intending passengers had reached it.

Another feature of the working at Torquay on these holiday Saturdays was that two bank engines were provided to assist the heavy trains up the 1 in 60 (ruling) gradient to Torre. If the train stopped at Torre the banker was coupled in rear but if it did not (and most didn't) it was not coupled on but banked the train uncoupled, 'dropping off' at Torre up advanced starting signal. The bank engine there reversed and returned in the wrong direction to the trailing crossover, the signalman observing its arrival by occupation of the fouling bar indicator for the points. He then had the difficult task of finding a path for the engine in the heavily occupied down line service, to return it to Torquay.

The working timetable did not show specific trains requiring to be assisted from Torquay to Torre and the use of the bankers depended on the load of the train and the type of hauling locomotive on the particular day. This meant numerous telephone calls to Torquay box from either Paignton or the station foreman at Torquay advising that a banker was required. The maximum passenger unassisted load from Torquay for the principal locomotive types was as follows (loads in excess of this had to be banked):

'King'	13 vehicles
'County' or 'Castle'	12 vehicles
'Hall' or 'Grange'	11 vehicles
'Manor', 'Mogul' or larger 2-6-2T	10 vehicles

Early and late turns were involved for Newton Abbot men on these bankers, normally pannier tanks, which were a 'junior' turn, one step up from the shunting yard and often carried out by passed cleaners (firing) and passed fireman (driving).

Such was the line occupation on Summer Saturdays that engines being sent from Newton Abbot to Paignton to start an up express were rarely sent 'light' but 'attached' to a down train. Firemen, when ringing the signalman at Newton Abbot West to advise the destination of the locomotive, tried to get a 'light' run down to avoid coupling and uncoupling, but the signalmen were wise to that move! On a

'51XX' class 2-6-2T No. 4174 on a down train at Paignton on 9th July, 1956. The bracket signal on the up platform controls down trains on that line; the movement across the crossover to the down platform is available for passenger trains but a small signal normally used on goods lines has been provided because of limited clearances.   *Philip J. Kelley*

The summer Saturday schedule will not be too demanding for 2-8-0 No. 3806, allocated to the 2.55 pm Paignton to Birmingham and here approaching Torre on the 1 in 55 climb from Torquay on 11th August, 1956.   *Peter Bowles courtesy Richard Woodley*

Saturday morning in the late 1930s as many as 40 engines would leave Newton Abbot shed to work trains all over the country, including some trains which started at Teignmouth, and assistant engines for down trains over the Devon banks. A standby engine was provided at Paignton.

After the last of the outward departures had ceased (by about 5 pm) and the late arrivals also had made their weary way to their hotel or boarding houses (by about 8 pm), there still remained a late night series of unadvertised 'Starlight Specials' which left Torbay for the North and Midlands in the peak few weeks of late July/August, conveying passengers at much cheaper excursion fares. Torquay box remained open until midnight on Saturday nights instead of its usual 9 pm closure, for these few weeks.

Freight was almost entirely banned from the line on Summer Saturdays, the only services in 1954 being a 3.05 am Hackney to Churston which called at Goodrington and a 3.25 am Hackney to Goodrington calling at Torre. In the up direction the 5.45 pm Goodrington to Newton Abbot had to suffice. In the summer of 1959 the 3.05 am Hackney to Goodrington was the sole freight train each Saturday.

The introduction of some additional lodging turns at Newton Abbot brought about an unofficial strike of footplate staff there from 17th May, 1954. This subsequently spread to several other Western Region depots until 2,500 men were involved resulting in loss of revenue of the order of £700,000. Many potential rail passengers took their custom elsewhere and freight services were drastically curtailed. Eventually the men were persuaded to resume work at midnight on 29th May. A national strike of Associated Society of Locomotive Engineers & Firemen (ASLEF) footplatemen in the summer of 1955 caused even more loss of traffic.

There was another crisis in the locomotive water supply arrangements at Kingswear in 1954. (In 1945 it had been stated that locomotive requirements were 400,000 gallons per month.) The railway was competing with Kingswear laundry which was taking 15,000 gallons daily from the same source. Following a meeting, it was agreed at times of shortage to plug the supply to the laundry at 5 pm each evening and they would unplug the next morning; fortunately they did not work at weekends. The year 1956 was again deficient for rainfall and on 4th July the 7.30 am Penzance to Crewe was delayed 14 minutes at Newton Abbot awaiting the Kingswear portion which had had to take water at Torre because of a shortage at Kingswear. In his explanation to Swindon, the CM&EE's representative at Plymouth, Mr Nightingale, said that the laundry had arranged to divert some more water to the railway, but not much else could be done. The new carriage sidings and engine facilities (*see below*) at Goodrington would, however, assist in reducing demand on the Kingswear supply.

There was an interesting development in 1956 which will not have helped with the water shortage. In March it was agree to bring steam crane No. 164 from Fremington to Kingswear as a temporary relief crane during repairs to electric cranes Nos. 3277 and 3278. It returned to Fremington when these repairs were completed, on 18th January, 1957.

British Railways announced a comprehensive Modernisation Plan in 1955, one part of which was the reinstatement of the pre-war idea to extend the carriage sidings at Goodrington and replacement of the level crossing at Tanner's Road by a road overbridge and a footbridge. The enlargement of Paignton station and the overbridge at Sands Road were abandoned, no doubt on the grounds of cost. As it was, the remaining part of the scheme, the work at Goodrington, cost the huge amount of £103,905, when the scheme was complete in 1960, bearing in mind the seasonal usage of the facilities. As part of this a contract was awarded in July 1955 to

The taxi queue on the downside of Torquay station in the 1950s. The holidaymakers all seem
very well dressed.   *Torquay Museum*

'Castle' class 4-6-0 No. 4098 *Kidwelly Castle* leaves Churston with the up 'Torbay Express'. A
short freight waits to continue its journey to Kingswear. No. 1466, unusually bunker first, is in
the Brixham bay. The date is pre-1957 when Churston Grammar School opened.

R. Blencowe Collection

Kingswear looking towards the buffer stops on 25th May, 1955.   *R.G. Nelson*

'Castle' class No. 7000 *Viscount Portal* leaves Kingswear with the 6.20 pm to Newton Abbot on 8th July, 1956. The elaborate work undertaken to preserve the public right of access to the seashore can be seen: the footpath alongside the railway leading to the huge iron footbridge over the station platforms.   *Philip J. Kelley*

Kingswear carriage sidings, Hoodown viaduct (*centre*) looking across the River Dart towards Dartmouth on 8th July, 1956.   *Philip J. Kelley*

On 26th July, 1956 'Castle' class 4-6-0 No. 7018 *Drysllwyn Castle* is turned on Kingswear turntable. The first of the class to be fitted with a double chimney, the locomotive had worked down with the 'Torbay Express' which included dyamometer car No. W7W (of 1901), seen in the background. The locomotive and car returned on the following day's 'Torbay Express'.

David Fish courtesy Mark S. Wilkins

The south end of Goodrington and Tanner's Lane crossing before the road bridge was completed in June 1956. The rather primitive ticket office (*right*) was formerly the crossing keeper's hut.   *NRM/SSPL*

The south end of Goodrington Sands Halt looking towards Paignton after completion of the road bridge and footbridge. The ticket office is now at the elevated road level.   *NRM/SSPL*

Right: Photographed from an unusual viewpoint, the Hennapyn Road bridge at the south end of Torquay station, the down 'Torbay Express' leaves for Kingswear.
Provenance unknown

Below: 'Castle' class 4-6-0 No. 5024 *Carew Castle* (a Newton Abbot engine) stands at Goodrington with a down 'A' headcode passenger train conveying a very mixed set of stock. The date will be pre-1956 as the road overbridge at the Paignton end has not yet been completed.
Provenance unknown

A nice shot of Kingswear looking towards the buffer stops is thought to have been taken in the 1950s. A short train is about to leave the bay line, 'the Torbay Express' coaches are at the main platform.   *J.H. Moss Collection*

This photograph of Kingswear looking towards Churston would appear to have been taken at the same time; the bay line 'starting' signal is lowered. On the right a locomotive has been turned and waits its turn to come into the station.   *J.H. Moss Collection*

The downside buildings at Torre, seen from the station approach, on 20th November, 1957.
NRM/SSPL

The downside buildings at Torre, seen on 20th November, 1957. The 'mushroom' water tank was moved to this position from its site opposite the goods shed in 1893. *NRM/SSPL*

Staverton Builders for some £41,700, which covered the construction of a 65 ft diameter turntable pit, a water tower, carriage washing hydrants, ashpit, engineers' and enginemen's cabins, a high level ticket office for Goodrington Sands Halt and all the necessary drainage works. The work at Goodrington required the signal box to be lengthened by about 6 ft, the 30-lever frame extended to 52 levers (a new frame) and the box rewired.

As the Modernisation Plan envisaged the eventual dieselization or electrification of the railway, it is difficult to understand the provision of the completely new steam engine facilities at Goodrington. The road overbridge was opened in June 1956 and the additional carriage sidings at Clennon Valley were brought into use later that summer. A new facing connection from the main lines into these carriage sidings was brought into use on 18th June, 1957. The turntable was completed on 9th July, 1957. Completion of these sidings meant that 200 coaches could now be stabled in the Paignton area. The scheme was 'signed off' by the Ministry of Transport in May 1958, with a stipulation that 'protective arrangements' should be provided on the footbridge steps at Goodrington to avoid children climbing onto the up home signal. A new refreshment room at Paignton station opened for the summer of 1956.

Torquay station shared in this modernization expenditure as follows:

1956 - provision of station name signs (£425)
     - replacement of gas lighting by electric (£6,550).
1957 - improved cloakroom facilities (£870)
     - alterations and improvements to booking office & hall and waiting room facilities on upside (£5,765)
     - raising platforms to 2 ft 9 in. minimum height (£2,700)
1958 - improvements to down side of station (£8,814)
1959 - provide and install ticket printing and issuing machines (£6,189)

Paignton was similarly dealt with in 1959 (*see below*).

In 1956 the replica of *Mayflower II* was launched in Upham's Yard, Brixham. The timber for her mast, good solid Devon oak 6 ft in circumference, had been brought to Goodrington by rail, unloaded and sent by road to Torquay Harbour and then dropped into the sea and towed to Brixham. *Mayflower II* commanded by Alan Villiers, set sail from Plymouth for America in April 1957.

The *Paignton Observer* for 5th July, 1956 printed some useful facts regarding traffic levels. Arrivals on the 23rd June had totalled 5,723 compared with 3,324 on the same Saturday in 1955. Outwards seat reservations on the same day had been 1,500 London, 850 South Wales, 550 Birmingham/Wolverhampton, 500 North Midlands and 400 for the North.

A Devon General bus strike in July 1957 meant that the trains were exceptionally busy. In the week 20th-27th July, the Brixham branch carried 15,192 passengers, equal to more than two-thirds of totals carried in three months of a normal summer.

A new grammar school adjacent to Churston station opened on 22nd October, 1957. At first it would accommodate 350 children, but numbers would be increased over the subsequent five years. Dartmouth Grammar School would close and its pupils be transferred to Churston. In planning the school, it was intended that the majority of pupils should travel by rail, hence its location.

On 26th April, 1958 there was another accident at Torre on the down line, quite similar to the 1946 collision but this time it was a driver's error that caused the mishap. Jack Eveleigh was on duty in Torre signal box that day. He had a short freight train detaching traffic in the meat siding (on the downside at the south end

The main station building behind the up platform at Paignton, *c*.1957.   *NRM/SSPL*

The parcels office at Paignton, *c*.1957.   *NRM/SSPL*

The downside booking office at Torquay, before and after modernization, 1957 and 1958. In 1959 a 'multiprinter' ticket printing and issuing machine replaced most of the card stock shown.

NRM/SSPL

Taunton-based Collett 0-6-0 No. 2275 shunts Torquay Gas Works with the remainder of its train standing on the up main line. *Derek J. Frost*

The 10.40 am Paddington to Paignton only ran for four Saturdays in 1957, calling intermediately only at Newton Abbot and Torquay, and this is the last one, 10th August, with 'Hall' class No. 4943 *Marrington Hall* about to pass Kingskerswell. Considering the peak demands at this time, it seems to have a reasonable set of coaches and a clean engine in good condition.

Peter Bowles courtesy Richard Woodley

The signalman leans out of his window to take the token from 'Grange' class 4-6-0 No. 6874 *Haughton Grange* with the 9.20 am Exeter to Kingswear service on 18th September, 1957. The third vehicle in the set is one of the 1935 Centenary vehicles noticeable by their bulbous sides and tapered ends. A couple of River Dart SP Co. paddle steamers are moored opposite Hoodown sidings and the Higher ferry is mid-river, in line with the first coach.

David Fish courtesy Mark S. Wilkins

An unusual photograph of the carriage sidings at Kingswear, also including the water tank, 1950s.   *J.H. Moss Collection*

Although there are two sets of coaches in the station area, there is not a locomotive to be seen, and the streets look deserted, so this may have been taken early on a Sunday morning. However, an unidentified vessel has just arrived at Kingswear pontoon and one of the River Dart paddle steamers would appear to be leaving its berthing station. © *English Heritage (Aerofilms Collection)*

of Torre station) which then had to be shunted to the upside coal siding. The shunt movement consisted of two coal trucks and a brake van, propelled by a pannier tank No. 9668. He brought the shunt to a stand at the south end of the trailing crossover from down to up main, to allow the 8.35 am Kingswear to Paddington to pass on the up line. At about the same time he had accepted the 8.55 am Newton Abbot to Kingswear from Kingskerswell, which was quite normal as Torre had two down home signals which permitted this arrangement.

After the up train had called at Torre it left for Newton Abbot and, as soon as he was able, signalman Eveleigh reversed the crossover to complete the shunt movement and lowered the shunt signal. The short train had not started to move when the 8.55 am from Newton Abbot, hauled by 'Castle' No. 7004 *Eastnor Castle* appeared on the steep incline from Lawes Bridge and smashed into the brake van, having passed both home signals at danger.

Fortunately there were no casualties and the Newton Abbot steam crane was soon on the scene to commence rerailing. The up 'Torbay Express' was allowed through specially at 12.35 pm behind 'Castle' No. 7029 *Clun Castle* (*Eastnor Castle* had been the engine allocated to this job) but nothing else was passed until the up line was re-opened at about 2.50 pm. Fortuitously the accident had occurred between the facing and southernmost trailing crossovers at Torre so the 'reversible signalling' was made full use of. Soon after 5 pm *Eastnor Castle* was towed back to Newton Abbot leaving just permanent way repairs to be effected, and normal working resumed thereafter.

Summer Saturday traffic levels remained high in 1958. The *Torquay Herald Express* stated that on June 14th and the nine following Saturdays, 75,951 passengers had arrived at Torquay, about 1,650 a week higher than in 1956, and a record, apart from the previous year (1957) when a bus and coach strike had artificially inflated the figures (80,838 had in fact arrived in the same 10 weeks of 1957). In December, Torquay's station master, Mr G.D. Collins, who had been there since 1950, was promoted to Exeter (St David's).

An empty Kingswear station, but with all facilities still in existence, *c.*1957.

GW Trust (M. Hale)

A busy summer Saturday scene at Newton Abbot on 2nd August, 1958. Train 855 in the down relief platform, 9.25 am Wolverhampton-Paignton, is due here 2.58-3.05 and should have preceded train 435, 7.43 Nottingham-Plymouth, due here 3.21-3.28, from Norton Fitzwarren. The Plymouth train is double-headed by 'Hall' class No. 6977 *Grundisburgh Hall* and '43XX' 2-6-0 No. 6397.
Peter Bowles courtesy Richard Woodley

'Castle' class 4-6-0 No. 5078 *Beaufort* makes a fine sight after leaving Greenway tunnel with the up 'Torbay Express' and heading for Churston on a lovely spring day, thought to be 26th May, 1958. *Peter Bowles courtesy Richard Woodley*

A fine shot of an up train on Noss curve (the Kingswear deviation). On Saturday 19th July, 1958 'Hall' class 4-6-0 No. 5967 *Bickmarsh Hall* is in charge of the 9.10 am Kingswear-Birmingham (Moor St) via Swindon.   *Peter Bowles courtesy Richard Woodley*

A down local service crosses Hoodown viaduct to arrive at Kingswear on 26th August, 1959.
                                                                                    T. Wright

'King' class 4-6-0 No. 6007 *King William III* leaves Churston with a Churston-Paddington relief (123) to the 'Torbay Express' (023) on Saturday 30th May, 1959. As this pre-dates the start of the summer service, the regular Saturdays-only 9.45 am Churston to Paddington will not yet be running. *Peter Bowles courtesy Richard Woodley*

On Saturday 4th July, 1959 '47XX' 2-8-0 No. 4706 leaves Churston heading for Kingswear on the 1.25 pm from Paddington, a regular turn for this class of locomotive. *David Fish courtesy Mark S. Wilkins*

As the booked diesel had been used to replace an earlier failure, 'Castle' class 4-6-0 No. 5032 *Usk Castle* had been sent to Kingswear to haul the up 'Torbay Express' (which had just been dieselized) on 28th July, 1959. However, as 'Warship' No. 805 *Benbow* later became available it was sent light to Torquay and replaced the 'Castle' here, much to many passengers' regret, one imagines.   *B.B. Williams courtesy P.W. Gray*

'Warship' class diesel No. 808 *Centaur* heads the down 'Torbay Express' past Gas House Sidings down distant signal in July 1959. Just over three years later this was the site of a collision between two passenger trains, after the second train passed Torquay down advanced starter (*seen in the distance*) at danger.   *B.B. Williams courtesy P.W. Gray*

'51XX' class 2-6-2T No. 5196 approaches Britannia Halt with the Kingswear portion of a down express on 17th September, 1959.   *R.G. Nelson*

Although the Paignton station enlargement scheme, abandoned in 1939, had not been reinstated, in November 1959 the General Manager submitted to HQ a scheme costing £50,565 to improve the 'antiquated' commercial facilities there. The existing parcels shed would be converted into a modern booking office and a booking hall (including a new ticket issuing machine), the existing booking office becoming a combined enquiry and seat reservations office. A verandah would be provided for passengers waiting for their seat reservation tickets and the station's gas lighting would be replaced by electricity. A new parcels office would be created. The work would be ready for the summer of 1961.

The *Western Morning News* gave the following interesting facts for traffic levels handled at Paignton in 1959:

Summer Saturday trains - 117 each week
Excursions/Reliefs dealt with during summer - 300
Tickets issued 190,000 pa and 75,000 seat reservations
Parcels dealt with 167,000 and 25,000 items of PLA
Freight - 24,000 wagonloads dealt with
Road vehicles based at Paignton goods station - 20
Passengers arriving at Goodrington Sands Halt - over 100,000

On an early spring afternoon in 1959, 'Castle' class 4-6-0 No. 4090 *Dorchester Castle* makes a stirring sight as it crosses Hookhills viaduct and climbs the ruling 1 in 67 gradient on the approach to Churston with the down 'Torbay Express'. *David Fish courtesy Mark S. Wilkins*

Chapter Nine

Into the 21st Century

Although this chapter has much to say about modernization. It also, unfortunately, outlines the contraction of the line. The reader will see the extensive facilities, so carefully built up by the GWR, closed or modified until the Kingswear line became, once more, a basic railway. In this of course it is not unique; it reflects what happened over the whole BR system as facilities provided in the Railway Age became redundant in the motor car age. Many lines closed entirely; at least the Kingswear line is still open, and, unusually, one half is worked by steam power.

Newton Abbot locomotive works completed its last steam engine overhaul on 15th July, 1960, when 2-6-2T No. 4566 was driven out of the shed by the Chairman of the local UDC and himself a driver there. Thereafter the works was altered to be able to deal with diesel locomotives. A diesel maintenance and servicing depot had been authorized in February 1959 at an estimated cost of £416,800. BR's *Western Divisional News* in reporting these facts gave some interesting details of Newton Abbot's then-current traffic levels which are worth recalling:

> Trains each weekday: 85 freight, 150 passenger (200 summer Sats: 120 Sundays)
> Passengers booked pa: 200,000 (and 53,000 platform tickets issued)
> Parcels forwarded pa: 27,000 (and 116,000 received)
> Wagons dealt with at Hackney: 7,500 weekly (3 pilot engines employed)

In May/June 1961 the road level crossing at the south end of Paignton station was resurfaced using steel rafts. This was done because of the heavy use of the crossing, particularly by coaches, leading to the need for frequent repairs.

The year 1961 was the first time there were no trains on Christmas Day. However, when it was announced that the Dartmouth Ferry also would not run, strong protests led to BR reinstating a ferry service from 8 am-12 noon and 2 pm-7.15 pm.

Torquay on a busy summer Saturday in 1962 was, most inconveniently for thousands of rail passengers, the location of another mishap. On 25th August, a dry day with intermittent sunshine, the down line to Torquay was heavily occupied in the afternoon so that as soon as one train unloaded its passengers at that station and cleared the platform, another train was offered from Torre. The 10.05 am Paddington to Kingswear that day comprised 14 coaches (476 tons) hauled by 'Warship' class diesel locomotive No. D833 *Panther*. On departure from Taunton the start was so slow that the driver suspected the train brakes were dragging but inspection showed this was not so. The train restarted at the second attempt using sand to assist adhesion. By the time the train reached Torquay it was 18 minutes late, as a result of signal checks.

Leaving Torquay at 2.30 pm the train made a very slow start. Despite application of maximum power and sand the train did not exceed 15 mph and was quickly brought to a stand as it reached the 1 in 56 rising gradient ¼ mile beyond Torquay station. It halted with its rear coach some 114 yards past the down advanced starting signal and thus clear of the track circuit on the approach to that signal. Knowing there was a bank engine at Torquay the secondman was immediately dispatched to ask the guard to obtain assistance.

237

On a bleak 5th January, 1960, '57XX' class 0-6-0PT No. 9678 heads the 10.35 am Hackney-Kingswear freight past Aller Vale, with Aller Junction signal box in the background. Had the proposed triangle been built (*see Chapter Seven*) it would have crossed these fields to join the Plymouth line in the left background.   *Derek J. Frost*

On the up line the driver of 2-6-2T No. 4105 running light is having a word with the Goodrington signalman before being turned into the yard. On the down line 'Grange' class 4-6-0 No. 6814 *Enborne Grange* on the 3.5 pm Exeter-Kingswear waits for the token for the section onwards to Churston, 8th April, 1960.   *Peter W. Gray*

One of the prestige Ocean Liner specials from Millbay Docks to Paddington passes Aller Junction at 5.19 pm on Easter Saturday 16th April, 1960. 'Castle' class 4-6-0 No. 5029 *Nunney Castle* leads Western Region vehicles 81015, 9112, 9598, 9113, 9114, 21447, the second, fourth and fifth being 1935 centenary stock. On a very quiet road Devon General route 12 (Brixham-Newton Abbot) nears its destination.   *Derek J. Frost*

The 6.30 am Newton Abbot to Kingswear parcels train, hauled by 'Hall' class 4-6-0 No. 4905 *Barton Hall* arrives at Churston on Saturday 2nd July, 1960. This had spent 32 minutes at Torre, 54 minutes at Paignton (much of this 'dead' time because of the business of the line) and was not due at Churston until 8.26 am. Here it would be held until 9.22 to allow two trains up from Kingswear. H31 is the engine's next working, the 12.15 Kingswear to Wolverhampton.

Peter Bowles courtesy Richard Woodley

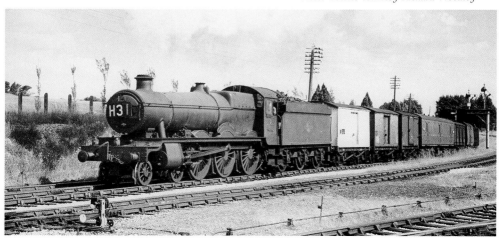

An unusual shot on Hookhills viaduct in July 1960; '14XX' 0-4-2T No. 1470 returns to Newton Abbot at the end of a day on the Brixham branch and has been coupled to '45XX' 2-6-2T No. 4566 to save on line occupation. This could well be the same day as the picture of No. 4566 in Churston down refuge.   *Peter Bowles courtesy Richard Woodley*

The mighty power of this BR Standard class '9F' No. 92248, seen here passing Noss siding on Saturday 30th July, 1960, will not be much in demand. The 5.30 pm Kingswear to Taunton on Saturdays called at every station except Silverton, Hele & Bradninch and Norton Fitzwarren, recessed at Exeter for nearly 40 minutes and was not due at Taunton until 9.15 pm.

Peter Bowles courtesy Richard Woodley

'45XX' class 2-6-2T No. 4566, the last steam locomotive to be overhauled at Newton Abbot factory, left there on 15th July, 1960, so this picture is likely to be later that month. It has possibly brought down the stock for the 9.45 am (Saturdays) Churston to Paddington which was stabled in the refuge siding there (seen here), or it may be a test train for the locomotive. A local dmu service to Kingswear ascends the steep gradient into Churston; note the backing signal (into the up loop). *Peter Bowles courtesy Richard Woodley*

A bad day for the 'Torbay Express' seen here near Aller Junction on Saturday 6th August, 1960 at 5.13 pm, 95 minutes late. The train had left Paddington behind North British 'Warship' diesel D604 which did reach Newton Abbot but had to be assisted by 'Hall' No. 6987 *Shervington Hall*. D604 was detached at Newton Abbot and sent light to Laira, the 'Torbay' continuing with No. 6987 and sister 'Hall' No. 4990 *Clifton Hall* (leading) which was attached as it was required at Paignton. *Derek J. Frost*

Crossing Maypool or Greenway viaduct on 27th August, 1960 is 'Hall' class 4-6-0 No 5992 *Horton Hall* with the summer Saturday 3.20 pm Kingswear to Cardiff.   *Peter W. Gray*

A classic shot of Torquay. On a fine sunny Saturday 9th September, 1960 'Hall' class 4-6-0 No. 4992 *Crosby Hall* leaves with the 9.05 am Swansea-Kingswear. In the middle road 2-6-2T No. 4165 waits its next turn of banking duty.   *Peter Bowles courtesy Richard Woodley*

'Warship' class No. D823 *Hermes* approaches Kingskerswell on 18th February, 1961 with the down 'Torbay Express'. In its winter schedule it left Paddington at 12.30 pm and with a call at Exeter was due at Torquay at 3.56 pm. *Derek J. Frost*

A David Fish masterpiece: on a Saturday in April 1961, Newton Abbot's own 'Castle' No. 5055 *Earl of Eldon* leaves Churston with the up 'Torbay Express'. The single car unit to Brixham is signalled out of the bay platform. *David Fish courtesy Mark S. Wilkins*

Probably on station pilot duties, '57XX' 0-6-0PT No. 9678 takes water on the down through line at Newton Abbot on Sunday 16th April, 1961. There were two station shunting engines on Sundays then, one for 24 hours and the other for 7 hours from 7.30 am.   *J. Attwood*

'County' class 4-6-0 No. 1012 *County of Denbigh* passes Torquay Gas Works on Sunday 18th June, 1961 with the 9.00 am Taunton to Kingswear. The engine has come on fresh at Newton Abbot and will next work the 1.08 pm Kingswear to Paddington (A92).   *J. Attwood*

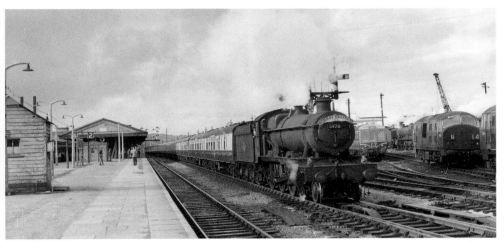

Although the 'Torbay' makes a fine sight as it passes Newton Abbot non-stop on Saturday 19th August, 1961, headed by 'Hall' No. 5978 *Bodinnick Hall*, appearances can be deceptive because it is almost 2 hours late. The shed yard is in the process of transition with steam still present, but also a dmu and two North British 'D63XX' diesels in view. *J. Attwood*

In its last year of service 'King' class 4-6-0 No. 6019 *King Henry V* makes light work of a 7-coach return party special 12.35 pm Torquay-Paddington on Torre bank, Sunday 1st April, 1962. Sadly, the locomotive was withdrawn in September. *J. Attwood*

A pleasing reminder of the Goodrington Model Railway that used to run behind the south beach; 27th May, 1962. The main line railway is out of sight to the left. *J. Attwood*

Leaving Paignton with the 11.22 am Kingswear to Newton Abbot (portion for the 11.8 am Plymouth to Cardiff), '45XX' class No. 4574 carries an 'A' headcode; 24th April, 1962. *J. Attwood*

When the 10.05 am had left Torquay platform, the signalman on duty there was immediately offered and accepted a following train. This was the 7.45 am Paddington to Paignton (via Bristol) which was running 46 minutes late following failure of its diesel locomotive at Taunton. This had been replaced by 'Hall' No. 4932 *Hatherton Hall* and the train comprised 13 coaches weighing 444 tons, slightly over the authorized load for 'Hall' class engines on the Kingswear line (24 tons over, not as has been written elsewhere 100 tons, the load limit for a 'Hall' being 420 tons between Newton Abbot and Paignton). The relieving driver at Newton Abbot had, however, agreed to take it, in view of the train 's lateness, and because he knew the engine was in good shape. The train received adverse signals all the way to Torquay and on running into the station at 2.34 pm the driver observed the starting signal on the platform end was at danger.

After station duties were finished, the signalman pulled off the starting signal to allow the 7.45 am to move down to the advanced starting signal to await acceptance. This was quite a normal procedure on Summer Saturdays and it allowed the Torquay signalman to admit another train to the platform. As the running time to the next box, Gas House Sidings, was only three minutes, most such trains in fact found the advanced starting signal 'clear' when they sighted it. A significant percentage were held here, however, because the train preceding them was in turn held at Gas House Sidings waiting acceptance by Paignton.

As soon as the 7.45 am started away *Hatherton Hall* started to slip despite the rail being dry, and the driver was fully occupied in driving the engine and getting up speed for the steep bank ahead and he missed the sighting of, and passed, the down advanced starting signal which was standing at danger. Because of line curvature the driver of a steam locomotive could only observe this signal at a range of 186 yds, and he lost sight of it at a range of 80 yards (it was then in the fireman's view). The driver was also slightly distracted by an employee of the Livermead House Hotel standing on a fire escape in line with the signal, and some 19 yards the Torquay side of it.

The guard of the failed 10.05 am was walking back to Torquay when he heard the following 7.45 am accelerating out of Torquay. He placed a detonator on the line and waved his arms to attract the driver's attention. The fireman looked up from his firing and saw the failed train three coach lengths away and its guard waving (both were out of the driver's vision). He shouted to the driver to stop, and an emergency brake application slowed the train from about 20 mph to between 5 and 10 mph, but *Hatherton Hall* collided heavily with the standing train ahead. The rear coach was forced off its bogies, and there was some telescoping of the leading two vehicles of the second train but no serious injuries. Single line working was introduced to clear the heavy incoming passenger traffic until 7.55 pm after which time the breakdown vans were given possession of the up line. From then until the line was cleared at midnight, a bus service was operated between Torquay and Paignton with a rail shuttle between Paignton and Kingswear. The down advanced starting signal was replaced by a colour light signal, slightly closer to Torquay, in 1963, as had been recommended by the MoT's Inspector.

This area of Western Region was one of the earliest to be cleared of steam locomotives because of the fierce gradients, Brunel's legacy, and consequent high cost of operation. In fact diesel working was the norm several years before other parts of the country finished steam working. Newton Abbot's steam shed was closed in June 1962 and replaced by a modern purpose-built diesel depot fashioned out of the former locomotive works. There were only two daily steam round trips to Kingswear during summer 1963 and steam had finished completely by early 1964.

Another load of coal for Torquay Gas Works leaves Kingswear yard on 12th June, 1962, with 'Hall' class No. 4978 *Westwood Hall* providing the motive power. The vessel from which the coal has been unloaded is the MV *Selectivity*.

Peter W. Gray

The accident near Torquay on Saturday 25th August, 1962, 'Hall' class 4-6-0 No. 4932 *Hatherton Hall* is embedded in the rear coach of the 10.05 am Paddington to Kingswear. *L.F. Folkard*

By 1962 the powerful 'King' class locomotives were becoming surplus to requirements. Here No. 6029 *King Edward VIII* makes possibly its last appearance at Torquay working the up 'Devonian' on 19th June, 1962 (it was withdrawn the following month). Note the fireman bringing his coal forward. The parcels van in the siding platform will be for theatrical scenery for a repertory company appearing in the town. *J.R. Besley*

Right: On the last day of operation of the Brixham branch, 11th May, 1963, a 3-car dmu leaves Churston for Brixham. The line of fish trucks in the siding will have to be loaded at this station in future.

Westcountry Publications Ltd

Below: Viewed from the footbridge at Paignton North, the crew of the 4.05 pm Kingswear to Taunton contemplate the long journey ahead, calling at all stations except Kingskerswell and Exminster; 'Hall' class No. 4902 *Aldenham Hall* provides the motive power in 1963.

J. Attwood

During the summer of 1962 it was announced that the Brixham branch would close at a date to be decided, this was one of a long list of Western Region lines to be proposed for closure just pre-Beeching. In the event the Brixham line did not close until 13th May, 1963. When the Beeching Report was made public in 1963 the Exeter-Kingswear service was shown to be a candidate for 'modification', nothing worse (although Kingskerswell was listed for closure*), but the Region was considering closure south of Paignton as early as March 1962.

The next few years were the then-familiar story of reduction of facilities. The former Aller siding was taken out of use on 8th March, 1964. Kingskerswell signal box closed at the end of the 1964 summer season on 28th September, and the station itself on 5th October, 1964 (it had ceased handling goods from 5th August, 1963). Two-way working over the up line at Torre was abolished with the removal of the facing crossover there on 1st November, 1964. Kingswear wharf, the source of so much of the line's freight traffic closed on 4th May, 1964, although the cranes remained available to unload ships until May 1968. One small piece of good news was that Britannia Halt would remain open; is costs were £50 pa and its annual revenue was estimated at £300 pa.

The Western Region tried an annual timetable for the first time in 1964; it ran from 15th June to 13th June, 1965. It was much criticized for its layout and received three large supplements before being superseded by a new timetable in January 1965. The September 1964 supplement cut back the Kingswear line Sunday service from 12 to 10 trains each way, only four of which ran beyond Paignton, and Torre and Churston lost their winter Sunday service; these changes were implemented on 4th October, 1964. On the following day a new 'rationalized' timetable was introduced with the Exeter-Kingswear (and vice versa) stopping trains withdrawn.

The two-way working through Torquay up platform was abolished on 14th February, 1965, and the facing crossover worked from Torquay ground frame taken out of use. On 31st October, 1965 the down refuge siding at Churston was taken out of use. In March 1965 the divisional manager Plymouth was again examining closure of the line beyond Paignton (Goodrington in the summer) and withdrawal of the Dartmouth ferry.

Messrs Philip & Son of Noss had their private siding agreement terminated on 18th May, 1965, the siding having been little used for some considerable time. BR said the firm would have to pay for the cost of removing the junction, but they would not do so (the firm, of course, had paid for it in the first place) and BR had to stand the cost itself. This was in any case a prelude to the withdrawal of freight facilities from Kingswear (also Torre, Churston and Paignton, apart from coal traffic) with the forthcoming implementation of the Newton Abbot freight concentration scheme (14th June, 1965).

There was a drastic alteration to the service at Kingswear with the annual timetable introduced 18th April, 1966. Henceforth the line was effectively cut in two with the section Paignton-Kingswear operated as a shuttle, apart from a few through trains at the beginning and end of the day. The number of Summer Saturday holiday trains running beyond Paignton was halved and the well-established 9.45 am Churston to Paddington now started from Paignton.

An interesting letter from the divisional movements manager at Bristol to Regional HQ dated 10th May, 1966 reveals that when this shuttle service was planned by the former Plymouth Division it was thought that the line beyond Paignton South would be operated as two separate single lines to Goodrington and Kingswear respectively, also that additional facilities would be provided at Paignton. This had not been done and the only way was for the train to run into the

* A winter census revealed only 33 passengers daily, with 45 during the summer.

British Railways Western Region

Divisional Headquarters
Plymouth Station
Plymouth Devon
Plymouth 62888 Ext.2313.

C. Hankins   Divisional Manager Plymouth

y/r
o/r XF75/78/M.

Date 17th May,1965.

Dear Sirs,

You will be aware that the closure of small freight stations is being undertaken in accordance with the Plan for the Re-shaping of British Railways under which freight concentration depots are being established at the larger centres.

I am now able to inform you of my proposals to withdraw general freight facilities from the following stations on and from Monday, 14th June, 1965 as a major step forward in the establishment of the Newton Abbot Concentration Scheme:-

Bovey	Teignmouth	Torre
Chudleigh	Totnes	Churston
Heathfield		Paignton
		Kingswear Wharves

Coal traffic will continue to pass to each of these stations, except Kingswear Wharves, pending implementation of the Coal Concentration Scheme at Newton Abbot, on which a separate advice will be issued in due course. Facilities for dealing with specific traffics will be retained at certain stations as indicated below:-

Bovey - Traffic for Messrs.Wyatt and Bruce Ltd. and Messrs.Vono Ltd.
Chudleigh - Gas oil in tank wagons.
Heathfield - Clay and private siding traffic.

Facilities will also be retained for serving the Quay lines at Totnes and Teignmouth.

With the exceptions listed, all wagon loads will be dealt with at Newton Abbot and I am confident that the service you will be given under these proposals will be satisfactory in every way. If, however, you have any questions regarding your particular traffic, or rail transport generally, please do not hesitate to communicate with me.

Yours faithfully,

Marketing and Sales Manager.

The divisional manager Plymouth's advice to traders that general freight facilities would be withdrawn from Torre, Paignton, Churston and Kingswear from 14th June, 1965.

Courtesy Peter Kay

(up) PLA bay platform involving the clipping and padlocking of points (and leading to delays at the Sands Road level crossing). This was particularly critical on Summer Saturdays when the scheduled timetable could not always be adhered to; the movements manager called for an urgent meeting to recast the timetable.

Torquay ground frame (the erstwhile North signal box) closed on 17th July, 1966, replaced by a one-lever ground frame on the upside working the remaining trailing connection from up main to up sidings. Torre lost its downside goods shed sidings in July 1966 and the meat sidings (south end of station) and south crossover in November 1966. In September 1966 a proposal was submitted for the complete closure of Torre station, although passenger revenue was £21,934 and staff costs £6,855. It was thought that the passenger revenue would transfer to Torquay.

Gas House Siding signal box closed on 4th December, 1966 and the layout was simplified so that the only main line connection remaining was a trailing lead from down main to the sidings, worked by a 1-lever ground frame. This meant that the sidings could only be served by down trains.

When Mr J.J. Donovan, BR's Devon & Cornwall Manager, addressed a joint meeting of the Torquay, Paignton and Brixham Chambers of Trade in October 1966, he told them that the railway's share of the West Country holiday traffic had dropped from 50 per cent, 10 years earlier, to 10-12 per cent currently. The private car had extracted the balance. Mr Donovan said that the line to Paignton covered its direct costs but the section onwards to Kingswear did not and was in a 'suspect position'. In his view there should be one station (at Torquay) serving Torbay (this met a very hostile reception from the press and traders and public and was not, fortunately, proceeded with). Mr Donovan told the meeting that with 30 through services on Saturdays from all parts of the country 'you have the best service of any holiday resort in the country'. The pages of history were turned back when one of Mr Donovan's listeners suggested that 'Torre might attract more holiday traffic if it was renamed 'Torquay North', and another that Churston should be renamed 'Brixham Road'! The latter idea was strongly supported by the Brixham representatives but neither was followed through.

From 24th September, 1967 Kingswear lost its winter Sunday train service, the four down and five up services being replaced by only two buses to and from Paignton. Following a meeting with the Town Clerk of Dartmouth and the Planning Officer of Devon County Council, two additional buses each way were put on from 26th November connecting with evening train services.

Since 14th June, 1965 Torre and Paignton's goods facilities had only been used for the reception of coal traffic, all other goods being delivered from Newton Abbot by road. Now, on 4th December, 1967 both stations, plus Churston, were closed to all goods traffic. Fish traffic from Brixham would be sent to Newton Abbot by road. In practice it probably went by road throughout, lost to BR. The Brixham branch line and branch sidings at Churston were recovered in 1968.

A group of Torquay schoolboys did a survey of the line in 1968 for a school project, and we must be grateful to them for their observations which are in the Torquay Reference Library.

Kingskerswell – The ticket hall and waiting room form a 2 storey building on the upside with outside access a first floor level. There are two flights of stairs from the booking office to the waiting room at platform level. There is another waiting/ladies room on the platform (the buildings had been completely demolished by April 1968 but the platforms remained intact).

Churston – Noted 14th June, 1968 track removed from the goods yard and Brixham bay [taken out of use 16th February]. Bay waiting hut removed [demolished during w.e. 2nd March] and gap filled with new fencing, different concrete posts and closer spaced wooden slats. 'Churston for Brixham' signboards intact on bay and up platform – latter not used except to cross trains (none were booked to cross there). Signal box still open and Booking Office open for enquiries. The siding behind the up platform is still in place.

Britannia Halt – Signal box and crossing are named Steam Ferry Crossing. Two trains per day stop for Philip's Boat Yard workmen. The halt consists of a low short, wooden platform with an all-over canopy and name board on the back wall. The crossing has two hand operated gates and the small ground frame operates 2 distant signals as well as locking the gates. There is also a gate keeper's house.

Kingswear – The quay sidings have been removed and the site fenced off and used as a car park entered via the bridge under the hotel. The turntable has been removed and well filled with rubble. The sidings nearer the turntable and two of those parallel to the main line (the two nearest the river) have been removed.

A letter from the Estate Surveyor, Slough dated 1st July, 1968 said that all loading and unloading of ships at Kingswear wharf had ceased two months ago 'with the withdrawal from use of the quayside cranes', which were being sold. 'No rail freight service now operates to Kingswear', although the goods shed was still in use as a store by crab fishermen and BR's marine department (for ferry operations' material). Kingswear docks had been profitable until 1963 as the following figures show:

1962 + £4,630; 1963 + £3,336; 1964 - £619; 1965 - £607; 1966 - £374
1967 - £1,649; 1968 - £1,198

The summer of 1968 saw the withdrawal of the Sunday service to Torre and Churston stations, and the buses between Paignton and Kingswear forming the winter Sunday service were not reintroduced. Conductor-guard working had been introduced on 20th May, leading to the withdrawal of booking clerks at Churston and Kingswear. There was no longer a need for a crossing loop at Churston, and this and the up siding and signal box were taken out of use on 20th October, 1968. The box at Kingswear was closed the same day but here a run-round loop was retained worked by two ground frames. The section Paignton-Kingswear was submitted to the TUCC for closure in November 1968,* that body dealt with the case in March 1969 and decided that hardship caused by closure would be substantially alleviated by additional bus services, although it recognised that some hardship would arise particularly during the holiday season. In the meantime BR applied to the Ministry of Transport for 'transitional grant' to keep the service running whilst the alterations to bus services were considered.

Although water under the bridge now, because the closure was not proceeded with at this time, at the meeting with staff representatives held on 30th October, 1968, the drivers' staff representative challenged Management's figure of £17,000 revenue earned, asking that 'surely there was a contributory revenue figure?' The management chairman replied that the figure of £17,000 was the revenue figure for the branch.

---

* This despite the fact that passenger counts in May and August 1968 revealed the following average number of daily users between Paignton and Kingswear; May (M-F) 961, (Sat) 622; August (M-F) 1,192, (Sat) 2,067, (Sun) 628. Costs were £54,500 and direct revenue £17,100 but significantly no allowance was made for contributory revenue (e.g. arriving passengers) which would be very substantial on this section. Some 271 objections to the closure were received by the TUCC.

The management chairman was misinformed, however; the file papers under 'contributory revenue' show 'no assessment made'. The figure of £17,060 was reached on the number of passenger miles over the section of line, 1,735,004 at 2.36*d*. per mile, equals £17,061.

Further questions must have been asked and a letter from the Chief Accountant to the divisional manager, Bristol dated 11th November, 1968 gives contributory revenue from three flows of traffic: local, Paddington-West of England and Birmingham-West of England, each for *just one week*, as totalling £1,066. None of these weeks included summer Saturdays and two of them were in the winter months. Also in the same file of papers, *originating* passenger revenue for Kingswear for the five years 1963-1967 is an average of £24,231 and for Churston £9,923. The Kingswear figure would have included ferry receipts but if £9,000 is allowed for this (1968 figure was £9,397) this still leaves these stations directly earning an average of £25,000 per annum, considerably more than the £17,000 the closure papers stated.

The closure proposal paper to the TUCC dated November 1968 also showed £17,100 as the earnings of this section but a statement attached to a letter from divisional manager Bristol to RHQ Paddington dated 11th December, 1968 for the first time included contributory revenue of £54,400; this sum effectively covered the costs of running the line (£54,500) and leaving a 'profit' of £17,000! However, their 'sums' showed that if the line closed £19,800 of the present total revenue (£71,500) was expected to lost but so would the expenses, meaning that BR was £34,700 better off from closure:

Before: Revenue £71,500	Expenses £54,500	Profit £17,000
After: Revenue £51,700	Expenses £ Nil	Profit £51,700

One suspects that the amount of revenue expected to be retained after closure is highly questionable; in any case expenses would not have been nil as Devon General advised in January 1969 that they would require a subvention payment of £7,600 to run replacement buses on an hourly service between Paignton and Kingswear. Why were these figures not put to either staff or TUCC? The answer can be found in *British Railways 1948-1973 A Business History* by T.R. Gourvish on page 437: contributory gross revenue figures were *only* given to the Ministry of Transport, even TUCCs being kept in the dark!

Torquay box was switched out semi-permanently in October 1968, in future only being brought into use on Summer Saturdays. However, there was an unexpected, but short-lived reprieve for the box on the night of 20th November, 1968, when the 10.05 am Bradford to Paignton, hauled by D1033 working on one engine, failed between Torquay and Paignton at about 5.45 pm. The 5.19 pm Exeter to Paignton (portion off the 2.30 pm Paddington) arrived at Torre at 6.05 pm but this was hauled by D816 also working on one engine and was considered inadequate to assist on the 1 in 56 gradient, so the Aller banker was called. However, during his enforced wait the driver of D816 managed to start his second engine and was allowed into the section to assist at 6.30 pm. On arrival at the failed train, it was found that the 10.05 Bradford had stopped on the catchpoint and it was considered that the train would slip backwards with only D816 to assist; the Aller banker was by now at Torre, but then a further complication arose! A contractor's inspector stationed at bridgeworks at 220¼ mp (Cockington Lane) said that the vibration from two engines assisting in rear might cause the bridge to partially collapse. Arrangements were made, therefore, for Torquay box to be reopened by the ex-signalman and the 10.05

The renewal of the Cockington Lane underbridge in January 1969 using two steam cranes.
L.F. Folkard

On the inaugural day for the Dart Valley Railway operations on the Paignton to Kingswear section, 31st December, 1972, 2-6-2T No. 4588 leaves Kingswear hauling three auto-trailers brought over from Buckfastleigh. *Peter W. Gray*

Bradford was drawn back to Torquay, arriving there at 8.10 pm. After attaching the Aller banker to the front it finally left 162 minutes late, having delayed the 5.19 pm Exeter 142 minutes and the 5.40 pm Exeter to Paignton 132 minutes!

A further deterioration in service was spelt out by the May 1969 timetable, whereby the Summer Sunday service between Paignton and Kingswear was withdrawn, but at least the threatened section of line remained open.

During 1971/2 talks took place between British Rail Western Region and the Dart Valley Railway Co., who ran the Totnes-Buckfastleigh branch, regarding the possibility of sale of the line below Goodrington to the Dart Valley Co. (DVR). BR said that the line made an annual deficit of £47,000 (costs £61,000, earnings £14,000) and that either the line must be subsidized, sold or closed. These figures were given in the closure publicity - note, still no contributory revenue! Eventually negotiations were concluded for the sale of the line below Goodrington (223 m.) to the DVR Co for £250,000, plus the cost of altering the layout at Paignton South which was £25,000. The date of purchase was 30th December, 1972. Included in the price was the Royal Dart Hotel at Kingwear (this was sold for £125,000 in 1979) and of course, all land. The independent company recouped most of their outlay by the sale of surplus land. The 1931 goods station at Goodrington accounted for 15 acres of land which was sold with planning permission to build flats.

The ensuing account of activities on the Paignton-Kingswear section does not purport to be fully comprehensive but only records the highlights.

Park Sidings behind the down platform at Paignton were also included in the sale and this became the site of Paignton Queen's Park station for the company, later retitled Torbay & Dartmouth Railway, later still the Paignton & Dartmouth Railway and in 2010 it became the Dartmouth Steam Railway and River Boat Company. The company had undertaken to keep a skeleton service going during the winter months and to take pupils to and from Churston Grammar School from Paignton and Kingswear. (For this latter arrangement they were paid by Devon County Council.)

Signalling alterations took place at Paignton between 5th and 13th November, 1972 to separate the Dart Valley operations from those of BR. The down BR line was slued into the up line at Paignton South box and continued as a single line to the carriage sidings at Goodrington. The former down BR line became the DVR single line with access to the new station at Queens Park only, although there was a crossover between the two single lines, south of the South level crossing, to enable BR trains to have access to the DVR (for specials, etc). The line between Paignton South and 223 milepost (north of Goodrington) still belongs to Network Rail and is used by the Dartmouth Steam Railway under 'running powers'. Goodrington signal box was closed on 1st November, 1972.

BR officially closed the route on 28th October, 1972 but for the next two months ran a reduced dmu service on behalf of the Dart Valley Railway. To enable the line to continue running without a break, Devon County Council had subsidized the cost of BR's operation whilst the DVR conducted the complex negotiations and obtained their Light Railway Order; the line passed into DVR ownership on 30th December, 1972. At last, on 31st December, 1972, 2-6-2T No. 4588 worked the inaugural DVR steam service from Paignton to Kingswear and back and two other return trips. A regular service of four return steam-hauled trains daily (including the school journeys) started on 1st January, 1973. Regrettably these trains ran for only the one season, after which the council subsidies were withdrawn, the service being found 'uneconomic'. Unfortunately the company did not possess a dmu which would have been a less costly proposition to run. But the new owner had found out for himself

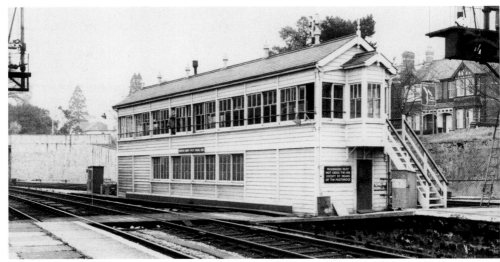

Newton Abbot West signal box, photographed on 13th April, 1971.   *S. Montgomery/D. Nicholas*

Newton Abbot West signal box interior with signalman Stan Rowe working the frame. This was a single-handed box with a booking boy, unlike East box which employed two signalmen and a booking boy.   *D.E. Canning*

On 30th May, 1971, a 3-car dmu stands in the former parcels bay at Paignton. This line was not normally used for passenger working as the points had to be clipped and padlocked.
The late John C. Gillham

After the removal of signalling at Kingswear and reduction to a basic shuttle service, a 3-car dmu leaves for Paignton on 18th September, 1971.   *D.H. Mitchell*

A family of holidaymakers, who have climbed the steps from Hollacombe beach, pause to watch 'Western' class diesel-hydraulic No. 1047 *Western Lord* hauling the 12.26 Paddington-Paignton pass the site of Torquay Gas Works on Saturday 6th September, 1975. The gas storage tanks were still standing although the rest of the works had been demolished.   *Mark S. Wilkins*

On Sunday 5th March, 1978 a railtour from Paddington to Par via Paignton brought 'Deltic' No. 55003 *Meld* onto the line. Here the locomotive, making light work of a heavy train and rising gradient, approaches Torquay up distant signal. (Until December 1966 this signal post carried the up home signal for Torquay Gas Works box as its top arm.) The 'Deltic' came off at Newton Abbot for servicing and was replaced by class '46' No. 46003 for the journey to Cornwall
                Mark S. Wilkins

what BR already knew; holiday lines conveying thousands of tourists in the summer did not usually 'pay' in the winter.

The summer 1973 DVR service was probably also too optimistic, and appeared to be trying to emulate the one-time BR peak service with departures from Paignton starting at 7.28 am and finishing at 7.35 pm (nine round trips). There was an even later 8.55 pm departure in July and August which did not arrive back at Paignton until 10.03 pm. By 1974 the service had been reduced to six round trips between 10 am and 6 pm from Paignton.

Reinstatement was the order of the day for the Torbay Steam Railway as it was known at this time, and the bay line at Kingswear was put back in the summer of 1976. A much bigger project was the re-installation of a passing loop and controlling signal box at Churston, to enable a two-train service to be worked at the busy summer peak. All the semaphore signalling and the brick-built signal box on the down platform had been removed by BR so it was necessary to start from scratch. It was decided to provide a power lever frame as this is much quicker to install and does not need the specialized skills necessary to maintain a mechanized locking frame. Furthermore it was decided to introduce colour light signalling 'after much heart searching' as the company's General Manager put it. The box was brought into operation for the peak service of July 1979. When Churston box was open the Paignton-Churston section was worked by Train Staff and Ticket with Telephone block whilst Churston to Kingswear was 'One Train Only' (or 'One Engine in Steam'). When Churston was closed the whole line was 'One Train Only'. In 1980 the Train Staff and Ticket Working (Paignton-Churston) was replaced by Electric Token Working. In November 1980 the bay line track at Churston was reinstated, but, sadly, not for Brixham branch trains as the branch trackbed had been built over. Churston box closed on 1st February, 1986, with control for the entire line passing to a signalling panel at Britannia Crossing. The loop points at Churston were set for the normal facing movements and self restored after trailing movements. Britannia Crossing signal box is only staffed during the operating season. During the winter the line is controlled by the Permanent Way & Civil Engineering supervisor who gives permission for every movement.

Summer 1981 saw the bringing into use of the turntable, formerly in use at Goodrington for the relatively short period of 1957-64, on a new site at Churston (old goods yard). The equipment was immediately used to turn coaches to even out the wear on wheels. Andrew Fiderkiewicz was part of the working party that moved the turntable from its original pit. He says:

The way we did it was an H&S nightmare. Sleepers were built up under the central pin, jacking and packing as we went until it tottered on a framework of sleepers. It was then dragged out by a tractor and winch and I think it went up to Churston after being loaded on a flat wagon by the steam crane that the DV railway had at the time (it had to be done on the BR metals that still ran into those extensive sidings). We then dug a pit with a tractor 'back actor' [shovel], laid a circular set of formwork and concrete was then poured for the base of the circular rail.

Back on the BR part of the line, there was a rather worrying incident on 5th September, 1980 when the 10.28 am Leeds-Paignton arrived at Torre at 5.22 pm with the diesel locomotive, class '45' No. 45038, on fire. After the fire was put out another class '45' was sent from Newton Abbot to assist the train forward, arriving at 6.25 pm. However, the Fire Officer, refused to allow the train to go forward with passengers and they had to be detrained and left Torre at about 7.10 pm on the considerably delayed 5.25 pm Exeter-Paignton. The Leeds coaching stock and disabled engine were taken back to Newton Abbot.

A minor plus point was the restoration of Torre's Sunday service from 29th January, 1984 - the first Sunday service there since September 1967, and the first Winter Sunday service since September 1964.

In May 1986 BR said they were considering a major facelift for Paignton station in about three years' time.

New 'Skipper' 2-car diesel units were introduced in 1986 but these are cramped and uncomfortable and have little luggage space.

The other source of investment has been in new signalling. All semaphore signalling has disappeared from the area. First to go of the remaining boxes was Torquay which closed on 15th November, 1984 (it had lost its crossover in 1974 and was only opened on Summer Saturdays after 1968). Torre closed on 5th October, 1986 (also having lost its last crossover in 1974) and latterly only being opened on Summer Saturdays. The block section was then Aller Junction to Paignton North which was 12 minutes running time, including calls at Torre and Torquay.

Newton Abbot also had to share in this misery and during the weekend of 25th/26th April, 1987 was reduced to a three-platform station, the former up main platform being taken out of use and the track lifted. The four-track section between Newton Abbot West and Aller Jn reverted to its pre-1925 arrangement, whereby the physical junctions at Aller were removed (and the signal box closed) and new connections put in at Newton Abbot West between the two pairs of lines. Reading from north to south the four lines between Aller and Newton Abbot are:

Up main (former up main)
Down main (former up relief)
Up Torbay (former down main)
Down Torbay (former down relief)

However, over ¼ mile of the former down relief between Newton Abbot West and Aller was removed so that down and up Torbay trains had to share a single line for this distance (to 214 m. 51 ch.), which seems a very small saving in infrastructure to balance the loss of flexibility when the timetable plan is upset by late running.

For a week the block section on the Torbay line was now Newton Abbot West to Paignton, and a special timetable was introduced to cope with this situation and the temporarily restricted layout at Newton Abbot, where only the down relief platform was available to Torbay trains.

But a week later it was Newton Abbot's turn, and the two majestic signal boxes were closed and large signal gantries removed* during the weekend of 1st/4th May, 1987. Exeter Panel took control of the signalling to Paignton North and Totnes (both exclusive).

The three remaining lines through Newton Abbot station, up main (former up relief), down main and down relief were all made bi-directional. The traffic handling capability of the Torquay line was improved by the installation of three intermediate signals in each direction. Paignton North box closed on 26th March, 1988, control of its level crossing (by CCTV) being transferred to Paignton South box.

An unexpected development in October 1987 was the withdrawal of all 13 'Skippers' allocated to Laira, which worked to Paignton amongst their duties, and their transfer to the North East and North West of England. They were replaced by

---

* One of the large gantries was preserved by the Chairman of David & Charles, publishers, and now graces their courtyard. It is still there in 2013 but is no longer 'David & Charles'.

conventional dmus, until they could be replaced by the more reliable and comfortable 'Sprinters'. Unfortunately, the 'Pacers', as the 'Skippers' later became known, were reintroduced to the area in the 2000s.

The Annual report of the Railway Heritage Trust for 1987/8 noted that they had made a grant of £20,000 to restore the 'heritage aspects' of Torquay station and a further £3,000 to repair or restore the nearby Hennapyn Road bridge.

Paignton South signal box was closed between 5th and 11th August, 1989, together with all mechanical signalling, and control transferred to a new panel located in the booking office. The level crossing at Sands Road, at the south end of the layout, became trainmen operated. The connection to the Torbay & Dartmouth Railway was controlled by a ground frame released by the new panel.

There was a tremendous coup for the Paignton & Dartmouth Steam Railway on Friday 10th April, 1992, when it hosted a Royal Train from Slough conveying the Duke of Edinburgh. The Duke was coming to take the salute at the Royal Naval College passing-out parade, and also to dedicate a Book of Remembrance to all special entry officers who had died or been killed in wartime. The Duke himself is the oldest surviving special entry wartime cadet trained at Dartmouth.

The Royal Train left Slough, two minutes early, at 10 pm the previous night and was stabled in Devon between 2.05 and 8.05 am. Calling at Exeter St Davids at 8.53 am, it was timed to run at only 40 mph between there and Paignton, presumably to fit in with the required arrival time at Kingswear (maybe the Duke wanted to enjoy the sea views of this attractive stretch of line!). At Paignton the preserved railway's pilot driver proudly stepped aboard to pilot the InterCity driver over the seven miles of private railway. Arrival at Kingswear was at 10.10 am where the Duke and his party detrained and crossed the river for his engagement at the College. After running-round its train, the class '47' diesel locomotive hauled the empty 5-coach Royal Train back to the London Midland Region via Bristol and Barnt Green, leaving at 10.35 am. This was just before the start of the steam railway's operating season so did not inconvenience them, although the local paper reported that Kingswear station had had an 'extra special buffing-up' and Torquay and Paignton stations had also been spruced up.

Marina level crossing, just outside Kingswear, was opened on 24th January, 1993. This is a private crossing for the use of an adjacent boat builder and is controlled by CCTV operated from Britannia Crossing signal box.

In March 1993, audacious thieves helped themselves to one of Torquay's heavyweight platform clocks, despite it being suspended 12 ft above the Paignton-bound platform. According to the local newspaper it was worth £5,000. Its twin, on the up platform, was swiftly removed and locked away in secure storage.

Adverse weather at the end of 1993 caused the Newton Abbot-Paignton line to close briefly due to flooding between 4 and 4.45 pm on 30th December, 1993. Less lucky was the line between Newton Abbot and Plymouth which closed at 5.39 pm from the same cause and did not open completely until 9.40 am on 31st December.

At 9.56 am on 25th March, 1994 the 9.40 am Paignton-Cardiff class '158' Sprinter unit was signalled, under permissive working arrangements, into the already occupied platform 3 at Newton Abbot where the late running 7.20 am Penzance-Edinburgh HST was standing. The Sprinter unit collided with the rear of the HST, injuring the Sprinter driver and 34 passengers, mostly from shock but one man with a suspected ruptured spleen was removed by air ambulance. Eventually the Sprinter driver was found to be at fault through not reducing his train's speed sufficiently. After this incident BR greatly reduced the number of locations where permissive working of passenger trains was permitted (i.e. two trains sharing the same stretch of line at a station).

The Exeter Rail Fair in May 1994 (celebrating 150 years of railways to Exeter) saw the reinstatement, for one day only, of the steam-hauled 'Torbay Express' in this case only between Exeter and Kingswear. However, in subsequent years the train became a regular feature, eventually running weekly on Sundays in the Summer season between Bristol and Kingswear.

Privatization of British Rail took place over the period 1994-1997, with all but one freight business sold by April 1997.

In November 1995 the *Western Morning News* reported a Devon County Council proposed to extend the (by then) Regional Railways local services between Exeter and Paignton to Churston with a major park and ride at Churston to cost £675,000. A separate scheme by the County Council suggested the re-opening of Kingskerswell station at an estimated cost of £410,000 (this idea would resurface many more times in subsequent years). The projects could be completed within four years but neither came to pass despite Kingskerswell being strongly supported by Regional Railways. Interestingly, in mid-2009, the Association of Train Operators floated a similar idea to extend First Great Western local services to Churston, but without the associated park and ride. The Dart Valley Railway (the owners of the line, although it traded as the Paignton & Dartmouth Steam Railway) complained it had not been consulted and that there was no spare track capacity in the summer holiday period. This makes it unlikely that this idea will succeed. A practical possibility, however, is an exchange or Parkway station at Goodrington if Happy Valley siding behind the up platform was upgraded to a running line and the platform made into an 'island'. There is a large car park adjacent, in the old carriage sidings area.

What started as a proposal early in 1997 to tidy up Torquay station, following complaints of vandalism there, developed into a plan by recently formed Railtrack to spend £450,000 on improvements. These would include new drainage, new tarmac in the courtyard and repainting of the station in red, green and gold. A 25-strong workforce was employed by contractor Dean & Dyball. In a separate action, the redundant signal box at Torquay was leased to a Torquay-based wine tours company as an office. It remains in private commercial use to this day.

The following year it was the turn of Torre, in its 150th birthday year to receive major expenditure from Railtrack (the press said £200,000) to resurface the platform, refurbish the footbridge, install CCTV and modern information signs. Additionally the Railway Heritage Trust gave £5,000 to replace the upside waiting shelter and Torbay Council £500 to re-roof the preserved Torre signal box. This was leased by the Torre Signal Box Preservation group, although it is no longer being used by them and is boarded up.

There was a brief re-use of Goodrington sidings for freight in the autumn of 1998 with shipments of 1,500 tons of stone every two weeks from Whatley Quarry in Somerset. The stone was to be used by communications firm Eurobell to fill in the holes left from the laying of their cable TV and phone network.

Consultants Halcrow, Fox, who were carrying out an in-depth study of road gridlock problems on behalf of the three South Devon councils and the rail firms in autumn 2000, came up with a proposal for a new station and park and ride at Kerswell Gardens, south of Kingskerswell village and at the start of the Torbay ring road. Nothing came of this scheme which, according to a local press report, would have cost about £2 million.

In March 2000 a new rail company name (Wales & West) and a new man at the top produced plans for a revamp of Torquay station, including turning empty offices into business units and a new waiting lounge on the up platform but it became, once again, a 'might-have been' as with so many other plans for the line since privatization.

In October 2001, vandals set fire to Torre Station footbridge, fortunately not destroying it but putting it out of use for a fortnight, during which time up direction passengers were conveyed by bus. The bridge had only recently been renovated at a cost of £150,000, according to the local press.

Also that month a long-standing member of the local railway community, Tom Punshon retired from the position of station supervisor at Paignton Queens Park (steam railway) after no less than 53 years' railway service. Starting with BR in 1948 at Torquay, Tom had progressed, including 21 years as a passenger guard at Newton Abbot, until being made redundant as station chargeman at Paignton (BR) in 1987. He missed the life so much he joined the steam railway four months later. As a passenger guard on BR Tom was well known to this author as he worked the Brixham branch in his regular duties.

Torre goods yard had lost its rail connection in 1969 but continued to be used for handling and distribution of coal by road. However, in May 2002 it was announced that its user, CPL Industries Ltd, was rationalizing its coal depots and that Torre was one of 10 that would be closed before October 2002 with a loss of 15 local jobs. In December Torre station celebrated its 154th birthday by the erection of new running-in boards painted chocolate with off-white lettering, thanks to a £1,000 donation from Midas Homes.

Members of the Dart Valley Railway (the Paignton to Kingswear operation) heard at their annual general meeting in July 2003 that the sale of the Totnes-Buckfastleigh operation to the South Devon Railway had resulted in a book profit for 2002 of over £1¼ million. Stripping out the sales proceeds from the figures left an operating profit of £208,021, compared with £68,707 in 2001. During the previous winter considerable relaying of track approaching and at Kingswear had taken place and repairs made to Greenway viaduct, Goodrington sea wall, river walls at Kingswear and to Churston station canopy. In August 2003 a plaque was installed at Kingswear station to commemorate the centenary of the death of Charles Seale Hayne who had done so much to bring the railway to Kingswear and who had founded the Dartmouth Harbour Commissioners.

'Routine maintenance work' one night in August 2003 was the cause of the Network Rail line shutting for more than eight hours. Maintenance gangs were using a rail grinding machine and it is thought sparks set fire to the sleepers. About 90 separate fires were discovered from 4.30 am onwards (another newspaper said 400 fires) along a seven mile stretch between Torre and Newton Abbot requiring 30 firefighters to deal with the problem. Train services were cancelled for most of the morning and Network Rail had to remove and replace the damaged sleepers. (Not something that would have occurred in BR days, I suspect.)

In 2004 Greenway tunnel walls were repaired and in 2005 the track through the tunnel was relaid. Despite its age the tunnel does not cause any particular problems; it receives a thorough check every year.

In September 2005 the Dart Valley Railway announced that it wished to spend £1.5 million upgrading its Paignton Queen's Park station which was 'unable to cope with rising visitor numbers'. A principal part of this upgrading involved turning the adjacent former Torbay Cinema (a Grade II listed building owned by the company) into a walk through terminal, café and souvenir shop. This proved highly controversial as local residents and conservationists are keen to see the building restored to its original purpose and at the time of writing has not taken place. The station rebuilding eventually took place during the winter of 2011/12 and was opened for the 2012 season at a cost of £1.2 million.

Thought to be the first time the Royal Train has run on privately-owned track, on 10th April, 1992 class '47' No. 47834 *Firefly* arrives at Kingswear with HRH the Duke of Edinburgh on board. The Duke was on his way to the Britannia Royal Naval College, Dartmouth (*top left*), for the annual passing-out parade. *Mark S. Wilkins*

Some 70 years separate the introduction of these two forms of traction. 'King' class 4-6-0 No. 6024 *King Edward I* (built 1930) climbs the bank out of Torquay with the 'Anniversary Limited' from Paddington to Kingswear on Saturday 2nd July, 2005, exactly 75 years to the day of its building. On the up line a Virgin 'Voyager' (built 2000) cruises past with the 12.30 Paignton to Glasgow. The Livermead House Hotel in the background (formerly Livermead House) was originally intended to be passed by the railway on the sea side (*see plan p.27*). *Mark S. Wilkins*

Minor improvements during the autumn period 2005 included a new cycle shelter at Paignton (Network Rail) station and the complete restoration of the footbridge at Torre, damaged in the arson attack in 2001.

Rail News reported that from 21st November, 2005 the line speed on the up line between Torre and Newton Abbot had been increased from 45 mph to 55 mph for passenger trains giving a 30 second saving in time between Paignton and Newton Abbot, reversing a reduction of speed imposed by BR in the 1980s to save money. The portion of up line between 217 m. 70 ch. and 215 m. 20 ch. was later raised to 60 mph and the down line from 216 m. 17 ch. to 217 m. 68 ch. was also raised to 60 mph, both speeds applicable only to passenger trains. Provision was made, and instructions issued, for First Great Western HSTs to call at Torre, with its fairly short platforms, from the December 2006 timetable onwards.

In March 2007 the local papers were full of the fact that the biggest investor in the Dart Valley Railway, David Barry, a millionaire living in the Channel Islands, had given an interview to the *Railway Magazine* commenting adversely on the way the railway was run. The Board had responded that they 'recognised what needed to be done and will do it in its own time, in a measured and humane manner'. It was intended to restore Paignton station, improve marketing and rebrand the company (the investor complained about the different titles the company used) – this was eventually done in 2010, the concern becoming the Dartmouth Steam Railway & River Boat Company. Later Mr Barry became a Directory of the company.

The same month the local newspaper reported that the roof sheeting of the station building at Kingswear was being replaced like-for-like. In October 2007, Churston Grammar School celebrated its 50th anniversary and the Dart Valley Railway gave them an anniversary present, worth £3,000, by providing a steam train for the day to take past and present pupils to the school - as used to be the daily routine when the school opened. The driver was Peter Roach, now 48, Churston's workshop foreman who was a student there in the 1970s. A few weeks later, long serving general manager Barry Cogar retired, he had been in charge ever since the line was bought from BR - possibly a record for a heritage railway?

The electric token working between Paignton and Churston was withdrawn in 2009 and the whole line became Track Circuit Block (Single line), after which it was possible to have two trains at Kingswear at the same time.

In August 2009 plans were published for the development at a cost of £175 million of Noss Marina, sited on the old Philip & Son shipyard. There would be 137 private homes, £12 million worth of affordable homes, a five star hotel, conference centre and offices. It was reported that the 'Paignton & Dartmouth railway' would be used to transport materials to the project, although I am informed no siding was envisaged. The development would create 330 permanent jobs. At the time of writing no development has taken place.

The year 2011 was the 150th anniversary of Churston station and the steam railway held a major heritage festival between 28th to 30th May to celebrate the fact, but also with a World War II theme. The paint shop at Churston station was given over to a display of model railways and photographs of the station. There was also a display of World War II military vehicles on the upside near the locomotive workshop which was open to visitors who could see work in progress inside. A special train ran conveying passengers dressed in World War II period uniforms and clothing. 'Manor' class 4-6-0 No. 7827 *Lydham Manor* was repainted black and masqueraded as No. 7800 *Torquay Manor* for the occasion. A blue plaque commemorating Churston's 150 years was unveiled by retired railwayman Rod

The year 2011 was the 150th anniversary of the opening of Churston station. To celebrate that event the Dartmouth Steam Railway staged a Heritage weekend and their locomotive No. 7827 was repainted in black and became No. 7800 *Torquay Manor*. On 29th May, 2011 'No. 7800' arrives at Churston with the 'Torbay Express'. There was a display of World War II vehicles in the upside yard area.   *S.M. Potts*

On 30th May, 2011 'Manor' class 4-6-0 No. 7800 *Torquay Manor* has just passed Britannia Crossing on its way to Churston. As explained above, this was really No. 7827 *Lydham Manor*, repainted in black and renamed and renumbered to celebrate 150 years of Churston station.

Mark S. Wilkins

Sanders and Jack Eveleigh, both of whom had worked at Churston in GWR and BR days.

Also in 2011 the Dartmouth Steam Railway restored the old up platform at Goodrington to use. Although regularly used, it is normally only used for crossing movements in the event of late running or special events.

In Autumn 2011 there was a welcome reduction in the number of trains on the national network locally covered by former BR ex-'Pacer' units and their replacement by class '150s' brought in from the Midlands. However, they are not yet entirely eliminated.

Some 100 years since the inhabitants of Greenway village asked for a halt, the Dartmouth Steam Railway opened one in 2012. It is able to accommodate two coaches and trains in either direction will call there, despite the fierce gradient in the up direction. Its principal purpose is to serve nearby Greenway House, once Agatha Christie's holiday home (and formerly that of Richard Harvey, see page 36), now a much-visited National Trust property. The halt was brought into service on 28th April, 2012, with a ceremonial opening on 26th July. I was told that use of the halt had been 'good, mainly by walkers, rather than people going to Greenway House, an unexpected source of income'.

The new halt at Greenway. On 5th July, 2012 'Manor' class 4-6-0 No. 7827 *Lydham Manor* leaves there with a train for Kingswear and will shortly enter Greenway tunnel.

Mark S. Wilkins

In May 2013 the local newspaper, the *Herald Express* announced 'A multi-million pound investment' for South Devon railway stations. Torre, Torquay and Paignton would share over £3.5 million pounds, to be spent on refurbishment and redecoration, the work mostly taking place between October 2013 and March 2014. At Torre, £150,000 would be spent on refurbishment of the platform canopy. At Torquay, canopies and the footbridge would be refurbished and building repairs would total £1.185 million. In addition Hennapyn Road bridge at the south end of the station would be refurbished and restored at a cost of £400,000; this latter work would start in May 2013 and last 18 weeks. Finally at Paignton restoration of the buildings, canopies and footbridge would cost £1.13 million. The improvements had been brought forward by Network Rail after an approach by the Torbay Mayor who had made 'cleaning up the gateway to Torbay' one of his priorities. Furthermore a team of volunteers from the Robert Owen Communities (ROC) organization had been working on restoring the landscaping around Torquay station (once famous for its station gardens). First Group paid for a project at Torquay which enabled the ROC team gain essential skills towards finding employment. Network Rail said that this work 'has already made a dramatic improvement to Torquay station and complements the structural and aesthetic renovation we have carried out'.

So this chapter will end on an optimistic note, as it appears that both the national and Heritage parts of the line can face the future with confidence, 150 years since Kingswear was reached by rail.

The modern form of local rail travel in Torbay. A 4-car 'Pacer', headed by No. 143619, and, unusually, with an additional class '153' in green livery at the rear, passes over the Cockington Lane bridge at Livermead with the 14.23 Exmouth to Paignton on 20th September, 2013. Quite frequently these trains are only two cars and can be very overcrowded in the summer months.   *Mark S. Wilkins*

Chapter Ten

A most important customer:
Torquay Gas Works

The Torquay Consumers Gas Company was formed in 1834 with its works at the head of what later became Torwood Gardens, but soon removed to Temperance Street. By 1855 this site was inadequate and another company, the Torquay Gas Co., was formed to acquire the old works and purchase land from the Ecclesiastical Commissioners on the border of the parishes of Cockington and Paignton. Their Act receiving the Royal Assent in June 1860, the foundation stone of the new Works at Hollacombe was laid on 28th July, 1860. Celebrations were held to mark the event but for a man named Holmes there had been a rather mournful ending: he became drunk and went to sleep on the railway line with his arm across the rail. Unfortunately a ballast train came along during the night and ran over his arm but such was the stamina of the man that he walked to the infirmary where the limb was amputated!

The works, built at a cost of some £3,000, started supplying gas in March 1861, the coal used to make the gas coming in by sea to Torquay harbour, thence by road to the works, a distance of about 1¾ miles. The initial capacity of the plant was 2,500 tons of coal pa. By February 1862 the company's correspondence mentions the possibility of a rail siding, but this could not be installed until the line reached Kingswear and access was gained to Dartmouth's natural harbour. With completion of the line near, the gas company wrote on 7th May, 1864, enquiring how much a siding would cost. But as we are aware the station at Kingswear did not, at first, include any facilities for coal traffic and goods working did not commence until 2nd April, 1866. The Torquay Gas Co. approached the SDR in September 1865 quoting expected tonnages of between 3-4,000 tons per annum, and was advised that the SDR would convey the trafffc for 1s. 4d. per ton (or 1s. if the gas company provided the trucks), which was rather more than they expected. They appealed to the D&T to intervene but the outcome is not known. They also wrote to Messrs Hennett & Spinks of Bridgwater asking 'on what terms they could furnish trucks' and as later correspondence refers to 'our trucks' it would seem they bought some.

A Private Siding agreement was drawn up between the gas company and the SDR on 26th July, 1866 and traffic may have started soon thereafter. In view of the traffic to be carried the annual rental was only 1s. By March 1867 the gas company was asking the SDR to ensure that the tarpaulins the gas company provided were used to sheet the wagons to keep the coal dry. However, the SDR required 2d. a wagon for this service, to which the gas company had to agree.

A note in the front of the 1876 Working Timetable said,

When the signals which protect Gas House siding (up direction) stand at danger, detonators (fixed on an iron rod attached to the base of the signals) will be placed on the line of rails, which the signals govern. When drivers run over the detonators, they must stop their train as speedily as possible.

The 1884 Working Timetable said,

Trucks for the Gas House Goods Siding may be pushed by engines of UP goods trains from Paignton to the Siding, but the speed of the trains, between these two places must not exceed EIGHT miles an hour.

In 1889 the annual contract between the Gas Co. and the GWR legislated for 10,000 tons of traffic being dealt with at the siding.* Some investigations took place that year as to whether a jetty should be built at Hollacombe to bring in the coal direct. Difficulty arose from the inadequacy of the single siding to deal with the traffic and in May 1891 Mr Compton (Plymouth superintendent) and Mr Jones from the GWR attended the gas company's Board meeting and said that a loop siding was necessary. However, the gas company, in reply, pointed out:

… that the gas company were under no obligation to extend it, that the ground formed part of the main line and that the gas company had already built the retaining wall and filled in the ground … that the Railway company ought therefore to assist if the extra accommodation was necessary particularly as it was not now required … in regard to the adjoining store but was rendered necessary on account of the insufficient accommodation at Kingswear and elsewhere …

The GWR officials undertook to report this back to the 'head office in London'.

Nothing was done until January 1892 when the Directors met the chief goods manager and it was agreed that a 'double' (loop) siding was required to which the GWR would contribute. A plan was later submitted for two parallel sidings on the up side of the line converging at each end of the layout into one, then into a connection with the main line, each connection worked by a 2-lever covered ground frame released by the electric train staff. The cost of the works was estimated at £1,093 (including gauge conversion costs) of which the GWR would pay one third. The Minutes record 'The cost of a signal box and locking arrangement to be avoided'. The GWR also undertook to provide ['narrow gauge'] wagons for at least six months. A new Agreement dated 16th November, 1892 superseded the 1866 one which was cancelled. The rental was now 5s. pa, and thus it remained until the end. The work was not carried out very speedily (in March 1893 the gas company complained of 'the wasteful manner in which the work was being done and protesting against the expenditure') but in September 1893 the GWR submitted the works for BoT inspection; they were passed in November. The final cost had been £1,055, of which the GWR paid one-third.

It looks as if we can narrow the timescale for completion to May 1893, thanks to a copy of a letter in Frank Hill's notebook dated 16th May, 1893:

FH 285/2   *May 16th 1893*

Dear Sir

I have been to Gas Siding, Torquay today as ordered and seen everything in working order, the fitting for the padlocks are not yet fixed. I have returned the lock you sent me and the one from the siding to Inspector Hockaday. Mr Gatfield (?) have given orders today for the fitting to be put on at once and when the locks can be used, the door keys I brought back to Torquay and left them in charge of the signalman on duty.

Mr Northcott

By 1894 the instructions as to working at Gas House Sidings had expanded to the following:

Gas House siding, situated between Paignton and Torquay
This siding is supplied with a ground frame worked by 'Annett's' key, and a 'throw-off' point is fitted to the siding.

---

* Appendix Five shows traffic dealt with at Hollacombe 1889-1906 and 1933-1948.

Each Electric Train Staff for the section between Torquay and Paignton is fitted with a key that opens the ground-frame lock, and the siding must be worked by the Guards of Goods trains, but it will, of course, be necessary for the driver of any engine or train doing work at it, to be in possession of an Electric Train Staff.

When the train or engine which has to stop at the siding has arrived there, the head guard must take the train staff from the driver, and, after unlocking the padlock, securing the door of the ground-box, he must insert the key in the lock at the foot of the levers inside the frame, and after unlocking the levers they will be free to be worked.

Guards must do the work they have to perform at the siding in a manner that will be most effective for carrying it out expeditiously, and after the work is over and the levers set, and locked, in their normal position, the door of the ground box must be padlocked and the train staff handed back to the driver.

The keys of the ground boxes are kept at the Signal Cabin, Torquay.

If at the time a goods train stops at the siding to do work, there should be any cart or carts loading or unloading in connection with trucks standing in the sidings, proper warning must be given to the person in charge of each, before any trucks are moved into or out of the siding.

Difficulty has arisen in connection with the working of Trucks to and from this Siding, resulting in the requirements of the Gas Company not being at all times met.

This has occurred in some cases from failure to observe the instructions given by the Torquay Station Master, and in order to avoid a similar difficulty in future, it must be distinctly understood by the Guards working Goods Trains over the Torquay Branch, that inasmuch as the Manager of the Gas Company makes his requirements known to the Station Master at Torquay, it will be the duty of the latter to give instructions to the Guards as to the loading and removing of trucks from the Gas siding.

In 1905 the GWR installed a winch and wire rope between the single line and the nearest siding, about 4 chains Torquay side of the 221 mp, for the purpose of hauling trucks along the sidings.

In a Report to the Traffic Committee dated 31st October, 1906 the General Manager stated that 'owing to an increase in the tonnage of sea borne coal dealt with at Kingswear, it would be more economical if the traffic were hauled in wagons of higher carrying capacity ... and he recommended the construction at Swindon of six 40 ton wagons ... at an estimated £2,250'. After authority from the Board these wagons formed Lot 552, dated 16th January, 1907.

As recorded elsewhere the line between Torquay and Paignton was doubled in 1910 and a new 26-lever signal box provided at Gas House Siding. Its proper name ws Torquay Gas Works but the operating instructions always referred to Gas House Siding, as they had since at least 1876. In 1923 the separate Torquay and Paignton gas undertakings amalgamated as the Torquay & Paignton Gas Company. The Paignton Works in Mill Lane, which was not rail connected but received its coal by road from Paignton station, closed down in the mid-twenties as soon as a gas main was laid to link the two systems.

Major improvements at the works in 1925 included the installation of a wagon tippler, which brought to an end the use of 40 ton coal wagons on the Kingswear run. The sidings were slightly extended. This work cost the gas company half the outlay, £253 10s. The works were now handling 25,000 tons of coal per annum and an electric capstan and guide pulleys replaced the winch installed in 1905.

In November 1930 the crossover road and single connection to the up main line were renewed at a cost of £137 to the gas company. The sidings themselves needed renewal in 1938 and the estimate for their replacement was £700 (again to be paid by the gas company). A wagon weigh bridge was installed alongside the tippler in 1940.

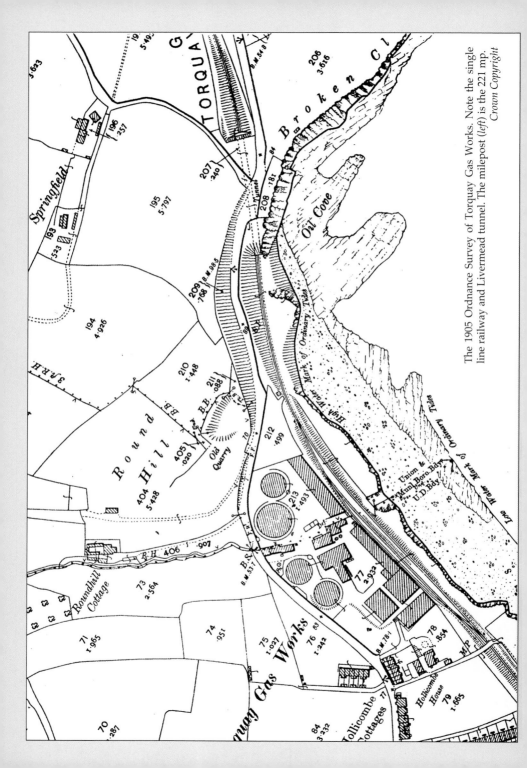

The 1905 Ordnance Survey of Torquay Gas Works. Note the single line railway and Livermead tunnel. The milepost (*left*) is the 221 mp.
Crown Copyright

Left: The electric cranes at Kingswear, a photograph taken in 1932 when they were installed.
NRM/SSPL

Below: I have included this photo because it shows the tunnel under the track at Torquay Gas Works that led to the beach (and still does) where the company used to tip their waste; preparations are here made for the foundations of the tar separator, February 1948.
British Gas

Problems which arose at this very exposed location when nature took a hand have already been described. In 1919 the telegraph pole route had to be moved due to sea encroachment. Difficulties of another sort were caused by gas fumes: in 1921 it was necessary to replace a ¼ mile length of iron telegraph wire only five years old, and decayed by the fumes, by copper wire. An aggregate of nine miles of wire was replaced at a cost of £190.

Vivian Lewis, formerly coal foreman at Hollacombe for the Torquay & Paignton Gas Co., has kindly allowed some of his memories to be put in print.

Known as 'Taffy' to his colleagues he worked at Hollacombe from the 1930s until he retired when the works closed in 1968. He was in charge of coal and coke movements in and out of the works and liaised closely with the GWR and then BR about train movements.

The sidings would hold some 32 loaded wagons and with overtime these could be emptied and the coal spread over the storage area by the telpher grab in one day. Normal time capacity was 26 trucks per day.

Before the war, Kingswear was used to import the coal and train loads had to be carefully matched with ship movements. He thinks that on rare occasions coal was held at Churston if he could not accept train loads because his sidings were full.

There were normally two trains per day and trucks would come and go back and forth in a shuttle. Renwick, Wilton and Dobson were the agents for supply of coal.

During the war Kingswear was not used and coal came by rail from the north. He would liaise with Hackney Yard to ensure that he had a regular supply of two trains per day, and if Hackney did not have the trucks they would have to be called forward from further up the line.

He would be charged £2 per day for standage when trucks were in the siding and he only requested the bare minimum from Hackney. This led to a finely balanced juggling act as he was very proud of the fact that when he was in control standage charges were minimal.

When a train was due a porter and porter/signalman would come from Torquay Station and switch in the box. The morning shunt was usually at around 8.00 am and as soon as it was complete the box was again switched out (usually by about 9.00 am). The afternoon shunt would start at about 2.00 pm.

Leaving the sidings would be coal empties and 15-20 trucks of coke per week together with 3 or 4 trucks of tar. 'Oxide' was received via the sidings as well. Oxide was used to purify gas in filter beds and was very heavy and difficult to manhandle on site. Coke was of course very light and was thrown into the wagons by hand using coke forks,

Two platoons of Home Guard (Nos. 2 and 3 Platoons - Torquay & Paignton Gas Company) were based at Hollacombe from early 1940 to 10th September, 1944. They were responsible for the defence of the gas works and railway sidings as the beach beneath was suitable for landing craft. The unit built its own defence works including several strongly-built pill boxes (which can still be seen today).

Patrols kept observation from dusk to dawn for 4½ years without a break. At first their sole defence was a solitary privately-owned shotgun but later were furnished with rifles, sten guns, machine guns, anti-tank rifles and an anti-aircraft battery consisting of an unrotating projectile radiator, or rocket projector. This was credited with shooting down a Focke-Wulf 190 on 30th December, 1942 when it and two companions approached the gas works at approximately 10.12 am. The unit afterwards received congratulations from the Home Guard District Commander, and painted a swastika, denoting a 'kill', on the projector!

The unit, 160 strong, despite long hours and difficult blackout conditions in the gas works, still managed on average seven shifts a week in the Home Guard, or an average 60 hours per week by the day workers. Additionally the officers and NCOs also performed full ARP duties and 'stood-to' on the 700-odd alerts in the Torbay area (not to mention attendance to broken gas mains and services, etc).

On 4th September, 1942 the gas works suffered damage by enemy action and a 1½ million cubic feet gas holder was set alight by cannon and machine gun fire. The Home Guard platoon were heavily involved in putting out the fire which was lighting up a passing convoy. Subsequently the Officer Commanding received the MBE and his Lieutenant and a Sergeant each received the George Medal.

Gas board records show that in the 1950s the sidings contained a 35 ton weighbridge and a 20 ton tippler, and two 1 ton telphers (overhead bucket system) which moved the coal around the Works. The Glover-West retort could handle 70 tons of coal per hour, as could the Woodall-Duckham retort. The tippler was restricted to wagons with a wheelbase not exceeding 18 ft 6 in. and body height between 3 ft and 8 ft 6 in.

For details of the Kingswear part of the coal-moving operation I was fortunate enough to meet Eric Bovey, who was in charge of the arrangements there on behalf of Renwick, Wilton & Dobson (RWD) from 1945 to 1963, when the traffic ceased. He lent me his register in which every ship is recorded and these details are extracted and summarized as *Appendix Six*.

Gas coal for Torquay Gas Works came from Yorkshire collieries (by ship) by way of the North Sea and the Channel. When war came in 1939 these seaborne movements had to stop as the passage via the Channel was too hazardous. For the duration of the war, therefore, apart from a few specialized loads (*see Appendix*) only household coal (which was transported via the Irish Sea and Lands End) was unloaded to rail wagons at Kingswear. Because of its weight and bulk this was more awkward to unload and a cargo of 600 tons could take as long to empty as 1,700 tons of gas coal.

After the war ended gas coal shipments did not immediately resume and in fact did not return to seaborne transport until 1951, after an intervention by the Government, Mr Bovey recalls. From then until 1956 the traffic developed until in that year 73 shiploads of gas coal were dealt with. But the previous year, 1955, was the actual peak year for total railborne traffic through Kingswear Docks as 79 vessels were handled (including 66 gas coal), more than one per week on average. Household coal by sea died away after 1955. Whilst it was being handled at Kingswear, trucks were loaded to Brixham, Paignton, Torre, Newton Abbot, Moretonhampstead, Christow, Dawlish and Teignmouth, although only small numbers of trucks were involved to each place.

The method of working with the gas coal was that when a ship left the Humber (Goole being the chief source of Kingswear's traffic), the time of departure and tonnage of coal was advised and Mr Bovey had two days to organize the necessary empty wagons. These were ordered from the Kingswear station master. The railway crane drivers were booked up to work in two days' time. Messrs Everards employed a fleet of about 100 vessels on coastwise shipping and their ships were employed on the Kingswear run, the most frequent visitor being the MV *Similarity*, but the register shows a variety of other vessels with names ending in '...ity' (e.g. *Angularity, Actuality, Ability, Continuity, Stability, Speciality*, etc., etc.). However, *Similarity* appears most frequently and the operation was geared to one vessel, week and week about, with one day's loading time, two days transit, two days unloading and two days return journey.

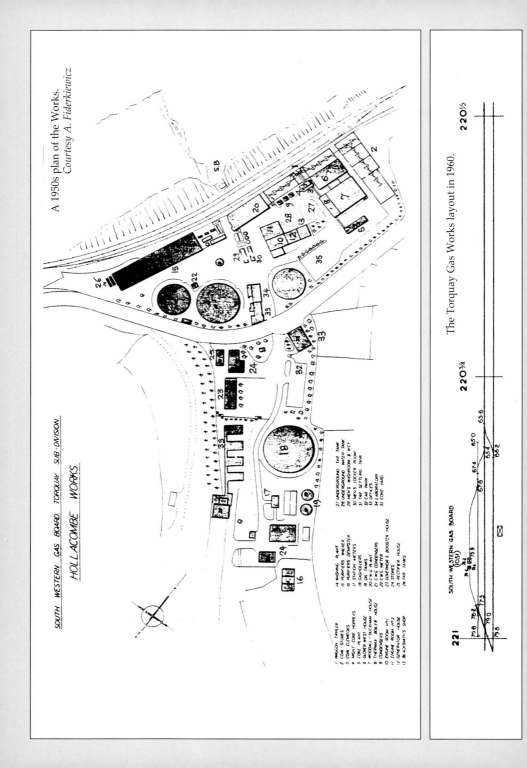

SOUTH WESTERN GAS BOARD TORQUAY SUB-DIVISION

HOLLACOMBE WORKS

A 1950s plan of the Works.
Courtesy A. Fiderkiewicz

1 WAGGON TIPPLER
2 COAL STORES
3 COAL ELEVATORS
4 COKE PLANT
5 NIGHT COKE HOPPERS
6 CORE PLANT
7 GUIDE-REST HOUSE
8 RETORT-OLDHAM HOUSE
9 THERMAL BOILER HOUSE
10 CONDENSERS
11 ENGINE ROOM N°1
12 ENGINE ROOM N°2
13 GENERATOR HOUSE
14 BLACKSMITHS SHOP
15 WASHING PLANT
16 PURIFIERS WALKER
17 PURIFIERS DEMISTER
18 STATION METERS
19 OIL TANKS
20 C.W.G. PLANT
21 C.W.G. CONDENSERS
22 C.W.G. METER
23 GOVERNOR & BOOSTER HOUSE
24 STORES
25 RECTIFIER HOUSE
26 TAR TANKS

27 UNDERGROUND TAR TANK
28 UNDERGROUND WATER TANK
29 PURIFIERS WASHROOM & W.C.'s
30 MEN'S LOCKER ROOM
31 TAR SETTLING TANK
32 CAR PARK
33 OFFICES
34 LABORATORY
35 COKE YARD

The Torquay Gas Works layout in 1960.

Hollacombe Gas Works in August 1931, showing the site following the 1925 rebuilding, and before the final enlargement in the late 1930s/early 1940s. The large building at left is the Retort House, to its right the wagon tippler. Running in front of the building is the telpher system that moved coal stocks around the site and eventually to the coal elevator behind the wagon tippler. Behind the Retort House is the Washing and Scrubbing plant (with chimney) where ammonia and tar was removed from the gas; these products were stored underground and sent away in rail tank wagons to chemical manufacturers. The single wagon in front of the Retort House is at the point where coke was loaded to rail wagons (using coke forks). The large buildings at the right-hand end of the premises are the purifiers where suphuretted hydrogen was removed from the gas. At the rear the Torbay Road is still lined with tram poles; the large gas holder remote from the works held 1½ million cu. ft of gas and had been erected in 1930.   *British Gas*

This picture shows the final state of the gasworks, seen here in 1947 looking towards Paignton. There are hardly any wagons on hand, which was very rare. The track at the Torquay end trailing crossover has been reballasted, perhaps indicating that the crossover has been renewed. Note the gun emplacement by the signal box and the allotments on the embankment. There are many more allotments behind the works, evidence of the wartime 'Dig for Victory' campaign. Today's road users would delight to see the Torbay Road (A3022) so empty of traffic.   *British Gas*

A close-up of the electric cranes unloading coal at Kingswear.   *E.A. Bovey*

By 1967 when this photograph was taken the up main line connection from the gas sidings at the Torquay end had been removed, after which only down trains could shunt there.

South West Media Group

When the ship docked at Kingswear the first of three empty trains, each of 30 wagons, ordered for that day, arrived at Kingswear between 6.15 and 6.30 am and was in place by 7 am. Eighteen wagons could be stabled on the jetty line of which 14 or 15 could be reached by the cranes without the wagons having to be moved. On the first day the coal lumpers employed by RWD on a freelance basis, plus the railway crane drivers, worked from 7 am to 7 pm with an hour's midday meal break. The vessels held 500 tons in the forward hold and 630 tons in each after hold. The two cranes worked simultaneously with six coal lumpers working with each crane, four in the hold trimming, one on the hatch directing the crane and one on the jetty dealing with spillage.

The second special of 30 empty wagons arrived later in the morning and ran into the platform loop until the first train, now loaded, was cleared. It was then positioned by its engine. There was no shunting engine available at Kingswear, any necessary movement of empty or loaded wagons being done by the train engine. Wooden wagons would hold 11½ tons of coal each and were of 6½ tons tare. Loads for single engine trains of such wagons from Kingswear were:

28XX - 23 wagons
43XX or 45XX etc - 17 wagons
57XX etc - 14 wagons
2251 - 10/11 wagons

If a banker to Churston was provided (the train engine of the next special which was being loaded) then loads were increased, e.g '28XX' to 33 wagons; '43XX' and '45XX' types were the most frequent engines provided. It took 150/160 wooden bodied wagons to clear a cargo, and when 7 ton tare, 14 ton payload steel-bodied wagons became general, the number required dropped to 120 as the proportion of these increased and their carrying capacity was uprated to 16 tons. Obviously the same sets of wagons shuttled to and from Gas House Sidings until the ship was empty. Wagons would also be conveyed by the daily outwards goods.

The third special of 30 empties arrived in the afternoon and unloading of the vessel continued until 7 pm. Next day two specials of 25/30 empty wagons each came down in the morning, whilst the third special was an engine and brake van to clear the last loaded special. Normally unloading of the vessel would be completed by 4 pm on the second day. Mr Bovey produced an example of the documentation made for each docking and this showed the cost of unloading the MV *Similarity*. The vessel arrived at 10.30 pm on 12th December, 1962, was discharged 7 am-7 pm 13th December and 7 am-11.30 am 14th December, sailing at noon having discharged 1,715 tons at a cost of £450.

The largest size of ship able to dock at Kingswear was 250 ft long, 36 ft beam and 15 ft draught. At spring tides 24 ft of water was available and 12 ft at neap tides. On 16th January, 1956 one of Everards much larger vessels *Superiority* docked after special permission was received to deal with her, and 2,691 tons of coal was discharged between 17th and 19th January instead of the usual 1,100 tons. On 8th February of that year MV *Seriality* discharged 1,700 tons, nearly 900 tons of which went by road because the gas board's wagon tippler had broken down. There was no gas coal sent by sea between September 1959 and January 1961, the coal lumpers at Kingswear being dismissed in consequence.

Similarity's last visit to Kingswear was on 17th/18th January, 1963 and the last vessel to unload its traffic to rail was MV *Fred Everard* on 25th/26th March, 1963, unloading 1,658 tons. The next line in the register is marked 'Coal traffic diverted to rail throughout' which was good news for British Railways corporately but not for the port of Dartmouth, and Kingswear wharf in particular. It was made possible because the gas board had changed their retorts to burn other than Yorkshire coal. In the peak years of the 1950s coal shipped through Kingswear and transferred to rail averaged 60-80,000 tons per annum.

In January 1966, with the rail facilities at Kingswear lying idle, it was reported that coal was being moved from Kingswear wharf to Newton Abbot electricity power station by road. It was thought that this was to build up stocks for use in any emergency.

The coal trains from Kingswear did not appear in the Working Timetables as they were organized around the arrival of the coal ships, and details of empty (code name 'Venlo') and loaded journeys were wired out by Newton Abbot Telegraph Office as details became known. It was up to the signalmen to regulate the movements in between the advertised train service. There was a carriage & wagon examiner from Newton Abbot located at Gas House Siding.

Coal for the gas works continued to be sent by rail via Newton Abbot until, sadly, the works closed in 1968 removing a major source of revenue from the line. The gas board's tenancy agreement terminated on 9th January, 1970.

The land on the seaward side of the main road is now a park. The land on the other side (the last gasholder was demolished in 2003) at the time of writing (2013) is going through the planning process as Midas Homes want to build a housing estate there, which is being resisted by the local community on the grounds of land pollution and traffic congestion.

This picture confirms the proper name of Torquay Gas Works signal box, rather than 'Gas House Siding' as referred to in the railway's operating instructions.   *Peter W. Gray*

Chapter Eleven

The Ferries

There were (and are) three ferries between the east and west banks of the Dart at Dartmouth, two of which were railway owned. These two used to be closely linked with the operation of the railway and they deserve, I feel, a separate chapter.

There is no road crossing over the Dart between the sea and Totnes Bridge, 10 miles to the north, only ferries and this has always been the case from ancient times. The first ferry was the Kingswear Ferry.

As early as 1365 there is a mention of this ferry across the Dart in the Close Rolls where it is described as a monopoly created by the crown as a safeguard, and acquired in that year by William Carey. The maintenance of the ferry was secured by a tithe impressed on the landowners. When Thomas Gale became Lord of the Manor in 1544, the purchase was subject to a payment to the Crown of 10s. 4½d. as a ferry tithe. By this time the contribution to this tithe and the upkeep of the ferry had become a perk of the owner.

By the 17th century the ferry rights were held equally by the Mallock family of Cockington and the Holway family. The passage money was now due from all the hamlets in the parish of Brixham. As for the actual conduct of the ferry, this was handed over to a tenant. In 1558 Robert Collyns held the ferry, as a lessee or tenant-for-life at a rent of 12s. with half the 'simba' or landing stage. Collyns probably ran the ferry from a slip or quay at Kittery Point (which was then an alternative to the slipway at the Square) at Kingswear (*see plan in Chapter Four*).

The ferry was a pulling ferry, usually a two-oared boat and the crossing was to the Ferry or Passage Slip at Bearscove on the Dartmouth side, some 300 yds away.

By the end of the 18th century this ferry had been moved to the northern side of Waterhead Creek under the style of the Hoodown passenger ferry, and here until 1927 stood The Ferry Inn, kept in 1863 by Mary Burgoine. The pulling ferry probably came to Hoodown sometime between 1558 (when it was at Kittery Point) and 1675, when a John Ogilby mentioned the greater width of the Hoodown crossing. Why it moved is not known - the Hoodown passage is some 600 yards wide (twice that of Kittery).

The village traffic continued to use the slipway by The Square (adjacent to the 'Plume of Feathers' Inn) right up to the coming of the railway in 1864, but maybe the carriage traffic went from Hoodown because the approach road at that time was better.

The Dartmouth & Torbay Act of 1857 authorized the establishing of a ferry or steam communication across the Dart from the intended terminus to Dartmouth, and to construct the necessary piers and landing places. The ferry was to be for the use of all, whether they had travelled by train or not, on payment of the usual toll, and to be within ½ mile of the Hoodown terminus.

As we have seen the railway was not extended beyond Brixham Road for several years. After failure of the 'Deviation Bill' it was at first intended to terminate at Hoodown, whence there was the aforementioned ferry to Dartmouth. In 1863 when it was decided to extend the line to Kingswear proper, an agreement was reached with George Fownes Luttrell for the rental of the necessary land to complete the line and purchase of the Hoodown and Kingswear ferries. The land was conveyed by a deed dated 18th November, 1873 at a rent charge of £54 pa in perpetuity (£1 an acre).

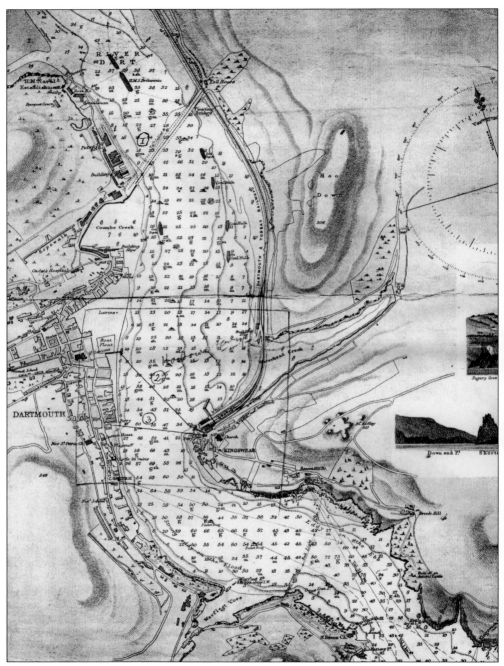

Extract from an Admiralty chart of 1880 showing the three ferry crossings; the Floating Bridge (marked 1), the Railway Steam Ferry (2) and the Horse, or Lower, Ferry (3). The route of the original Hoodown Ferry is also shown hatched (- - - -) just above the number 2. Note the two moored naval training vessels in the river (top of chart) and the various coal hulks.

The ferries' conveyance is also dated 18th November, 1873, after the absorption of the D&T by the SDR although the document shows conveyance to the D&T: the price was £3,100.* The Hoodown ferry or 'pulling ferry' from Hoodown Ferry House to the New Ground, Dartmouth, was discontinued by the railway in 1864, extension of the railway to Kingswear having made it redundant.

Kingswear Ferry

Apart from the pulling ferry , there was from the early part of the 19th century a horse or 'waggon' ferry. This ferry ran from a slip leading out of The Square south-east of the station at Kingswear to a landing at Bayards Cove, Dartmouth. It was referred to by the D&T company as the Kingswear Ferry or the Horse Ferry and locally also as the Lower Ferry. Originally a float propelled by two men with long oars, it was capable of carrying one horse and cart at a time, hence its name.

Before the purchase of the ferry rights under the 1863 Heads of Agreement, the tenant of the ferry had for some years been the landlord of the 'Plume of Feathers' inn at Kingswear. In the early 1850s it was a Mr Cox, but in March 1855 the new landlord, Thomas Sandover, took over the running of the Lower Ferry. The *Dartmouth Chronicle* noted at the time that it hoped that 'the ferry will be conducted with more regard to the public'. Sandover remained the lessee of the ferry until 1864, and probably until October 1865 when the ferry was released.

The D&T Act 1857 gave the Postmaster General (PMG) powers to send mails by any boats run by the company and the latter were to run boats for such mails after notice by the PMG, on penalty of £20 for failing to do so. From October 1865, the Kingswear Ferry was leased to Messrs Avis & Son of Kingswear, the local postmaster, so doubtless the penalty clause was never invoked! Three boats were worked by Avis, two (rowing) for passengers, one kept each side, the other solely for luggage (the 'horse boat' which was supplied by the D&T). The ferry was converted to steam operation in April 1867 when Avis' steam launch *Pioneer* was placed in the service. (She had struck an unmarked rock at Weymouth whilst en route to the station earlier in the year and had to put in for repairs.)

The *Pioneer* could carry 30 passengers and had a speed of 8 knots. Her crossing time was 1½ minutes solo, or 3¼ minutes with the horse boat. Her principal dimensions were: length 30 ft overall, breadth 7 ft, draft 2ft 11 in. max. *Pioneer* had a high pressure engine on White's patent and a 4-bladed propellor. The complete boat was built by J. Samuel White of Cowes.

The new horse boat was built to the order of the D&T at the beginning of 1865 and could carry a wagon with a 4 ton load and two horses. It had a loading prow at each end for ease of working.

In October 1867 the ferry slip at Kingswear was improved by the SDR with the addition of a small quay in communication with the new Yacht Club Hotel. This enabled passengers to land direct at high tides without going under the old archways as before. To improve night working of the ferry, Avis placed a red light at the slip.

From Monday 25th June, 1877 the Kingswear Ferry was leased to G.A. & J.W. Casey Brothers for five years at £73 pa. *Pioneer* must have ceased operations by then, for the *Dartmouth Chronicle* drew attention to the fact that a steam launch would be

---

* The most likely reason for the 10 year delay in the sale of the land and ferries is that G.F. Luttrell was tenant-for-life but after the death of his father in 1867, obtained agreement from his father's executor to change his title to sole owner in fee-simple (freehold). The purchase price also included the land for the 1864 embankment and the properties affected along the foreshore at Kingswear, including the small shipyard leased by Mr Alford.

The beautiful mouth of the River Dart, looking towards Dartmouth with the railway pontoon in the centre of the picture and a River Dart Co. paddle steamer moored at the landing stage to the left. The Royal Naval College is prominent at top right, photographed in September 1928.
GWR (BR Records Centre)

The GWR slipway at Kingswear, south of the station, formerly used by Casey & Heal's horse ferry, from 1927 by the Dartmouth Council ferries. *GWR (BR Records Centre)*

provided on Sundays (the busiest day in the summer) instead of the usual rowing boats, which, however, provided the service on other days. 'During the winter a covered steam launch now in course of construction, will be put on the ferry, thus according passengers better accommodation than hitherto'. (From a reference in a 1901 Agreement with Casey's, and the GWR timetables, it is known that the GWR did not run its own steam ferry on Sundays. However, in 1903, passenger traffic was such that the GWR had to agree to operate its own boat on Sundays in future.)

After only a fortnight's operation under the new lessees the *Dartmouth Chronicle* was much impressed with the 'greatly improved service' at the ferry:

> Instead of only one boat being kept on as formerly, from 12 to 2, and again in the tea hour, two boats are now regularly in attendance, as well as a light and fast steam launch when required. This latter is in attendance to each train on Sundays which in itself is a great boon to a large number of persons. We trust that Messrs Casey will receive the support their spirit and energy so deserves.

A new steam launch *Forester* was brought into use early in 1878, certificated for 30 passengers it could make the double crossing in six minutes.

The *Dartmouth Chronicle* drew attention to the hazards of being a ferry passenger at this time. Apparently 'fly' boatmen traded illegally at the passenger slip at Dartmouth. They kept clear until Casey had pulled away and then waited for unwary passengers. Once aboard, these unfortunate travellers were held in midstream until they paid up to 4*d*. for the crossing, against the official ½*d*. charge. However, this practice stopped after one or two of the 'flyboys' were thrown overboard by their intended victims!

When Casey's lease was renewed for a further three years from 24th June, 1882 the rent was raised to £100 pa and this sum was maintained for several years but in November 1894, following the opening of the Kingsbridge branch in December 1893 (which extracted a lot of traffic) they successfully negotiated a reduction to £89 pa.

Casey's were in trouble again in 1896 and wanted to terminate their agreement from Michaelmas 'because receipts continued to diminish and they could not afford to work the ferry', but because the GWR could not find another tenant they were persuaded to continue for another 12 months at a rental of only £1 per week. Things must have looked up for in May 1897 Casey's took on the ferry for another five years at £80 pa. This was cancelled in August 1901 on the death of John Casey, when Tom Casey entered the partnership, and replaced by an agreement for a further six years, still at £80 pa. This period may have been linked to the need to renew the horse boat, for in August 1907 the GWR contracted with Messrs Philip to construct a new horse ferry boat at a cost of £360, delivery to be in 4½ months' time. In 1909 George Casey died and Tom Casey took F.C. Heal as a partner. The rental was maintained at £80 until September 1913, when the lease agreement, with Tom Casey and F.C. Heal, was raised to £85 pa for a further seven years. The rowing ferry ceased in 1915 and a steam launch *Relief* was bought by Casey & Heal as a replacement.

Messrs Casey and Heal asked to be relieved of the obligation to run a Sunday service with the horse ferry in March 1918, to which the GWR agreed 'subject to adequate provision being made for the transport of goods etc. for the Naval College and of any other traffic of which notice may be given'. The GWR's agreement to the suspension was given, however, 'for the time being'.

The GWR was making large outpayments to Messrs Casey & Heal in respect of conveyance of their own parcel delivery vehicles to Dartmouth by the horse ferry

Casey's motor launch disembarking passengers at the private steps alongside the GWR slipway.
GWR (BR Records Centre)

A rather lightly loaded Lower Ferry, in the last year of Dartmouth Council's ownership, arrives at Kingswear, 31st March, 1973.   *The late John C. Gillham*

(2s. 4d. per vehicle in 1921). It decided to strengthen the pontoons on both sides of the river and adapt its steam ferry *The Mew* (*see later*) to carry its own vehicles. In August 1921 the GWR agreed to reduce Casey and Heal's annual rental from £85 to £50 pa and increase the vehicle crossing payments from 2s. 4d. to 3s. until September 1922, when they no doubt intended to withdraw Casey and Heal's tenancy. Possibly there were just too many calls on the GWR's money, for a fresh agreement was drawn up for three years from 1st October, 1922 to 30th September, 1925 whereby the rental remained at £50 pa but the vehicle payment was reduced to 2s. 6d. per crossing.

Meanwhile the GWR strengthened the pontoons (in 1924/5 at a cost of £1,096) and adapted *The Mew*; Messrs Casey and Heal lost their tenancy from 1st October, 1925 after an unbroken 48 years of operation.

The GWR closed the service down on 30th September, 1925 and seemed to expect everyone to use *The Mew* in future, including cattle and sheep, even though it only ran at about 30 minute intervals. There was a storm of protest in Dartmouth and on 20th October, 1925 a high powered deputation, led by Torquay MP Mr C. Williams, met General Manager Sir Felix Pole at Paddington. As the local papers reported, the deputation 'were told there was no need to go into detail … and the impression was that the Railway Company had already considered the matter … Sir Felix asked them if they would be content to accept the horse ferry from the Railway Company'. The only charge would be a nominal payment of £5 per annum for the use of the Kingswear slip. This was confirmed to the council in a letter.

The *Torquay Herald Express* in its 20th May, 1926 edition reported that the horse ferry service had not yet restarted 'by reason of the refusal of the MoT to give consent to the transfer of the ferry under the Ferries (Acquisition by Local Authorities) Act on the present terms of agreement proposed to be entered into between the GWR and the Corporation of Dartmouth'. The formal Agreement with the Council is dated 30th July, 1926; there is no price mentioned except that the fee for use of the slipway at Kingswear had been made a one-off payment of £100. No restart date for the ferry service has been found.

The GWR sold the ferry rights to Dartmouth Corporation in a conveyance dated 28th March, 1927, the 'transaction not exceeding £500' (which seems to have been something of a smokescreen!), together with a payment of £100 for use of the GWR's slipway at Kingswear. Tom Casey would not tender for the new lease as the conditions were onerous. Instead he ran a 'private' service from Collins Quay, Kittery for a few years with his motor boat *I'll try*.

The Corporation lessees were Peters and Hesseltine, with a change of leaseholder to General Estates of London in 1932. Dartmouth Borough Council operated the service from 1949 after the leaseholder decided it was no longer viable. Following local government reorganization, ownership transferred to the South Hams District Council on 1st April, 1974. The ferry, being an 'ancient ferry' or 'franchise ferry', there is a legal duty on its owner to maintain the ferry in existence.

The GWR Steam Ferry

The 'Steam Ferry' is how the GWR's official documents refer to the passenger ferry which crossed the Dart from the GWR's own pontoon at Kingswear station to a similar pontoon at Spithead, Dartmouth. The rights of ferry remained with the railway right up to 1972 but until 1872 the actual daily operation was carried out by

PS *Dolphin* at Kingswear pontoon at a very early date; the trucks look to be broad gauge.
Totnes Image Bank

PS *Dolphin* dressed overall and conveying royalty, 7th March, 1902 (*see Chapter Six*).
Courtesy Brixham Museum

Charles Seale Hayne's Dartmouth Steam Packet Co. Ltd (DSP) formed in 1859, with W.E. Froude as a partner.

The first railway ferry steamer was the *Perseverance*. However, as she was not ready until 1st October, 1864 when she took up station, the DSP Co. ran the service with the two standby boats, viz the *Louisa* (built 1856) and the *Newcomin* (built 1864). These two boats were employed in the summer season on the run to Totnes. The *Perseverance* was overhauled and converted by Lewis & Stockwell of Thameside (the builders of the *Newcomin*). Expected to cost £500-£800, she proved difficult to handle owing to her double-ended construction and double-ended steering. A paddle steamer of some 50-60 tons register, *Perseverance* had a high wind resistance and even in the sheltered waters of Dartmouth harbour this disadvantage was most marked. In addition her 'overhauled' engines began to give trouble and in March-May 1865 she was off-station for an extensive overhaul to her machinery and boiler at the works of the Plymouth Foundry Co. During this time, *Louisa* was the ferry boat.

The true cost of the *Perseverance* was revealed at the D&T meeting on 3rd March, 1866. Seale Hayne, referring to the high cost of the ferry steamer said they had expected to pay £800-£1,050 for the boat and had made 'arrangements' with the firm carrying out the conversion. Subsequently a dispute arose over the cost of the work and an arbitrator made an award against them, bringing the total cost to £1,769 13s. 8d. *Perseverance* was off-station from February to September 1868 for overhaul but the D&T had an agreement with the Dartmouth Steam Packet to provide a replacement as and when required. Soon after return to service, in November 1868, she was in collision with a coal lighter on the Dart, due to a shortage of steam. The coal lighter sank and a court action ensued against the SDR.

In December 1868 the *Dartmouth Chronicle* announced that a new steamer was being built for the South Devon Railway by Messrs Harvey of Hayle. She was being built specifically for the Kingswear Steam Ferry and the engine and boiler from *Perseverance* would be transferred to her after overhaul. She was *Dolphin*, a double-ended iron-hulled steamer with paddle wheels, weighing 61 tons and 105 ft long. She was able to carry a substantial number of passengers (331) and took up service on 24th August, 1869. Her average crossing time was four minutes.

The South Devon Railway decided, in June 1872, to take over the operation of the ferry boat from the Dartmouth Steam Packet Co. ('who worked the *Dolphin* at a loss'). This was possibly because of Seale Hayne's resignation from the SDR and the consequent loss of good relations. A new boiler was authorized for *Dolphin* at a cost of £500. However, as usual, the Dartmouth Steam Packet provided a replacement whilst *Dolphin* was overhauled and she returned on 14th September, 1873.

The *Dolphin* was off-station again in January 1875, awaiting new engines which were being made by Harvey's of Hayle. These were a pair of low pressure condensing engines of 25 hp (nominal) and were intended to make *Dolphin* easier to handle. The new engines were fitted in early February; in the interim *Royal Dartmouth* was the standby boat. In July 1880 the GWR Board approved the sum of £110 for a new gridiron at Kingswear, to be used for repairs to the *Dolphin*. The private slips on which the vessel had previously been docked were no longer available.

In 1889 the GWR was paying the now renamed (from 1877) Dartmouth & Torbay Steam Packet Co. £5 a day for replacement vessel and crew when the *Dolphin* was not available, with a guaranteed minimum of £150 pa. This was increased to £6 per day, £180 minimum in 1898. The Steam Packet Co. ('River Dart Steam Boat Co. Ltd'

Just a month before withdrawal after 46 years' service, *The Mew* arrives at Kingswear on 4th September, 1953.   *Peter W. Gray*

The naming ceremony at Kingswear for the two 'Gilberts', 18th March, 1957.   *NRM/SSPL*

from 1906) was required to keep a boat in readiness at all times and the boats to be made available had to be either *Berry Castle*, *Dartmouth Castle*, or *Totnes Castle*.

In 1900 £720 was spent providing a glazed deckhouse on *Dolphin*, giving passengers some shelter for the first time, and removal of deck gear to allow luggage to be wheeled on board, also necessary repairs to plating, etc.

An internal GWR report in 1903 mentions that the GWR ferry was 'only worked in connection with our train service', most inhabitants using the Kingswear ferry (horse ferry). This was still the case in 1925.

In 1904 the funnel of the *Dolphin* was lengthened, presumably to give better boiler draught at her low speed.

After nearly 40 years of reliable and steady service the GWR decided to replace *Dolphin* and a contract was entered into with Messrs Cox of Falmouth on 5th November, 1907 for a new vessel, *The Mew*, at a price of £5,100. Her principal dimensions were: length 90 ft., breadth 22½ ft, depth 8½ ft. She was a twin screw steamer with two engines capable of 250 hp and a speed of 10 knots. The main deck provided covered accommodation whilst the promenade deck was completely open and free of obstructions to maximize her passenger-carrying capacity. Altogether *The Mew* could carry 547 passengers, 216 more than the *Dolphin*. After extensive testing when her manoeuvring and speed capabilities were found to be better than the builder's guarantee, *The Mew* entered service at Kingswear on 31st May, 1908. As already related, she was altered to carry the GWR's road vehicles in 1924.

The *Brixham Western Guardian* carried an interesting piece in its 25th October, 1928 edition regarding the Roper family of Dartmouth who had served the GWR for a combined total of 100 years. Fred Roper (now 90) had served 40 years; formerly engineer on the *Dolphin* he had actually commenced his duties as early as 1866 with the *Perseverance*. His son Edwin had joined *Dolphin* as engineer in 1894, later bringing *The Mew* to Dartmouth to replace *Dolphin*. His other son Philip had joined *The Mew* as fireman in 1908. Finally grandson Fred Roper (junior) joined *The Mew* as fireman in 1922. That was really keeping it in the family!

When Fred Roper (senior) died in July 1932, *The Mew* flew its flag at half-mast for the weekend.

Destined to have an even longer tenure of the GWR Steam Ferry service than *Dolphin*, *The Mew* 'did her bit' for the war effort on 31st May, 1940 (her 32nd birthday) when she answered the call for help at Dunkirk. Piling extra coal on her deck and steaming at her full speed, 10 knots, continuously for over 24 hours her boilers became red hot, but, alas, all to no avail. When she arrived she was dismissed as unsuitable for beach work and returned, with less haste to her normal Devonshire occupation. By 1940, the GWR was paying the steam boat company £15 per day for a replacement for *The Mew*, whenever needed. In 1941 this became £18 a day, but when the steam boat company tried for £25 in 1942 the GWR declined and said that, for the duration of the war, GWR traffic would have to use the lower ferry (Kingswear ferry) if *The Mew* were unavailable.

The Mew made her final run, after no less than 46 years, on 8th October, 1954 to the sound of ships sirens and rockets and witnessed by crowds of people lining the banks of the Dart. Rather than hire one of the River Dart Steamboat Company's paddlers, a large 50 ft hired motor boat *Lady Elizabeth* or in her absence a River Dart Steamboat Co. vessel had to suffice until the arrival of two purpose-built 58 ft wooden motor vessels in 1957. These 35 ton diesel-engined craft were named *Adrian Gilbert* and *Humphrey Gilbert* and were officially named at a ceremony at Kingswear on 18th March, 1957, entering service immediately.

Humphrey Gilbert arrives at Dartmouth on 29th May, 1976. The cover over the landing pontoon has subsequently been demolished (as it has at Kingswear, opposite).

J. Woods, courtesy John Gillham

The Dart Pleasure Craft vessel *Kingswear Belle* leaving Kingswear on 10th September, 1993, before the ferry service was sold to the steam railway.   *Peter W. Gray*

In a bid to help keep the BR ferry in operation, Dartmouth Corporation gave up the use of its own passenger launches, afterwards operating carfloats only from this date.

The first mention of consideration of closure of the BR ferry was as early as 1960. A financial statement for the period 1913-1947, which covered 1913, 1922 and then every year from 1924 onwards showed the ferry only made a profit from 1933-1939 and in 1943 and 1944. The figures do not make clear whether they include any contributory revenue (through tickets), although it is likely they did. Bringing the story up to date, the average annual loss between 1958 and 1962 was £2,048 (and these receipts did include contributory revenue). The chief solicitor at British Railways Board (BRB) was unclear of the legal status of the ferry; at one stage the local superintendent was asked to ask the Dartmouth Town Clerk if he knew of its status! (Had those concerned looked at the Marine Superintendent Fishguard's file they would have found that it was the Kingswear ferry (sold to Dartmouth Corporation in 1926/7) that was required to be kept running by law.) The chief solicitor decided that, despite the uncertainty, BR 'will be justified in taking any risk there may be and proceeding on the assumption that there is no legal objection to the Kingswear-Dartmouth ferry being closed'.

A full unrenumerative services investigation was carried out in 1962, which recommended increased fares and shortened hours in service, neither of which were implemented. In 1965 a draft proposal to close the ferry was drawn up, but on learning that Dartmouth Council would object to this most strongly, BR had a change of heart and decided to try and sell the ferry.

From 21st February, 1966 single journey fares on the ferry were doubled from 3d. to 6d., through rail/ferry tickets were withdrawn, as were season tickets, although BR reversed the decision on season tickets after strong complaints from local education authorities. On 3rd October, 1966 the booking clerk at Dartmouth was withdrawn and station staff reduced to a porter between 9 am and 5 pm. On 17th April, 1967 coin operated turnstiles were introduced at Kingswear, which proved rather troublesome in practice and required staff to be available in case of their (frequent) failure. On 9th January, 1969 Paddington informed BR's Shipping Division of the intention to discontinue rail services between Paignton and Kingswear. In November of that year, the Shipping Division told Paddington that they intended to sell the ferry to Dartmouth Council. Almost exactly two years later, the *Western Morning News* of 30th November, 1971 reported that the ferry was being sold to the council for £9,000.

Withdrawn by BR in 1972, when they sold the Goodrington-Kingswear section of railway to the Dart Valley Railway, and the ferry service to Dartmouth Council, both *Adrian Gilbert* and brother *Humphrey Gilbert* later by sheer chance returned to their original station. The ferry was run by Dartmouth Borough Council (utilizing 'the Gilberts') from 1972-74 and by S. Hams District Council from 1974-76, following which Dart Pleasure Craft Ltd took over the ferry. Both former BR vessels were tried out on the St Mawes Ferry in Cornwall in 1976 but proved unsuccessful and were sold back to BR in 1977, who re-engined them. *Adrian Gilbert* was bought from there by Dart Pleasure Craft in 1978 and resumed the Kingswear-Dartmouth ferry work. *Humphrey Gilbert*, by then renamed *Edgcombe Belle*, did not return to Kingswear until 1985 having been employed in the meantime on the Drakes' Island ferry and the Cawsands ferry. *Adrian Gilbert* was sold in 1996.

Appropriately, in 1999 the ferry came back into railway ownership when it was bought by the Dart Valley Railway as part of a payment of £1.2 million for six ferries

The 1856 Floating Bridge pulled by two horses working a treadmill.

Courtesy Brixham Museum

The Dartmouth side slipway of the Floating Bridge, photographed from the ferry.

GWR (BR Records Centre)

and ships. *Dartmouth Princess* (built 1990) has become the main railway ferry, but *Kingswear Belle* (built 1972) and *Edgcombe Belle* are also available for this service.

In 2012 the Dartmouth Steam Railway & River Boat Company brought back the *Kingswear Castle* paddle steamer, once owned by the River Dart Steamboat Company and built at Philip's Noss Works in 1924, to her old home. She is the last paddle steamer of her generation and, following refurbishment, runs pleasure trips from Dartmouth to Totnes.

The 'Floating Bridge'

Up to the year 1831, the only regular ferry across the Harbour was from Kingswear in connection with the old road from Brixham, which for centuries had been maintained and was the private property of the various owners of the lands known as the Luttrell Estate. In 1830 an Act of Parliament was obtained for the purpose of 'establishing and maintaining a Floating Bridge across the Harbour of Dartmouth' and 'for building, erecting … proper piers, wharfs, quays … and convenient roads to and from the said bridge on each side of the harbour' (etc). The project formed part of a scheme for connecting South Devon from Torquay to Plymouth with the main coach road to London, and was promoted by Earl Morley and other landowners. Sir John Seale, promoter of the Floating Bridge Bill, took a great interest in the scheme and was the principal shareholder. Like so many other Dartmouth ventures it was a financial failure. Unfortunately, a clause had been inserted in the Act exempting the Post Office from payment of tolls. One clause involved paying a £60 annuity to the Luttrell family for loss of earnings on the Kingswear ferries.

As well as providing the ferry, Sir John Seale also built the road on the eastern side which stretched some two miles to the Brixham turnpike at Hillhead. The authorizing Act of 1830 forced the owners to run even at a loss and it became a millstone to the Seale family. One reason for its poor performance was the poor road approach on the western side. During the period 1855/6 when the Floating Bridge was inoperative after it sank at its mooring following a violent storm, the company declared itself insolvent leaving the mortgagee Sir H.P. Seale Bt in possession. Sir Henry continued to pay the Luttrell annuity until 1861 after which it fell into arrears. Subsequently the D&TR and its successors agreed to take over the Bridge annuity should the Floating Bridge be abandoned. As far as is known this clause is still extant. A new ferry was built, launched on 16th October, 1856 and brought into service on 31st October. This was much lighter than its predecessor and powered by two horses in the centre of the ferry working a treadmill. The crossing took seven minutes. A steam engine was re-introduced in 1867 with a new ferry built by Philip & Son (steam used earlier in the ferry's history (1831-5) had been replaced by a single horse power for economy's sake) and the crossing time reduced to three minutes. In 1873 the Floating Bridge was sold to the Trustees of the Raleigh Estates at Dartmouth, as mortgagee.

They closed the bridge for reconstruction in 1874 and ordered a new bridge from Messrs Willoughby and Co. Plymouth. The *Dartmouth Chronicle* of March 1876 had this to say about the new Floating Bridge:

> The Bridge across the Dart, which was at first worked by steam power, was, after a few years, worked by hand. This, in time, gave way to horses being employed, and again

return was made to steam. The old Bridge, although repeatedly altered, was too heavy and clumsy, and very difficult from the present structure, which has been built by Messrs Willoughby and Co. Central Foundry Engine Works and Hammer Mill, Plymouth, to the order of the Trustees of the Raleigh Estate, whose property the Ferry became, by purchase from Sir Henry Seale.

The following are the dimensions of the bridge: - length 52 feet: breadth 28 feet; depth 5 feet to top of roadway: 2 prows, each 19 feet 6 inches long. The bridge is divided longitudinally into three sections, viz: centre roadway, 12 feet wide; one side containing engine and cabin, and the other side the boiler and cabin. It is also divided transversely by two water tight bulk heads. She is driven by a pair of horizontal high pressure surface condensing engines (12 in. diameter cylinders, 18 in. stroke). and cylindrical multitubular marine type boiler, and seems admirably adapted for her work. She has done the passage across in three minutes, with a strong breeze blowing. This is good work, as the distance is over 1,100 feet! Traffic has been entirely suspended at this Ferry for nearly two years, and it is a matter of surprise that during the past six months, whilst the New Bridge has been in course of construction, the slipways and approaches have not been put in order, as, although the chains are fitted, the Bridge cannot be worked until this necessary work is done. If the traffic which has been so long diverted is to be restored and increased, it will only be by efficient management and regular periods of departure.

After four years out of service (replaced by a rowing boat), Raleigh Estates sold the Bridge in 1912 to the owner of the Torpoint Chain Ferry who brought in a new bridge. In 1921 it became the property of Philip & Sons. A new steam-operated paddle bridge entered service in 1921 and ran until 1960 when it was replaced by a diesel-electric paddle vessel. The ferry is mostly used by through traffic to and from the South Hams, etc. In 2009 the Floating Bridge, which had been in use for the last 48 years, was replaced by a larger model capable of carrying twice as many cars.

The Floating Bridge vessel *Philip*, with its chains visible, arriving at Dartmouth, 29th May, 1976.   *J. Woods, courtesy John Gillham*

Chapter Twelve

The Line described and Operating details

(Note: The line is described is the 1930s after doubling etc. was completed, but reference is made to later additions also. The gradients quoted are those shown in the Sectional Appendix.)

Kingswear station managed to cram the maximum facilities into a very cramped site which curved from south-west to north. Alongside the jetty were sidings which handled the coal traffic imported though the port in considerable quantity. Travelling cranes grabbed the coal from the ships' holds, a boat taking two days to unload with the electric cranes. Often another boat was waiting the clearance of the boat at the jetty before it could be berthed for discharge.

Behind the jetty sidings was a small goods shed and goods yard and then the passenger platform, an island, either face of which could be used for arrivals or departures. The longer face of the island was covered in for the last 100 ft by an overall roof which also sheltered all the station offices. Partway down the length of the shorter face of the island a connection led off to the former engine shed site, coal stage and water column, turntable and carriage sidings, all on ground formed by the railway on the mud of Waterhead Creek.

At the platform end was the all-wood 38-lever signal box which was provided with a new locking frame in 1960. The line straightened to cross Waterhead, or Hoodown, viaduct which was renewed as a double line viaduct in 1927. Beyond this a facing connection to the left led to Forwood's sidings, the site of the near-disastrous passenger train diversion in 1870. To the right lay the connection to Hoodown siding where the coaches of the 'Torbay Express' were always stabled. From here to beyond Britannia Halt the single line is just above sea level on a narrow shelf with high cliffs behind. Now approaching Steam Ferry Crossing or Kingswear Crossing (later Britannia Crossing) protected by distant signals, the line then passes over the wide slip leading to the Higher Ferry (or Floating Bridge) and continues past the very short Britannia Halt, first used by the Prince of Wales in 1877. The crossing keeper here was provided with a small ground frame with bells repeating the block signals between Churston and Kingswear signal boxes; he was also given a cottage alongside the line and a more pleasant place of employment it is difficult to imagine. In 1988 the level crossing gates were removed and replaced by lifting barriers. The halt also was removed as it was declared to be unsafe.

A short distance after the crossing the previously level line inclines sharply as the foot of the 1 in 66 ruling gradient to Greenway tunnel is encountered (the gradient is between 1 in 80 and 1 in 57). Some 300 yds beyond the halt the line curves to the north-east to take the 1923 deviation avoiding the Noss and Longwood creeks and then curves slowly back to the north-west as can best be judged in the appropriate photograph. As the curve is traversed , the quays and works of Philip's boatyard can be seen to the left whilst the leafy green of Noss Plantation is to the right. The line regains the very edge of the Dart as it straightens out from the 'deviation' and the attractive Long Wood stretches high above it on the right. Finally the line curves away from the Dart to the north-east and crosses the impressive curved Maypool, or Greenway, viaduct, entering soon afterwards the 495 yd Greenway tunnel situated on a slightly easier 1 in 100 rising gradient. The new Greenway Halt was built just beyond the tunnel in 2012. Travelling in the opposite direction, towards Kingswear,

MAXIMUM LOADS OF GOODS TRAINS BETWEEN
NEWTON ABBOT AND PENZANCE AND BRANCHES.

KINGSWEAR BRANCH.

FROM	STATION.	Tender Engine.				Tank Engine.				REMARKS.
		Coal.	Goods	Mix'd	Emps.	Coal.	Goods	Mix'd	Emps.	
DOWN TRAINS.										NOTE.—Three Empties to count
Newton Abbot ..	Torquay	22	32	38	40	24	34	40	45	as two Loaded Trucks. With
Torquay	Churston	12	18	21	24	14	21	24	28	two Engines double loads may
Churston	Kingswear ..	25	30	35	40	25	30	35	40	be taken, but no Train must
Kingswear	Churston	13	18	22	26	15	21	26	30	exceed 45 Vehicles.
UP TRAINS.										
Churston	Paignton	25	36	40	45	25	36	40	45	
Paignton	Torquay	16	24	28	32	16	24	38	42	
Torquay	Torre	11	17	19	22	13	18	23	36	
Torre	Newton Abbot ..	15	21	26	30	17	25	29	34	

Maximum loading of goods trains, as shown in the October 1898 Working Timetable.

Gradient profile.

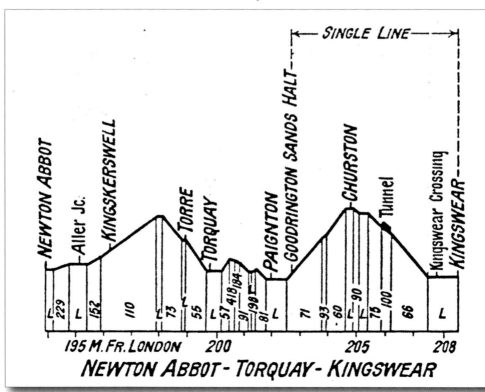

NEWTON ABBOT - TORQUAY - KINGSWEAR

this part is particularly attractive as one leaves the tunnel and catches a first glimpse of the Dart sparkling in the sunlight through the thickly wooded area.

The gradient steepens again on leaving the tunnel to 1 in 74 for just over ¼ mile and first Brim Hill plantation and then Brim Hill itself are passed on the left, the line soon being crossed for the first time by an overbridge carrying the Galmpton to Greenway Quay road. The houses of the large Galmpton village appear on the left, the line levels, climbs again at 1 in 120 for a spell and then levels again as Churston is reached, the White House noticeably prominent above the station.

Until 1963 Churston was a junction for the Brixham branch and an important station as many trains 'crossed' here, and it was responsible for attaching the trucks of fish received from Brixham to the up trains. After the 1912/13 extension the platforms were 700 ft long, capable of dealing with the heavy summer trains. The signal box was resited at the same time from its position beyond the road overbridge to the down platform; it was a substantial brick-built box containing 48 levers. Behind the Brixham bay on the downside was (and is) the former Railway Hotel, fortuitously close for a spot of liquid refreshment between trains! A short siding behind the up platform was used for horse boxes, and, before the introduction of auto-train working on the Brixham branch (in 1929), for stabling loaded fish trucks which were picked up by up trains. Beyond the overbridge at the Paignton end of the station (until 1978 an attractive stone structure now replaced by a modern concrete erection), the Brixham branch curved away to the east past the small goods yard which dealt with coal and agricultural, etc., traffic. There was a tiny goods shed of which I have not, so far , traced any photograph.

An up train restarting from Churston regains the single line just past the overbridge and quickly reaches the steep descent of 1 in 67 for the next two miles. The down refuge siding which parallels the single line for a short distance is seen above the height of the carriage roofs , such is the gradient here. This refuge was used to stable the 9.45 am Churston to Paddington (Saturdays only) in the summer. To the left, but also above the line which is now in cutting, is the broad expanse of Churston Golf course. Passing under the bridge carrying a minor road from Windy Corner to Brixham the line, which has been curving from south-west to north-west, straightens out and crosses the mighty Hookhills viaduct, high above Broadsands Road leading to Broadsands beach which can be seen to the right, Tor Bay coming into view for the first time. Following the viaduct the line takes very long curve from north-west to north-east then the line straightens and crosses the shorter Broadsands viaduct. After a short cutting the line steers towards the coastline and at Oyster Bend hugs it very closely, once again in cutting. Passing Armchair Rock and Saltern Cove the line closely parallels the profile of the coastline, being now on a high embankment descending steeply. Our imaginary up train would now be braking heavily, for even if it did not call at Goodrington Sands Halt it would be necessary to slow to 15 mph to hand over the single line token at the 52-lever wooden signal box.

The large 1957 carriage siding yard (now a car park) was on the left just before the platforms at Goodrington where the single line became double and remained so to Aller Junction. The halt which was only used in the summer months (apart from the 'thirties' until 1941), was very basic with a single shelter on each 600 ft-long platform, but there is a booking office on the new overbridge (previously a window in the former crossing keeper's hut at Tanner's Lane served this purpose). Beyond the station the layout expanded considerably as on the upside were the sidings provided for the 1931 goods yard and railhead depot and carriage sidings. There was also a bi-directional goods loop on the upside between Goodrington and

ENGINE LOADS FOR PASSENGER, PARCELS, MILK, AND FISH TRAINS FOR ENGINE WORKING PURPOSES

SECTION — Branch Lines.		60XX	Class 9F 2-10-0 92XXX (C); B.R. Standard Class 7 (70XXX); 10XX; 4037, 4074—4099, 50XX, 70XX	B.R. Standard Class 5 (73XXX); 49XX, 59XX, 69XX, 79XX; 68XX	B.R. Standard Class 4 (75XXX and 76XXX); 78XX; 53XX, 63XX, 73XX, 41XX, 51XX, 61XX, 81XX; 56XX, 66XX	B.R. Standard Class 3 (2-6-2T) (82XXX); 45XX, 55XX; 36XX, 37XX, 46XX, 57XX, 77XX, 87XX, 96XX, 97XX; 34XX, 84XX, 94XX
From	To	Tons	Tons	Tons	Tons	Tons
Churston	Brixham	—	—	—	—	220
Brixham	Churston	—	—	—	—	196
Exeter	Bampton	—	—	—	—	240
Bampton	Dulverton	—	—	—	—	220
Dulverton	Bampton	—	—	—	—	220
Bampton	Tiverton	—	—	—	—	240
Tiverton	Exeter	—	—	—	—	260
Newton Abbot	Paignton	485	450	420	394	320
Paignton	Kingswear	390	360	340	300	290
Kingswear	Paignton	410	365	340	320	300
Paignton	Torquay	460	450‡	420‡	364	308
Torquay	Newton A. unassisted	390	360	340	300	280
Torquay (Assisted to Torre Up	Newton Abbot Advanced Starting Signal)	500	455	420	420	420

C—At speeds not exceeding 60 m.p.h.

‡—Allowed one minute extra running time from Paignton to Torquay when the load for "Castle" and 10XX Class engines exceeds 420 tons and for 49XX, etc., when it exceeds 392 tons.

Engine loads as shown in the 1962/63 winter timetable.

SECTION — Branch Lines.		22XX 32XX; 0-6-2T "B" Group	0-6-0T "A" Group	S.R.—M.7	0-4-2T 14XX
From	To	Tons	Tons	Tons	Tons
Churston	Brixham	—	190	180	—
Brixham	Churston	—	168	144	—
Exeter	Bampton	—	190	150	—
Bampton	Dulverton	—	170	130	—
Dulverton	Bampton	—	170	130	—
Bampton	Tiverton	—	220	150	—
Tiverton	Exeter	—	240	180	—
Newton Abbot	Paignton	250	220	140	—
Paignton	Kingswear	220	220	140	—
Kingswear	Paignton	250	220	140	—
Paignton	Torquay	280	252	196	—
Torquay	Newton A. unassisted	220	210	130	—
Torquay (Assisted to Torre Up	Newton Abbot Advanced Starting Signal)	392	364	198	—

Paignton South boxes and a down goods loop, controlled by Goodrington, which was principally used for stabling coaching stock. The line was level to Paignton.

Entering Paignton over Sands Road level crossing, controlled by the 60-lever South box, the cramped nature of the layout was very obvious. To the left was the small goods area, displaced in 1931 by the new goods station at Goodrington, and to the right Park carriage sidings, now the site of Queen's Park Dartmouth Steam Railway station. In between were the two platforms which had to suffice for Paignton. Even though the up platform was bi-directional delays were heavy here in the summer months, because so many trains terminated and had to be unloaded and cleared to the sidings before the next could arrive.

At the north end of the platform was another level crossing very heavily used as the road, Torbay Road, was right in the centre of the town. Soon after an up train crossed the road and passed the little 13-lever North signal box the gradient changed from level to 1 in 80 rising. North box up main starter was a good train length from the crossing so that if on busy Saturdays the previous train had not cleared the section, it was possible to wait here and allow another up train in to load-up at Paignton. The gradients between Paignton and Torquay were undulating but about 1½ miles of the 2 miles distance was rising in the up direction, then falling, the last ¼ mile of which was at 1 in 55 before reaching Torquay which was on the level.

Shortly after the site of Preston Platform (221 m. 13 ch.) and roughly midway between the two stations was Torquay Gas Works, which was just inside the Paignton boundary. The works and the railway were squashed between the road and the sea and the 26-lever wooden signal box was perched very close to the edge of the cliffs. Two double-ended sidings were provided on the upside of the line and it was possible to serve the works from either the up or down line. A wagon tippler was provided on the siding nearest the works, and in the period when the author was regularly travelling over the line (1950s and 1960s), a small green 0-4-0 diesel shunter was employed by the gas board to shunt out the empty trucks, etc.

The line has been fairly close to the sea all the way from Paignton but at Hollacombe (also spelt Hollicombe) it is only a matter of yards from the cliffs; the line curves to the east and it is still possible to see the end walls of Livermead tunnel, opened out in 1910. Passing under the substituted road overbridge the railway is then the landward side of the road so they run in parallel past Livermead Sands, from where a brief view of Torquay harbour and the houses on Park Hill can be glimpsed. Then the line bears north and turns slightly inland to reach Torquay station, which, however, is only just off the sea front.

Torquay boasted two long platforms built on a curve with a centre line (middle siding) in between, which connected into the down main at the south end, and the up main at the north end of the layout. This was probably installed originally to hold the passenger trains that terminated at Torquay before their return journey, but was also available as a short refuge for goods trains and the bank engines in summer. At the south end of the station the small stone-built signal box containing 27 levers was a Saxby & Farmer original, never rebuilt by the GWR. At the north end the former North signal box was of similar design and lasted as a 14-lever ground frame until 1966, being demolished thereafter. As no goods traffic was handled at Torquay other siding accommodation was limited, consisting (after 1925) of two dead-end sidings behind the up platform at the north end. These were used chiefly in the 1960s for 'theatrical traffic' (the 'props', of repertory companies visiting the Pavilion and, later, Princess Theatres) which often necessitated the opening of Torquay box for a short turn on winter Sundays to pick up the trucks.

ENGINE RESTRICTIONS (PRINCIPAL MAIN ROUTES)

7(c) NEWTON ABBOT TO KINGSWEAR. Route Colour—'Red'.

All types of Western Region Engines are permitted:—
The following restrictions apply in Sidings in respect of the engines authorised over the route:—

Stations	Connections and Sidings	Engines Prohibited
Torre	Down Sidings alongside Loading Bank	All except 0-6-0T, 32XX, 55XX, 41XX, D.8XX, D.63XX, D.70XX permitted at slow speed.
	Up Side—Mileage Sidings at the rear of the Signal Box and Weighbridge Siding	'Red' engines (except D.8XX).
	Down Side No. 4 Meat Sidings and Crossover leading to it.	'Red' engines.
Torquay	Gas Works Siding	Engines not to pass over Tippler.
Kingswear	Noss Siding	All beyond stop goard.
	Mileage and Wharf Lines	'Red' and 'Blue' engines.
	Mileage Siding	All beyond stop board opposite the buffer stop of adjacent Jetty Siding, to the buffer stop of Mileage Siding.

KINGSWEAR BRANCH—The speed of all Up and Down Trains between Aller Junction and Kingswear must not exceed 50 miles per hour and must be further restricted to a lower speed as shewn below :

Aller Junction :			
215 m.p. to 215¼ m.p.	All Down and Up Trains to and from Torquay Line and Relief Lines		50
Through Facing Crossovers	Down Main Line	Down Relief Line	25
	Up Relief Line	Up Main Line	30
Between Kingskerswell and Torre	All Down and Up Trains		45
(218 m.p. to 219 m.p.)			
Torre—			
Torre (218m. 76ch. and 219m. 20ch.)	{ Down Trains from Down Line to Up Line		15
	Down Trains from Up Line to Down Line		15
Torre (219 m.p. and 219m. 20ch.)	All Up and Down Trains over Reverse Curves		30‡
Between Torre and Torquay			
Down Line (219m. 20ch. to 219 m. 66ch.)	All Down Trains		45
Up Line (220 m.p. to 219m. 20ch.	All Up Trains		45
Torquay—			
Down Line (219m. 66ch. and 219m. 79ch.)	Down Trains to Down or Up Platform		20‡
220m. 9ch. and 220m. 5ch.	Down Trains from Up Platform to Down Line		15
Torquay and Torquay Gas House Sidings—			
Down Line (220 m.p. and 221 m.p.)	All Down Trains over curves leaving Station		40
Up Line (221 m.p. and 220 m.p.)	All Up Trains over Curves approaching Station		35
Paignton—			
Down Line (222 m.p. and 222m. 4ch.)	Down Line to Up Line		20
Between Paignton and Goodrington Sands Halt (222 m.p. and 222½ m.p.)	All Down and Up Trains		40
Goodrington Sands Halt			
222m. 73ch. and 223 m.p.	Down Line	Single Line	15
Goodrington Sands Halt and Kingswear			
(223 m.p. and 227m. 8ch.)	All Down and Up Trains		30‡
(227m. 8ch. and 227m. 70ch.)	All Down and Up Trains		35‡
(227m. 70ch. and 228m. 45ch.)	All Down and Up Trains		40

‡—Permanent Speed Restriction Boards which are illuminated at night.

ENGINE LOADS FOR PASSENGER, PARCELS, MILK, AND FISH TRAINS FOR ENGINE WORKING PURPOSES

SECTION		CLASS OF ENGINE			
Branch Lines.		Diesel D63XX	Diesel D70XX	Diesel D6XX	Diesel D8XX and D1XXX
		A	A	A	A
From	To	Tons	Tons	Tons	Tons
Churston	Brixham	—	—	—	—
Brixham	Churston	—	—	—	—
Exeter	Bampton	—	—	—	—
Bampton	Dulverton	—	—	—	—
Dulverton	Bampton	—	—	—	—
Bampton	Tiverton	—	—	—	—
Tiverton	Exeter	—	—	—	—
Newton Abbot	Paignton				
Paignton	Kingswear				
Kingswear	Paignton	245	420	490	525
Paignton	Torquay				
Torquay	Newton A. unassisted				
Torquay	Newton Abbot				
(Assisted to Torre Up	Advanced Starting Signal)				

A – Unassisted

Extracts from the Working Timetables for 1962 and 1963.

From almost the platform end an up train immediately faces a fearsome 1 in 60 gradient which extends ¾ mile to Torre station. The line is heading north and away from the sea, but a last glimpse may be had of Tor Bay as our train slowly ascends the steep embankment leading to Torre. This is practically straight with a bend to the left just before Torre is reached. Until Paignton goods station was built in 1931, Torre had the biggest layout of all the stations on the line. On the upside behind the platforms were the coal merchants' sidings; behind the down platform were four short sidings, two of which had loading platforms, and a 10 ton hand crane. Beyond the down platform (Newton Abbot end) was a large two-road goods shed, in front of it was a long refuge siding. Like Paignton and Torquay the up platform was bi-directional. The station was built on a sharp curve and to help the signalman oversee operation the signal box (rebuilt in 1921) was a three-storey affair containing 42 levers.

Torre station was on a short level stretch but a steam engine having blasted its way up from Torquay now had to traverse almost ¾ mile of 1 in 75 rising. Firemen on this line had to know what they were doing! The line was now in cutting as our up train passed Torre up advanced starting signal (where the bank engine, if any, would 'drop off') and under Shiphay bridge.

The line, still climbing, is practically straight and heading due north for ⅓ mile passing the large Devon General Omnibus depot on the right, until at Lowe's Bridge (also spelt Lawe's bridge) it bears quite sharply to the left. At the midpoint of the curve the line passes Longpark Pottery, with its tall chimney, on the left, originally the atmospheric pump house built for the section between Newton and Torre but never used for this purpose. The line becomes level briefly and then, a welcome change for the fireman, a long decline begins at 1 in 120 which extends to beyond Kingskerswell station. At first heading almost due west, at Scott's bridge the line bears north-westwards and is gently curving and embanked until Kingskerswell is reached.

The most unusual feature of this station was that the road level was considerably higher than the railway so that a two-storey station building was provided on the up platform with access at first floor level to the booking office. From here one descended two flights of stairs to gain the platform, first using the road overbridge to cross the line if wanting to catch a down train. Kingskerswell was no more than a village and a single siding on the upside at the Torquay end of the layout was all that was necessary to deal with goods traffic. The platforms had been extended to 600 ft in 1911, but one presumes this was to enable the station to handle without delay the longer seasonal trains using the line, rather than any recognition of its traffic generating potential! A small Saxby & Farmer signal box containing 17 levers graced the up platform.

Beyond Kingskerswell the terrain was not particularly striking, continuing on embankment (and at a slightly easier grade of 1 in 150 falling) apart from a cutting about ¼ mile long leading up to Aller bridge. About ⅓ mile further on was Aller siding (connected to the down line) which served Aller Vale sand pits. The line became level and the Kingswear line comes to an end at Aller Junction, where our up train crosses the down main line (on the level) and enters upon the up relief line. This it follows for the remaining mile to Newton Abbot, passing the two large gantries controlled by West box just south of the Torquay Road overbridge, where the two up lines become three, and finally stops in Newton Abbot station.

Tables showing speed restrictions, permitted engine loads and engine route availability are included in the text.

List of Signal Boxes

Distance Box to Box.		NAME OF BOX.	TIMES DURING WHICH BOXES ARE OPEN.					Whether provided with Switch.
			Week Days.			Sundays.		
			Opened.		Closed at	Opened at	Closed at	
M.	C.		Mondays.	Other days.				
1	72	Exminster	6. 0 a.m. 9.30 a.m.	— 9.30 a.m. **TThO** 10.45 a.m. **WFSO**	5.30 p.m. **MTThO** 10. 45 p.m. **WFSO**	—	10.30 p.m.**E**	Yes.
1	74	Powderham				—	—	Yes.
1	66	Starcross	6. 0 a.m. —	5. 0 a.m.**SX**	11. 0 p.m.**B**	10. 0 a.m. 6.30 p.m.	5. 0 p.m. 10.30 p.m.**E**	Yes.
1	71	Dawlish Warren		Continu	ously.	—	—	Yes.
1	52	Dawlish	4.30 a.m. 9.30 a.m.	4.30 a.m. **SX** 9.30 a.m. **TThO** 9.30 a.m. **WFSO**	11. 0 p.m.**C** 5.30 p.m. **MTThO** 9.30 p.m. **WFSO**	10. 0 a.m. 6.30 p.m.	5. 0 p.m. 10.30 p.m.**E**	Yes.
1	39	Parsons Tunnel				—	—	Yes.
1	32	Teignmouth	—	Continu	ously.	—	—	Yes.
—	22	Old Quay	8. 0 a.m.	8. 0 a.m.	4. 0 p.m.**S**	—	—	Yes.
1	64	Bishopsteignton	7.50 a.m.	6.15 a.m. **SX**	11.30 p.m.**G**	11. 0 a.m.	9.15 p.m.**R**	Yes.
2	19½	Newton Abbot (Hackney)	5. 0 a.m.	—	—	—	11.15 a.m.	Yes.
—	41½	Newton Abbot (East)	—	Continu	ously.	—	—	No.
—	31½	Newton Abbot (West)	—	Continu	ously.	—	—	Yes.
1	3	Aller Junction	—	Continu	ously.	—	—	Yes.
1	15	Kingskerswell	6. 0 a.m.	§6. 0 a.m.	10. 0 p.m.**J**	11. 0 a.m.	8. 0 p.m.	Yes.
2	54	Torre	3.15 a.m.	—	—	7.30 a.m.	1.40 a.m. 11.15 p.m.**P**	Yes.
—	75	Torquay	6.30 a.m.	6.30 a.m.**K**	10.30 p.m.**K**	7.30 a.m.**T**	9.30 a.m.	Yes.
—	68	Gas House Siding	10. 0 a.m. 1.30 p.m.	10. 0 a.m. 1.30 p.m. **SX** 8. 0 a.m. **SO**	11.30 a.m. 5.30 p.m.**L SX** 8. 0 p.m. **SO**	—	—	Yes.
1	12	Paignton, North	3.30 a.m.	—	—			No.
—	19	Paignton, South	3.50 a.m.	—	—	**M**		No.
—	37	Goodrington Box	3.50 a.m.	3.50 a.m.	**A**	‡	1. 10 a.m.	No.
2	13	Churston	4. 0 a.m.	4.0 a.m.	**A**	‡	1. 10 a.m.	No.
3	58	Kingswear	4.20 a.m.	4.20 a.m.	**A**	‡	1. 0 a.m.	No.

A—To remain open until 12.5 a.m. Light Engine (12.30 a.m. Light Engine Friday nights) ex Kingswear has cleared. **B**—To remain open on Friday nights and to 12.0 midnight on Saturdays. **C**—To remain open on Friday nights, and until 11.30 p.m. on Saturdays. **D**—To remain open until 9.50 p.m. on Fridays and Saturdays. **E**—Or until 9.16 p.m. Plymouth has cleared. **F**—7.35 p.m. on Saturdays. **G**—To remain open on Friday nights. **J**—On Friday nights to remain open until 11.0 p.m. Kingswear cleared, and on Saturdays until 10.0 p.m **K**—To remain open until 11.30 p.m. on Friday nights and to open at 5.0 a.m. on Saturdays. **L**—Or until 3.30 p.m. Kingswear Goods has cleared. **M**—Closed on Sundays after completion of Train Service. **P**—Or until 10.30 p.m. Kingswear has cleared. **R**—Or until 5.0 p.m. Penzance has cleared. **S**—To close on Saturdays after both parts 3.30 p.m. ex Paddington has cleared. **T**—When required for theatrical traffic only. **§**—Open 4.0 a.m. on Saturdays. **‡**—Open as required on Sundays for Train Service.

Opening of signal boxes from the 4th July to 25th September, 1938 Working Timetable when the Kingswear line was probably at its peak of business, certainly in GWR days. Torre is open continuously except for about 10 hours on Sunday and Sunday/Monday, the Paignton boxes are continuous apart from about four hours Sunday/Monday and Goodrington, Churston and Kingswear are open for about 20 hours out of 24 on weekdays. Even Kingskerswell is required for 18 hours on Saturdays and nine hours on Sundays.

Operating Details

Kingswear

Heavy freight trains, mainly the loaded coal trains for Torquay Gas Works, needed banking up the steep gradients between Kingswear and Churston. The bank engine was required to be coupled to the rear of the train and engines of the 'King', 'Castle', 'County' or '47XX' classes were not allowed to assist in this way.

Noss siding at 227 m. 32 ch. was situated on a stretch of line at 1 in 80 falling towards Kingswear and could only be used in daylight. Trains were propelled, brake van leading and not more than 10 wagons, from Kingswear to the siding, the guard being accompanied by one of the station staff. On arrival at the facing points (which were worked by a ground frame released by the token) the wagons were uncoupled from the van, which was left on the main line with the person assisting the guard remaining inside. The wagons for the siding were propelled into the siding on a falling gradient of 1 in 53 and any outwards wagons pulled out and attached to the brake van, being spragged and braked. Finally the inwards wagons could be placed in the siding and the engine returned to the train waiting to be taken back to Kingswear. Obviously the operation occupied the whole section from Kingswear to Churston and could only take place when sufficient time was available.

Jack Eveleigh was lad porter at Kingswear from 1937-41 and worked 8 am-5 pm (1 hr lunch) and 12 noon-9 pm (with two ½ hr breaks) alternate weeks. His duties were cleaning, filling and changing signal lamps, reversing the tail lamp on terminating trains, delivering parcels to the village with a handbarrow and watering the coaches and dining cars. In those days, before the war, Kingswear was an open station, two porters from Churston joined each down train and collected tickets but the station was made 'closed' at the beginning of the war.

Most places had their own unusual names for certain sidings and Kingswear was no exception. The loop line off the longer platform face, used by engines to run-round was called the New Found Out. This led over Waterhead viaduct into Forwood's siding used for coaling from 1865 onwards and opposite was Hoodown siding, used to hold the 'Torbay Express' coaches. Behind the bay platform was the Cattle Pens Road (under the water tank), next was the Middle siding and nearest the creek was the Water Line.

The water supply for the locomotive water column and the siding came from a reservoir situated about a mile from the station, above Kingswear cemetery. In the autumn the outlet pipe from this reservoir often became choked with leaves, cutting off the supply. The cemetery caretaker, Albert Tabb, obligingly cleared the leaves and for this service the company granted him one free pass annually for himself and his wife. By the early 1960s the C&W Examiner at Kingswear had the job of keeping the pipe clear. The water was also sold to boats calling at the jetty to be used as ballast, but was not good enough to drink.

In August 1941 Jack went to Brixham as porter and then enlisted in the RAF. After the war he became signalman at Brixham, Churston and Torre in turn, returning to Kingswear as signalman in August 1958 (until February 1967). By this time the signalmen's weekday hours were 5.15 am-12.15 pm, and 3.15 pm to finish, which was after the 10.35 pm (10.45 pm summer) ex-Kingswear cleared Churston, except on summer Saturdays when an empty stock train left at 11.15 pm. The intervening three hours 12.15-3.15 pm were covered by a porter-signalman, whose other duties involved operating the electric cranes unloading coal (together with a porter from

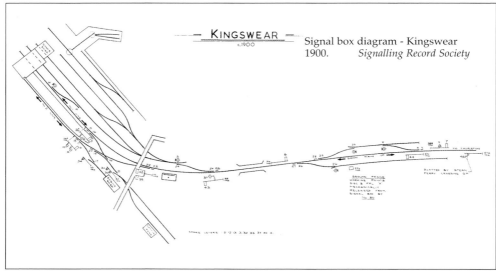

Signal box diagram - Kingswear
1900.   *Signalling Record Society*

Signal box diagram - Kingswear 1900.   *Signalling Record Society*

A diagrammatic layout of Kingswear in 1960.

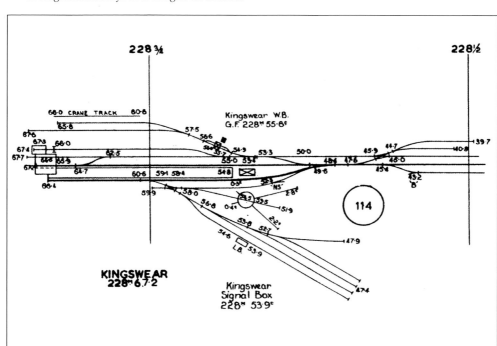

The wharf at Kingswear with a line of coal trucks standing in front of the goods shed; 24th June, 1958. *NRM/SSPL*

Kingswear station building with the entrance to the goods yard near the Royal Dart Hotel, left: 24th June, 1958. *NRM/SSPL*

A view from the buffer stops at Kingswear, June 1958.   *NRM/SSPL*

A fine study of Kingswear signal box on 25th May, 1955.   *R.G. Nelson*

the station). When thus occupied his hours in the box were covered by the signalmen on overtime. Coal came from Goole shipped by Everards and Jack remembers the boat most regularly in use called *Similarity*. Often a second boat would be waiting to unload. Only one coal train at a time could be loaded at Kingswear and the next train of empties would be held at Churston refuge until called forward.

Until Kingswear signal box lever frame was renewed in 1960, there were no track circuits at all at Kingswear but the new frame made provision for this. During the war the box was equipped with an air raid shelter: this looked like a steel cupboard and accommodated one person. One signalman had all the waste off the dining cars to feed his pigs. During the war when a bomb fell close to his property, the old tins and bottles which he had stored came in very handy to fill the crater - maybe one day someone will dig them up and class them as an archeological find!

Alan Babbage was an S&T lineman working on the Kingswear line from 1948 to 1959, at first as assistant to Charlie Rawlings. After 1954 the line was cut in two administratively and from then until 1959 he was the lineman covering from Paignton North to Aller Junction.

> I recall that during an inspection at Kingswear by officials it was 'discovered' that the crossover between the main platform line and the adjacent siding, which was used among other things for an engine to run round its train, was in fact being run over in the facing direction (at the 'B' end) by passenger trains departing for Churston. The points were very soon clipped and padlocked, and at some later date fitted with a facing point lock, operated from a ground frame.
>
> The signal box locking frame was of the twist and pinion type, unlike most of the others on the line which were of the 3 or 5 bar vertical tappet.
>
> There was a very unusual finial fixed to the Kingswear (fixed) down distant signal. It incorporated a pulley wheel which enabled the keeper to lower the complete signal lamp case and bracket to ground level for filling and cleaning. It was not a very successful arrangement, however, as the two contacts for the lamp repeater circuit to Kingswear box invariably became bent, or picked up dirt from the signal post, causing the indicator to show 'Lamp Out' incorrectly.
>
> As linemen we were issued with a train pass (also available on goods trains with the guard's permission) and an engine pass with which to check the correct operation of the ATC equipment. In order to provide a little relief from what could sometimes be a rather mundane job, we would take an occasional trip across the river to Dartmouth on *The Mew*, ready with an answer, if challenged, that we were going to check the Dartmouth station clock, the only piece of S&T equipment there. We never had to use this excuse!

After coal for Torquay Gas Works ceased to be imported through Kingswear (1963), the cranes were used for a short time to offload coal into lorries destined for Newton Abbot Power Station but this did not last long. The coal wharf sidings were closed on 4th May, 1964. The cranes were dismantled for scrap in 1969.

John Polyblank was chief clerk at Kingswear until made redundant in 1968 when the station was run right down. He remembers Royal Trains bringing Royal visitors to the Naval College. If, however, they came by Royal Yacht they landed at the GWR pontoon. Attempts were made about 1948-9 to reintroduce the overnight use of the Royal Dart Hotel for liner traffic but this was unsuccessful. The property was, however, still in use as an hotel in 1968, still railway owned and used for railway functions, retirement presentations etc. Before Torquay Gas Works closed, coal went by road for a short period because rail was becoming too expensive but this method was unsatisfactory.

Philip & Son Ltd, Dartmouth – Noss Yard (c.1960)

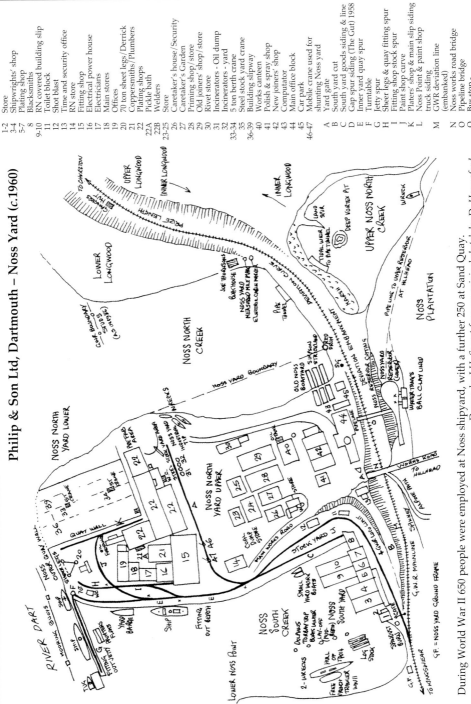

1-2	Store
3-4	Shipwrights' shop
5-7	Plating shop
8	Blacksmiths
9-10	RN covered building slip
11	Toilet block
12	Shot blast
13	Time and security office
14	RN store
15	Fitting shop
16	Electrical power house
17	Electricians
18	Main stores
19	Offices
20	70 ton sheet legs / Derrick
21	Coppersmiths / Plumbers
22	Plating shops
22A	Pickle bath
22B	Welders
23-25	Store
26	Caretaker's house / Security
27	Caretaker's Garden
28	Priming shop / store
29	Old joiners' shop / store
30	Rivet store
31	Incinerators – Oil dump
32	Incinerators – yard
33-34	5 ton berth crane
35	Steel stock yard crane
36-39	Building slipway
40	Works canteen
41	Polish & spray shop
42	New joiners' shop
43	Computator
44	Main office block
45	Car park
46-47	Mobile crane used for shunting Noss yard
A	Yard gate
B	South yard cut
C	South yard goods siding & line
D	Gap spur siding (The Gut) 1958
E	Inner yard quay spur
F	Turntable
G	Jetty spur
H	Sheer legs & quay fitting spur
J	Fitting shop stock spur
J	Paint shop curve
K	Platers' shop & main slip siding
L	Noss Point & paint shop truck siding
M	GWR deviation line (embanked)
N	Noss works road bridge
O	Pipeline bridge
P	Bus stop -
Q	Devon General & Burton

During World War II 650 people were employed at Noss shipyard, with a further 250 at Sand Quay.

Drawn by I.H. Smart from an original sketch by D. Hannaford.

Churston

The regulations required the signalman to exchange the token with the driver of a down train 'whenever possible' but a suitable person would be dispatched to do this at busy times. However, if the 'Warning' bell signal (section clear but station/junction blocked) was received from Kingswear the signalman then personally had to hand over the token and verbally warn the driver. The down line at Churston was also signalled for up trains and this line was used for this purpose except when two trains required to 'cross'.

Coupling and uncoupling of train engines terminating at or starting from Churston was carried out by the fireman. If for any reason the Brixham branch was not worked by an auto-engine, the fireman had to uncouple/couple at each end of the line. However, during any shunting operations, the station staff or guard was responsible for such work.

Jack Eveleigh recalls that the upside siding (always known as 'the cattle pens') was also used for horse boxes and for loading pit props.

Alan Babbage recalls:

One of the regular signalmen was George Snell who had a very strong Devonshire accent. He referred to the kettle as the 'Tay Ketto', usually kept permanently on top of the Valour oil stove, except when he was having one of his massive 'fry ups'!

A certain fireman on the Brixham branch used the water tank on the bay platform for an occasional dip or cooling off during the hot summers we used to have, but he did so very discreetly.

One morning a relief signalman was using one of the bus circuits to relay a long message to Newton Abbot when the exchange operator sent out the 11 o'clock time signal. This proved to be so uncomfortable and painful to his ear that he scattered the message papers, and everything within his grasp all over the signal box floor accompanied by a stream of curses and abuse! This chap was a keen motorcyclist and had a very powerful machine. On one occasion he offered to take one of our assistants back to Paignton to collect some battery jars which needed replacement. I don't think the man will ever forget the experience; he returned looking very pale, but with the glass jar remarkably intact.

On another occasion, Jack Eveleigh recalls, this same relief signalman set fire to the pampas grass on the downside bank using paraffin, 'because it annoyed him!' The flames were so intense that they blistered the paint on carriages in a down train.

Jack Eveleigh recalls an occasion in the 1950s when he had an empty stock train at Churston waiting to go to Goodrington. He had run it into the down (reversible) platform and accepted another train from Kingswear. On offering the empty coaching stock (ECS) to Goodrington the latter signalman refused it as he had a train waiting to come to Churston. In Jack's words, he was therefore 'snookered'.

The Brixham branch had shut for the day and he asked the driver of the ECS if he was prepared to shunt onto the branch, the down refuge siding also being occupied. Fortunately the driver agreed; to clear the points the train had to pass under Bridge Road bridge at the end of the long curve from the station. Farmer David Fish was working in his fields and saw the unexpected sight of a large tender engine and main line coaches appearing from under the bridge. Amazed, he went home for his camera and captured the picture. Fortunately for Jack, David told him about the picture and Jack managed to stop him sending it off for publication.

It may be noticed from the hours of opening of signal boxes set out earlier, that at least until the 1930s Churston and Kingswear boxes were open for about 20 hours out of 24 but by the 1950s and 1960s the service could be contained in an 18 hour period (or so). Like Kingswear, the midday period at Churston was covered by a porter-signalman.

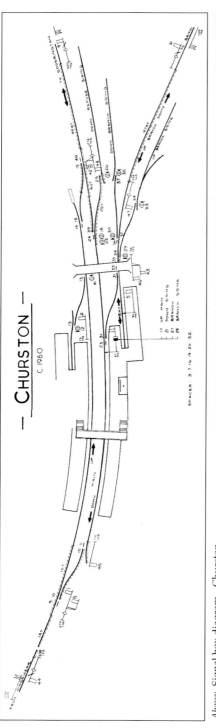

— CHURSTON —

c.1960

SPACES 3. 7. 16. 19. 20. 32.

Above: Signal box diagram - Churston c.1960.

Signalling Record Society

Right: Churston station and signal box, probably seen in the mid-1930s. A train in the Brixham bay is propelling onto the branch line for the engine to run-round its coaches. In the 1930s trains from Exeter ran through to Brixham on summer Sundays.

Lens of Sutton Collection

The Churston side of Greenway tunnel on 25th May, 1955.   *R.G. Nelson*

'41XX' class 2-6-2T No. 4150 and brake van, possibly making their way to Kingswear for a coal train for Torquay Gas Works, cross Hookhills viaduct and approach Churston passing its fine down fixed distant signal on 4th September, 1959.   *T. Wright*

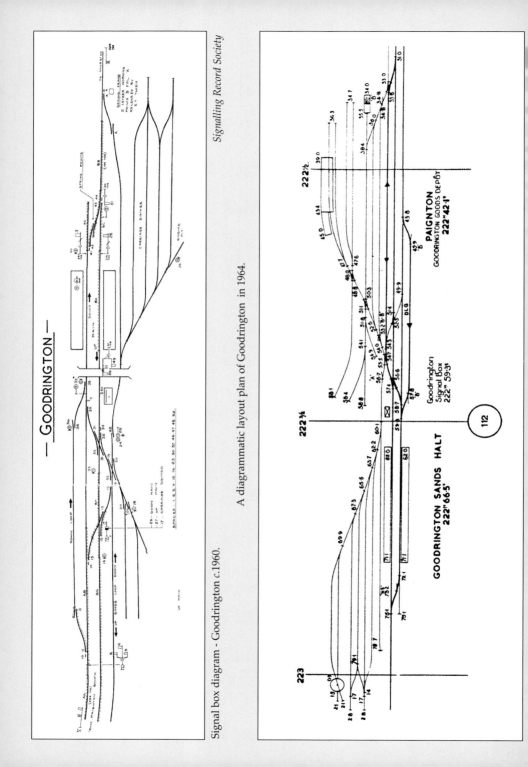

— GOODRINGTON —

Signal box diagram - Goodrington c.1960.

Signalling Record Society

A diagrammatic layout plan of Goodrington in 1964.

Goodrington

There was an auxiliary token instrument at the Churston end of the own platform so that trains booked to call at the halt could unload their passengers, and await the clearance of the section to Churston by another train, without the need for the fireman to walk back 200 yards to obtain the token from the signal box. The auxiliary token instrument, like the halt, was only used in the summer.

The yard accommodation for empty coaches was as follows:

Goodrington Yard		New Sidings (1957)	
Down Loop	10	Happy Valley	17
Up Loop	15	No. 1	16
No. 2	14	No. 2	14
No. 3	12	No. 3	12
No. 4	11	No. 4	10
Crane Road	10		
Coal Road	10		

Goodrington was the focus of the freight working on the line as the following example of freight working shows (winter 1961/2 timetable).

	Goodrington arr.	Goodrington dep.
	am	*am*
3.45 am Hackney	4.28	–
	–	5.17 to Brixham MWFO
6.15 am Brixham MWFO	6.52	–
6.35 am Hackney	7.16	–
8.15 am Gas House Siding	8.21	–
8.20 am Hackney	9.38	–
	–	10.05 to Hackney (call Torre, Kingskerswell)
	–	10.15Q to Gas House Siding
10 am Hackney to Kingswear	10.41	(11.56)
10.50 Gas House Siding Q	10.56	–
10 am Hackney to Kingswear	(10.41)	11.56 call Churston if required
	pm	*pm*
1.35 pm Kingswear to Hackney	1.59	5.45
	–	8.45 to Hackney

MWFO = Mondays, Wednesdays and Fridays only. Q = runs when required

Martin Kelland has kindly supplied some reminiscences of his grandfather, Henry Kelland, who was a signalman at Goodrington for almost 30 years.

My grandfather Henry Kelland was born in 1899 and joined the GWR in 1913. He started as an oil lamp boy at Paignton, progressed to St Thomas, Exeter in some capacity and then became signalman at Cadleigh & Bickleigh on the Exe Valley Line. Exempted from war service due to this essential occupation he spent 10 happy years here before accepting a move to Moretonhampstead as signalman in 1925.

The foundation for the turntable provided by Ransomes & Rapier at Goodrington in 1956; today the turntable is at Churston on the Dartmouth Steam Railway and the area is a Council car park. Goodrington Sands Halt is behind the carriages on the right. *NRM/SSPL*

Above: Goodrington Sands Halt seen in 1956 with the additional carriage sidings being built and the access to the turntable and water tower bearing right beyond the fourth telegraph pole. The line immediately behind the up platform could be used for trains on the national rail system, and Goodrington become a Parkway station, if it was so desired. *NRM/SSPL*

Right: Goodrington signal box, seen on 19th August, 1972, just a few months before closure.
S. Montgomery/D. Nicholas

In 1930 he was offered promotion and the opportunity to take up a new position at either Paignton or Goodrington signal boxes. He chose the latter and ran the box until 1958 when his first heart attack forced him to take on lighter duties as ticket collector at Paignton. He died in 1968.

Henry (Harry to his friends), worked an 8-4-8 shift system of 4 am-noon, noon-4pm, 4pm to midnight. Various members of my family remember Fred Harker and Harry sharing the 'eights' and a porter-signalman called Disney taking the four hour midday slot as part of his other duties.

Harry had a rather uneventful career which must be the pinnacle of achievement when one is a signalman! However, this means the family recollections portray a quiet routine rather than a life packed with accidents and derailments.

Tanner's Crossing was, of course, very busy during summer periods and in the days of the horse and cart Harry was assured of a plentiful supply of fresh manure to assist the growth of his enormous marrows kept beside the box. Every so often during a quiet spell, he would descend armed with a shovel and collect what was needed. As a keen gardener he also grew a rambling rose up the side of the box and no doubt kept a keen ear on the telegraph whilst tending his crops.

On the other hand Tanner's Road users could often become annoyed at having their progress towards the sea interrupted and on one occasion an irate visitor climbed the steps to give Harry a piece of his mind.

Harry's spare moments were not confined just to gardening - he also occupied himself disentangling swans from the signal wires which ran along by Goodrington Park and providing hot tea for my father and uncle when they picnicked there as boys.

During the war, routine and practice were suspended with unscheduled troop train movements requiring the presence of a signalman at all hours. Later in the war, a section of negro US Army soldiers were camped at Goodrington and a number made friends with Harry and his colleagues, providing welcome supplies of tinned food, sweets and tobacco. Joe Louis the boxer was among them.

Paignton

The up platform was signalled for bi-directional working and if a down train terminated in the up platform an engine was permitted to run 'up' the down platform line to run-round (or for any other purpose). Because the station is in the town centre, a bell plunger was provided from the up platform to Paignton North signal box to avoid drivers whistling for the signal. Similarly drivers were advised that a track circuit was provided to the rear of North box's down home signal to avoid them whistling for this signal.

Until the winter of 1957/8 Paignton North and South signal boxes were open continuously, as there was only a short spell during the night hours when no trains ran. In the next winter timetable (1958/9) both boxes closed after the last up train on Saturday night (just after midnight) until 6.25 am Sunday morning and again from just after midnight Sunday night until 4 am Monday morning. The continuous opening in the summer timetable was, however, maintained until 1965 inclusive. The 1966 timetable showed Saturday and Sunday night closings, both summer and winter. The 1968 annual timetable showed both Paignton boxes to cover the period 04.30/05.00 (Mon) to 23.00/23.15 (Sat) and 'open for train service Sundays', but an amendment for the winter period reduced Paignton South to a two-turn box, 05.00-21.20 weekdays and 14.00 to 17.00 Sundays. Outside these hours only dmus were run and these could be reversed in the up platform at the Paignton North end. This was not the case in the summer months, however. Details are not available

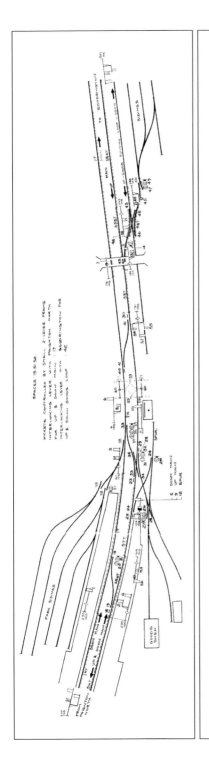

Top: Signal box diagram - Paignton South c.1950.
Signalling Record Society

Above: Signal box diagram - Paignton North.
Signalling Record Society

Right: Paignton South signal box seen on 30th May, 1971.
The late John C. Gillham

Looking from Sands Road level crossing (Paignton South) towards the station on 30th May, 1971.   *The late John C. Gillham*

The interior of Paignton South signal box, and signalman Bill Drake, seen on Sunday 9th July, 1961. Many signalmen wore slippers while on duty but Bill's shoes are on the bench should he need to go outside. Notice also the comfortable chair in front of the fire (and kettle) and the pile of completed block registers on the shelf above the window - these would be 'gold dust' today!
                                                                                                    J. Attwood

An unusually quiet scene at Paignton looking from the down platform to the up platform.

GW Trust (M. Hale)

Everything is looking smart and tidy as 'Hall' class 4-6-0 No. 5976 *Ashwicke Hall* arrives at Paignton with a portion of a down express, strengthened by two coaches for local passengers, 3rd September, 1959.   *T. Wright*

concerning the hours of duty in the intervening years, but by May 1971 Paignton North was open 04.30-23.20 weekdays (still worked by three signalmen but one man had to cover certain platform duties) and 08.20 to 22.30 Sundays. Paignton South was open 05.00-20.50, 04.35 to 21.00 summer Saturdays. Sunday hours were 10.50 to 19.25 in the summer and just 16.00 to 17.15 in the winter. The level crossing gates at Paignton North were converted to lifting barriers in 1976 and those at Paignton South in 1989.

As Goodrington was the hub of the freight working for the line, so was Paignton the centre of passenger operations. On summer Saturdays there was invariably an assistant district inspector located at Paignton to coordinate the working, which could become dislocated in the event of serious late running in the down direction. Although the rolling stock and engine workings were not as 'tight' as they are these days, most of the down trains brought in the engines needed for up departures and in many cases the stock was required to make a return journey, as the following examples from the 1961 summer Saturday timetable show:

Arriving train	Due am	Engine works	Coaches work
10.10 pm Leicester	4.35	7.45 am to Newcastle	7.45 am to Newcastle
10.40 pm Wolverhampton	5.15	?LE to Newton Abbot	10.35 am to Wolverhampton
10.00 pm Nottingham	5.25	6.50 am to Bradford	8.40 am to Nottingham
10.15 pm Sheffield	5.47	8.52 am to Sheffield	8.52 am to Sheffield
8.45 pm Bradford	7.03	10.58 am to Nottingham	10.58 to Nottingham
10.44 pm Manchester	7.12	9.45 am Churston/Padd.	12.05 pm to Cardiff
10.05 pm Hull	8.15	9.30 am to Swansea	(following week)
11.23 pm Manchester	8.35	10.35 am to W'hampton	12.30 pm to Manchester
9.05 pm Newcastle	8.45	12.05 pm to Cardiff	2.25 pm to Sheffield
6.05 am Cardiff	10.35	1.55 pm to W'hampton	1.55 pm to Wolverhampton
7.40 am Paddington	11.56	LE to Newton Abbot	1.30 pm to Paddington
	pm		
8.10 am Newport	12.08	1.55 pm Torquay/Padd.	1.55 pm Torquay/Padd

A standby engine was kept at Paignton between 6.30 am and 5 pm on summer Saturdays and a shunting engine from 4 am until 9 pm. A number of trains which started from Kingswear attached additional coaches at Paignton (e.g. in 1961):

8.45 am Kingswear to Bradford 'The Devonian'	- attached 2 rear (August)
10.20 am Kingswear to Manchester	- attached 4 rear
11.20 am Kingswear to Paddington 'Torbay Express'	- attached 4 rear
1.40 pm Kingswear to Paddington	- attached 2 rear
4.35 pm Kingswear to Paddington	- attached 2 rear if required

As at Churston there were special instructions regarding coupling and uncoupling of engines to/from trains. A shunter was provided after 9.30 am on weekdays in the winter and at all times in the summer for the purpose. At other times and on Sundays, it was the fireman's responsibility.

John Polyblank recalls that the last through service to London which, except on summer Saturdays, left Paignton between 4.30 pm and 5 pm for many years, was very popular with newly-marrieds going on honeymoon. One day in 1968 a man just married missed the train and hurried up to John to tell him that he was the bridegroom and that the train had left carrying the bride and the best man!

Paignton North signal box and level crossing, 30th May, 1971. *The late John C. Gillham*

Paignton North signal box interior, 1981. The small block instrument (*right*) is for down trains travelling over the bi-directional up line through the station. *Author*

Alan Babbage remembers that at Paignton North,

The method of working the facing points and lock on the down to up main scissors was rather unusual and employed a 'Princes Lock', a device which operated the points and FPL from one lever. I believe there were no spares in the locking frame to enable them to be worked separately.

Apart from S&T apparatus we also had to maintain the old mechanical chain-operated platform ticket issuing machines, and the PA system on the platforms. This was operated by one Harry Farthing, the train announcer, who I remember consistently referred to Newton Abbot as 'you can have it'. I don't think the public were aware of what he really said; it certainly sounded like 'Newton Abbot' through the loudspeakers!

Adjacent to the signal box was a footbridge crossing the road, which could be used by pedestrians when the level crossing was shut for a train to pass. Under the footbridge steps on the down side was located the 'Odd Spot' café; this was a firm favourite for some railwaymen to take refreshment, and it certainly was in an odd spot!

Paignton station was graded 'special A' and the station master normally came from Kingswear on promotion. However, in the 1950s the then station master at Kingswear was very happy there and would not move, which opened the door to men from other areas of the Region. A.E. Pallett was appointed from the Midlands and became the last station master, becoming the only appointment to the post of Area Manager, Paignton, *circa* 1964/5, the post later being swallowed up in the Newton Abbot Area.

Torquay

At this station only handled passenger traffic there were no special operational instructions, and the arrangements for banking heavy trains have already been described. The two up home signals were built on concrete posts and I have been told that these were made because of a shortage of timber after World War I, so much having been used for trench supports.

The 1903 Plymouth Divisional Appendix to the Working Timetable (the Kingswear line was part of the Plymouth Division until October 1904) makes it clear that the former North signal box at Torquay was a ground frame by this date.

Gas House Sidings came under the Torquay station master and Alan Babbage recalls it posed special problems for the S&T staff and the signalmen:

Here was a place which presented special problems from an S&T point of view. The combined action of fumes from the works and salt air played havoc with almost all our equipment. I remember at one stage a special paint containing fish oil was used to protect point ends and cranks etc., it didn't seem to do a lot of good as most of the apparatus was badly corroded before being treated. Instruments in the signal box also suffered, any brass items turned black, and polishing the lever handles was practically impossible. Overhead line wires also suffered from corrosion being mainly of copper, and the life of signal wires, and wire rope slings were pretty short. Everywhere had a distinctive smell about it, as I well remember.

On a more personal note, many was the time that I would take my bicycle to the works to obtain a huge bag of coke for 2s. 6d. and push it up the hill to our home in St Paul's Road, Preston.

Signal box diagram - Torquay Gas Works.
Signalling Record Society

— TORQUAY GAS WORKS —

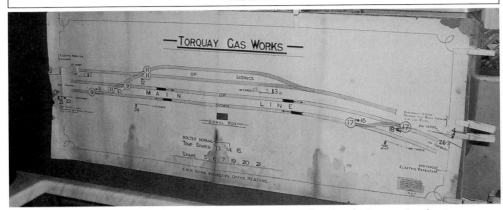

The signal box diagram for Torquay Gas Works signal box, showing the layout after the Torquay end (*right*) connection with the sidings had been removed (levers 13, 14, 15).   *Bruce Bennett*

'Castle' class 4-6-0 No. 7000 *Great Western* passes Gas Works down distant (only just visible behind the tender) with the 8.55 am Newton Abbot to Kingswear on 19th May, 1956. The locomotive is carrying the train reporting number for its next working, the up 'Torbay Express'. The third coach is passing over Cockington Lane bridge which was replaced in January 1969.
Peter W. Gray

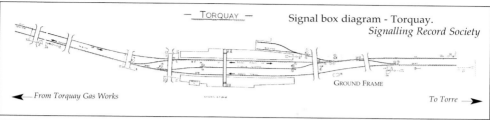

— TORQUAY —

Signal box diagram - Torquay.
Signalling Record Society

GROUND FRAME

◄— *From Torquay Gas Works*

To Torre —►

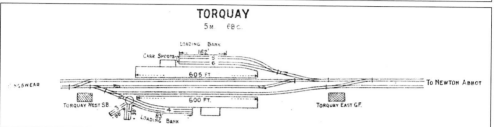

TORQUAY

5 M 68 c.

LOADING BANK

162'

CARR SPOTS

605 FT.

NSWEAR

To NEWTON ABBOT

TORQUAY WEST SB

600 FT.

TORQUAY EAST GF.

LOADING BANK

Torquay track layout in the 1920s.

Torquay signal box interior, photographed in 1981. At this time it was only normally in use on Summer Saturdays. *Author*

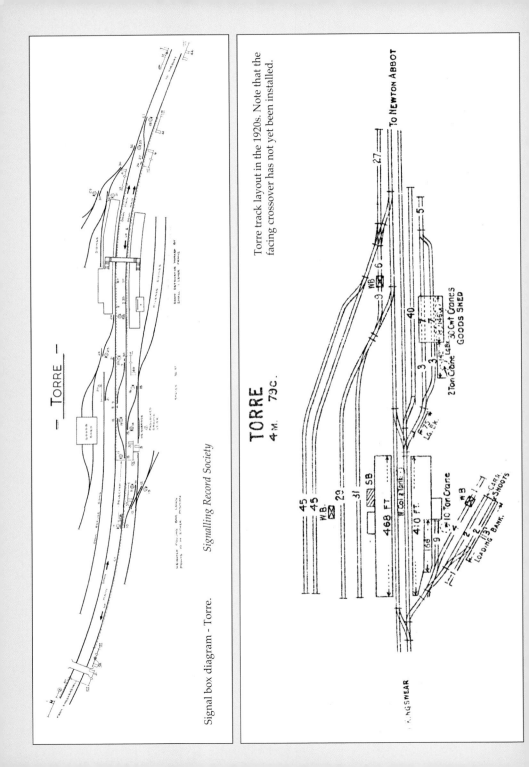

— TORRE —

Signal box diagram - Torre.   *Signalling Record Society*

Torre track layout in the 1920s. Note that the facing crossover has not yet been installed.

TORRE
4 M. 79 C.

Torquay station looking from the up platform to the down, view towards Newton Abbot, 1960.
Stations UK

Torre

From the 1894 Working Timetable:

When Down Trains or Empty engines are run on the Up Line from Torre to Torquay, they must be stopped dead before arriving at the Facing Catch Point at the South-side of Torre Station, 410 yards from the signal Cabin: and, before proceeding, Drivers must satisfy themselves that the Facing Catch Point is held over for the main line.

Torre station was sited on a short plateau between two very steep gradients and for this reason the appendix instructions were almost exclusively about securing vehicles and trains to prevent runaway. A down freight train calling at Torre to detach or attach vehicles had first to be stabled in the down refuge, braked and spragged. Not more than 15 vehicles could be propelled from the down to up line whence they were gravitated into the up sidings. No other shunting by gravitation was permitted. The meat sidings, or Lower Yard, were out of sight behind the down platform, and a code of rings on a special telephone was employed between the shunter and signalman to control shunting movements. The goods train which left Goodrington about 5.45 pm for Hackney (incidentally worked by the engine off the down 'Torbay Express' for many years) called at Torre to pick up traffic from the meat sidings. Even in the late 1950s it was so busy at Torre that it was almost impossible to get the engine across from the upside to pick up the outwards traffic.

Until 1921 Torre signal box was sited at the London end of the up platform at the foot of the ramp. In conjunction with the extensive alterations carried out in that year (*see Chapter Seven*), the box was rebuilt as a three-storey structure on the up platform close to the footbridge. For many years the box was open continuously, but by the winter of 1957 it closed from 8.50 pm Sunday to 4 am Monday. The following winter,

A panoramic view of Torre looking towards Newton Abbot, 17th September, 1959.

R.G. Nelson

Torre signal box interior, with its forest of spare (white) levers, seen in 1981.   *Author*

1958, the signalmen lost their Sunday duty as the box closed at 12.55 am Sunday until 4 am Monday, and this winter arrangement continued until 1966. In the summer months the opening hours remained continuous from 4 am (Mon)-8.50 pm (Sun) until April 1966, when the hours became 4 am (Mon) - after last train Saturday night , and 8.45 am-10.40 pm Sunday. From October 1966 the night turn of duty was discontinued and hours were 4 am to after the 8.35 pm Newton Abbot clears daily and, as usual in the winter, no Sunday turn was worked. I have no details for 1967 but certainly from Summer 1968 onwards the box was no longer open continuously on weekdays in the summer period, opening from 4.30 am-9.35 pm daily and 9.30 am-9.20 pm Sundays. In 1971 and 1972 (and possibly before this) it closed for an hour at midday so the two signalmen did not meet, but by 1974 the evening closing time had been brought forward and the box was now in switch from 4.15 am to 8 pm. By 1981 a single eight hour shift was being worked, and at the end the box was only open on summer Saturdays.

Alan Babbage has two particular memories of Torre:

It was here that I was asked to 'lift' the electric lock for the up starting signal (against Rule 83) by a certain relief signalman (now deceased) to let an up passenger train proceed to Kingskerswell. We were working on the middle floor at the time. I remember going upstairs to check the supposed electric lock 'failure' and spotted the track circuit to the rear of the up advanced starter was showing 'occupied'. When questioned, the relief signalman suddenly remembered that he had a light engine waiting 'line clear' out there. Could have been nasty if I had been tempted to carry out his original request!

On 26th April, 1958 the 8.55 am Newton Abbot to Kingswear hauled by 'Castle' No. 7004 *Eastnor Castle* (which was the engine to work the up 'Torbay') overran signals at Torre and collided with a short freight train. I remember the S&T inspector arriving soon afterwards and accompanying him to the down distant signal and ATC ramp. We were to carry out tests for a 'wrong side' failure as the driver and fireman both stated that they had got a bell at the ramp and that the distant, home and inner were all in the 'off' position. No fault was found, and the train crew's statements were later retracted at the subsequent inquiry, having been told that what they claimed was a physical impossibility by virtue of the mechanical and electrical protection given whilst the goods was shunting within station limits.

Kingskerswell

At Kingskerswell the signal box footnotes said that only the Torre-end crossover should be used to cross a train from one line to the other but there was no apparent reason for this. One day in the early 1950s, the signalmen on duty, Clifford Pearce, had no alternative but to use the crossover. A Plymouth-bound train was wrongly signalled down the Torquay line and surprisingly the driver went as far as Kingskerswell before stopping. It was necessary to use both crossovers to run the engine round the train and the forbidden crossover was clipped and padlocked before the train used it to cross to the up line. Later signalman Pearce received a visit from the Torre station master (who was also responsible for Kingskerswell) but the latter could offer no explanation for the restriction. However, at a later date when the box was being painted the footnotes were taken down and the offending instruction was found to be dated 1910, since when the track had been relaid with modern British Standard material! The footnote was sent in to Exeter District Office and henceforth the restriction was ignored.

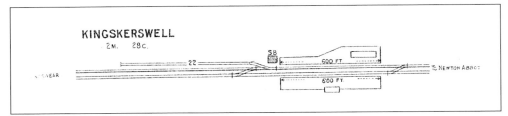

Kingkerswell track layout in the 1920s.

Signal box diagram - Kingskerswell.　　　*Signalling Record Society*

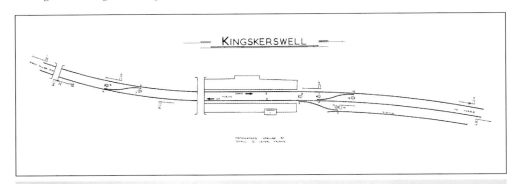

Kingskerswell station, looking towards Newton Abbot from the rear of a down train, 1st November, 1958.　　　*Hugh Davies (Chris Gammell)*

Alan Babbage's final memories include an anecdote concerning Clifford Pearce:

The amusing incident of signalman Clifford Pearce's determined effort to get his WC I remember well. He had asked me whether a space could be found under the box for this, and I told him that if the battery cupboards were moved a little there would be room. Armed with this information he told the 'powers that be' that the lineman said that there was room for it. The rest is history; Clifford got his way but not before stopping the 'Torbay' to attend to the wants of nature!

Telephone Circuits
These were the lifeline of the railway, used for both official and unofficial messages.

We had a working arrangement with most of the signalman who would notify us if either the S&T inspector or sub-inspector were seen on any down train from Newton Abbot. The message referred to them as either 'large' parcel or 'small' parcel on the so-and-so train coming our way. This was the signal to make sure we were out of the box and making ourselves look busy! An inspector appointed at a later date was given the codeword 'Bluebird', derived from the model of Datsun car that he drove.

The bell code for the lineman was 4-2 on any of the bus [telephone omnibus] circuits, this was the signal that we were urgently needed somewhere.

Joe Trethewey was a fireman at Newton Abbot in the late 1930s/1940s and has kindly penned these memories of the line:

We used to start off the 3.25 am freight to Kingswear stopping at Goodrington to shunt most of the Brixham traffic off and then we would carry on to Churston and eventually Kingswear. We used to return from Kingswear with a through passenger service for Bristol (winter), Swansea (summer). The next service was the 4 am parcels to Paignton and Churston and this was the engine for the Brixham branch. After that came the Torre Goods which was always very heavily loaded, which mostly served Torre and Torquay.

From then on there were several passenger services to Paignton, some returning as through services to London. There was a service where the locomotive worked the 8.25 am to Kingswear and returned with the famous 'Torbay Express'. The footplate staff on this train used to 'double home' to London.

The day time freight train used to carry coal for Torquay Gas Works and Goodrington and also some for Kingswear and when returning in the afternoon, used to pick up freight at Goodrington and empties at the Gas Sidings, we also used to work coal trains from Kingswear to Torquay Gas Sidings.

During the summer season Torquay and Paignton were always busy with special excursions, but of course on Saturdays it was extremely busy with holiday trains from all over the country. They started at 3.25 am and were continuous to and from Paignton until 5 pm. During that period there could have been about 70 to 80 trains in each direction and I have known a Saturday when we have had up to 100 arriving and 80 trains out, especially during 'Wakes weeks'. A lot of the locomotives were serviced at Newton Abbot as there wasn't then a turntable at Goodrington. Before they extended Goodrington Yard coaches were brought back to Newton Abbot and were stabled for the following Saturday. Some coaches were sent as far away as Exminster - these were used for trains starting at Teignmouth. Summer Sundays were also very busy, there were so many excursions.

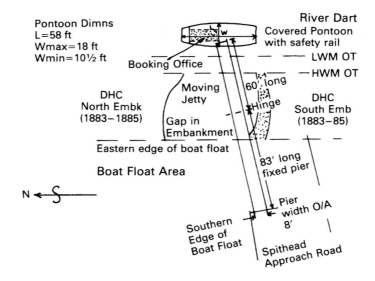

The original Dartmouth 'station' and its 1889 replacement.

From originals drawn by I.H. Smart

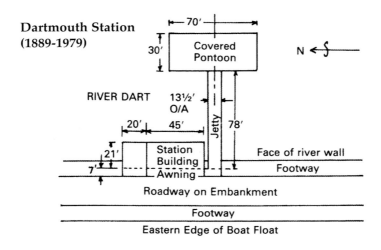

Appendix One

Dartmouth Station (1858-1889) *by I.H. Smart*

The siting and completion of the Dartmouth end of the railway was a complex and long drawn out business for the authorized terminus of the line was at a point on the eastern bank of the Dart above the Hoodown ferry or Passage House Inn, directly opposite an embanked and reclaimed area in Dartmouth known as the New Ground. To the north of the New Ground about ½ mile distant was the western end of the Floating Bridge at Sandquay. Between the New Ground and Sandquay there was neither a direct nor a satisfactory carriage road. The New Ground itself was centrally placed to the residential and commercial areas of Dartmouth.

As early as April 1858 there was local discussion as to the siting of the Dartmouth station and Robert Cranford, editor of the *Dartmouth Chronicle*, confidentially reported that the site chosen was at Coombe (Sandquay), but that a good road was wanted. The northern portion of the existing road belonged to Sir H.P. Seale, whilst the southern portion was under the control of the Town Council. If true the report would mean that the Directors intended the railway terminus to be at the eastern end of the Floating Bridge ferry. To have built a terminus here would have been expensive as there was only a narrow strip of land at the base of the riverside cliffs between the Floating Bridge and Hoodown, approximately 1¼ miles. In the event the railway was built in the river between high and low water marks.

By September 1858 the *Dartmouth Chronicle* carried a report that the railway terminus would be at the Floating Bridge, the Luttrell family* having agreed to give the D&TR land at that point for a terminus , provided the D&TR built a carriage road to Kingswear along the foreshore within 12 months. There would be no charge for the land below the Floating Bridge, whilst that above the Floating Bridge would be made available at a reduced cost. During the summer of 1858 the people of Dartmouth, ever money conscious, wanted their station to be at the New Ground, which would save the expense of widening Clarence Street and other roads.

In reply the D&T Directors, through Charles Seale Hayne, pointed out that they had no power or money to build a road on the Dartmouth side and proposed to consider the matter in about 12 months time (i.e. late 1859) after the Greenway tunnel was complete. No firm decision, indeed, had taken place as yet.

The matter was still unresolved in May 1862 when the matter was discussed at a Board meeting, but no decision was then taken. By this time the Dartmouth town improvement scheme had been published. This was a plan for, amongst other things, a new carriage road from Southtown to Sandquay, with the intention of giving vehicle access across Dartmouth in as straight a line as then seemed possible.

If the Dartmouth station was to be below the Floating Bridge the upper part of Mr Bell's new road would be unnecessary. (William Bell had been Resident Engineer of the D&TR (1857-1861) and would become Engineer of the Torbay & Brixham line in 1864.)

The editor of the *Dartmouth Chronicle* went on to state that since the cost of continuing [the railway] down to the Hoodown Ferry is small compared with the cost of the local improvement and the cost of a road from the Floating Bridge to the New Ground, the two schemes should be taken together and the local Board of Health and the D&TR act together.

However, as a result of the visit of the East India Shipping Co. Directors in September 1862, to discuss with the D&TR the use of the harbour as a port of call for the Cape Mail boats, the position changed dramatically. The railway Directors now decided on the extension of the railway to Kingswear, using a board of Harbour Commissioners - themselves - to obtain the Dartmouth Harbour Act (1863).

When in November 1862 the Local Board wrote to the D&TR Board asking for information on the site of the Dartmouth station, Charles Seale Hayne replied that the

---

* The Luttrell's were Lords of the Manor of Kingswear and owners of Nethway Estate up to 1874.

Dartmouth station at a very early date, with vintage GWR parcels delivery lorry outside.
Lens of Sutton Collection

Dartmouth station photographed from the Boat Float (foreground), 31st March, 1973.
The late John C. Gillham

D&TR Board wanted to know the views of the inhabitants of the Town; the Local Board replied that they wanted the station as central as possible, and that the ferry should carry horses and carriages. However, by April 1863 with the railway approaching the Floating Bridge, no decision had been taken as to the site of the station.

At the end of July a meeting was held between the Engineers and Directors of the D&TR and it was decided that Mr Brereton should carry out a survey for a station site and report back within 7-10 days. This he did in a letter to the Board dated 4th August, 1863. After discussing the needs for the site of the station, Brereton stated unequivocally the neighbourhood of the New Ground was the desirable site with a pontoon and landing stage to allow the ferry to operate at all states of the tide. But that place was also planned to be the outlet of the main sewer and Brereton therefore recommended an even better site, projecting less into the river, and interfering less with river traffic, at the point just to the south known as Spithead. This would be the passenger station which would be built on a small area to be enclosed in front of the Quay (i.e. in the boat float). Goods traffic would be dealt with at a wharf lower down the river. Brereton's report was adopted at once so that work below the Floating Bridge and on to Hoodown might commence (August 1863) and by December 1863 had reached Waterhead Creek. Yet in January and April 1864 the D&TR asked the Town Council if they could moor the pontoon off the New Ground.

A portion of the foreshore in front of the Quay was purchased from the Duchy of Cornwall for a nominal sum (measuring 125 ft east/west and 100 ft north/south) on the southern side of the boat float at Spithead, up to the New Quay or Castle Hotel steps. From this was to be built a pier and floating jetty to a moored position in the river. The booking office was a 'box on the pontoon' (*see page 334*). Another proposed development was the erection of a new booking office at Dartmouth station. This would have replaced the 'box on the pontoon'. The South Devon Railway had purchased a portion of the foreshore in front of the New Quay in 1871, and sought to develop it in October 1874, when they wrote to the Dartmouth Urban Sanitary Authority asking permission to build a booking office on shore at the commencement of the gallery leading from Spithead.

After discussion on the merits or demerits of the South Devon proposal, it was resolved to refuse the SDR permission on the grounds that the company, with the agreement of the BoT and the Dartmouth Harbour Commissioners (DHC), could build on that position of the foreshore that they bought in 1871. In view of this refusal nothing developed for a further decade.

In 1880 the DHC still basically representing railway interests as most of the Commissioners were ex-D&TR Directors, their relations or friends, decided to promote a Bill to enable them to build a sea wall, 600 yds long from Bearscove (Bayards Cove) to the Gas Works in the north , as well as to dredge the river. The Act of 1882 provoked extreme opposition in the Town and radically altered the membership of the DHC still led by Charles Seale Hayne and Sir H.P. Seale. The Embankment story does not concern us except for the GWR portion (100 ft in width) at Spithead. The total cost of the embankment and roadway was to be £24,000, whilst the small GWR portion was estimated by R.P. Brereton, acting now as the Commissioners' Engineer, to cost £1,160.

In December 1881, when the Bill was published, GWR officials expressed their approval and said that GWR would cooperate in their portion of the scheme. As all actions regarding GWR property were under the Bill (and Act of 1882) to be by mutual agreement, the DHC entered into negotiation with the GWR and reached a friendly agreement (July 1882) in writing between Seale Hayne and Mr Hubbard (GWR). All was agreed but the Directors of the GWR would not formalize the agreement as the DHC wanted to move the pontoon and station from the Spithead to the New Ground. Indeed in 1881 the GWR were putting in a petition against the Bill and appointing a barrister, Nathanial Baker, to join their other representative on the DHC, Capt. Toms of Kingswear, to make known their case. This petition was withdrawn before the House of Lords proceedings in May 1882, but the dispute dragged on and in September 1883 the GWR asked the Court to grant them an injunction to prevent the DHC moving their pontoon.

The case was heard before Mr Justice Pearson in the Chancery Court and it was concluded by counsel for the DHC that they could move the pontoon as the ferry was illegal, not having been made as described and authorized by the Act of 1857. It should have gone from Hoodown to Kingswear ferry slip and thence to Dartmouth, said the DHC. The Judge did not accept this argument, considering it to be irrelevant, and granted an injunction to the GWR, preventing the DHC moving the pontoon except by mutual agreement. There the matter rested as did the pontoon!

The editor of the *Dartmouth Chronicle* commented that the decision deprived ratepayers of use of the embankment behind the GWR pontoon. A gap would have to be left in the embankment preventing it from being continuous unless the DHC spent £1,100-1,200 for sole benefit of GWR, 'who have never treated Dartmouth favourably, although they have a monopoly'. The agreement of 1882 was favourable to both parties - why would not the GWR Board sanction it? It was not until his resignation in 1885 that the reason was divulged by Charles Seale Hayne.

By February 1884 whilst work proceeded on the embankment, north and south of the GWR portion, there was some prospect of an agreement with the GWR. By October 1884, the tradesmen of Dartmouth and Kingswear were prepared to memorialize the GWR Board and the Board of Trade which they did claiming, *inter alia*, inadequacy of both pontoons and inability to take goods, horses, or carriages from them, excessive traffic rates and the early close down of the ferry (9 pm). The GWR also came under pressure from the Board of Trade, who, following inspection, considered Dartmouth pontoon 'extremely dangerous'.

The GWR obviously considered the memorial and in March 1885 applied to the Town Council for permission to move their station to the New Ground - the very thing they refused to do in 1882/3. Permission was refused by the council as they considered Spithead to be the best site. It is to be presumed that the Council were of the opinion that the GWR would not then complete their section of the embankment. They could also have pointed out that their agreement with the Duchy of Cornwall forbade the erection of commercial buildings on the New Ground (since 1861).

By the end of 1885 the embankment was complete except for the GWR portion, but the acrimony of the anti-embankment faction in Dartmouth, both on the Council and from their representatives on the DHC, had been sufficient to induce Seale Hayne to resign from the Harbour Commission, handing over the chairmanship to his uncle, Sir H.P. Seale, Bart. In the same year, the GWR withdrew its nominees on the DHC and did not replace them (Capt. Toms and Mr Baker).

In his letter of resignation, dated 18th February, 1885, Seale Hayne warned the DHC against allowing the GWR to avoid building their portion of the embankment, alleging that the GWR wanted to save the expense of building three retaining walls around their property which should have been done long ago. Seale Hayne pointed out that DHC

Dartmouth railway pontoon with the station building behind, seen from the river on 22nd January, 1954.   *NRM/SSPL*

Dartmouth station decorated for the 1956 Royal Regatta seen on 31st August. There is a very well presented display of timetable and fare posters in evidence. In other years these boards were taken up with colourful scenic posters. *NRM/SSPL*

would derive nothing from building the GWR portion and also that DHC should maintain strict neutrality as to siting of the GWR station. Again, according to Seale Hayne, the area of boat float owned by the D&TR was to have been the site of Dartmouth station but a lack of money meant that it was not built and the 'box of a booking office' made on the pontoon instead.

In January 1886 the DHC went bankrupt and a Receiver was appointed - none other than Charles Seale Hayne, MP. Towards the end of 1886 the GWR put forward plans for a new station, but these were rejected by the DHC as the pontoon would interfere with river navigation and the proposed station interfere with the embankment roadway. Matters continued to drift until the middle of 1887 when the GWR put forward fresh proposals which were approved on 12th August, 1887, with the proviso that the GWR give up the western half of their land in the boat float and the portion on which the embankment roadway was to be built.

Apparently this matter could not be mutually agreed and so Col. Rich (BoT) was appointed as arbitrator in February 1888 as to the site of the station. His decision was that the portion of the boat float might be filled in by the GWR, but only for buildings required for passenger traffic to the ferry boats. In fact this was never carried out, but the station building was erected on the river side of the embankment. After further discussions between the GWR, the DHC and the Corporation of Dartmouth to whom the embankment was to be conveyed, an agreement respecting the siting of the new station was made (October 1888). This satisfied the judgements of Mr Justice Pearson (in December 1883) and confirmed that the DHC would convey the GWR portion of the embankment and foreshore immediately in front of it to the GWR, which was done in December 1889. The GWR completed the embankment when they rebuilt the station (authorized in 1888 at £4,680), opened on 31st March, 1890. Dartmouth's last station master is thought to be Mr A.J. Bradridge who was promoted to Moretonhampstead in 1909 and replaced by an inspector. The station building still stands as the 'Station Restaurant' being leased from the South Hams DC as successors to the Dartmouth Corporation.

Appendix Two

Summary of Sir Roundell Palmer's Award, 1871

After reciting the Heads of Agreement for the lease of the Dartmouth & Torbay Railway (see Chapter Three) and the reason for the reference to him for umpirage, Sir Roundell Palmer* makes 16 awards, as follows (summarized). References to the meaning of 'Rent (B)' and 'Rent (A)' can also be established from Chapter Three (pages 56/7).

1 That the sum of £200,000 is the amount of Debenture Debt and Preferential Capital of the Dartmouth Co., raised or authorized to pay off the liabilities of the Dartmouth Co. existing at 10/10/1865, and bearing interest at 5 per cent p.a.

2 The Rent (B) payable by the SDR to the D&T under the Heads of Agreement for the 5th year of the term, commencing 1/1/1870 was £10,000.

3 The sum of £12,000 is the amount by which the Rent (A) paid to the Dartmouth Co. during the first 4 years of the lease was insufficient to meet the interest on the Debenture Debt and dividends on the Preferential Capital during those 4 years.

4 The sum payable from 1/1/1871 shall be the yearly sum of £10,600.

5 The two companies shall be amalgamated on the following terms.

6 In place of the yearly rent of £10,600 the SDR would create and issue £140,410 South Devon £5 per cent rent charge stock and would take over the entire debenture debt of the D&T amounting to £71,587 with interest at 5 per cent p.a. Any authorized unissued debentures of the Dartmouth Co. remaining at the date of amalgamation would be bought by the SDR at face value, and cancelled.

7 The South Devon rent charge stock hereby authorized to be created to be exchanged on an equal (i.e. £ for £) basis to holders of Dartmouth Preference shares issued prior to 10/10/1865, or issued subsequently with the SDR's consent, the Dartmouth shares then to be cancelled. The balance of the rent charge stock to be held by two Trustees (one nominated by the D&T, the other by the SDR) and used to pay off the lawful debts and liabilities of the Dartmouth Co., other than their debenture debt, as existed at 10/10/1865.

8 The SDR to pay in cash £4,700 plus interest at 5 per cent p.a. from 1/1/1871 for the following D&T Assets:
i) D&T expenditure on works since 10/10/1865
ii) The *Perseverance* steam boat
iii) The rent payable by the Post Master General in respect of telegraphs and apparatus
iv) The gridiron in the River Dart
v) Surplus lands and property at Torquay; mudland in the River Dart; shipbuilding yard, dwellinghouse and ferry at Hoodown; the Yacht Club Hotel Kingswear; the [horse] ferry, landing slips etc at Kingswear, the SDR receiving the rent from 1/1/1871.
vi) Anything else the Dartmouth Co. might wish to claim

9 Houses at Kingswear belonging to the Dartmouth Co. and the leasehold security of the Brixham Road Hotel and surplus land shown on an attached plan should be conveyed to Trustees upon trust for sale, the proceeds passing to the Trustees set up in clause 7 (above), being used to pay off the D&T debts.

10 All D&T land and property not specifically mentioned in clauses 8 or 9 to pass to the South Devon Railway.

11 Sets out the mechanism by which any cash payable by the SDR under this (Sir R. Palmer's) Award and proceeds from application of clause 9 be used to pay off the D&T liabilities.

12 Arrangements for paying dividends on the South Devon rent charge stock issued under clause 6.

13 Dartmouth Co. to be allowed £150 for office expenses in 1870 and 1871.

14 The SDR to be indemnified by Deed against all outstanding liabilities of the Dartmouth Co. This Deed to be executed before the amalgamation takes effect.

15 The amalgamation to take effect after the execution of the said Deed and the performance of the other conditions of this document.

16 Each company to pay their own costs in the arbitration and share the costs of [his] umpirage equally.

* Later Lord Selborne (1812-1895). Lord Chancellor 1872-4 and 1880-5.

Appendix Three

Correspondence relating to Charles Seale Hayne's resignation from the SDR Board

MR. SEALE HAYNE AND THE SOUTH DEVON BOARD
The following correspondence, with reference to Mr Seale Hayne's resignation as a Director of the South Devon Railway, has just been published:-
TO THE SHAREHOLDERS OF THE SOUTH DEVON RAILWAY.
3, Eaton-square. London. S.W.

December 14th, 1871

Ladies and Gentlemen, - Having been honoured with your confidence at the last contest for a seat at your Board, it is due to you and to myself that the reasons of my resignation should be explained.

The following letters will supply the needful information.

The manner in which the prosperity of the Company has long been retarded by the exclusive and illiberal policy in traffic matters, which has been pursued by your Board, is well understood by a large body of Shareholders. The narrow gauge competition, imminent at Plymouth, has become a public necessity in consequence of this policy. The causes therefore, which lead to its continuance, now deserve the special attention of the Shareholders, in order that the arrangements, if beneficial, indicated by the public notices recently advertised. may not be thrown over, as in 1867, by disputes, which in no way concern this company; and that their interests may be no longer treated as subservient to those of other Companies, without adequate compensation.

The other matter is one which I expose with much reluctance; but knowing, as I do, the opinion which is entertained as to the character of these transactions of your Board, reticence on my part would be far more injurious than an open statement of the facts; as to the accuracy of which I challenge the strictest investigation. Premising that prior to the date of the following correspondence the Chairman had written to me stating that certain letters, which I had addressed to the Board, had 'produced painful impressions', and that the Directors thought my 'charges ought to be withdrawn', and hence my offer to do so if I should be found to be in error by any unbiassed authority; I have but to add that this offer and my last letter, given below, remain unnoticed.

I have the honour to be, your most obedient Servant,

C. Seale Hayne.

* *

Kingswear, Dartmouth,

November 4th, 1871.

Gentlemen, - I regret that it has twice been my duty to differ from you in matters of grave importance. On the first occasion, in reference to the injurious effect upon the interests of your shareholders and the public of working the South Devon Line for the exclusive benefit of particular Companies; of offering impediments to the free interchange of traffic with the South Western Company, to and from certain stations; and of unjustly continuing this system without adequate compensation from those companies in whose interests these restrictions are maintained, as a dispute affecting the Bristol and Exeter Company, in which South Devon interests are in no way concerned, has been the means of depriving your shareholders and the public of a most beneficial arrangement with the South Western in reference to future competition and increased railway accommodation.

On the second occasion, in regard to the honesty of the course which has been adopted towards the Dartmouth Company and its Directors; I must, therefore, decline further connection with your Board.

In explanation of my views upon the first matter you have before you, my written statement made in October, 1869, when my proposal, so obviously beneficial to the South Devon, to establish through booking for passengers and goods with the South Western Company, to London and all stations, found not a single advocate among you. In regard to the second, my desire is that there should be no uncertainty as to the ground of my complaint, I therefore make the following statement, the accuracy of which is well known to you. In the month of August, 1865, when the connection between the South Devon and Dartmouth Companies was merely a working arrangement, and the Directors of the latter Company were promoting an important extension into the South Hams, and contemplating alliances with narrow gauge interests, your Chairman and Secretary, with your instructions, attended a meeting of the Dartmouth Board, for the purpose of setting the terms of a lease and amalgamation of the South Devon and Cornwall Railways. Having announced the object of their visit, they were informed by me, as requested by my colleagues, that we declined to go into the question at that time, unless it was first distinctly understood that such amalgamations should have the effect of indemnifying the Dartmouth Directors personally against the debts of their company, for which they are liable. Your Chairman and Secretary then left the room to consider the matter. On their return they informed us that 'this point was conceded;' your Chairman adding these words: 'You gentlemen, must, of course, be held personally harmless.' 'If we cannot give you the money, we can give you the money's worth'. The negotiation then proceeded; the Dartmouth Directors undertaking to withdraw their support from new lines in the district, and to assist financially with their credit, in order to keep down interest charges, until the South Devon Company was in a position to carry out the amalgamation. £200,000, in round numbers, was stated to be the debt then owing. As the Dartmouth line was to become South Devon property, and having at that time full confidence in the good faith of those with whom they were dealing, my Directors left the legal arrangements in your hands. The bill and agreement, which I was informed would carry out the above settlement, in passing through Parliament received many alterations; notably the rate of South Devon guarantee, which was to have been attached to Dartmouth Preference Shares, was reduced from 6 to 5 per cent; but a distinct assurance was given, at an interview of the Committees of the two Boards, that these alterations should not in any way prejudice the arrangements and understanding which existed between us. Up to a certain date these arrangements were duly observed. You gave your guarantee to the Devon and Cornwall Bank for loans to the Dartmouth Company; and, at your Secretary's request, in the great financial panic, Mr Belfield and Mr Froude lent large sums of money to the Dartmouth Company upon your guarantee.

Owing to the difficulties occasioned by this panic and obstacles raised by yourselves to arrangements made in concert with your own officers, for the payment of Dartmouth creditors, the charges connected with the £200,000 estimated debt of the Dartmouth Company amounted to more than either party had anticipated. After protracted negotiations, it was not until certain letters and documents had been forced upon your notice, in a manner which ought not to have been necessary, by my letter and enclosures of January 7th last, producing the 'painful impressions' alluded to in your Chairman's last letter to me, that concessions were made in the terms which you had long been endeavouring to impose on my Directors. These concessions enabled them to accept a settlement, although involving great pecuniary loss, the sacrifice of a per centage of Mr Froude's and Mr Belfield's loans, and utterly at variance with the original arrangements. Instead of the Dartmouth Directors being held harmless, they are charged with the sole responsibility of settling the debts of the Dartmouth Company, with much less than the money's worth of your rent charge stock; and an indemnity is extorted from them in respect of those very debts against which they were to have been indemnified, and a release relieving your Company from its pecuniary liabilities in respect of the amalgamation.

In December, 1869, you repudiated a deed of guarantee, under seal of your Company, upon faith of which Dartmouth debentures had been raised, and subscriptions invited , upon the

Stock Exchange for Guaranteed Preference Shares, by public circular, signed by your ovvn Secretary, with your approval. Upon the security of these shares large loans had been made within your knowledge. That circular states, as is true , that no debts had been incurred by the Dartmouth Company at that date, except by your consent. The terms of the arrangement being that you are liable for debts incurred with your consent, you, by your Secretary's letters of January last, refuse to acknowledge and decline to provide for your liability in regard to heavy expenses consequent upon a loan from the Devon and Cornwall Bank, negociated and guaranteed by yourselves prior to the date of the circular: and such charges, in excess of 5 per cent, are virtually extorted from the private purses of the Dartmouth Directors. You are in possession of all particulars in regard to the origin of this loan, and I need not again drag them to the light. I can only say that a Board, which has refused to acknowledge this debt, in the face of the letters of the Secretary, which are before you, clearly indicating the understanding that existed in regard to it, has been guilty of dishonesty.

In my former letters I have referred in greater detail to these and other matters, which reflect no credit upon your good faith. I have therefore only to say that the statements I have made I am able to prove by letters and documents; and in regard to what passed at the two intervals of the Boards above alluded to, I have witnesses; and the facts I have now given, when publicly stated at various Directors' interviews, have never been questioned.

For the above reasons I have affirmed that there has been a gross breach of faith, and decline to withdraw my letters, as you suggest; but if, in the opinion of any unbiassed person, or fairly chosen committee of Shareholders, having regard to the simple question of what honourable dealing in pecuniary matters demand, I am wrong, I would freely do so, and acknowledge my error. As it is , I have been accustomed to consider that the same rules of conduct in money matters should guide the dealing of companies as of individuals. Requesting you to accept the resignation of my seat at your Board,

I remain, your obedient Servant,

C. Seale Hayne

To the Chairman and Directors of the South Devon Railway.

* *

South Devon Railway.

Plymouth, 29th November, 1871.

Sir, - I am desired by my colleagues to inform you that they have unanimously accepted the resignation of your seat at this Board as requested in the concluding paragraph of the printed letter you have sent them under date of the 4th instant.

My colleagues and I decline to follow you through the offensive remarks and unfounded allegations of your letter. It is sufficient for us to know that the agreement between this and the Dartmouth and Torbay Company was reduced to writing after the careful consideration of both parties; was submitted to and approved by the proprietors of the both Companies, and was finally ratified by Parliament.

My Board has always been willing to abide by this agreement although they have differed with you as to its meaning and effect. In compliance with your own request these difficulties have been referred to the arbitration of Sir Roundell Palmer whose award has proved the correctness of our views, and the unsoundness of your own.

Your complaints against my Board really absolve themselves into this - that we have declined to sacrifice the interest of our Shareholders by adopting, in your personal favour, an interpretation of the agreement which Sir Roundell Palmer has declared to be erroneous and illegal.

The Board will be prepared to justify their conduct both in regard to the Dartmouth agreement and the general policy whenever and wherever it may be impeached.

I am, Sir, your obedient Servant,

Tho. Woollcombe , Chairman

C. Seale Hayne, 3, Eaton-square, London.

Kingswear, Dartmouth,

November 14th, 1871.

Sir, - I have received your letter, inadvertently dated November 29th, which appears to have been written in some haste.

As it ignores the matters referred to in my letter of resignation, it is unnecessary for me to reply further than to contradict the gratuitous mis-statement, terminating with the assertion that I complain 'that you have declined to sacrifice the interest of your Shareholders by adopting, in my personal favour, an interpretation of the agreement which Sir Roundell Palmer has declared to be erroneous and illegal.' If you will refer to my letters, you will observe that I have specially avoided expressing any opinion upon the legal interpretation of the so-called agreement, to which his consideration was confined, except upon the question of your liability for the debts of the Dartmouth Company on amalgamation, in regard to which the terms of the award prove that I have been entirely correct.

I have affirmed that honesty and fair dealing require the due observance of the arrangements, made when you met my Board at Dartmouth in August 1865, and subsequently acted upon by both parties, a question which you took care to exclude from Sir Roundell Palmer's consideration by insisting upon limited terms of reference.

At your Board I have invariably left the room when matters affecting my personal interests were being discussed. After it became obvious to my Dartmouth colleagues and myself that your conduct was inconsistent with honourable dealing, and they had expressed their opinion that 'my continuance at your Board would be open to misconstruction', having had no previous opportunity of officially expressing my views, I conceived it to be my duty, before leaving, to state them (in the letters which you have since desired me to withdraw), and to make suggestions for a compromise consistent in principle with good faith. I have yet to learn that you have submitted, or will submit those statements to the judgment of any impartial authority; and in reference to my suggested compromise, so far from desiring you to sacrifice the interest of your Shareholders in my personal favour, it would possibly have been equally costly to myself as the present settlement; and certainly could not have differed so widely in pecuniary results as to justify an accusation which is unworthy of my notice, and, as far as I am concerned, shall not have the probably desired effect of diverting attention from the subjects of my letter of resignation.

As you do not scruple to use Sir R. Palmer's award as a cover to transactions which have never been before him; and, as it appears from the concluding paragraph of your letter, that you prefer mere bluster to accepting my offer to submit our differences upon matters of good faith to the judgment of impartial persons, further comment is unnecessary from

Your obedient Servant,

C. Seale Hayne

T. Woollcombe, Esq, Chairman South Devon Railway.

Appendix Four

Coal Bunkering at Dartmouth *by I.H. Smart*

The supply of large amounts of coal into steamships calling with empty or near-empty bunkers grew as a formal business at most UK ports of significance in the second half of the 19th century. This trade known as the 'bunkering trade', began in Dartmouth by 1850, although at this stage it was carried on by the principal coal merchants of the town, who imported house and gas coal for domestic use. The earliest recorded call for coal that the writer has found is by a Capt. John Moody of Goole in 1852. He was so impressed by the calm natural harbour of Dartmouth, a pre-requisite for bunkering, which involved the transfer of coal between two ships , that he stayed on for some years , eventually founding the Dartmouth Steam Packet Co. in 1859.

By this time there were a number of steamships plying on the Dart, who took coal from lighters moored abreast the New Ground and Coombe Mud on the western side of the River Dart. Before the coming of the railway and the growth in tonnage of steam vessels, the coal was brought in by collier brigs from South Wales and the North and North East of England. Some of the cargo was landed over the quays of Dartmouth and some into lighters.

The bunkering trade grew slowly at first since the earliest steamships were small and often used engines in an auxiliary capacity on long journeys. One of the earliest hulks was moored in the harbour in the early 1860s for the Dartmouth Steam Packet Co. ships and another in the late 1860s for the steam trawler fleet of Lake and Armeson. In 1871 a major development took place when the Cape & Natal Steam Navigation Co., later Donald Currie's 'Castle Line' of Cape mail steamers, began to use Dartmouth as a port of call and moored a store ship and hulk combined off the quay at Kingswear. After 1864 'domestic' coal for Torquay, Paignton, Ashburton etc. was being off-loaded at Kingswear wharf having been brought in by sea, and although a coal jetty and sidings for off-loading coal had existed at Hoodown since 1865, it was not much used for rail borne coal until after the opening of the Severn Tunnel.

The beginning of the major growth phase in the bunkering trade at Dartmouth was in 1876, when the major coal merchant in the town, George H. Collins & Co., asked the Harbour Commissioners for permission to moor a coal hulk, capable of holding several hundred tons of coal, in the harbour. The hulk was moored in midstream so as to command a great depth of water for the larger steamers now being built, and the coal steamers bringing in South Wales coal from Newport and Cardiff. These ships belonged to the Powell Duffryn Co. whose agent in the port was Geo. Collins & Co.

Shipping was attracted to Dartmouth to coal by the sheltered nature of the harbour and by the low tonnage rate charged for using the harbour as a port of refuge or calling for orders. This rate of ½d. per ton was introduced in 1870 and after 1880 called the 'bunkering rate'. These dues helped to pay for the 1883 Embankment Scheme and the continued dredging of the harbour, when combined with the income from laid up shipping in 1920s and 1930s.

During the next four years two other agents entered the bunkering trade, Messrs Fox & Co. of Plymouth, and R.L. Hingston & Co. who were also consular agents. These companies had their own hulks and acted for such companies as Dowlais Iron and the Cwmaman Company amongst others. The bunkering coal was still brought in by sea as was the gas and house coal. Tabulated below are typical annual tonnages. [*Source: Custom House register*] :

Year	Total coal inwards by sea (tons)	Including coal re-exported by sea (tons)	Including bunkered coal (tons)
1877	33.784	1,211	1,397
1878	37,856	5,660	3,095
1879	* 56,212	4,053	4,321
1880	38,000	5,000	7,211
1881	58,000	(est.) 7,000	(est.) 20,000

* An error, probably 36,212.

Not all the coal brought in was used locally , much of it went forward. For example in 1880 it was stated at a public meeting in Kingswear that in the previous year, coal brought into Dartmouth was broken down thus:

	tons	tons*	
Dartmouth	10,000	7,000	(incl. gas works).
Totnes	5,000	5,000	Totnes up river
Coal hulks	6,000	7,000	Coal hulks
Torquay, Paignton & Ashburton, etc	18,000	14,000	Torquay etc. incl. Kingswear
Kingswear	683		
Re-export	5,000	5,000	Re-export
Totals	approx 45,000	38,000	

* My estimates taken from other sources including DHC minutes.

It will be seen that more than ⅕ of the tonnage brought in by sea was transferred for rail transit to the area of Torbay, rather than being brought into such places by rail direct.

The rapid rise of the bunkering trade after 1879, was brought about by Powell Duffryn, though their Chairman Sir George Eliot and their agent George H. Collins. The latter circulated promotional literature listing the advantages of Dartmouth as a natural harbour and bunkering port. Bunkering really took off in 1880 and rose to a peak in 1890 reckoned on a basis of ships coaling - from 357 to 797. During this time the economics of steam power for ships was increased multifold by means of compound, triple and quadruple expansion engines, consumption falling from 6 lb. of coal/ihp-hr to 1¼ lb./ihp-hr during the 1880s and 1890s. Ship tonnage too, was increasing, so that by the 1890s the maximum tonnage was above that capable of entering Dartmouth. These factors caused a decline in the bunkering trade so that by 1896 the-number of vessels coaling had dropped to 404, and, although it rose to 600 in 1907, the previous peak was never reached. With the wartime sinkings (1914-18) coupled with the rise of the diesel-powered ships the trade gradually declined, although some bunkering continued even after World War II.

The companies engaged in the bunkering trade changed as outside influences became predominant. In 1882 the Plymouth firm of J.A. Bellamy moored a hulk in the harbour to be joined in the late 1880s by the Cwmaman Company who had been supplying Fox & Co. of Plymouth; their agent was Thomas Wilton. The Dowlais Iron & Coal Co. also moored a hulk in Dartmouth, whilst Nixon Steam Navigation Coal Co. were suppliers to Hingston & Co. Two of the local companies soon dropped out, Hingston by 1886, Fox later in the same decade, and by 1893 Wilton with his partner R.D. Renwick of Torquay were in business for themselves, competing with the Channel Coaling Co. and G.H. Collins & Co. These three bunkering companies were supplied by colliers bringing coal by sea from South Wales and off-loaded into the hulks by floating grabs.

However, in 1902 the Liverpool based company, Forwood Bros, began shipping steam coal by rail into their newly opened sidings with a small jetty and tipping shute at

Hoodown ('Forwoods'). The coal was taken by barge and unloaded by grabs into the hulk itself. Meanwhile Renwick, Wilton and G.H. Collins were shipping sea borne gas and house coal, mainly from the North and North East over Kingswear wharf and by rail to Torquay Gas Works. A new stage in bunkering started in 1908 when the Dartmouth Coaling Co. was formed, fathered by Forwoods, who transferred the lease of the sidings and equipment to that company. At about the same time G.H. Collins and Renwick, Wilton exchanged interests; Renwick, Wilton gave up bunkering whilst G.H. Collins ceased supplying Torquay Gas Works. In 1910-11 this latter firm was absorbed by the Channel Coaling Co. whilst Dartmouth Coaling were taken over by Evans, Thomas, Ratcliff of Cardiff (later Evans & Reid Steam Coal Co. Ltd). Forwoods dropped out of the picture, although the hulk supplied by them continued to be known as 'Forwoods'. The lease of the sidings was given up in 1912, although the equipment was not removed until 1921/4. After 1912 all coal was seaborne; both to the hulks and over Kingswear wharf from where Renwick, Wilton supplied Torquay Gas Works until 1963. At its peak, 80,000 tons per year were loaded on to rail at Kingswear wharf.

This trade provided work for the 'coal lumpers' of Dartmouth as the bunkering trade declined after the Great War and the shipping slump of the early 1920s. Although three hulks were still moored in the river (namely Forwoods, Channel Coaling and Dartmouth Coaling) they all belonged to the same organization after *circa* 1923 when Evans & Reid took over Channel Coaling but allowed them to operate under their own names. Final integration took place about 1937 and the one company remained until the end of bunkering in 1950. In this year, the last three hulks Dagney, Juno and Sorkness - were towed away for scrap together with the Philip's-built Grab No. 4. Thus ended the 'bunkering era' in Dartmouth history. The coal company offices at 22 South Parade are now the Dartmouth Yacht Club.

A Renwick & Wilton coal wagon, built by Gloucester Railway Carriage & Wagon. Co.
OPC Collection

Traffic handled at Hollacombe Gas Works
1889-1906 and 1933-1948

Year	Inwards			Outwards			
	Coal		Sulphate				Ammoniacal
	Common	Cannel	of ammonia	Coke	Tar		liquor
	tons	tons	tons	tons	galls		galls
					'000		'000
1889	10,700	400	100	7,400	113		226
1890	11,700	–	81	7,800	118		200
1891	13,400	–	100	8,200	125		252
1892	11,800	250	105	8,400	127		242
1893	13,400	280	111	8,700	133		238
1894	15,200	225	120	9,100	122		271
1895	13,000	826	123	9,700	127		295
1896	14,000	316	35	9,800	136		300
1897	16,200	319	121	10,000	146		350
1898	13,600	–	105	10,200	144		303
1899	16,500	–	116	10,200	136		332
1900	14,800	320	89	10,400	148		342
1901	15,700	–	115	10,900	153		355
1902	18,000	–	132	11,200	115		276
1903	14,700	542	120	11,200	141		332
1904	17,500	820	131	11,300	135		337
1905	17,000	309	106	11,300	154		335
1906	15,500	–	141	12,000	176		508

Notes:
Coal was rail-borne; sulphate of ammonia was probably rail-borne. Tar and ammoniacal licquor were rail-borne as was some coke.
Cannel is a bituminous coal which burns with a bright flame and is rich in volatile matter; it can be cut and polished like jet.

Year	Inwards			Outwards		
	Coal				Tar	Benzole
	Common	Oil	Breeze	Coke	galls	galls
	tons	galls	tons	tons	'000	'000
1933	34,700	86,000	905	16,500	552	–
1934	38,600	34,800	884	15,800	584	–
1935	38,300	45,500	1,355	18,400	731	91
1936	41,500	63,900	1,074	19,300	682	94
1937	43,900	103,900	824	17,300	688	90
1938	44,200	121,300	823	20,200	681	89
1939-43	No figures available					
1944	49,600	48,200	1,566	22,900	915	42
1945	55,600	117,800	1,326	25,700	934	30
1946	63,300	108,000	2,770	30,500	1,120	22
1947	69,000	359,600	2,629	25,700	1,138	2
1948	65,600	207,800	2,966	28,800	1,148	–

Notes:
Oil was used for making carburetted water gas. Benzole was related to the horizontal retorts and napthalene production (unwanted by-product). Breeze was a very low quality coke (used in force fed boilers).
Products coming in: coal, cannel coal, gas oil and oxide. Products going out: sulphate of ammonia, ammoniacal licquor, coke, breeze, tar and benzole.

Source: British Gas, South Western. Courtesy A. Fiderkiewicz

Appendix Six

Traffic shipped through Kingswear Wharf and transferred to rail, 1939-1963

Year	Shiploads	Remarks
1939	33 coal, 1 timber	
1940	24 coal, 1 potatoes, 1 cement, 1 fuel oil	
1941	41 coal, 1 manure	
1942	22 coal	
1943	8 coal	
1944	4 coal, 4 scrap iron	
1945	6 coal, 2 scrap iron	
1946	26 coal	
1947	44 coal, 1 oil	
1948	41 coal, 4 oil	
1949	8 coal, 1 timber	
1950	14 coal, 1 timber	
1951	26 house coal, 4 gas coal, 1 oil (loaded)	First load of gas coal 6th Nov. MV *Speciality*
1952	11 house coal, 44 gas coal	
1953	17 house coal, 46 gas coal	
1954	5 house coal, 47 gas coal, 2 coal bunkering (transferred to barges)	
1955	12 house coal, 66 gas coal, 1 chocolate (66 tons)	Some gas coal ex-Rotterdam
1956	2 house coal, 73 gas coal	Gas coal from Goole, Tyne, Antwerp
1957	3 house coal, 52 gas coal	Gas coal from Goole, Tyne
1958	1 house coal, 42 gas coal	Gas coal mostly from Goole
1959	28 gas coal, 2 coal bunkering (172 tons each, transferred to barges).	No ships docked between 10th September-30th December
1960	Nil	BR succesful in obtaining traffic by rail throughout
1961	23 gas coal, 1 load SWEB N. Abbot (unloaded to road vehicles)	
1962	38 gas coal	
1963	9 gas coal, 17 loads SWEB N.Abbot (half by rail half by road). 3 loads SWEB road only. 1 load SWEB rail only	Last ship 25th/26th March after which coal traffic diverted to rail throughout

Notes:
Household coal normally 600 ton cargoes, gas coal varied from 1,100-1,700 tons but latterly 1,700 tons on average. During wartime only household coal handled, gas coal went by rail because unable to use Channel. Household coal shipped at Workington and via Irish Sea and Lands End. Gas coal restarted via Kingswear 6th November, 1951. During 1954 2 ships diverted to Plymouth and Exmouth because of ASLEF strike. During 1955 two ships unloaded to road lorries because of ASLEF strike. Household coal ceased in 1958.
'SWEB N. Abbot' is the electricity power station at that place.

Source: Records held by E.A. Bovey

Appendix Seven

Broadsands Halt (not built)

These details are extracted from Chief Engineer's file W4/44718, letter dated 15th February, 1939. Accompanying this was a Memorandum of Steps dated 27th January, 1933, which details the divisional engineer had obtained from the divisional (traffic) superintendent. As this Memorandum covers two sheets of paper, the more important details are abbreviated below:

1924 A halt suggested Churston side of Broadsands viaduct, at 224¼ mp (the viaduct mid-point was at 224 m. 8 ch.).

Feb. 1928 Lord Churston did not think this the best site, but it was the only one with access to Lord Churston's private road leading to Broadsands beach.

Mar. 1928 'Lord Churston would not put any impediment in the way, but he could not guarantee that the private road from the viaduct to Broadsands would be open to the public for ever …'

Apr. 1928 Divisional engineer did not think it desirable to extend the private road to the main road (Dartmouth Rd) - which it did not reach at present - as GWR might be called upon to maintain its full length. It might, at a later date, be necessary so to extend the private road. In other words, at the start, the GWR did not intend to have access to the halt other than by train.

28.4.1928 Halt authorized by the Board.

Aug. 1928 Lord Churston was willing to give authority for use of his road only if the halt was used by 'inhabitants in the locality' and did not result 'in a large influx of excursionists' .

Nov. 1928 Paignton Council had promoted a Bill asking for powers of control over the sands and would not be happy with a halt being opened until 'proper sanitary conveniences' (at the beach) had been provided. The Council had entered negotiations with Lord Churston for the acquisition of land and construction of roads. This would also give public access to the halt and GWR decided to postpone provision of a halt until this sorted out.

Jul. 1929 Lord Churston 'could not see that the proposals would be of any benefit to the [his] Estate' and could not agree to the intended use of the private road. The following month the General Manager said that the Paignton Council town planning scheme, which would provide road access, was currently at the Ministry of Health for consideration.

Mar. 1931 (a) Paignton Council would not agree to anything which would bring 'a great number of people to the place' until sanitary conveniences were available.
(b) The Council scheme provided for a bridge over the railway, avoiding Lord Churston's land and 'if the scheme materialised' would mean the halt being at a point nearer Paignton. Scheme in abeyance. .

Mar. 1932 A plan had been produced showing the halt in a new position relative to the footbridge which would be created by Paignton Council 'when the land passes into their possession'.

Aug. 1932 The land the Council had been negotiating for had changed hands 'having been purchased by a Builders' Estate' and the Council would have to re-open negotiations with the new owner. (Written in January 1933:) 'Since that date no steps have been taken'.

By February 1939 things had reached a state whereby the council and the GWR were about to agree a 'Heads of Conditions' for building and use of the halt. The Council reached agreement with the owners to purchase the Broadsands estate. However, the start of World War II stopped Paignton Council sealing the conveyance of the lands. The Broadsands estate, 28.6 acres in the Urban District and 87.6 acres in Totnes Rural District plus a Crown lease of the foreshore, was finally purchased by Paignton Council in May 1948, by which time, and following nationalization, the provision of a halt had probably been forgotten. A long and sorry saga, but at least we now know the truth about Broadsands Halt.

Index

351

---

* These are combined as many entries refer to both stations.